1993 EDITION

THE STATES AND SMALL BUSINESS

A DIRECTORY OF PROGRAMS AND ACTIVITIES

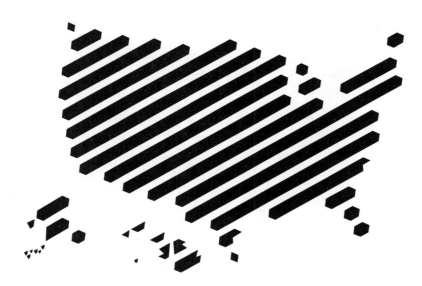

OFFICE OF ADVOCACY

U.S. SMALL BUSINESS ADMINISTRATION

U.S. Government Printing Office
Washington, D.C.: 1993

For sale by the Superintendent of Documents
U.S. Government Printing Office
Washington, DC 20402
GPO Stock No. 045–000–00266–7

ISSN 0742–843X
ISBN 0–16–041654–X

Foreword

As part of its mandate to represent the interests of small business within the federal government's legislative and regulatory processes, the U.S. Small Business Administration's Office of Advocacy has, since its creation by Congress in 1976, followed developments in small business assistance and regulation at the state level. *The States and Small Business: A Directory of Programs and Activities*, along with the periodic legislative conferences sponsored by the Office of Advocacy, is one of the primary products of this effort.

Since the appearance of the first edition of *The States and Small Business* in 1979, the number of state programs to assist small businesses has exploded. This growth has mirrored the astonishing rate of business formation that took place over this 12-year period, when the number of business tax returns filed with the Internal Revenue Service grew from 12.5 million in 1979 to 20.5 million in 1991, a 165-percent increase.

The structural changes to the U.S. economy that took place over this period—the source of much of this growth—will continue through the 1990s. For this reason, the fostering of new businesses will become an even more crucial strategy for state governments to pursue in order to promote diversified, growing economies in their jurisdictions.

The successful state programs described in this new edition of *The States and Small Business* can point the way for state legislators, economic development officials, and other policymakers who wish to take similar approaches in their own states. Needless to say, potential and existing business owners seeking management, financial, or procurement assistance will also find *The States and Small Business* to be a valuable resource for locating these services.

It is our hope that in providing the information collected in this new edition of *The States and Small Business* we will be contributing to the continued growth of a vigorous small business economy in the United States during the 1990s.

Acknowledgments

The States and Small Business: A Directory of Programs and Activities was written under the direction of Thomas P. Kerester, chief counsel for advocacy. The Small Business Administration's regional advocates were responsible for gathering the information contained in this directory. In this work, they had the cooperation of SBA district directors and state small business assistance offices.

The directory was edited by Susan Johnston of the Office of Information, with the assistance of Sarah Fleming, Kathy Tobias, Lisa Kunze, Valérie Johnson, and Melinda Crossley. John Ward was the production editor. Staff support was provided by Clara Myhill, Mary Sanders, and Darlene Moyé.

Appendix A, the listing of Small Business Development Centers, was provided by the SBA's Office of Small Business Development Centers.

Introduction

This directory is designed to identify state and local programs, agencies, laws, and other activities that aid in the nurturing of small business in the United States. Information is included for all 50 states, as well as the District of Columbia, Puerto Rico, and the U.S. Virgin Islands.

The directory listings for each state are divided into five broad categories:

Small Business Offices, Programs, and Activities. Lists executive departments and agencies, independent boards, and semipublic corporations that serve small business interests through loans, loan guarantees, joint ventures, minority assistance, counseling, assistance with regulatory requirements, or other such development assistance. This section is usually divided by administrative unit of government.

Governor's Advisory Council or Task Force. Provides a listing of small business advisory boards, councils, or task forces for the states that have them. A brief description of the board's functions is given along with the name, address, and telephone number of a contact person.

Legislative Committees and Subcommittees. Lists legislative committees, subcommittees, and joint committees of both chambers of each state that are concerned with small business issues and business regulation.

Legislation. Contains an informal, nontechnical summary of recent state legislative actions that affect small business. Depending upon the length and frequency of a state's legislative session, this will generally cover activity in 1990 and 1991.

State Small Business Conferences. Highlights state-sponsored conferences that focus on small business issues. In addition, there are a number of conferences cosponsored by state development agencies and the private sector that are oriented toward such issues as entrepreneurship, procurement, business development, and trade. Where there have been such conferences, they are noted in this section, along with a report on conferences that may be planned in the near future and the name of a contact person.

In addition to the information contained in the state-by-state listings, an additional source of small business information will be found in the appendices to this directory. Appendix A is a complete listing, as of September 1992, of all Small Business Development Centers throughout the country. Appendix B contains a brief report on the status of the regulatory flexibility acts that exist in 25 states. Appendix C contains the names, addresses, and telephone numbers of the Small Business Administration's 10 regional advocates. Appendix D contains a list of all SBA district offices. A glossary of commonly used business development terms appears at the end of the book.

Comments, corrections, or requests for further information regarding this publication should be directed to: Editor, The States and Small Business, Mail Code 3114, U.S. Small Business Administration, Washington, DC 20416; telephone (202) 205–6531; FAX (202) 205–6928.

Contents

Alabama

Small Business Offices, Programs, and Activities

The Alabama Development Office

Contact:
Mr. Fred Braswell, Director
Alabama Development Office
State Capitol
401 Adams Avenue
Montgomery, AL 36130
(205) 242–0400

The **Alabama Development Office** provides technical and management training programs, as well as financing through industrial revenue bonds (IRBs). Through IRBs, businesses can receive financing for land, buildings, and equipment. The office is responsible for the Alabama Industry Development Program, which provides technical services such as screening of personnel, upgrading of skills, and on-the-job training free of charge to businesses.

Contact:
Mr. Bill Brock, State Advocate
Small Business Office of Advocacy
Alabama Development Office
State Capitol
401 Adams Avenue
Montgomery, AL 36130
(205) 242–0400

The **Small Business Office of Advocacy** was created to aid, assist, counsel, and protect the interests of small business concerns in order to preserve free enterprise, maintain a healthy state economy, and to provide information and assistance to citizens interested in entering into commercial activity in Alabama.

Contact:
Mr. Mark Warsham, Acting Director
Research Division
Alabama Development Office
State Capitol
401 Adams Avenue
Montgomery, AL 36130
(205) 242–0400

The Alabama Development Office's **Research Division** prepares cost and feasibility studies for clients as well as cost analyses of labor, transportation, utilities, and state and local taxes. The division prepares studies, reports, and promotional brochures containing information on natural resources, quality of life, demographics, economics, and training. The division maintains a comprehensive industrial research library.

Loans and Capital Formation

Contact:
Mr. James Allen, Jr., Chief of Staff
Southern Development Council
671 South Perry Street, Suite 500
Montgomery, AL 36104
(205) 264–5441

Alabama has an **Economic Development Loan Program** available to all businesses.

Procurement

Contacts:
Mr. Kent Rose, Director of Purchasing
Department of Finance
Division of Purchases and Stores
11 South Union Street, Room 200
Montgomery, AL 36130
(205) 242–7250

Mr. Roger McKean,
   Small Business Representative
Department of Finance
Division of Purchases and Stores
11 South Union Street, Room 200
Montgomery, AL 36130
(205) 242–7256

The **Alabama Small Business Assistance Act of 1975** directs each state agency to obtain a minimum of 10 percent of its purchases from small businesses—defined as those businesses with less than $1 million in sales and fewer than 50 employees. A recent study indicates the state is doing more than 50 percent of its business with small firms. The State Purchasing Office maintains approximately 18,000 firms on its bidders' list, with one third being small. A small business representative is available for primary contact with small firms.

Office of Minority Business Enterprise

Contact:
Mr. Jack P. Crittenden, Director
Office of Minority Business Enterprise
Alabama Development Office
State Capitol
401 Adams Avenue
Montgomery, AL 36130
(205) 242–0400

The **Office of Minority Business Enterprise** coordinates minority business efforts at the state level. Its program includes procurement, technical assistance, and advocacy on behalf of minority businesses.

SBA 504 Statewide Certified Development Company

Contact:
Mr. James Allen, Jr., Chief of Staff
Southern Development Council
671 South Perry Street
Montgomery, AL 36130
(205) 264–5441

Certified Development Companies (CDCs) are certified by the U.S. Small Business Administration to package, process, close, and service 504 loans. CDCs obtain loan funds by issuing bonds guaranteed by the SBA. The SBA 504 loan program can provide long-term, fixed-asset financing to eligible small businesses for acquisition, construction, expansion, or renovation of land and buildings or purchase of long-life equipment.

Alabama Small Business Development Consortium

Contacts:
Mr. John Sandefur, State Director
Alabama Small Business Development
  Consortium
University of Alabama at Birmingham
1717 11th Avenue South, Suite 419
Birmingham, AL 35294
(205) 934–7260

The **Alabama Small Business Development Consortium** (ASBDC), headquartered at the University of Alabama in Birmingham, provides managerial and technical counseling and training at no cost to current and potential small business owners. These services are provided through 11 Alabama Small Business Development Centers (ASBDCs) located in university schools of business and at the Alabama International Trade Center. Additional services are provided through the Alabama Technology Assistance Program and the Alabama Small Business Procurement System (ASBPS). ASBDC consultants provide assistance in business planning, international trade, government procurement, engineering and technical assistance, rural development, and business start-up. The agency also provides research and other support for state economic development activities. A list of SBDCs in Alabama is in Appendix A of this directory. (These can also be contacted for assistance and information pertaining to Alabama Small Business Development Consortium Procurement System.)

The Alabama Small Business Development Consortium also provides **Small Business Innovation Research** (SBIR) information to entrepreneurs. The SBIR assistance program is delivered to entrepreneurs, SBIR award applicants, and SBIR award recipients through partnerships established between private companies and public universities. SBIR activity is promoted through seminars and workshops presented across the state, and the consortium maintains an SBIR library for the use of people interested in participating in the program.

Governor's Advisory Council or Task Force

The **Governor's Rural Development Task Force** was established in an attempt to deal with the critical levels of unemployment in rural distressed counties in Alabama. The governor formed a task force of individuals from state and federal agencies and the private sector to examine these problems and identify potential for economic development. The effort is coordinated by the Division of Planning and Economic Development in the Alabama Department of Economic and Community Affairs in cooperation with the Alabama Development Office.

Contact:
Dr. Don Hines, Division Chief
Division of State Planning and Economic Development
Alabama Department of Economic and Community Affairs
3465 Norman Bridge Road
Montgomery, AL 36105–0939
(205) 242–8672

Legislative Committees and Subcommittees

Alabama has small business committees in both houses of the legislature.

Contacts:

Representative Frank McDaniel
Chairman
Committee on Small Business
House of Representatives
State Capitol
Montgomery, AL 36130
(205) 242–7697

Senator Walter Owens
Chairman
Committee on Small Business
State Senate
State Capitol
Montgomery, AL 36130
(205) 242–7870

Legislation

No recent legislation targeting small business has been enacted.

State Small Business Conferences

Contact:
Mr. Bill Brock, State Advocate
Small Business Office of Advocacy
Alabama Development Office
401 Adams Avenue
Montgomery, AL 36130
(205) 242–0400

There is ongoing activity for a collaborative effort between the Small Business Office of Advocacy and the International Division of the Alabama Development Office in the next fiscal year for Alabama to host an international small business conference.

Alaska

Small Business Offices, Programs, and Activities

Department of Commerce and Economic Development

Contact:
Mr. Jamie Parsons, Director
Division of Business Development
Department of Commerce and Economic
   Development
P.O. Box D
Juneau, AK 99811–0800
(907) 465–2017

The **Alaska Department of Commerce and Economic Development** promotes an active, healthy, and expanding business community. This goal is accomplished by formulating and implementing policies and programs that develop, strengthen, and diversify Alaska's economic base, increase employment opportunities, and stimulate private enterprise.

The **Division of Business Development** works to strengthen and diversify the state's economy and establish a positive business climate that is conducive to commercial and industrial investment and development. The division's responsibilities include developing commercial fisheries, forest products, and mining industries; providing assistance to regional development organizations; analyzing the state of the economy; providing small business assistance; and encouraging import substitution and venture capital investment.

Contact:
Mr. James E. Wiedeman,
   Development Officer
Division of Business Development
Department of Commerce and Economic
   Development
3601 C Street, Suite 722
Anchorage, AK 99503
(907) 563–2165

The **Business Assistance Program** in the Division of Business Development is charged by statute to promote and develop business within the state, promote economic development activities on the state and regional levels, and provide technical assistance, counseling, and advice to small business.

Contacts:
Mr. Greg Winegar, Loan Manager
Division of Investments
Department of Commerce and Economic
   Development
P.O. Box D
Juneau, AK 99811
(907) 465–2510

Mr. Bob Richardson, Loan Manager
Division of Investments
Department of Commerce and Economic
   Development
3601 C Street, Suite 778
Anchorage, AK 99503
(907) 582–3779

The **Division of Investments** offers a Small Business Economic Development program (A.S. 44.88.400–430) designed to provide private sector employment in areas designed by the U.S. Department of Commerce's Economic Development Administration. Financing under this program is available to support the origination and expansion of businesses that will create significant long-term employment and will help diversify the economy. Emphasis will be made on projects that show the greatest long-range economic impact on a community. Applicants must meet the criteria of "small business" as established by the U.S. Small Business Administration and must obtain additional private, non-public financing of at least twice the amount requested.

The Division of Investments also offers a program that assists purchasers to assume existing small business loans. Applicants must demonstrate financial responsibility and good character, must have sufficient collateral, and must demonstrate knowledge of Alaska's economic conditions. Other factors considered are the business' potential for growth, its ability to repay the loan, and the potential to create more jobs and provide additional services to the community. If the existing loan is for a building that was built, purchased, or refinanced under the state's small business loan program (A.S. 45.95.010–080), the building must be at least 50-percent occupied by the applicant. Applicants must be Alaskan residents 18 years old or older. Corporations, partnerships, limited partnerships, or any other association of applicants must be 100-percent owned by a resident of Alaska.

Office of International Trade

Contact:
Mr. Robert G. Poe, Director
Office of International Trade
Office of the Governor
3601 C Street, Suite 798
Anchorage, AK 99503
(907) 561–5585

The **Office of International Trade** was created to encourage the development of new markets for Alaskan resources, expand existing markets, locate sources of investment capital, increase the visibility of Alaska and its products in the international marketplace, and improve communication among members of the Alaskan and international business communities. The office also makes referrals and provides technical assistance to Alaskans interested in developing business abroad.

Umbrella Bond Program

Contact:
Mr. Bert Wagnon, Executive Director
Alaska Industrial Development and Export
   Authority
480 W. Tudor Road
Anchorage, AK 99503–6690
(907) 561–8050

The **Umbrella Bond Program** is designed to provide long-term financing for capital business projects, such as buildings, plants, property, and equipment. Any business located in the state may apply. Businesses may obtain indirect loans up to $10 million plus whatever portion the originating lender will retain. (The minimum originating lender participation amount is 20 percent. Interest depends on the cost of the bonds.)

Small Business Development Centers

Contact:
Ms. Jan Fredricks, State Director
Small Business Development Center
430 West 7th Street, Suite 110
Anchorage, AK 99501
(907) 274–7231

The Department of Commerce and Economic Development, in conjunction with the University of Alaska–Anchorage, has joined with the U.S. Small Business Administration to fund a **Small Business Development Center** (SBDC). The SBDC operates small business centers in Anchorage, Fairbanks, Juneau, and Matanuska-Susitna Borough. A listing of all Small Business Development Centers and subcenters in Alaska is in Appendix A of this directory.

Small Business Consulting Center

Contacts:
Mr. Gary Selk, President
Alaska Business Development Center
821 N Street, Suite 103
Anchorage, AK 99501
(907) 279-7427

Mr. Bob Keller, Director
Economic Development
Fairbanks Native Association, Inc.
310½ First Avenue
Fairbanks, AK 99701
(907) 452–1648 or 456–5151

The **Small Business Consulting Center** (SBCC) is a joint venture of the Fairbanks Native Association, Inc., and the Alaska Business Development Center. The SBCC provides a full range of technical assistance to small businesses across the state. Services are available to all small businesses with special attention given to rural and minority businesses. Offices have been established in Juneau, Anchorage, and Fairbanks.

Alaska Business Development Center

Contact:
Mr. Gary Selk, President
Alaska Business Development Center
821 N Street, Suite 103
Anchorage, AK 99501
(907) 279-7427

The **Alaska Business Development Center** (ABDC) began as a part of the Alaska Native Foundation in the early 1970s and incorporated independently in 1979. Since then, ABDC has used a variety of state, federal, and other funding sources. ABDC was awarded a contract by the Alaska Department of Commerce and Economic Development to operate small business support centers in Anchorage and Juneau. Services are not limited to minority businesses.

Department of Community and Regional Affairs

Contacts:
Mr. William Mailer,
    Program Manager, JTPA
Rural Development Division
Department of Community and
    Regional Affairs
949 East 36th Avenue, Suite 400
Anchorage, AK 99508
(907) 563–1955

Mr. Mark Mickelson,
    Program Coordinator, JTPA
Rural Development Division
Department of Community and
    Regional Affairs
P.O. Box BC
Juneau, AK 99811
(907) 465–4890

Alaska's **Department of Community and Regional Affairs** assists businesses through its training and rural development programs.

The **Rural Development Initiative** (REDI) provides technical and financial assistance for economic and community development.

The **Job Training Partnership Act** (JTPA) program provides job training and related assistance to economically disadvantaged individuals, with the ultimate goal of moving trainees into permanent, self-sustaining employment. Grants are awarded for state vocational coordination, older workers' training, youth summer employment and training, the dislocated worker program, and discretionary training. Eligible applicants include state and local governments, public and private nonprofit agencies, community-based organizations, and educational agencies.

The **State Employment and Training Program** provides job training and other related services to eligible participants to reduce current and future claims against unemployment benefits, foster new jobs due to the availability of a skilled work force, and increase training opportunities to the state's workers.

Governor's Advisory Council or Task Force

In January 1989, the governor, in response to a campaign pledge and recommendations of Alaskan delegates to the 1986 White House Conference on Small Business, named a statewide task force of small business persons to plan and implement the Governor's Conference on Small Business. This task force, known as the **Steering Committee for the Governor's Conference on Small Business**, generally followed the format of the White House Conference on Small Business.

Legislative Committees and Subcommittees

The first Joint House and Senate Economic Recovery Subcommittee was formed in January 1988 to consider small business legislation.

Contact:
Ms. Linda Wild, Deputy Commissioner
Department of Commerce and Economic
 Development
P.O. Box D
Juneau, AK 99811
(907) 465–2500

Legislation

In 1989, the governor signed Administrative Order 117 establishing the Business Development Information Network, a one-stop shop for inter- and intrastate businesses or prospective businesses. The coordinator can provide information, answers, booklets, and forms from 10 to 15 different state agencies, alleviating the need for multiple phone calls.

In the 1990 legislative session, a resolution passed supporting the Governor's Conference on Small Business process and findings. Senate Concurrent Resolution No. 53 requested that the governor (1) implement, to the extent possible, the final recommendations made by the Governor's Conference on Small Business; (2) hold a similar conference every two years; (3) appoint at least one person from the small business community to each state board and commission that handles issues relevant to small business; and (4) direct the Division of Business Development to coordinate the handling of small business issues by state agencies.

State Small Business Conferences

Contact:
Mr. Bill Paulick, Development Specialist
Division of Business Development
Department of Commerce and Economic
   Development
P.O. Box D
Juneau, AK 99811–0800
(907) 465–2017

To spur the development of technology and innovation in Alaska, the U.S. Small Business Administration initiated an annual conference to bring members of the technology community together with sources of assistance and expertise. Started in 1990, the Annual Alaska Technology and Innovation Conference is sponsored by the SBA, the state of Alaska, the Alaska Science and Technology Foundation, the Alaska Small Business Development Center, and the Alaska Inventors Association.

In 1989, 13 regional conferences were conducted to define the top 24 problems in each region of the state and select delegates to represent their region at the state conference. The top 20 problems for small business were identified and a final set of recommendations developed. The recommendations included changes to state laws, programs, and policies that the delegates believed would benefit and strengthen small business in the state. A final report was submitted to the governor and to the legislature, which responded by passing a resolution (S.C.R. 53) supporting the concept of a governor's conference every two years.

Arizona

Small Business Offices, Programs, and Activities

Arizona Department of Commerce

Contact:
Mr. James E. Marsh, Director
Arizona Department of Commerce
3800 North Central, Suite 1500
Phoenix, AZ 85012
(602) 280–1306

The responsibility for Arizona state small business programs resides with the **Arizona Department of Commerce**. The department offers assistance to companies in various growth phases, packages expansion financing for established companies, assists businesses establishing operations in Arizona, and helps with export financing and other export logistics. The *Guide to Establishing a Business in Arizona*, published by the Department of Commerce, provides information on registering a business, licensing requirements, taxation, environmental regulations, labor regulations, sources of funds for business development, and a list of sources for additional information.

Contact:
Ms. Patty Duff
Business Finance
Arizona Department of Commerce
3800 North Central, 15th Floor
Phoenix, AZ 85012
(602) 280–1341

Small Business Financing Programs are administered by the Department of Commerce to encourage the expansion of existing and newly-formed businesses. The staff analyzes loan requests and assembles application packages on behalf of small businesses for submission to the funding sources. A revolving loan program is administered for businesses in economically distressed counties of the state. Financing available through the agency includes SBA 504 loans and 7(a) loans, and the U.S. Department of Housing and Urban Development's Community Development Block Grant loan funds.

Business Assistance Center

Contact:
Mr. Joe Dean, Program Manager
Business Assistance Center/Business
    Connection
Arizona Department of Commerce
3800 North Central, Suite 1500
Phoenix, AZ 85012
(602) 280–1480
(800) 542–5684 (toll-free, in-state)

A top recommendation of the Governor's 1989 Small Business Conference, the **Business Assistance Center** was created by the legislature and began operating in June 1990. The center serves as a one-stop shop for individuals who are either starting or expanding a business. Information is available on the permits and licensing necessary to open a business in Arizona, as well as the various state, county, and city statutes relating to business.

Contact:
Dr. Bill Tompkin, Manager
Business Retention and Expansion
Arizona Department of Commerce
3800 North Central, Suite 1500
Phoenix, AZ 85012
(602) 280–1335

A **Business Retention Activity**, designed to stimulate community ownership and participation, begins with a local needs assessment. A sampling of retail, service, and basic industry companies is surveyed by questionnaire and subsequently contacted by phone or in person to determine the local perception of the business climate and services available. Activities to improve the business climate may be instituted. A simple economic indicator is established and evaluated quarterly to monitor the continuing health of the area's established businesses.

Through **Business Expansion Programs**, eligible companies that have existed for two or more years and meet certain sales requirements may receive business counseling and assistance. The program also sponsors the development of various nontraditional agriculture industries, including pistachios, aquaculture, wine grapes, pecans, apples, native plant seeds, and value-added processing of agronomic and horticultural products.

Contact:
Mr. Charles Deaton, Director
Business Development/National Marketing
Commerce and Economic Development
    Commission
3800 North Central, Suite 1500
Phoenix, AZ 85012
(602) 280–1328

The **Commerce and Economic Development Commission** oversees a statewide financial assistance program for business, both in-state and out-of-state. The five-member commission is appointed by the governor and chaired by the executive director of the commission. The program is financed by two lottery scratch-games called "Arizona Pay Day," enacted by the legislature in 1989. The primary focus of the program is to aid distressed economic areas. The financing available includes grants, as well as low-interest loans. The loan program requires a 50-percent match, with funding from a private source.

Statewide SBA 504 Certified Development Company

Contact:
Ms. Patty Duff, Executive Director
Arizona Enterprise Development Corporation
3800 North Central, 15th Floor
Phoenix, AZ 85012
(602) 280–1341

The **Arizona Enterprise Development Corporation** was certified by the U.S. Small Business Administration to operate on a statewide basis. It offers financing to independently owned businesses with a net worth of less than $6 million under the SBA's Section 504 loan program. A 504 loan is a guaranty loan that requires a 10-percent cash down payment by the loan applicant. The SBA will guarantee the funds advanced by the corporation up to the lesser of 90 percent of the loan or $750,000. The interest rate for a 504 loan is the market rate.

Small Business Development Centers

Contact:
Mr. Dave Smith, State Director
Arizona Small Business Development Center
Gateway Community College
108 North 40th Street, Suite 148
Phoenix, AZ 85034
(602) 392–5224

The **Arizona Small Business Development Center** (SBDC) provides start-up and existing businesses with information and management and technical assistance. The lead center in Arizona is at Gateway Community College in Phoenix, and there are 10 subcenters located throughout the state. A complete listing of all Small Business Development Centers and subcenters is in Appendix A of this directory.

Governor's Advisory Council or Task Force

Contact:
Mr. Don Cline, Chairperson
Economic Planning and Development
   Advisory Board
3800 North Central
Phoenix, AZ 85012
(602) 280–1300

The governor and the Department of Commerce are advised on small business issues by the Economic Planning and Development Advisory Board, consisting of representatives from local governments, chambers of commerce, and the business community. This group was instrumental in organizing the Arizona White House Conference on Small Business and in sponsoring a statewide forum and 10 areawide workshops on "Shaping Arizona's Economic Future."

Legislative Committees and Subcommittees

While there are no legislative committees focusing solely on small business, two legislative committees regularly deal with small business issues: the Senate Commerce and Labor Committee and the House Commerce Committee.

Contacts:

Senator Manuel Peña, Jr.
Chairman
Senate Commerce and Labor, and
    Insurance and Banking Committees
State Capitol
Phoenix, AZ 85007
(602) 542–4171

Staff aide to the committee:
Ms. Patrice Kraus
(602) 542–3171

Representative Brenda Burns
Chairperson
House Commerce Committee
State Capitol
Phoenix, AZ 85007
(602) 542–3255

Staff aide to the committee:
Mr. Blake Anderson
(602) 542–5480

Legislation

The 1991 Arizona Legislature passed H.B. 2027, which allows small group health insurance policies to be written exempt from the mandated benefits required of insurers, hospitals, medical service corporations, and health insurance policies.

State Small Business Conferences

Contact:
Ms. Pat Schroeder, Program Manager
Community Development
Arizona Department of Commerce
3800 North Central, 14th Floor
Phoenix, AZ 85012
(602) 280–1300

Contact:
Ms. Rita Anne Johnson
Community Development Specialist
Arizona Department of Commerce
3800 North Central, 14th Floor
Phoenix, AZ 85012
(602) 280–1350, Ext. 2054

In 1989, the first **Governor's Conference on Small Business** was held. Planning for the meeting was coordinated by an 18-member steering committee, appointed by the governor and chaired by the deputy director of the state Department of Commerce. The conference allowed small business owners an opportunity to meet together and discuss important policy issues. One of the main recommendations of the conference was the creation of a one-stop shop to provide information and assistance to individuals starting or expanding a business. This resulted in the creation by the legislature of the Business Assistance Center, which began operations in the summer of 1990.

The governor's annual **Rural Economic Development Conference** is held each September. The conference focuses on the "how-to's" of economic development, with a primary emphasis on business retention and expansion. Workshop topics include how to obtain public and private sector financing, how to evaluate a community in making a location decision and how to market a community.

Arkansas

State Offices, Programs, and Activities

Arkansas Industrial Development Commission

Contact:
Mr. Windell R. Adams, C.I.D., Coordinator
Small Business Programs
Arkansas Industrial Development
  Commission
One State Capitol Mall
Little Rock, AR 72201
(501) 682–5275

The **Arkansas Industrial Development Commission** (AIDC) was established in 1955 and is guided by an advisory board of 16 commissioners appointed by the governor. The agency publishes the *Arkansas Journal* and the monthly *AIDC Review*, which highlights industrial activities throughout the state. The agency also publishes a *Manufacturers Exchange Bulletin*, which is mailed to manufacturers every other month. The bulletin provides a communications tool to help firms find work for idle machinery, sell surplus materials and equipment, and to announce educational seminars and meetings.

The **Small Business Information Clearinghouse** was established in 1988 to assist new or expanding small businesses by providing a counseling and referral service. Detailed information is available for all state, federal, nonprofits, and privately sponsored assistance programs in the state.

Contact:
Mr. James Hall, Director
Minority Business Development
Arkansas Industrial Development
  Commission
One State Capitol Mall
Little Rock, AR 72201
(501) 682–1060

The objective of the **Minority Business Development Program** is to facilitate the growth, expansion, and development of minority business. The office acts as an information clearinghouse, providing information on procurement and contract opportunities, the identification of financial resources, and limited management and technical assistance. Working through the Community Assistance Division of AIDC, the Minority Business Development Program assists minority businesses in obtaining loans from AIDC's economic development fund. These loans are available for businesses located in certain areas of Arkansas, primarily for manufacturing and wholesale distribution businesses.

Contact:
Mr. Roger Chinn, Coordinator
Arkansas Enterprise Zone Program
Arkansas Industrial Development
   Commission
One State Capitol Mall
Little Rock, AR 72201
(501) 682–7384

The **Small Business Section** of AIDC administers an enterprise zone program that provides tax incentives for new or expanding industry to create jobs in economically depressed areas.

Contact:
Mr. Steve Cochran, Marketing Manager
Arkansas Industrial Development
   Commission
One Capitol Mall
Little Rock, AR 72201
(501) 682–6103

The **Agricultural Export Development Program** promotes export sales of Arkansas agricultural products and assists producers and manufacturers in developing foreign markets.

The **Good Work Arkansas** program helps increase sales of Arkansas-produced products that are found in grocery stores within the state. Point-of-purchase materials are displayed below Arkansas products on grocery shelves.

Procurement

Contact:
Mr. Ed Erxleben, Director
Office of State Purchasing
P.O. Box 2940
Little Rock, AR 72203
(501) 371–2336

The **Office of State Purchasing** helps companies wishing to sell their goods or services to the state. The office maintains a bid list, classified by commodity, of firms in good standing with the state. The office does not handle highway, transportation, or university contracts.

Arkansas Capital Corporation

Contact:
Mr. Sam Walls, Executive Director
Arkansas Capital Corporation
800 Pyramid Place
221 West Second Street
Little Rock, AR 72201
(501) 374–9247

The **Arkansas Capital Corporation** is organized as a non-profit institution and funded by the state. The corporation provides intermediate and long-term financing for fixed assets, land, and working capital. The average loan is between $350,000 and $500,000.

Small Business Development Centers

Contact:
Mr. Paul McGinnis, State Director
Small Business Development Center
University of Arkansas at Little Rock
100 South Main Street, Suite 401
Little Rock, AR 72201
(501) 324–9043

The Arkansas **Small Business Development Center** (SBDC) provides management and technical assistance to the small business community, linking federal, state, and local resources with those of the university and the private sector. The SBDC counsels and trains small businesses in organizational, financial, marketing, technical, and other skills.

The lead SBDC in Arkansas is in Little Rock, at the University of Arkansas. Subcenters are located in Arkadelphia, Beebe, Conway, Fayetteville, Jonesboro, Searcy, and State University. A listing of all Small Business Development Centers and subcenters is in Appendix A of this directory.

The Arkansas Science and Technology Authority

Contact:
Mr. Chuck Myers, Research Program
    Manager
Arkansas Science and Technology Authority
100 Main Street, Suite 450
Little Rock, AR 72201
(501) 324–9006

The **Small Business Innovation Research Grants Assistance Program** assists Arkansas small businesses in capturing available federal research and development funds.

The **Business Incubator Program** increases the survival rate of new, technology-based businesses in Arkansas.

Contact:
Ms. Anita Millard, Fiscal Officer
Arkansas Science and Technology Authority
100 Main Street, Suite 450
Little Rock, AR 72201
(501) 371–3554

The **Research and Development Tax Credit Program** provides incentives to Arkansas industry to participate in the Applied Research Grant program or similar research programs. The program encourages investment by industry in the transfer of science and technology from Arkansas colleges and universities.

Contact:
Mr. James T. Benham
Vice President, Finance
Arkansas Science and Technology Authority
100 Main Street, Suite 450
Little Rock, AR 72201
(501) 324–9006

The **Seed Capital Investment Program** fosters the formation and development of innovative technology-based business enterprises that will stimulate the economy of Arkansas through increased employment and leveraging of private investment.

Rural Development Action Program

Contact:
Mr. Mike Gauldin
Ms. Susan Whitacre
Office of the Governor
State Capitol
Little Rock, AR 72201
(501) 682–2345

The **Rural Development Action Program** improves the quality of life in all of Arkansas' most distressed rural counties. Action teams comprised of directors from numerous agencies will target and coordinate assistance efforts.

Governor's Advisory Council or Task Force

Contact:
Mr. Phil Price
Senior Assistant for Economic Development
Governor's Office
State Capitol, Room 238
Little Rock, AR 72201
(501) 682–2345

The governor has an economic development board of agency directors that covers small business issues and other economic development concerns.

Legislative Committees and Subcommittees

Small business legislation is handled by the committees on insurance and commerce in both houses of the legislature. Staff support is provided by the Bureau of Legislative Research.

Contacts:

Senator W.D. Moore, Jr.,
 Chairman
Senate Committee on Insurance and
 Commerce
State Capitol
Little Rock, AR 72201
(501) 682–1937

Representative Ode Maddox,
 Chairman
House Committee on Insurance and
 Commerce
State Capitol
Little Rock, AR 72201
(501) 682–1937

Mr. Kern Treat, Director
Bureau of Legislative Research
315 State Capitol Building
Little Rock, AR 72201
(501) 682–1937

Legislation

The following legislation was enacted in Arkansas in 1991:

- Act 3 raised sales and use taxes on all items by ½ cent and imposes a sales and use tax on the sale of used automobiles of more than $2,000 in value.

- Act 219 replaced truck weight-distance tax with a 4 cents per gallon fuel tax, increased registration fees, and permit fees.

- Act 342 established laws for the control of ground water resources.

- Act 442 reappropriated more than $15 million for public works and job training projects.

- Act 454 authorized the denial of permits, licenses, and operational authorizations to applicants who have a record of environmental noncompliance.

- Act 544 established the state minimum wage at $3.65 per hour effective July 1, 1991, and $4.00 per hour effective July 1, 1992.

- Act 561 established a Workers' Compensation Insurance Plan for risks rejected by insurance companies.

- Act 645 authorized cities and counties to finance economic development, educational, and museum audiovisual facilities by the use of bonds.

- Act 671 established a linked deposit program to help finance small business and agricultural enterprises.

- Act 695 appropriated $300,000 to be used to establish two new field offices of the Small Business Development Center program.

- Act 698 established an annual procurement goal of 10 percent for state agencies with minority businesses, and establishes monitoring procedures.

- Act 707 established an inventors assistance program within the University of Arkansas.

- Act 748 provided for an income tax credit of 30 percent of the purchase price of solid waste reduction, reuse, or recycling equipment.

- Act 749 created a solid waste recycling board and sets rules for disposal of batteries, tires, paper, and used motor oil. Also sets fees to cover disposal costs, and amends laws on recycling fund use.

- Act 756 authorized the establishment of a workers' compensation private sector self-insurer guaranty fund.

- Act 775 amended the Arkansas Development Finance Authority Small Business Act of 1989 to target resources to rural areas, technology-oriented small business, minority-owned enterprises, and agriculture-related enterprises.

- Act 909 appropriated $139,678 for use by the new Office of Rural Advocacy for FY 1991–1992 and $140,256 for FY 1992–1993.

- Act 1029 authorized county or regional industrial development corporations, and sets guidelines for economic development efforts.

- Act 1057 increased the criminal and civil penalties for environmental violations.

- Act 1067 established and appropriated funds for services and operating expenses for a small and disadvantaged business program of the Arkansas Industrial Development Commission.

- Act 1202 appropriated more than $10 million to the Arkansas Science and Technology Authority for use in funding research grants for product or technology development, business incubators, and to establish centers of excellence.

- Act 1211 imposed a tax of one cent per pack of cigarettes with revenues to be used exclusively for transportation services for the elderly.

- Act 1244 created the Arkansas Technical and Community College System, expanded the State Board of Education, and transferred responsibility for technical and community colleges to the State Board of Higher Education.

State Small Business Conferences

No recent statewide small business conferences have been reported.

California

Small Business Offices, Programs, and Activities

California has several offices to assist small enterprises, most notably the Office of Small Business and the Office of Local Development, both within the Department of Commerce; the Office of Small and Minority Business in the Department of General Services; and the State Small Business Advocate.

State Small Business Advocate

Contact:
Ms. Grace T. Daniel
State Small Business Advocate
1120 N Street, Suite 2101
Sacramento, CA 95814
(916) 654–3390

The **Small Business Advocate**, appointed by the governor, serves as California's principal advocate on behalf of small businesses, advising policymakers on legislative and administrative measures. One of the primary responsibilities of the advocate is to receive and respond to complaints from small businesses concerning the actions of state agencies and the effects of state laws and regulations.

Department of Commerce

Contact:
Mr. William Harper, Executive Director
Office of Small Business
Department of Commerce
801 K Street, Suite 1600
Sacramento, CA 95814
(916) 324–1295

Within the California Department of Commerce, the **Office of Small Business** (OSB) provides the following services to small businesses: advocacy, seminars, general information, management and technical counseling, and loan programs. The OSB helps small businesses deal with regulatory agencies, provides guidance on license requirements, and acts as a link to the resources needed to solve business problems.

Among the loan programs coordinated through the Office of Small Business are the following:

- Through the **Small Business Loan Guarantee Program**, loan guarantees are available to small firms unable to obtain financing at reasonable cost and terms. Guarantees are issued by affiliated regional corporations up to $350,000 or 90 percent, whichever is less, for a maximum of seven years. Most are short-term loans under $100,000, revolving lines of credit, or agricultural loans.

- In the **New Product Development Program**, qualified affiliated regional corporations are authorized to make royalty-based investments in small firms to bring to the market new products and processes that are beyond the theoretical development stage. Implementation procedures and regulations are being developed.

- **Energy Reduction Loans** are available to small business owners for the purpose of retrofitting their operations to be more energy efficient. Low-interest loans are available for up to $150,000 and a maximum term of five years. Applicants can obtain financing through any of the eight Regional Development Corporations (RDCs) located statewide.

- **Hazardous Waste Loans** provide small businesses with a way of financing the acquisition and installation of hazardous waste reduction equipment or processes. Loans are available from $20,000 to a maximum of $150,000 for up to seven years. A small business owner can apply directly through one of eight RDCs located throughout the state.

- The **Farm Loan Program** is available to farmers in the Salinas and Fresno areas who need working capital, want to purchase land, or need to purchase additional equipment. A line of credit or term loan of up to $350,000, a portion of which is guaranteed by a federal agency, is now available at the RDCs in the Salinas and Fresno areas.

- **Underground Storage Tank Loans** are available to small businesses to upgrade, repair, or replace tanks used to store petroleum or for minor cleanup of the site. The maximum loan is up to $350,000 with up to 20 years to repay. Interested small business owners can contact any of the RDCs and a number of Small Business Development Centers located throughout the state to complete applications or to receive general information on the loan program.

- The **Small Business Air Pollution Loan Program** was made available in September 1990 to small rural gas station owners for installation of vapor recovery systems on their pumps. The loan program will also provide financing for small business chrome platers to purchase equipment or change their processes which will reduce air emissions. Loans are available from $10,000 up to a maximum of $500,000 with up to 10 years to repay. The implementation procedures and regulations are currently being developed.

Small Business Development Centers

Contact:
Dr. Edward Kawahara, State Director
California Small Business Development
  Center
Department of Commerce
Office of Small Business
1121 L Street, Suite 600
Sacramento, CA 95814
(916) 324–9234

Small Business Development Centers (SBDCs) provide in-depth counseling and technical assistance in the areas of business planning and management, financing, and marketing to existing and prospective small business owners. Other services include workshops and conferences for existing and new businesses as well as information dissemination. There are 20 SBDCs located throughout the state. A complete listing of Small Business Development Centers and subcenters is in Appendix A of this directory.

Office of Local Development

Contact:
Director
Office of Local Development
Department of Commerce
801 K Street, Suite 1600
Sacramento, CA 95814
(916) 322–1398

The **Office of Local Development** and the public and private sectors work together to diversify and strengthen local economies and to provide jobs for local residents. The office promotes economic development as an ongoing function of local government by providing case studies, handbooks, slide shows, and other information on topics such as downtown revitalization, the streamlining of the permit process, and the formation of local development corporations. The office also provides direct loan development through the state's revolving loan program and some limited loan application packaging assistance.

Financing mechanisms from the Office of Local Development include the following:

- Through the **Community Development Block Grant Nonentitlement Program**, eligible cities with populations of less than 50,000 and counties with populations of less than 200,000 may obtain funds for a variety of activities that benefit small businesses, including the acquisition, rehabilitation, and construction of public works facilities; housing clearance and rehabilitation; and economic development.

- The **Small Business Revitalization Program** provides loan packaging assistance for eligible businesses applying to the U.S. Small Business Administration and the Department of Housing and Urban Development.

26

- The **California Statewide Certified Development Corporation** (CSCDC), allied with the Office of Local Development, assists small businesses in accessing public financing programs. Formed in 1988, the corporation provides 90-percent real estate financing for healthy growing businesses throughout California. Using the SBA 504 loan program, CSCDC creates employment opportunities by enabling expanding businesses to attain long-term, fixed rate loans. Although CSCDC targets the industrial/manufacturing sector, commercial and retail businesses are served as well.

In addition, the office assists municipalities in financing public infrastructure improvements necessary to accommodate the retention and expansion of businesses.

The **Rural Development Infrastructure Program** funds rural/public infrastructure projects that serve a specific business and result in the creation/retention of permanent private-sector jobs.

In addition to the Office of Small Business and the Office of Local Development, the Department of Commerce offers services or assistance to California firms through the **Office of Business Development** and the **Office of Economic Research**.

Contact:
Mr. Calvin Young
Department of Commerce
801 K Street, Suite 1600
Sacramento, CA 95814
(916) 322–1398

Contacts:
Ms. Janet Turner, Director
Office of Business Development
Department of Commerce
801 K Street, Suite 1600
Sacramento, CA 95814
(916) 322–3502

Mr. Lance Barnett, Director
Office of Economic Research
Department of Commerce
801 K Street, Suite 1600
Sacramento, CA 95814
(916) 322–3562

Office of Administrative Law

Contact:
Mr. Marz Garcia, Director
Office of Administrative Law
555 Capitol Mall, Suite 1290
Sacramento, CA 95814
(916) 323–6225

The **California Office of Administrative Law** (OAL) conducts a legal and technical review of all state agency actions to adopt, amend, or repeal regulations. OAL is responsible for ensuring that each regulation is necessary, can be easily understood, does not duplicate or conflict with other laws, and gives the agency the authority to take action. Agencies must also consider alternatives to imposing unnecessary burdens and paperwork. Regulations failing the review process are disapproved. Public notices and other materials are available.

Office of Small and Minority Business

Contact:
Ms. Alice Flissinger, Chief
Office of Small and Minority Business
Department of General Services
1808 14th Street, Room 100
Sacramento, CA 95814
(916) 322–5060

The **Office of Small and Minority Business** (OSMB) has the responsibility to aid, counsel, assist, and protect the interests of small, minority, and women-owned firms that do business with state agencies and to ensure that a fair proportion of state purchases, construction contracts, and service contracts are placed with such businesses.

Within OSMB, the **Small Business Section** assists state agencies in identifying resources, establishing goals and policies, disseminating information, and providing liaison services with small businesses. It conducts quarterly meetings of the Business Expansion Council, compiles and maintains comprehensive bidder lists, assists in the implementation of the small business bid preference provisions, verifies preference eligibility of firms, and engages in outreach programs, such as small business conferences and seminars.

The **Minority- and Women-Owned Business Section** encourages women and minority participation in business ownership by offering technical assistance, identifying specific business opportunities, and working with state agencies to establish goals for a greater share of state business to be placed with such firms.

Through a twice-monthly publication, the **California State Contracts Register Section** presents a centralized source of state contract opportunities and activities to the business community. In addition, the office assists state agencies in complying with contracting procedures through the promotion of open government; increases competition by small, minority, and women-owned businesses; and protects state revenues through efficient and prudent use of taxpayer monies.

Business and Industrial Development Corporations

Contact:
Mr. John Paulus
Deputy Superintendent of Banks
State Banking Department
111 Pine Street, Suite 1100
San Francisco, CA 94111
(415) 557–8686

Business and Industrial Development Corporations (BIDCOs) provide financial assistance to California firms in cooperation with the U.S. Small Business Administration, pursuant to section 7(a) of the federal Small Business Act. They are publicly chartered and privately funded corporations for small business development, regulated by the State Banking Department.

SAFE–BIDCO

Contact:
Mr. Paul Cormier, President
State Assistance Fund for Enterprise
Business and Industrial Development
   Corporation
145 Wikiup Drive
Santa Rosa, CA 95403–1337
(707) 577–8621

The **State Assistance Fund for Enterprise, Business and Industrial Development Corporation** (SAFE–BIDCO) is a state-owned nonprofit corporation. Like other BIDCOs, it issues loans in conjunction with SBA's guarantee program. It can also assist small firms working with the state's Export Finance Office and provides loan guarantees as part of the state's Small Business Development Corporation program. SAFE–BIDCO also provides access to other state loan programs designed to help small businesses meet environmental standards.

Firms are eligible for SAFE–BIDCO loans so long as they meet the SBA guidelines. Terms are flexible—loans can range from $25,000 to $875,000 for 5 years to 25 years. These loans can help a firm acquire assets, provide working capital, or restructure existing debt. In some cases, loans can be made to acquire or start a business. SAFE–BIDCO works with many other agencies to boost economic development, job creation, minority opportunity, energy conservation, and export growth.

California Pollution Control Financing Authority

Contact:
Ms. Annette L. Porini, Executive Director
California Pollution Control Financing
   Authority
P.O. Box 942809
Sacramento, CA 94209-0001
(916) 445–9597

Created in 1973, the **California Pollution Control Financing Authority** is an independent state agency. Companies that must comply with air and water quality regulations or have waste disposal projects are eligible for tax-exempt financing. The authority will fund the cost of a project including land, buildings, equipment, engineering, and related professional expenses.

Alternative Energy Source Financing Authority

Contact:
Ms. Annette Porini, Acting Director
Alternative Energy Source Financing
   Authority
P.O. Box 942809
Sacramento, CA 94209–0001
(916) 445–9597

Established in 1980, the **Alternative Energy Source Financing Authority** assists companies using new energy projects developed by private businesses.

California State World Trade Commission

Contact:
Mr. Gregory Mignano, Executive Director
California State World Trade Commission
801 K Street
Sacramento, CA 95814
(916) 324–5511
fax: (916) 324–5791

The **California State World Trade Commission** is the state's leading agency for export promotion, organizing overseas trade shows and missions, and maintaining computerized export trade leads—available on-line through the Automated Trade System.

Contacts:
Ms. Irene L. Fisher, Director
California Export Finance Office
107 South Broadway, Suite 8039
Los Angeles, CA 90012
(213) 897–3997
fax: (213) 897–0915

The **California Export Financing Office** (CEFO), a unit of the California State World Trade Commission, provides both working capital (preshipment) and accounts receivable (post-shipment) loan guarantees to assist in the financing of California exports. Applicants must have a solid export order in hand and at least one year of experience.

Mr. J.H. Dethero, Regional Manager
California Export Finance Office
425 Market Street, #2838
San Francisco, CA 94105
(415) 557–9812
fax: (415) 557–7710

CEFO can guarantee up to 85 percent of a qualified loan, with a maximum guarantee of $500,000, for as long as 360 days. Past CEFO guarantees have supported transactions ranging in size from $25,000 to $5 million. A preshipment guarantee can provide working capital needed to finance the cost of labor, material, and other expenses leading to an export sale. A post-shipment guarantee enables an exporter to extend terms to a foreign buyer.

The CEFO became operational in mid-1985. To date, the office has supported more than $220 million in California export sales. A recent pilot agreement with the U.S. Small Business Administration created a joint loan guarantee agreement by the two agencies that can provide for a working capital loan of up to $822,000.

Economic Development Department

Contact:
Ms. Kaye R. Kiddoo, Director
Employment Development Department
800 Capitol Mall
Sacramento, CA 94280–0001
(916) 445–9212

The **Employment Development Department** (EDD) joins with other members of a statewide employment and training system to provide a wide range of services to small businesses. With EDD's Job Service program, employers can take advantage of a network of information and services provided in nearly 200 cities throughout California.

Governor's Advisory Council or Task Force

Contact:
Mr. Ron Matik, Chairman
Small Business Development Board
Department of Commerce
801 K Street, Suite 1600
Sacramento, CA 95814
(916) 324–1295

The governor has established a 36-member **Small Business Development Board** to identify and discuss the needs and concerns of small business, consisting of 21 voting and 15 non-voting members. The main objective is to encourage a favorable small business climate in the state. Their findings—such as recommendations for new legislation or regulatory changes—are reported directly to the governor. The board replaces the governor's former Small Business Advisory Council.

Legislative Committees and Subcommittees

There are no legislative committees or subcommittees that meet specifically on small business issues. The committees were eliminated as a result of reductions in committees and staff mandated by passage of Proposition 140.

Legislation

Legislation passed in California in 1989 includes the following:

- S.B. 1005, which covers rural economic development. S.B. 1005 increases the number of potential projects eligible for funding to include private developers; it also streamlines the application process. This bill also expands the number of small business development centers in rural counties.

- A.B. 324, which covers relocation assistance. This bill brings state law into compliance with federal law on the issue of relocation assistance for small businesses. It provides that a small business may receive state assistance when it is determined by a public entity that the displacement is permanent.

- A.B. 1588, the Small Business Incubator Grant, appropriated $25,000 from the General Fund for allocation to the Hoopa Valley Business Council of the Hoopa Valley Tribe for use as a small business incubator grant to fund small businesses that make and merchandise native American crafts.

- A.B. 28 extends the sunset of the Employment Training Program to January 1, 1994, and restructures the program. Among other changes, the bill revises the Employment Training Panel's priorities to include retraining of eligible participants employed by small businesses and requires that the Small Business Development Center program in the Department of Commerce provide specified information on the program to its clients.

- S.B. 1629 expands the purposes of the State Assistance Fund for Energy, California Business and Industrial Development Corporation (SAFE–BIDCO) to include all types of businesses eligible for government-guaranteed loans. It also provides SAFE–BIDCO the option to function as a regional corporation under the Department of Commerce.

- A.B. 1542 recasts and revises the law that authorizes the Small Business Development Board. Among the various other provisions, it would require regional small business development corporations to present a one-year plan instead of a four-year plan to the board and revise the criteria for the making of a loan or loan guarantee.

- A.B. 2444, which covers environmental quality, requires the South Coast Air Quality Management District to allocate and expend approximately $1 million collected from penalties for financial assistance to small businesses and employers of minorities and low-income persons to further their compliance with air quality regulations.

- A.B. 60 establishes the California Major Medical Program to provide health insurance to state residents who are unable to obtain adequate health insurance and would provide for the scope of coverage, rate limitations, method of operation, and subscriber eligibility and enrollment.

- S.B. 906 which, among other provisions, requires the California State Lottery Commission to report annually to the legislature on the level of participation of small businesses, socially and economically disadvantaged businesses, and California businesses in all contracts awarded by the commission.

- S.B. 1517 requires that any state governmental agency that awards contracts for professional bond services, construction, procurement, and services have annual participation goals of not less than 3 percent for disabled veteran-owned small business enterprises.

- A.B. 307 extends the size requirement for the small business preference to contracts for delivery of services.

- A.B. 457 makes it unlawful for a person to fraudulently obtain acceptance or certification as a minority or women business enterprise. It would subject them to a civil penalty of up to $5,000 and from further contracting with any state agency.

- A.B. 1717 clarifies participation goals for minority business enterprises (MBEs) and women business enterprises (WBEs) established by A.B. 1933 (Chapter 61, statutes of 1989). Among other provisions, this bill requires state agencies to award contracts to bidders that meet or make good faith effort to meet the current 15/5 participation goals for MBEs andWBEs.

- A.B. 1829 provides that in a tie between lowest reasonable bids from a disabled veteran-owned business and a small business, the disabled veteran-owned business shall be awarded the contract.

- A.C.R. 67 urges the Department of General Services to reject proposed emergency regulations concerning self-certification by minority and women business enterprises and would urge the department to develop new statewide certification regulations.

- A.B. 724 expands the definition of the telephone seller who must register with the Department of Justice. Among other definitional changes, the bill requires the registration of telemarketers who are engaged in the offering of any item or service at a price that the seller states or implies is below the regular price of the item or service.

- S.B. 432 and A.B. 1308 establish, among other provisions, a tax credit program for machinery used to manufacture products from waste materials. A credit of 40 percent of the cost of "qualified property" (new machinery) would be spread over four years for the property purchased within a specified period.

- A.B. 446 expands the state's existing tax credit program for employer-incurred child care expenses. Specifically, the bill allows employers to claim the credit for contributions associated with dependent care centers providing specialized care of mildly ill children.

- A.B. 982 waives the imposition of a minimum franchise tax in the taxable year in which the taxpayer ceases doing business, if certain conditions are met.

Legislative action in 1990 that affects small business includes the following:

- A.B. 107 redefines "storage facility" to provide that a hazardous waste facility is not a storage facility in such a case if the quantity of hazardous waste does not exceed 5,000 gallons or 45,000 pounds, whichever is greater. It would also require the owner of an underground storage tank to maintain evidence of financial responsibility and would require the owner to pay a monthly storage fee of $0.006 for each gallon of petroleum stored. Signed by the governor on April 11, 1990.

- S.C.R. 46 covers capital formation. This bill requests that the Small Business Development Board within the Department of Commerce conduct a comprehensive study on financial obstacles to small business development and an overview of the public/private approaches that may be used to overcome these obstacles. This measure requests that the Small Business Development Board create a Task Force on Small Business Capital Formation to provide input into this study. Signed by the governor on May 1, 1990.

State Small Business Conferences

Contact:
Mr. William Harper, Executive Director
Office of Small Business
Department of Commerce
801 K Street, Suite 1600
Sacramento, CA 95814
(916) 445–6546

The Office of Small Business within the Department of Commerce participates in many local conferences in conjunction with state legislators, promoting state assistance programs and services to small business owners.

Colorado

Small Business Offices, Programs, and Activities

Office of Business Development

Contact:
Mr. Rick Garcia, State Director
Colorado Small Business Development
  Center
Office of Business Development
1625 Broadway, Suite 1710
Denver, CO 80202
(303) 892–3809
Hot Line: (800) 333–7798
        (toll-free, in-state)
fax: (303) 892–3848

The **Office of Business Development** serves as the primary contact point for private sector business development inquiries and initiatives, and is the single point of contact for business-to-business assistance, retention, expansion, and recruitment activities. The office houses the Colorado Small Business Development Center, the Minority Business Office, the Business Development Office, and administers the Colorado FIRST training program.

The **Colorado Small Business Development Center**, in conjunction with the **Office of Regulatory Reform**, offers information, management assistance, and referrals to small businesses across the state. The office maintains a computerized data base of business-related information on training workshops, public financing resources, business regulations, and license and permit procedures. In addition, businesses seeking management or technical assistance are referred to the local Small Business Development Centers located throughout the state. A listing of all Small Business Development Centers and subcenters in Colorado is in Appendix A of this directory.

Contact:
Mr. Rick Garcia, State Director
Small Business Development Center
Office of Business Development
1625 Broadway, Suite 1710
Denver, CO 80202
(303) 892–3809 (administration)
Hot Line: (800) 333–7798
        (toll-free, in-state)
        (303) 592–5920
        (Denver metropolitan area)
fax: (303) 892–3848

The **Colorado Leading Edge Program** is part of a statewide initiative to improve the business success rate for Colorado businesses. The program includes an all-day overview seminar and follow-up intensive training—50 to 70 hours of classroom work, with 6 to 8 hours per business of one-on-one consulting. By the end of the course, each graduate is expected to have completed a business plan and be qualified to manage a small business, including being able to secure capital, market products, and manage personnel.

Contact:
Mr. Ron Montoya, Director
Minority Business Office
Office of Business Development
1625 Broadway, Suite 1710
Denver, CO 80202
(303) 892–3840
fax: (303) 892–3848

The **Minority Business Office** assists minority-owned businesses in securing federal, state, and corporate contracts. It also provides a resource referral service and facilitates networking between majority and minority businesses to promote joint business activities. The office is an advocate for minority business and provides a point of contact for current bid information to match with the data base of minority businesses maintained by this office.

Contact:
Ms. Susan Blansett, Business Development
   Coordinator
Office of Business Development
1625 Broadway, Suite 1710
Denver, CO 80202
(303) 892–3840
fax: (303) 892–3848

The **Business Development Office** provides information and assistance to local economic development organizations, assists in retaining and expanding existing businesses, and responds to out-of-state business inquiries concerning expanding or relocating in Colorado.

Contact:
Ms. Susan Blansett, Director
Colorado FIRST
Office of Business Development
1625 Broadway, Suite 1710
Denver CO 80202
(303) 892–3840
fax: (303) 892–3848

The **Colorado FIRST Customized Training Program** is jointly administered by the Office of Business Development and the Colorado Community College and Occupational Educational System. The program provides job training assistance for nonretail companies locating to, or undertaking a significant expansion in, Colorado.

Colorado International Trade Office

Contact:
Mr. Morgan Smith, Director
Colorado International Trade Office
1625 Broadway, Suite 680
Denver CO 80202
(303) 892–3850
fax: (303) 892–3820

The **Colorado International Trade Office** has two principal goals: (1) to promote the export of Colorado goods and services, and (2) to attract the kind of foreign investment that will create jobs for Coloradans. Export promotion activities include individual counseling, market research, participation in seminars and educational programs, organizing trade shows and missions, and bringing buying missions to Colorado. The office also maintains a worldwide network of investment prospects. Overseas offices are located in Japan, Korea, and Taiwan.

Office of Consumer Counsel

Contact:
Mr. Ron Binz, Director
Office of Consumer Counsel
1580 Logan Street, Suite 700
Denver, CO 80203
(303) 894–2121
fax: (303) 894–2117

The **Office of Consumer Counsel** (OCC) is Colorado's advocate for the residential, small business, and agricultural communities in utility rate cases before the Public Utilities Commission (PUC). When utility companies seek rate increases, the OCC analyzes the request and represents consumers in hearings before the PUC to ensure that utility rates are reasonable.

Office of Regulatory Reform

Contact:
Mr. Greg Romberg, Director
Office of Regulatory Reform
1560 Broadway, Suite 1530
Denver, CO 80202
(303) 894–7839 Director's Office
Hot Line: (303) 592–5920
        (800) 333–7798
fax: (303) 894–7885

The **Office of Regulatory Reform** (ORR) serves as a small business advocate by identifying and eliminating duplicative, burdensome, and unnecessary government regulation and providing one-stop license and permit assistance to new and expanding businesses.

ORR works in a number of ways to keep governmental requirements on small businesses reasonable. Under the Regulatory Flexibility Act, ORR reviews all proposed regulations of state agencies to make sure they are not unduly burdensome on small businesses. Businesses with specific problems or concerns should contact ORR.

In conjunction with the Colorado Small Business Development Center, ORR operates the **Small Business Hotline**, a one-stop location for businesses and potential businesses to get regulatory, financial, and management information.

Contact:
Ms. Debra A. Martinez, Administrator
Office of Certification
1560 Broadway, Suite 1530
Denver, CO 80202
(303) 894–2355
fax: (303) 894–7885

A part of the Office of Regulatory Reform, the **Office of Certification**, reviews—according to standards and regulations developed by the U.S. Department of Transportation—the applications of firms that want to be certified as disadvantaged business enterprises. This office currently provides certification for firms wanting to do work for the Colorado Department of Highways, the Regional Transportation District, and the Denver Water Board. It is expected that it will provide certification for other programs in the future.

Colorado Division of Employment and Training (Job Service)

Contact:
Mr. Robert Hale, Director
Colorado Division of Employment and Training
600 Grant Street, Suite 900
Denver, CO 80203
(303) 837–3819
fax: (303) 837–3956

The **Colorado Job Service** refers applicants to local training and job opportunities. Employers may list job orders with the Job Service for statewide recruitment, screening, and referral of workers. Employers providing training opportunities may be eligible for a tax credit for wages paid through the Targeted Jobs Tax Credit.

Job Training Partnership Act

Contact:
Mr. Leslie Franklin, Director
Governor's Job Training Office
728 South Colorado Boulevard, Suite 550
Denver, CO 80222
(303) 758–5020
fax: (303) 758–5578

The **Job Training Partnership Act** is a federally funded program authorizing training for economically disadvantaged individuals. Activities include basic skills training, classroom training, on-the-job training, youth employment, and job creation through economic development. Also, the **Governor's Summer Job Hunt** is designed to develop jobs for Colorado youth (ages 16 to 21). Tax credits are available to employers who hire young workers. Colorado has 10 service delivery areas:

Adams County Employment Center
7190 Colorado Boulevard, 5th Floor
Commerce City, CO 80022
(303) 289-6500

Arapahoe County Employment and Training
11059 Bethany Drive, #201
Aurora, CO 80014–2617
(303) 788–1080

Boulder County Private Industry Partnership
2040 14th Street
Boulder, CO 80302
(303) 441–3985

Mayor's Office of Employment and Training (Denver)
1391 North Speer Boulevard, #500
Denver, CO 80204
(303) 893–3382

Colorado Springs/El Paso County Industrial Training Administration
702 East Boulder
Colorado Springs, CO 80903
(719) 578–8871

Jeffco Employment and Training Services
900 Jefferson County Parkway
Golden, CO 80401
(303) 271–4600

Larimer County Employment and Training Services
3842 South Mason
Fort Collins, CO 80525
(303) 223–2470

Office of Rural Job Training
655 Broadway, Suite 900
Denver, CO 80203
(303) 620–4800

Pueblo County Consortium SDA
720 North Main Street, #320
Pueblo, CO 81003
(719) 543–2951

Weld County Department of Human Resources
P.O. Box 1805
Greeley, CO 80631
(303) 353–3800

Enterprise Zones

Contact:
Mr. Evan Metcalf, Enterprise Zone
    Coordinator
Department of Local Affairs
1313 Sherman Street, Suite 518
Denver, CO 80203
(303) 866–2205
fax: (303) 866–2251

Colorado's Urban and Rural Enterprise Zone Act offers the following tax incentives for businesses within designated enterprise zones:

• a 3-percent investment tax credit;

• a $500 job tax credit or refund;

• a double job tax credit or refund for agricultural processing businesses;

• a $200, two-year job tax credit for employer-sponsored health insurance;

• a 3-percent credit for increased research and experimental expenditures;

• a 25-percent credit, up to $50,000, for qualified expenditures to rehabilitate buildings that are at least 20 years old and that have been vacant at least two years;

• a 50-percent credit, up to $100,000, for contributions to designated enterprise zone projects and for contributions to promote child care in enterprise zones;

• exemption from the 3-percent state sales and use tax on purchases of manufacturing equipment; and

• local government property tax incentives on a case-by-case basis.

An enterprise zone newsletter and annual report is distributed by the Department of Local Affairs. State law, which authorizes 16 zones, expires February 15, 1998.

40

Business Advancement Centers

Contact:
Ms. Karen Eye, Director
CU Business Advancement Centers
4700 Walnut Street, Suite 101
Boulder, CO 80301
(303) 444–5723
(800) 369–1243 (toll-free)
fax: (303) 447–8748

Subcenter locations:
PRO–BID, Denver
(303) 571–4215
fax: (303) 595–0027

PRO–BID, Colorado Springs
(800) 544–7516 (toll-free)
(719) 591–1104
fax: (303) 550–1011

The **University of Colorado Business Advancement Center** (CU–BAC), based in Boulder, provides business management and specialized consulting services to small businesses throughout Colorado. The following services are offered by the center:

- **Federal procurement assistance:** PRO–BID, a procurement technical assistance program, is available in all counties of Colorado to assist businesses interested in selling a product or service to the federal government. Contract specialists work with businesses on interpretation of solicitations, federal regulations, bid preparation, and other aspects of the procurement process.

- **Business Research and Information Network:** BRAIN is a state-of-the-art technology transfer program that brings computerized information retrieval and technical transfer capabilities to all areas of Colorado. BRAIN is currently accessed through CU–BAC offices and BRAIN associates throughout Colorado.

- **Small Business Innovation Research** (SBIR) program: CU–BAC assists Colorado's small research and development firms in competing for federal contracts from the Small Business Innovation Research program. BRAIN and the CU–BAC's business consultants help firms gain access to technical experts and commercialization strategy. Assistance is also provided for commercialization of federal and university laboratory technologies.

- **Consultant data base of expertise:** staff and faculty are registered by area of expertise, consulting interest, and availability. Business and industry seeking to utilize CU–Boulder expertise can be matched with an appropriate consultant.

- **Publications and workshop presentations** are also available upon request.

Colorado Housing and Finance Authority

Contact:
Ms. Colleen Schwarz, Director
Commercial Program Division
Colorado Housing and Finance Authority
1981 Blake Street
Denver, CO 80202
(303) 297–2432
fax: (303) 297–2615

Colorado Housing and Finance Authority (CHFA), a quasi-government corporation, was established in 1973 to finance housing through the issuance of tax-exempt securities. In 1982, the Colorado General Assembly authorized CHFA to develop and operate programs to assist small business. Currently, CHFA offers the Quality Investment Capital program, the bank participation (ACCESS) program, the Colorado Export Credit Insurance program, and the Quality Agriculture Loan program, and provides staffing and partial funding to Colorado International Capital (CIC), Colorado Invesco, Strategic Equity Funds, and the Rural Seed Fund.

The **Quality Investment Capital** (QIC) program is administered by CHFA to provide fixed-rate financing for small business loans guaranteed by the U.S. Small Business Administration. Loans are extended for working capital needs, equipment purchases, business expansions, and real estate acquisitions. Firms seeking funds under this program must be for-profit, have less than $750,000 outstanding on any SBA loans, with no defaults of CHFA or state of Colorado loan programs, and cannot be retail/wholesale establishments where more than 25 percent of income is derived from alcohol sales. The SBA guarantees up to 90 percent of loans up to $155,000, and up to 85 percent of loans up to $750,000. Loan terms extend seven years for working capital, 10 years for equipment, and 25 years for real estate purchases.

The **ACCESS** program is a small business financing tool for fixed assets, created through participation in a bank-generated first mortgage funded as part of an SBA 504 financing package. ACCESS borrowers receive a fixed-rate mortgage for 20 years.

Colorado, through CHFA, was the first state to offer exporters a way to insure their foreign receivables under the umbrella policy of the Foreign Credit Insurance Association (FCIA). FCIA is an agent of the Export-Import Bank of the United States; this insurance is backed by the federal government. A **Colorado Export Credit** insurance policy will cover 90 percent of commercial risk and 100 percent of political risk, based on the gross invoice amount.

Colorado International Capital is a public/private partnership that provides preshipment and post-shipment financing for international sales by Colorado firms.

Colorado Invesco is a minority enterprise small business investment company (MESBIC) that provides equity to disadvantaged businesses.

The **Strategic Equity Funds Program** is a venture capital fund for start-up and early stage Colorado businesses. The fund is managed by Colorado Venture Management and the investors are from both the public and private sector.

The **Rural Seed Fund** is a venture capital fund for start-up and early stage businesses located in rural Colorado. This fund is managed by Colorado Venture Management and the investors are from both the private and public sectors.

Colorado Agricultural Development Authority

Contact:
Mr. Jim Rubingh, Secretary
Colorado Agricultural Development Authority
700 Kipling Street, Suite 4000
Lakewood, CO 80215–5894
(303) 239–4114
fax: (303) 239-4125

The **Colorado Agricultural Development Authority** (CADA) runs the **Beginning Farmer Program**, which offers low interest financing to Colorado farmers and ranchers. Lenders receive a tax-exempt bond for financing a qualifying agricultural project, resulting in lower interest rates for borrowers. The maximum loan amount is $250,000 and proceeds can only be used for the purchase of land and equipment.

CADA's **Quality Agricultural Loan** (QAL) program offers additional financing to Colorado agricultural producers. Through this program, administered by the Colorado Housing and Finance Authority (CHFA), state farmers and ranchers can obtain competitive, fixed-rate financing for terms of up to 25 years. Loans are made by the existing lending community, utilizing the Farmers Home Administration (FmHA) guaranteed loan program. Once a lender has received a loan guarantee from FmHA, CHFA can purchase the guaranteed portion of the loan.

SBA 504 Certified Development Companies

Four Colorado development companies—two in Denver, one in Colorado Springs, and one in Pueblo—lend to small and medium-size businesses at fixed rates for terms of 10 to 20 years. Companies must create one job for every $35,000 they receive in financing. A 504 loan is funded through the sale of a debenture that is guaranteed by the U.S. Small Business Administration for up to $750,000 or 40 percent of the total cost of land, buildings, and equipment.

Contacts:

Statewide

Mr. John Burger, Executive Director
Community Economic Development
   Company of Colorado
1111 Osage Street, Suite 110
Denver, CO 80204
(303) 893–8989
fax: (303) 892–8398

City and County of Denver

Mr. Dick Jones, Economic Development
   Specialist
Denver Urban Economic Development
   Corporation
303 West Colfax Avenue, Suite 1025
Denver, CO 80204
(303) 575–5540

El Paso County

Mr. James Coffey, Executive Director
Pikes Peak Regional Development
   Corporation
P.O. Box 9867
1112 West Colorado Avenue
Colorado Springs, CO 80932–9867
(719) 578–6962

*Pueblo County, San Luis, and
   Arkansas Valley*

Mr. Gil Baca, Program Officer
SCEDD Development Company
P.O. Box 1900
Pueblo, CO 81002
(719) 545–8680

*Adams, Arapahoe, Boulder, Denver,
   Douglas, Jefferson, Larimer, Morgan,
   and Weld counties*

Mr. Rudolph D. Bianchi, Executive Director
Front Range Regional Economic
   Development Company
Denver West Office Park,
   Building 19, #400
Golden, CO 80401
(303) 233–6598
fax: 237–1103

Small Business Incubators

Small Business Incubators are designed to encourage business start-ups and help struggling young firms survive their early years. Business incubators provide services to teach business skills and to improve knowledge of business operations and opportunities. Assistance offered includes workshops; formal and informal networks of business assistance; information about local business consulting services; multi-tenant office space; shared office services; and improved business access to capital. The Colorado Bio-Venture Center and the Boulder Technology Incubator are targeted incubators that seek to provide resources to build profitable new bio-businesses in Colorado.

Contacts:

Mr. Lewis T. Kontnik, Executive Director
Colorado Bio-Venture Center
860 Clermont, Suite 101
Denver, CO 80220
(303) 320–5651
fax: (303) 320–4965

Dr. Robert Calcaterra, Executive Director
Boulder Technology Incubator
1727 Conestoga Street
Boulder, CO 80301
(303) 449-3323

Ms. Marty Wilcoxson, Manager
Pueblo Business Technology Center
301 North Main Street
Pueblo, CO 81003
(719) 546–1133
fax: (719) 546–1942

Mr. Hugh Blevins, Director
Business Innovation Center of
    Jefferson County
1667 Cole Boulevard,
 Building 19, #400
Golden, CO 80401
(303) 238–0913
fax: (303) 237–1103

Mr. Skip Dyer, Executive Director
Canon City Business Incubator
402 Valley Road
Canon City, CO 81212
(719) 275–8601
fax: (719) 275–4400

Mr. Richard Reimer, Director
Mesa County Small Business Incubator
304 West Main Street
Grand Junction, CO 81505
(303) 243–5242
fax: (303) 241–0771

Mr. David Gonzales, Director
Denver Growth Center, Inc.
3003 Arapahoe Street
Denver, CO 80205
(303) 296–9400
fax: (303) 296–5542

Colorado Advanced Technology Institute

Contact:
Dr. Phillips V. Bradford, Executive Director
Colorado Advanced Technology Institute
1625 Broadway, Suite 700
Denver, CO 80202
(303) 620–4777
fax: (303) 620–4789

The **Colorado Advanced Technology Institute** (CATI) is a state agency created to encourage sponsorship of advanced technology research by the state's research universities and high technology industries. This cooperative effort is expected to produce new jobs by attracting, creating, and expanding Colorado industries involved in advanced technologies.

The state of Colorado appropriated $2.9 million for CATI in 1990. Matching funds, required to support CATI's programs, come from private industry and the federal government. In 1991, CATI provided seed funds for the creation of a targeted incubator, the Colorado Bio-Venture Center.

Governor's Advisory Council or Task Force

Contact:
Mr. Rick Garcia, State Director
Small Business Development Center
Office of Business Development
1625 Broadway, Suite 1710
Denver, CO 80202
(303) 892–3840

The **Small Business Council**, consisting of small business leaders from throughout the state, provides a forum for small business owners to bring their views to the attention of the state. The council seeks to identify small business problems, recommend solutions, and generally advise the governor on small business matters.

Legislative Committees and Subcommittees

The Colorado Legislature has no committee or subcommittee focusing solely on small business issues. Small business matters typically are considered by the House and Senate Business Affairs and Labor Committees.

Contacts:

Senator Jack Fenlon, Chairman
Senate Committee on Business Affairs
    and Labor
State Capitol
Denver, CO 80203
(303) 866–4866

Representative Paul Shauer, Chairman
House Committee on Business Affairs
    and Labor
State Capitol
Denver, CO 80203
(303) 866–2946

Legislation

Legislation adopted in the 1989 session affecting small business included the following:

- S.B. 195 balances Colorado's workers' compensation laws to benefit both injured workers and their employers. S.B. 195 reduced the statute of limitations for injuries from three to two years, reducing business owners' exposure to liability claims. Cost savings for business owners should flow from the requirement that the director of the division of labor promulgate rules establishing a time schedule within which hearings should be held.

- H.B. 1321 established, as of July 1, 1989, that employees who quit one job for a "better" job that they ultimately lose are no longer eligible for unemployment insurance benefits. H.B. 1321 continues benefits for construction workers under certain limited circumstances. Business owners will eventually save on their unemployment insurance premiums, as this change will eliminate $9 million annually in unemployment compensation costs.

- S.B. 211 affirms a recent Colorado Supreme Court decision that requires group health insurance policies to provide coverage for normal pregnancy and childbirth. However, S.B. 211 further provides that small businesses with 15 or fewer employees may self-insure for the coverage separate from group health policies. S.B. 211 requires that all future legislative proposals for mandatory benefits include a cost/benefit analysis prior to the adoption of such mandatory benefits.

Legislation adopted at the 1990 session of interest to small business included the following:

- H.B. 1222 requires that more than 1,700 dealer firms and 55,000 securities brokers doing business in Colorado be licensed by the state. The legislation also eliminated loopholes in securities registration practices and broadened state enforcement powers.

- H.B. 1033, which took effect in 1991, gives those restoring historic properties a state income tax credit not to exceed $50,000 per property or 25 percent of the total cost of the renovation, whichever is less.

- H.B. 1305 creates a pool of funds to be used to insure between 2,500 and 4,000 people who have been classified as uninsurable because of certain health problems. The bill calls for the collection of an income tax surcharge to fund the program.

- S.B. 161 would allow businesses setting up on-site child care to follow different regulations than those established by the state Department of Social Services. A company seeking to establish on-site care would be required to set up a panel of employees, which would then draft regulations for the child care center to follow.

- S.B. 81 prohibits the taxation of computer software, and exempts a company's computer software from property taxation assessments.

- H.B. 1212 allows employers to receive a reduction in premium rates if the companies institute risk management plans to reduce the number of job-related injuries.

Legislation adopted at the 1991 legislative session of interest to small business included the following:

- S.B. 218 streamlines the administrative process of workers' compensation, including medical cost containment measures; tightens the definition of what constitutes permanent partial disability; and increases benefits to more seriously injured workers. Some of the changes made in Colorado's workers' compensation law include the following:

  Permanent Partial Disability. If an employee has an injury enumerated in the schedule of injuries, the employee is limited to the medical impairment benefits specified in the schedule.

  Mediation. Mediation is required for disputes involving a claimant's average weekly wage, change of health care provider, or authorized medical benefits. Voluntary mediation is not precluded. This bill authorizes the imposition of penalties for failure to attend or participate in mandatory mediation.

  Binding Arbitration. Binding arbitration may be used as an alternative to the present hearing procedures for workers' compensation.

  Data from Insurance. The director of the Division of Workers' Compensation and the Insurance Commissioner are to collect data and statistics that will establish a Colorado data base to be used in determining the cost of the workers' compensation system and the reasonableness and fairness of rates for workers' compensation coverage.

  Definitions. "Employment" shall not include participation in a voluntary recreational activity, regardless of whether it is promoted, sponsored, or supported by the employer.

  Maximum Medical Improvement. "Maximum medical improvement" is a point at which any medically determinable physical or mental impairment resulting from injury has become stable and further treatment cannot improve the condition. This definition helps to eliminate needless medical costs.

  Physical Impairment Ratings. All physical impairment ratings shall be based on the revised 3rd edition of the "AMA Guides to the Evaluation of Permanent Impairment."

- H.B. 1279 amends the Colorado Employment Security Act to make it easier for employers to demonstrate that a person working for them is an independent contractor rather than an employee. The bill permits contractual agreements to include provisions spelling out working conditions, training requirements, and other points that previously would have been construed as conditions of employment, thus requiring an employer to provide unemployment insurance benefits.

- S.B. 18 provides for the continuation of the Office of Regulatory Reform (ORR). This office offers small businesses one-stop permitting and licensing information and acts as an advocate within state government for the interests of small business. ORR has been especially effective when state agencies propose rules that may affect small business.

- S.B. 231 restores the right of taxpayers whose properties are over-valued by an assessor to have their property taxes reduced by an abatement. The Colorado Court of Appeals took away that right in a 1990 decision. If this bill had not passed, property taxpayers who failed—for any reason—to protest the over-valuation of property by an assessor would have been unable to secure a reduction in property taxation through an abatement.

- H.B. 1262 lowers the statutory limits on growth in state spending of general fund money. This measure covers about half the state's budget and should encourage efficiency in government operations.

- H.B. 1168 will allow health insurance carriers to offer small businesses (with 25 or fewer employees) a policy without the mandatory coverage currently required of policies sold in Colorado. As passed, the bill does not allow employers to drop mandated coverage they already provide. The bill will enable more small businesses to provide health insurance to their employees.

- H.B. 1198 creates a Colorado Department of Transportation to coordinate statewide transportation planning.

State Small Business Conferences

Contact:
Office of Business Development
1625 Broadway, Suite 1710
Denver, CO 80202
(303) 892–3840

In 1990, the Governor's Economic Development Strategic Plan called for a Statehouse Conference. Eleven regional conferences were held in advance of a statewide **Colorado Small Business Statehouse Conference**, which was conducted in November 1991. Objectives of the conference were, in part, to (1) increase awareness of the contributions of small business to the economy; (2) identify issues creating obstacles for small business development; and (3) identify local and state leaders in advance of the 1994 White House Conference on Small Business.

Women's Economic Summits were conducted in March 1988 and June 1990. Each conference brought together hundreds of women from across the state to address the role and status of women in the Colorado economy.

Connecticut

Small Business Offices, Programs, and Activities

Department of Economic Development

Contact:
Ms. Martha A. Hunt, Executive Director
Business and Regional Development
Office of Small Business Services
Connecticut Department of Economic
    Development
865 Brook Street
Rocky Hill, CT 06067–3405
(203) 258–4200

Through various program offices, the **Office of Small Business Services** provides financial, technical, and management assistance to small firms, as well as specialized information in areas such as procurement and international trade. The office directs set-aside programs for small business procurement; administers funds for the state's Small Business Development Centers; coordinates the flow of information with technical and management assistance programs sponsored by the department; and encourages lending to small firms by the Connecticut Development Authority. The office also serves as a liaison between federal, state, regional, and local government agencies concerned with small business matters.

Contact:
Ms. Patricia E. Koch, Development Agent
Connecticut Department of Economic
    Development
865 Brook Street
Rocky Hill, CT 06067–3405
(203) 258–4200

The **Procurement Assistance Program** helps small firms interested in contracting with the government. State law requires that a minimum of 25 percent of state-funded purchases be set aside for Connecticut small business; 25 percent of that amount is to be allocated to minority- and women-owned firms. To be eligible, a small business must be Connecticut-based, in operation for at least a year, and have gross sales of less than $3 million. By law, firms participating in the program are to be paid within 30 days after completion of the contract.

Contact:
Mr. Graham Waldon, Business Ombudsman
Office of State Business Ombudsman
Connecticut Department of Economic
    Development
865 Brook Street
Rocky Hill, CT 06067
(203) 258–4200

The **Office of Business Ombudsman** was established within the Department of Economic Development by executive order of the governor. The purpose of the Ombudsman office is to settle business owners' complaints about any service provided by Connecticut state government. The office has 72 hours to inform the business owner of the status of the complaint.

Contact:
Mr. Andy Hammer, Director
International Division
Connecticut Department of Economic
   Development
865 Brook Street
Rocky Hill, CT 06067
(203) 258–4200

The **International Division** encourages both foreign and domestic companies to locate or invest in Connecticut. The division promotes trade through a lead program, publishes a licensing and joint venture brochure, sponsors trade missions, and participates in trade shows. Also available are an Exporters Revolving Fund to encourage export opportunities for small to medium-sized companies, and other incentive programs.

Connecticut Technology Assistance Center

Contact:
Mr. Eric Ott, Director
Connecticut Technology Assistance Center
845 Brook Street
Rocky Hill, CT 06067
(203) 258–4305

The **Connecticut Technology Assistance Center** (CONNTAC) maintains a complete listing of technical, financial, research and educational services, programs, and other state resources to help potential business owners turn their ideas into viable products. CONNTAC offers a wide range of assistance in addition to being an information warehouse, including developing and writing business plans; planning, managing, marketing, and sales functions; federal, state, and local financing; and educational and training assistance to upgrade employees' skills, recruit employees, and develop training programs.

Connecticut Development Authority

Contact:
Mr. A. Searle Field, Executive Director
Connecticut Development Authority
217 Washington Street
Hartford, CT 06016
(203) 522–3730

The **Connecticut Development Authority** is a public agency established to assist in capital formation for small business. The authority is governed by a board of directors that includes the state treasurer, the commissioner of economic development, and the secretary to the Office of Policy and Management. The authority assists businesses through a number of programs, including the following:

The **Connecticut Growth Fund** provides up to $1 million of fixed asset or working capital financing to businesses with sales of $10 million or less on terms of 5 to 20 years.

The **Comprehensive Business Assistance Fund** provides up to $500,000 of financing to certain targeted businesses with sales of $3 million or less.

The **Naugatuck Valley Revolving Loan Program** provides supplemental financing in amounts up to $200,000 to industrial businesses in the Naugatuck Valley area and certain other areas of Connecticut.

Through the **Umbrella Bond Program**, the authority issues bonds on behalf of small firms to cover small issues.

Under the **Credit Insurance Program**, the authority can insure both bonds and privately financed loans. The program is especially effective in helping small and medium-sized firms, because the insured portion of the loans is backed by the full faith credit of the state. The authority is responsible for the statewide SBA 504 program.

Connecticut Innovations, Inc.

Contact:
Mr. Eric Ott, Director
Connecticut Innovations, Inc.
845 Brook Street
Rocky Hill, CT 06067
(203) 258–4305

A quasi-public, nonprofit organization, **Connecticut Innovations, Inc.**, makes risk capital investments in Connecticut firms developing new products. Up to 60 percent of development costs are provided in exchange for royalties, typically 5 percent, on the sale of sponsored products. Capitalized by general obligation bonds of the state, the goal of the organization is self-sufficiency based on royalty income. Loans of up to $300,000 at favorable interest rates for terms up to six years are offered to provide working capital for market introduction of new products. Loans must be matched dollar-for-dollar from the private sector.

Connecticut's **Small Business Innovation Research** (SBIR) program is also administered by Connecticut Innovations, Inc. Connecticut augments the federal SBIR program by providing a bridge grant of up to $20,000 to companies that have received a Phase I grant and are awaiting a decision on Phase II. The state grant enables companies to continue their research work during this critical period.

In addition to being Phase I winners, candidates for a Connecticut SBIR Assistance Grant must: be independently owned and operated, employ 250 or fewer people, submit their Phase I Final Report, submit their Phase II proposal and not be rejected at the time of the Connecticut award, and show potential for commercialization of product or service in Connecticut.

Connecticut Small Business Development Center

Contact:
Mr. John O'Connor, State Director
Connecticut Small Business Development
  Center
University of Connecticut
School of Business Administration
Box U-41, Room 422
368 Fairfield Road
Storrs, CT 06269-2041
(203) 486–4135

The Connecticut network of **Small Business Development Centers** (SBDCs) is headquartered at the University of Connecticut in Storrs, with branches in Bridgeport, Groton, New Haven, Waterbury, and West Hartford. The centers provide management and technical assistance to Connecticut small businesses. In addition to workshops and seminars, the SBDCs can provide in-depth counseling in problem areas such as marketing, cash flow management, accounting, and product development. A complete listing of all Small Business Development Centers in Connecticut, including addresses and telephone numbers, is in Appendix A of this directory.

Governor's Advisory Council or Task Force

Contact:
Ms. Patricia E. Koch, Development Agent
Connecticut Department of Economic
  Development
865 Brook Street
Rocky Hill, CT 06067
(203) 258–4200

The **Connecticut Small Business Advisory Council**, which is part of the Department of Economic Development, serves as a line of communication between the governor and the small business community. The 11-member body studies problems of small business, evaluates proposed and existing programs and legislation, and makes recommendations as appropriate.

Legislative Committees and Subcommittees

Contacts:
Senator George Jepsen, Chairman
Ms. Ellen Roman, Clerk to the Committee
Joint Committee on Planning and
  Development
Legislative Office Building, Room 2100
Hartford, CT 06106
(203) 240–0550

The Connecticut Legislature has in place a Joint Committee on Planning and Development that focuses primarily on small business issues. The legislature meets from January through June during odd-numbered years and February through May during even-numbered years.

Legislation

The 1989–1990 legislature enacted P.A. 90–253 to tighten and change language and definitions, helping eliminate "front" activity with respect to minority- and women-owned small business. In addition, the legislation allocated $50,000 for a study of discrimination in state construction contracts.

The 1991 legislature passed P.A. 91–201 in an effort to make health insurance more available to small business. All health insurers offering benefits to small businesses in Connecticut are mandated to participate in a reinsurance pool for small employers. The law requires insurers to accept small businesses into the Small Employer Health Plan, and makes special programs available to previously uninsured small businesses.

During 1992, the legislature passed P.A. 92–236, concerning capital investment. The act authorizes $110 million in state bonding for the Connecticut Development Authority to be used to leverage private lending through the following four programs:

- The Loan Guarantee Program allows the Authority to issue loan guarantees to eligible financial institutions for any new eligible project to encourage the growth and retention of manufacturing firms and other small businesses.

- The Business Line of Credit provides a two-year pilot program for small and medium-sized businesses wherein loans and loan guarantees are available to assist small businesses with their short-term working capital needs.

- The Capital Access Program lets the Authority provide portfolio insurance to participating financial institutions to assist them in making somewhat risky—or riskier than normal—loans.

- Under the Regional Corporation Revolving Loan Program, the Authority can make grants to no more than four regional corporations that will in turn use the funds to provide financial assistance to business for projects that demonstrate a substantial likelihood of providing increases in jobs or retaining jobs.

This initiative included other programs to increase the capabilities of creating and retaining jobs in the state. These programs include the following:

Defense Diversification: Changes the local match requirement under the Defense Diversification Program. The new law broadens the availability of defense diversification funds to companies that increase employment opportunities for former employees of a contractor or subcontractor doing defense work.

Flexible Manufacturing Network: Provides $1 million in bonds for grants to groups of firms that form flexible manufacturing networks for joint product and technology development.

Surety Bond Guarantee Program: Provides an incentive to encourage sureties (people or companies) to post bonds for small businesses to bid on contracts. The state will reimburse surety companies for up to 90 percent of any losses they incur on bid, performance, or payment bonds they post for small contractors and subcontractors.

Entrepreneur Program for Low-Income People: The Commissioners of Economic Development and Income Maintenance are required to establish a three-year demonstration program to train low-income people to become entrepreneurs and to provide them with access to capital.

- P.A. 92–193 makes changes in sales, property, and corporate income taxes paid by manufacturers. The act phases in tax savings over a five-year period, and expands the four-year property tax exemption for manufacturing machinery and equipment to include used machinery after July 1, 1992.

- P.A. 92–162 streamlines the permitting process through the Department of Environmental Protection. The bill aims to reduce delays, thereby allowing companies to correct potential problems in a more timely manner and get their products to market more quickly.

- S.B. 92–54 requires the Department of Economic Development, in concert with the Department of Environmental Protection, to select two environmentally contaminated sites to be cleaned up and reused for economic development. The bill is intended to promote the reuse of urban facilities that have been environmentally contaminated but would otherwise make good locations for inner city jobs development.

State Small Business Conferences

No recent statewide small business conferences have been reported.

Delaware

Small Business Offices, Programs, and Activities

Delaware Development Office

Contact:
Mr. Gary Smith, Small Business Advocate
Delaware Development Office
99 Kings Highway
P.O. Box 1401
Dover, DE 19903
(302) 739–4271

The director of the **Delaware Development Office** reports to the governor and has cabinet status. The office was established in 1981 specifically to encourage the expansion of existing industry and to attract new business and tourism to the state. The office has professional specialists in the following areas:

Business Development—The office recruits new business and industry to Delaware and maintains contact with existing businesses and industry to encourage growth and expansion. Business development representatives also provide assistance to firms experiencing regulatory problems with government agencies, and recommend improvements in state programs that affect the business community.

Education, Training, and Recruitment—This division assists employers with recruitment, develops and underwrites training programs, and provides information regarding the labor situation.

Business Finance—Several financing programs are available to assist businesses and increase Delaware's employment base. Representatives of this office assist businesses in processing applications for financial aid. Entire financings can be closed within nine weeks when the borrower's needs are not unusual.

Business Research—This division collects, analyzes, and distributes statistical data on the state's economy and business climate, and develops research that responds to client concerns. Producing and distributing travel and business-related publications are also part of this group's responsibilities.

Tourism—The Delaware Tourism Office develops and implements a regional, national, and international tourism marketing program promoting Delaware as a travel destination. This division commissions travel research, promotes the development of Delaware's travel industry, and also administers the Delaware Development Office's Matching Grants Program.

Small Business—The Small Business Office offers advisory assistance to small business persons, coordinates the small business efforts of various organizations statewide that serve small business persons, and sponsors small business events and programs. It also provides staff assistance to the Governor's Council on Small Business, the Urban Community Revitalization Study Task Force, and the Governor's International Trade Council.

Publications available from the Delaware Development Office include *Small Business Start-up Guide*, *Selling to the State*, *Solutions for Delaware Small Business*, and *The Workforce Resource*.

Contact:
Mr. John J. Casey, Jr., Director
Delaware Development Office
99 Kings Highway
P.O. Box 1401
Dover, DE 19903
(302) 739–4271

The **Small Business Development Section** of the Delaware Development Office was established to help the state's new and existing small businesses participate in economic development programs. Assistance is provided in financing, advocacy, management, and procurement.

Financial Help

Contact:
Mr. Gary Smith, Small Business Advocate
Delaware Development Office
99 Kings Highway
P.O. Box 1401
Dover, DE 19903
(302) 739–4271

The **Small Business Revolving Loan and Credit Enhancement Fund Program**, which became effective December 31, 1989, provides financing through the Delaware Economic Development Authority. Financing may be in the form of a loan at below-market rates, may not exceed 25 percent of the total capital required to finance an eligible project, and may not exceed $100,000 for working capital and fixed-asset purposes. Financing may also be in the form of credit enhancements purchased by the authority in order to support loans made by or through private financial institutions.

The **Land Acquisition Fund** was created to help Delaware businesses reduce their land acquisition borrowing costs through the issuance of below-market rate loans by the Delaware Economic Development Authority. Business applicants must provide at least $200,000 capital investment in, or secure at least $200,000 of, capital leases for buildings and/or equipment in Delaware. The maximum size loan is $250,000; the maximum term is 20 years. Applicants must meet an employment standard requirement, which includes the number of permanent, quality, full-time or part-time jobs created or retained as a result of the loan.

Delaware's **Small Businesss Innovation Research** (SBIR) program offers businesses bridge grants that match, dollar-for-dollar, the funds received in Phase I. Small business seminars are offered to promote the SBIR program, and help is available with Phase I proposals. Delaware is currently identifying and targeting the types of companies that would be interested in the SBIR program or that have had awards in the past. Although there was no money allocated for Fiscal Year 1993, the program will continue to serve small businesses in an SBIR advisory capacity.

Loans and Capital Formation

Contact:
Mr. James P. Lisa, Director of Business
   Finance
Delaware Development Office
99 Kings Highway
P.O. Box 1401
Dover, DE 19903
(302) 739–4271

The **Business Finance Section** of the Delaware Development Office offers several special financing programs to assist small businesses in commercial, industrial, and agricultural projects. State-administered industrial revenue bonds are used to finance the lending program.

Industrial Revenue Bond Financing

Contact:
Mr. John Casey, Chairman
The Delaware Economic Development
   Authority
99 Kings Highway
P.O. Box 1401
Dover, DE 19903
(302) 739–4271

The **Delaware Economic Development Authority** provides statewide financial assistance to new or expanding businesses through the issuance of Industrial Revenue Bonds (IRBs). IRBs are purchased by investors at low interest rates because interest from the bonds is exempt from federal income taxes and state income taxes for Delaware residents. The business person benefits by obtaining long-term financing at interest rates below the prime rate. IRBs can be especially cost-effective for projects involving over $250,000 in fixed assets.

To initiate financing through an IRB, the applicant details his or her business history and proposed project in an application to the Delaware Economic Development Authority.

Projects eligible for financing with industrial revenue bonds include the following major categories:

• Manufacturing—This can include office and warehouse space as long as it is a related part of the overall manufacturing facility.

- Agriculture—Projects involved in the acquisition of equipment to be used for farming purposes by an individual who has not at any time had any direct or indirect ownership interest in substantial farmland.

- 501(c)(3) Organizations—Projects involved in supporting the exempt activities of 501(c)(3) organizations.

Industrial revenue bonds financing is limited to a maximum of $10 million for each manufacturing or agricultural project within a single political jurisdiction. However, the total amount of tax-exempt financing that may be outstanding at any one time with respect to a 501(c)(3) organization, other than a hospital, is $150 million.

Applications are reviewed by the authority's staff for their financial feasibility and impact on Delaware's economy. In a public hearing, the Council on Development Finance determines whether the applicant's proposal is authorized for issuance of IRBs. After approval, the applicant is responsible for locating a buyer for the bonds. The tax-exempt nature of the bonds makes them an attractive investment for a variety of institutions. While the authority's staff can provide assistance, it must be stressed that the applicant has the responsibility to locate prospective investors so that the final closing and funding of the IRB can occur.

Delaware Development Corporation

Contact:
Mr. James P. Lisa, Director of
  Business Finance
Delaware Development Office
99 Kings Highway
P.O. Box 1401
Dover, DE 19903
(302) 739–4271

In 1982, Delaware, through the **Delaware Development Corporation**, became the second state to obtain certification under the U.S. Small Business Administration's Section 504 loan program. This program offers long-term, fixed-asset financing at fixed rates to the growing small firm. In addition to land, building, and equipment, many of the out-of-pocket expenses associated with construction—interim financing costs, architectural drawings, etc.—may be included in the 504 loan package.

To be eligible, a small business must be a "for-profit enterprise" with a net worth of less than $6 million and average net profits of less than $2 million for the past two years. In addition, the project must create one new job for approximately every $40,000 in total project cost. The SBA will allow some latitude in the employment requirement.

The 504 program can provide long-term financing for projects totalling $200,000 to $1,500,000 for the acquisition of land and buildings; the construction, expansion, or renovation of facilities, including leasehold improvements; and the purchase of machinery and equipment. Funds are not available for working capital, inventory, debt consolidation, or debt repayments. The applicant must be the user of the facilities.

A 504 fixed-asset financing involves a mixture of funding from the small business, a private sector lender (bank, savings and loan, or insurance company), and the Delaware Development Corporation. A typical project would involve 50-percent funding from the private lender, 40 percent from the Delaware Development Corporation up to a maximum of $500,000, and 1 percent from the small business. For a start-up small business, the business may need to contribute 20 to 25 percent in equity to the project.

The small business loan is actually funded by the Delaware Development Corporation's issuing a debenture—a bond secured by the project's real estate. While the interest rate and term for the private sector portion of the loan are negotiated, the interest rate for the debenture portion is fixed at the market rate at time of sale, and the term may be either 10 or 20 years, depending on the economic life of the assets being financed. If the project involves construction, interim financing will be arranged and the debenture issued after a Certificate of Occupancy has been obtained.

Small Business Development Centers

Contact:
Ms. Linda Fayerweather, State Director
Delaware Small Business Development
    Center
University of Delaware
Purnell Hall, Suite 005
Newark, DE 19716
(302) 451–2747

Small Business Development Centers (SBDCs) provide practical management and technical assistance to present and prospective small business owners. They offer courses, seminars, and one-on-one counseling as well as access to information on marketing, managing, and financing a small business. SBDCs are partially funded by the U.S. Small Business Administration, and are usually affiliated with a state college or university. In Delaware, an SBDC is located in Newark, at the University of Delaware.

Governor's Advisory Council or Task Force

Contact:
Mr. John J. Casey, Jr., Director
Delaware Development Office
99 Kings Highway
P.O. Box 1401
Dover, DE 19903
(302) 739–4271

The **Governor's Council on Small Business** was formed in 1987. The council is made up of 16 members, five from each of the three counties, plus the director of the Delaware Development Office, who serves as chairman.

Legislative Committees and Subcommittees

Both houses of the legislature have standing committees to address state small business issues during the annual session from January through June. Committees are appointed for two years in the December following a November election.

Contacts:
Senator Robert Venables, Chairman
Senate Committee on Small Business
Legislative Hall
Dover, DE 19903
(302) 739–4298

Representative Mary Beth Boykin, Chairman
House Committee on Small Business
Legislative Hall
Dover, DE 19903
(302) 739–4449

Legislation

No recent legislation targeting small business has been enacted.

State Small Business Conferences

Contact:
Mr. Gary Smith, Small Business Advocate
Delaware Development Office
99 Kings Highway
P.O. Box 1401
Dover, DE 19903
(302) 739–4271

No recent statewide small business conferences have been reported.

District of Columbia

Small Business Offices, Programs, and Activities

The government of the District of Columbia has two major offices assisting small businesses: the Office of Business and Economic Development and the Department of Human Rights and Minority Business Development. The Office of the Deputy Mayor for Economic Development also coordinates activities dealing with small business policy.

Office of Business and Economic Development

Contacts:
Mr. Charles Countee, Executive Director
Office of Business and Economic
    Development
717 14th Street, N.W., 10th Floor
Washington, DC 20005
(202) 727–6600

Mr. George Brown, Deputy Director
Office of Business and Economic
    Development
717 14th Street, N.W., 10th Floor
Washington, DC 20005
(202) 727–6600

The **Office of Business and Economic Development** (OBED) was established in 1978 to promote the growth of business that will expand the city's tax base, generate jobs, and make commercial corridors more vital. Through the many programs administered by OBED, small businesses in the District receive technical and management help, business site location assistance, financial assistance, and other important business information.

Through OBED, the District of Columbia government provides a broad range of financing programs. There are 12 distinctive programs that include the SBA 504 fixed asset financing program, a revolving loan program for short-term working capital and equipment financing, a business development loan program that can be used for equipment gap financing, leasehold improvements and inventory, a facade loan program, and several other real estate and development financing programs.

The Department of Human Rights and Minority Business Development

Contact:
Ms. Marjorie Utley, Executive Director
Department of Human Rights and Minority
  Business Development
2000 14th Street, N.W., Room 324
Washington, DC 20009
(202) 939–8780

The **Department of Human Rights and Minority Business Development**, established in 1976, monitors District of Columbia government agencies' compliance with requirements for minority participation in agency contracts. It also implements the sheltered-market program, under which selected contracts are designated for certified minority business enterprises through competitive bidding or negotiation. The certified minority business enterprises receive technical assistance through group orientation, periodic seminars, and referrals to local technical assistance agencies.

Loans and Capital Formation

Contact:
Ms. Pamela Vaughn-Cooke-Henry, Chief
Financial Services Division
Office of Business and Economic
  Development
717 14th Street, N.W., 10th Floor
Washington, DC 20005
(202) 727–6600

The government of the District of Columbia offers a wide range of loan and other financing programs. The District-wide SBA 504 loan program is operated through the **Washington, D.C., Local Development Corporation** (W/LDC), which is staffed by the Office of Business and Economic Development. SBA 504 loans are offered for fixed-asset financing for terms of up to 25 years and for amounts of up to $500,000 or 40 percent of total project cost, whichever is less. Eligible uses of funds include the purchase of land, buildings, machinery, and equipment, building renovation, and construction and leasehold improvements.

The OBED offers several direct loan programs. The **Revolving Loan Fund** provides a source of limited financing to small and medium-size businesses. The fund offers direct, short-term loans in conjunction with private lenders. Typical fund uses are short-term financing for equipment and inventory purchases. The OBED also offers the **Participation Loan Program** (PLP), designed to broaden the spectrum of businesses eligible for financing. The PLP offers direct loans for periods of one to 20 years, depending on the use of funds.

Contact:

Mr. George Brown, Chief
Neighborhood Commercial Services Division
Office of Business and Economic
   Development
717 14th Street, N.W., 10th Floor
Washington, DC 2000
(202) 727–6600

The **Neighborhood Commercial Services Division** of OBED, under its Neighborhood Commercial Revitalization Program, offers a number of services to small businesses located in neighborhood commercial corridors that have been targeted for revitalization and to businesses interested in locating in economically distressed areas of the city. These programs range from acquisition and real estate development loans to a variety of other business loans, technical and management assistance, and capital improvement program opportunities.

Small Business Incubator Facility Program

Contact:

Mr. Joseph Bender, Chief
Development Services Division
Office of Business and Economic
   Development
717 14th Street, N.W., 10th Floor
Washington, DC 20005
(202) 727–6600

The **Small Business Incubator Facility Program**, administered by the Office of Business and Economic Development, encourages establishment of business incubator facilities in the District of Columbia by offering use of city-owned property and credit support to participating businesses. Small business incubators support new and small firms by providing affordable space, shared office services, and management help. Assistance is given to companies through their conceptual, start-up, and early growth stages. Incentives are offered to ensure that costs to the participating businesses for space and services are kept at a minimum. The OBED is developing three incubator facilities in the District of Columbia.

Economic Development Finance Corporation

Contact:

Mr. Lloyd Arrington, Acting President
District of Columbia Economic Development
   Finance Corporation
1660 L Street, N.W., Suite 308
Washington, DC 20036
(202) 775–8815

The **Economic Development Finance Corporation** (EDFC), established in 1984, is a quasi-public, nonprofit organization that operates as a venture capital firm to foster the growth of small businesses in the District of Columbia. The EDFC provides both capital and management assistance.

Contact:
Mr. Lloyd Arrington, Acting President
District of Columbia Economic Development
   Finance Corporation
1660 L Street, N.W., Suite 308
Washington, DC 20036
(202) 775–8815

The **Business Purchase Assistance Program** (BPAP) is designed to directly stimulate business and commercial revitalization in the District's neighborhood commercial corridors. Under the BPAP, the Real Property Acquisition Loan Program (RPA) provides loans for acquisition of primarily vacant real property in certain targeted areas of the District, and the Business Acquisition and Expansion Loan Program (BAE) provides loans for acquisition of for-profit corporations, partnerships, or proprietorships.

Office of the Deputy Mayor for Economic Development

Contact:
Mr. Austin Penny, Deputy Mayor for
   Economic Development
The District Building
1350 Pennsylvania Avenue, N.W.,
   Suite 401
Washington, DC 20004

The **Office of the Deputy Mayor for Economic Development** (DMED) was established by Mayor's Order 83-13 on January 3, 1983. The office oversees and coordinates all programs, policies, proposals, and functions related to economic development in the District of Columbia, including those that deal with small business development.

Office of International Business

Contact:
Mr. Clifford Lee, Director
Office of International Business
1250 I Street, N.W., Suite 1003
Washington, DC 20005
(202) 727–1576

The **Office of International Business** was formally established in October 1987. The office provides a channel of support, technical and reference assistance, and information to businesses interested in international trade. The office also organizes seminars, trade shows, and trade missions.

Small Business Development Centers

Contact:
Ms. Nancy Flake, Director
Metropolitan Washington Small Business
   Development Center
Howard University
2600 Sixth Street, N.W.
Washington, DC 20059
(202) 806–1550

Small Business Development Centers (SBDCs) provide practical management and technical assistance to existing and prospective small business owners. SBDCs are partially funded by the U.S. Small Business Administration, and offer courses, seminars, and one-on-one counseling, as well as access to information on marketing, managing, and financing a small business. A complete listing of Small Business Development Centers and subcenters, including addresses and telephone numbers, is in Appendix A of this directory.

Governor's Advisory Council or Task Force

Contact:
Mr. Joseph Bender, Chief
Development Services Division
Office of Business and Economic
    Development
717 14th Street, N.W., 10th Floor
Washington, DC 20005
(202) 727–6600

The **Business Incubator Advisory Board** advises the City Council and the OBED on "ways in which the District can best support business incubator development and the delivery of services and resources to tenant businesses by public and private entities." The five-member board has met regularly since 1987 to carry out this mandate and to assist new and growing small businesses in the District.

Legislative Committees and Subcommittees

Contact:
Councilmember Charlene Drew Jarvis,
    Chairperson
Committee on Economic Development
The District Building
1350 Pennsylvania Avenue, N.W.
Washington, DC 20004
(202) 724–8052

The Council of the District of Columbia, which acts in many ways as a state legislature, does not have a designated small business committee. However, the Committee on Economic Development has oversight for small business legislation and programs in the District of Columbia.

Contact:
Mr. Eric McFarland, Committee Clerk
Committee on Public Services
The District Building
1350 Pennsylvania Avenue, N.W.
Washington, DC 20004
(202) 724–8045

The Committee on Public Services has oversight of the Minority Business Opportunity Commission (MBOC). The MBOC was established to ensure minority participation in public contracting and to foster local minority business opportunities. The commission also provides certification to minority-owned businesses in the District, and monitors their participation in the sheltered markets program.

Legislation

The Council of the District of Columbia has passed several pieces of legislation pertaining to small business, including the following:

- The District of Columbia Government Quick Payment Act of 1984, which requires the District government to pay its contractors within 30 days.

- The District of Columbia Business Incubator Facilitation Act, which authorizes the establishment of small business incubator facilities in the District.

Small Business Conferences

The District of Columbia offers a variety of workshops and small business conferences.

Contact:
Ms. Joan Moore, Manager
Research, Information, and Marketing
Office of Business and Economic
    Development
717 14th Street, N.W., 10th Floor
Washington, DC 20004
(202) 727–6600

Florida

Small Business Offices, Programs, and Activities

Bureau of Business Assistance

Contact:
Ms. Mary Helen Blakeslee, Chief
Bureau of Business Assistance
Florida Department of Commerce
443 Collins Building
107 West Gaines Street
Tallahassee, FL 32399–2000
(904) 488–9357

The **Florida Department of Commerce's Bureau of Business Assistance** helps new and expanding businesses. Various services are offered in financing, business services, and entrepreneurship.

Contact:
Ms. Bridget Merrill, Supervisor
Bureau of Business Assistance
Florida Department of Commerce
443 Collins Building
107 West Gaines Street
Tallahassee, FL 32399–2000
(904) 488–9357

The **Community Development Section** encourages business and economic development in small Florida communities by providing technical assistance for industrial recruitment and by assisting in incubator development. The section administers a retention and expansion program to assist communities in specific areas of need by providing departmental staff to serve as community consultants. The section also can help organize local venture capital pools and encourage support of an entrepreneurship club network consisting of lawyers, bankers, accountants, venture capitalists, entrepreneurs, and others who support and promote entrepreneurship.

Contact:
Supervisor
Business Finance Section
Bureau of Business Assistance
Florida Department of Commerce
443 Collins Building
107 West Gaines Street
Tallahassee, FL 32399–2000
(904) 487–0463

The **Finance Section** helps businesses locate financing alternatives to meet their needs; assists communities in locating financing for economic development efforts and projects; and administers the Economic Development Transportation Fund, which makes financing available for public road improvements needed to support business starts or expansions. The section also assists with loan packaging for the U.S. Small Business Administrations's SBA 504 program and provides information on the SBA 7(a) loan program. The SBA 504 loan program provides long-term, fixed-rate financing for fixed assets when the loan results in job creation. The 7(a) loan program provides user financing for start-up, expansion, and property.

The **Florida First Capital Finance Corporation** (FFCFC), a nonprofit organization certified to issue debentures, offers financial assistance to Florida businesses in conjunction with the SBA 504 loan program. The Florida Department of Commerce provides loan packaging assistance. An SBA 504 loan may be used to buy land, construct buildings, buy existing buildings, buy machinery and equipment, modernize, renovate, and restore an existing facility including leasehold improvement. The borrower must not have a net worth over $6 million or an average net profit for the previous two years of over $2 million, and within two years of loan closing must create one job for every $15,000 provided.

Contact:
Ms. Doris Malloy, Supervisor
Bureau of Business Assistance
Florida Department of Commerce
443 Collins Building
107 West Gaines Street
Tallahassee, FL 32399–2000
(904) 488–9357
(800) 342–0771 (toll-free, in-state)

The **Business Services Section** operates a toll-free information and referral service for small businesses and individuals interested in starting or operating a business in Florida. The section also coordinates regional small business forums and a statewide conference to identify small business issues, and leads an annual Florida small business development workshop, which brings together resource people from local, state, and federal agencies and private organizations. The section distributes and publishes information to assist small businesses in Florida, including the *Florida New Business Guide* and *Checklist*.

Contact:
Mr. Maury Hagerman, Development
  Representative
Bureau of Business Assistance
Florida Department of Commerce
443 Collins Building
107 West Gaines Street
Tallahassee, FL 32399–2000
(904) 488–9357

The **Entrepreneurship Network** program encourages the affiliation of venture capitalists, bankers, lawyers, accountants, business consultants, successful entrepreneurs, university resource people, and others who provide assistance to entrepreneurs. Currently, 20 such local organizations are located throughout the state.

Contact:
Mr. Roger Griesbaum, Development
  Representative
Bureau of Business Assistance
Florida Department of Commerce
443 Collins Building
107 West Gaines Street
Tallahassee, FL 32399–2000
(904) 488–9357

Florida has established a support program to increase the number of firms in the state competing in the federal **Small Business Innovation Research** (SBIR) program. The SBIR program stimulates new product development among small technology-based firms.

Bureau of Industry Development

Contact:
Mr. John Robbins, Senior Development
   Representative
Bureau of Industry Development
Florida Department of Commerce
325 Collins Building
107 West Gaines Street
Tallahassee, FL 32399–2000
(904) 488–9360

The Business Supplier Program in the **Bureau of Industry Development** helps Florida companies locate other Florida-based companies that can be used as suppliers of goods and services. Existing businesses in selected industries are visited to ascertain specific needs.

Bureau of International Trade and Development

Contact:
Mr. Tom Flattery, Chief
Bureau of International Trade and
   Development
Florida Department of Commerce
331 Collins Building
107 West Gaines Street
Tallahassee, FL 32399–2000
(904) 487–1399

The **Bureau of International Trade and Development** assists Florida firms interested in exporting. The bureau encourages the state's domestic trade and exports and assists foreign companies investigating Florida business locations and opportunities.

Bureau of Economic Analysis

Contact:
Mr. Nick Leslie, Economist Supervisor
Bureau of Economic Analysis
Florida Department of Commerce
305 Collins Building
107 West Gaines Street
Tallahassee, FL 32399–2000
(904) 487–2971

The **Bureau of Economic Analysis** provides support information, research, and planning assistance for community and economic development in Florida. The office maintains a comprehensive computer data bank of state and local economic information.

Industry Services Training Program

Contact:
Mr. Lawrence Taylor, Director
Industry Services Training
Division of Vocational Education, Adult, and
    Community Education
Florida Department of Education
1102 Florida Education Center
Tallahassee, FL 32399–0400
(904) 487–1040

The **Industry Services Training Program** in the Department of Education trains employees of new, expanding, and diversifying industries in the state. On-site training is available in addition to training at vocational-technical centers, community colleges, or departments of comprehensive high schools.

Small Business Development Centers

Contact:
Mr. Jerry Cartwright, State Coordinator
Florida Small Business Development Center
University of West Florida
11000 University Boulevard
Pensacola, FL 32514–5750
(904) 474–3016

The **Small Business Development Center** (SBDC) program is a partnership between the state university system of Florida and the U.S. Small Business Administration. Twenty-three SBDCs are located around the state and offer training programs and free counseling to practicing and potential business owners on topics such as recordkeeping, procurement and contracting assistance, commercial loan packaging, and business plans. A complete listing of all Small Business Development Centers and subcenters, including addresses and telephone numbers, is located in Appendix A of this directory.

INFO-BID is a statewide data bank program offered by the SBDCs to help Florida's small and minority businesses locate bid opportunities to sell to federal, state, and local governments and participating commercial firms.

The **Statewide Contracts Register** was created to increase the capability of small and minority businesses to participate in government purchases. State agencies are required to submit all bids to the SBDCs for inclusion in the statewide contracts register. The information on bids is distributed to interested small and minority businesses to assist them in identifying their markets.

High Technology

Contact:
Mr. Ray Iannuci, Executive Director
Florida High Technology and Industry
   Council
111 Collins Building, Room 128
107 West Gaines Street
Tallahassee, FL 32399–2000
(904) 487–3136

The **Florida High Technology Innovation Research and Development Fund** is a $1.5-million venture capital pool with up to $50,000 in equity financing for the research and development of new and existing high-tech businesses in the state. Patterned after the federal SBIR program, this fund encourages innovation in designated high-tech areas.

The **Florida High Technology and Industrial Council** coordinates the needs of high technology businesses and industries with the resources of universities and vocational schools.

Minority Purchasing Councils

Minority Purchasing Councils are private-sector corporations interested in providing opportunities and business environments conducive to the development and participation of minority vendors. The councils encourage firms to procure goods and services from minority business enterprises and assist minority businesses in a variety of certification, technical assistance, and referral activities.

Contacts:
Mr. Don Foster, Executive Director
Florida Regional Minority Purchasing
   Council, Inc.
99 Northwest 183rd Street, Suite 203
Miami, FL 33169
(305) 757–9690

Mr. Robert L. Gault, President
Purchasing Council of Florida's First Coast,
   Inc.
P.O. Box 43132
Jacksonville, FL 32202–3132

Mr. Malik Ali, President
Greater Florida Minority Development
   Council
P.O. Box 640
Malabar, FL 32950–0640

Ms. Heritza Rovira, Executive Director
Minority Business Council
120 University Park Drive, Suite 170
Winterpark, FL 32792
(407) 679–4147

Minority Business Assistance Office

Contact:
Ms. Carolyn Wilson-Newton
Minority Business Assistance Coordinator
Department of General Services
2737 Centerview Drive
Knight Building, Suite 201
Tallahassee, FL 32399–0950
(904) 487–0915

The **Minority Business Assistance Office**, created by the Small and Minority Business Assistance Act of 1985, was established within the Department of General Services to assist minority enterprises in becoming vendors to state agencies and to certify them as minority business enterprises. All state agencies are encouraged to spend 15 percent of their funds for the purchase of commodities, contractual services, and construction from certified minority businesses.

State Procurement Assistance

Contact:
Mr. George Banks, Director
Department of General Services
Division of Purchasing
2737 Centerview Drive
Knight Building, Suite 110
Tallahassee, FL 32399–0950
(904) 488–1194

The **Florida Department of General Services** (DGS), Division of Purchasing, coordinates and regulates purchases of commodities and contractual services used by state agencies. The department publishes *Doing Business with the State of Florida*, a guide designed to help small and minority-owned companies. Not all goods and services used by state agencies are purchased through the DGS, and potential vendors should direct their marketing efforts to each state agency's purchasing office. Each agency maintains a vendor file, as well as a listing of vendors for contractual services provided by DGS.

Job Training Partnership Act

Contact:
Mr. R. Hayden Gray, Assistant Chief
LET Administration II
Bureau of Job Training
201 Atkins Building
1320 Executive Center Drive
Tallahassee, FL 32399–0667
(904) 488–9250

The federal **Job Training Partnership Act** (JTPA) program provides job training and related assistance to economically disadvantaged individuals and others in special need of training. These training programs are planned and carried out through a partnership between the private sector and government at local and state levels. Funds are allocated to service delivery areas and may be used for administration and training purposes. Local Private Industry Councils (PICs) coordinate these public/private endeavors and can reimburse employers for up to 50 percent of wages paid during job training.

Sunshine State Skills Program

Contact:
Mr. Don Magruder, Director of Economic
   Development
Sunshine State Skills Program
Economic Development and Industry
   Programs
State Board of Community Colleges
Florida Department of Education
325 West Gaines, Room 1314
Florida Education Center
Tallahassee, FL 32399–0400
(904) 487–4943

The **Sunshine State Skills Program** provides grants to establish training partnerships between community colleges and employers with specific training needs for employees in new, expanding, or diversifying businesses in Florida. The state has appropriated funds for training grants to be matched by industry with cash, equipment, or facility use. Training is offered to develop skills in mechanical assembly, computer use, secretarial skills and word processing, basic electrical work, critical-care nursing, marketing, and management.

Governor's Advisory Council or Task Force

Contact:
Ms. Laurise Thompson, Advocate
Small and Minority Business Advisory
   Council
Florida Department of Commerce
679 Collins Building
107 West Gaines Street
Tallahassee, FL 32399–2000
(904) 487–4698

The **Small and Minority Business Advisory Council** was created by the Florida Small and Minority Business Assistance Act of 1985 to identify the concerns and needs of small and minority-owned businesses in Florida. The council serves as a liaison between the business community, state agencies, and the legislature. A Small and Minority Business Advocate serves as staff and spokesperson for the council. The advocate presents viewpoints of small and minority business on legislation and state agency rules affecting them.

Contact:
Ms. Judy R. Jones, Executive Director
Florida Black Business Investment Board
519 East Park Avenue
Tallahassee, FL 32301
(904) 487–4850

The **Florida Black Business Investment Board**, also created by the Florida Small and Minority Business Act of 1985, concentrates on obtaining financial assistance for Florida's black-owned and operated firms. The state appropriated $5 million for this purpose; direct loans are provided.

Legislative Committees and Subcommittees

A Small Business Subcommittee exists within the House of Representatives' International Trade and Economic Development Committee.

Contact:
Representative Mary Brennan, Chairman
Economic Development Subcommittee
232 House Office Building
Tallahassee, FL 32399–1300
(904) 488–6197

Legislation

The 1991 legislature passed an amendment to the Florida Small and Minority Business Act of 1985 that refined and strengthened the Act. Changes include the following:

- Small businesses are defined as having fewer than 51 full-time employees.

- The bill eliminates "physically disabled" as a minority group.

- The bill simplifies the certification process by allowing state certification of small or minority business to be accepted by local governments and provides for a study of allowing local government certification to be used by the state.

- For state procurement, the bill breaks down the categories of small and minority businesses and state agency spending goals in each category.

State Small Business Conferences

Contacts:
Ms. Mary Helene Blakeslee, Chief
Bureau of Business Assistance
Florida Department of Commerce
443 Collins Building
107 West Gaines Street
Tallahassee, FL 32399–2000
(904) 488–9357

Ms. Laurise Thompson, Advocate
Small and Minority Business Advisory
  Council
107 West Gaines Street, Room 519
Tallahassee, FL 32399–2000
(904) 487–4698

Small Business Regional Forums and a statewide **Florida Conference on Small Business** are conducted during the year to formulate legislative recommendations on these issues. The forums and conferences give policymakers an opportunity to learn first-hand from small business owners about their needs and concerns.

Georgia

Small Business Offices, Programs, and Activities

Small Business Development Centers

Contact:
Mr. Hank Logan, State Director
Georgia Small Business Development
 Center
The University of Georgia
Chicopee Complex
1180 East Broad Street
Athens, GA 30602
(404) 542-5760

Contact:
Mr. Marvin Doster, Division Head
Special Programs
Georgia Small Business Development
 Center
The University of Georgia
Chicopee Complex
1180 East Broad Street
Athens, GA 30602
(404) 542-5760

Contact:
Mr. Marvin Doster, Division Head
Special Programs
Georgia Small Business Development
 Center
The University of Georgia
Chicopee Complex
1180 East Broad Street
Athens, GA 30602
(404) 542-5760

The **Small Business Development Center** (SBDC), head-quartered at the University of Georgia in Athens, can be considered the state small business office. Branch offices are located in Albany, Athens, Atlanta, Augusta, Brunswick, Columbus, Gainesville, Lawrenceville, Macon, Milledgeville, Morrow, Rome, Savannah, Statesboro, Valdosta, and Warner Robins. The centers are jointly funded by the U.S. Small Business Administration and the state of Georgia. A complete listing of these centers, with addresses and telephone numbers, is in Appendix A of this directory.

The SBDC is scheduled to begin a **procurement program** for small business in cooperation with the Department of Administrative Services. Requests for bids are matched with interested vendors. The program is being expanded to include selected municipalities and will eventually include large private firms that might be served by small business.

The SBDC also has an **International Trade Development Center** that provides seminars and counseling for small businesses interested in international trade.

Cooperative Extension Service

Contact:
Dr. Richard Schemerhorn, Department
  Head
Economic Development Department
The University of Georgia Extension Service
The University of Georgia
Athens, GA 30602
(404) 542-0534

The **University of Georgia Agricultural Extension Service,** through its Economic Division, provides information and advice to rural communities and agribusiness firms.

Department of Community Affairs

Contact:
Mr. Bobby Stevens, Special Assistant
Community Programs Section
Community and Economic Development
  Section
Georgia Department of Community Affairs
1200 Equitable Building
100 Peachtree Street
Atlanta, GA 30303
(404) 656–3872

Georgia's Department of Community Affairs assists small firms through small business revitalization and rural development programs.

The **Small Business Revitalization Program** provides technical assistance to small businesses, with an emphasis on finding capital for expansion projects that will create new jobs.

Contact:
Ms. Winfred Ownes, Assistant
  Commissioner
Office of Rural Development
Georgia Department of Community Affairs
1200 Equitable Building
100 Peachtree Street
Atlanta, GA 30303
(404) 656–9790

The **Office of Rural Development** was established in 1988 in response to recommendations of the Rural Development Policy Advisory Committee. The office serves as an ombudsman to local government on all matters affecting rural community and economic development, and focuses and coordinates existing programs of technical financial assistance to enhance rural development efforts.

Contact:
Mr. Paul D. Radford, Assistant
  Commissioner
Executive Division
Georgia Department of Community Affairs
40 Marietta Street N.W.
Atlanta, GA 30303
(404) 656–3836

The **Community and Economic Development Division** provides financial packaging assistance for grant applications being made to state and federal agencies.

Contacts:
Mr. Stuart Dorfman, Senior Consultant
Mr. George Fields, Senior Consultant
Government Information Division
Georgia Department of Community Affairs
40 Marietta Street N.W.
Atlanta, GA 30303
(404) 656–5526

Information about federal and state funding sources is available from most Area Planning and Development Commissions (APDCs) and from the **Government Information Division.**

Rural Development Initiative

Contact:
Mr. R.A. Foss, Executive Director
Rural Development Initiative
P.O. Box 28
Soperton, GA 30457

The **Rural Development Initiative** began operations in August 1986, and now serves six rural counties in south central Georgia. The organization works with industry and trade groups to encourage economic development in rural areas, and it has helped finance business start-ups and expansions. The Rural Development Initiative is funded by the state legislature and the counties it serves.

Office of Small and Minority Business Affairs

Contact:
Mr. Hooper Wesley
Small and Minority Business Affairs
Department of Administrative Services
200 Piedmont Avenue S.W.
West Tower, Suite 1302
Atlanta, GA 30334
(404) 656–6315

The governor has publicly encouraged state agencies to increase procurement from small businesses to promote economic development. The **Office of Small and Minority Business Affairs** was established to facilitate that goal.

Special Assistant for Minority Affairs

Contact:
Rev. Jackey Beavers, Executive Assistant
Special Assistant for Minority Affairs
Office of the Governor
State Capitol, Room 245
Atlanta, GA 30334
(404) 656–1794

The governor's advisor on small and minority business concerns also serves as a **Special Assistant for Minority Affairs** to assist in the development of small and minority-owned firms.

Department of Industry, Trade, and Tourism

Contact:
Mr. Randy Cardoza, Commissioner
Department of Industry, Trade, and Tourism
P.O. Box 1776
Atlanta, GA 30301
(404) 656–3556

The state encourages businesses to engage in international trade. **The Department of Industry, Trade, and Tourism**, promotes the interest of small business at trade fairs.

High Technology Business Emphasis

Contacts:
Mr. Wayne Hodges, Director
Advanced Technology Development Center
Georgia Institute of Technology
430 10th Street N.W., Suite N-116
Atlanta, GA 30318
(404) 894–3575

Mr. Bert Fridlin, Director of Government
  Relations
National Federation of Independent
  Business
1447 Peachtree Street N.E., Suite 1008
Atlanta, GA 30309
(404) 876–8516

Contact:
Mr. Michael Cassidy
Small Business Innovation Research
  Manager
Advanced Technology Development Center
Georgia Institute of Technology
430 10th Street, N.W.
Atlanta, GA 30318
(404) 894–3575

In 1980, the governor and the General Assembly established the **Advanced Technology Development Center** (ATDC), part of the State University System and located on campus at the Georgia Institute of Technology. The ATDC encourages high-technology growth in the state by supporting technology-based entrepreneurs and small businesses, helping existing businesses with new product development, assisting in the formation of venture capital, and providing educational programs. A consortium of Emory University, the University of Georgia, the Georgia Institute of Technology, and the Advanced Technology Development Center has been established. The ATDC serves as the focal point of these efforts and provides the staff to coordinate research at the three universities.

Georgia's **Small Business Innovation Research** (SBIR) effort is operated as part of the Advanced Technology Development Center's overall budget. Annual seminars offer SBIR information to interested small firms.

Georgia Tech Research Institute

Contact:
Dr. Donald J. Grace, Director
Georgia Tech Research Institute
Centennial Research Building
Corner of 10th and Dalney
Atlanta, GA 30332
(404) 894–3400

The **Engineering Extension Program** provides technical services to businesses from its field offices throughout the state.

Governor's Advisory Council or Task Force

Contact:
Dr. Lorraine Walton, Chairman
Governor's Small and Minority Business
    Development and Advisory Committee
c/o Country Place Restaurant
300 South Tennessee Street
Cartersville, GA 30120
(404) 386–8040

In 1983, the governor announced the formation of the **Governor's Small and Minority Business Development Committee.** The group includes 40 citizens who meet quarterly to work on improving state procurement purchasing, prompt pay, rural development, and other issues and activities of interest to small and minority firms. The committee also sponsors an annual Governor's Conference on Small and Minority Business.

Contact:
Mr. Larry L. Clark, Commissioner
Department of Administrative Services
Twin Towers West, Suite 1520
Atlanta, GA 30334
(404) 656–5514

Members of the **Governor's Interagency Council for Minority and Small Business** include the Department of Community Affairs; the Department of Industry, Trade, and Tourism; the Department of Administrative Services; the Secretary of State; the Small Business Development Center; the Department of Labor; the Commissioner of Insurance; the Department of Transportation; and the Department of Revenue. The council considers the impact of the activities of member departments upon small business.

Contact:
Mr. Robert Mabry, Deputy Commissioner
Planning and Development
Georgia Department of Technical and Adult
    Education
Suite 660, South Tower, One CNN Center
Atlanta, GA 30303-2705
(404) 656–5845

The **Governor's High Technology Advisory Council** consists of 12 members: 10 from private industries within the state and one representative each from the Advanced Technology Development Center and the State Board of Industry and Trade. The council recommends measures to attract and retain high technology firms.

Contacts:
Mayor Lace Futch, Chairman
Rural Development Policy Advisory
    Committee
P.O. Box 508
Willacoochee, GA 31650
(912) 534–5152

The **Rural Development Policy Advisory Committee** has conducted rural development studies and has made recommendations to the Georgia General Assembly and the governor.

Legislative Committees and Subcommittees

Contacts:
Senator Bill Harris, Chairman
Senate Subcommittee on Small Business
State Capitol
Atlanta, GA 30334
(404) 656-0071

Representative George Hooks, Chairman
House Industry Subcommittee on Small
    Business
Suite 608, Legislative Office Building
State Capitol
Atlanta, GA 30334
(404) 656–5115

Both the Senate and House have Subcommittees on Small Business.

Legislation

The 1987–1988 Georgia Legislature enacted the following legislation:

- A Small Minority Business Development Corporation was created to provide support for firms with annual gross sales of $6 million or less, 51 percent minority control, and fewer than 300 employees.

- A Seed Capital Fund was created for small business loans for innovative technology, manufacturing, and agriculture.

- The university system became associated with small business and economic development, leasing of laboratories, research facilities, and authorized lease when not in use.

• Product sellers were determined not liable as manufacturers in certain product liability tort actions.

The 1989–1990 legislative session created the Georgia Export Expansion Study Committee to improve global marketing competitiveness.

The 1991–1992 session enacted the following:

• Increased the amount of the Underground Storage Tank Trust Fund, the environmental assurance fees on petroleum products.

• Created the Southeast Growth and Economic Development Study Committee.

• Created the Joint Task Force on Workers' Compensation to study high business costs and low benefits to workers.

State Small Business Conferences

Contact:
Rev. Jackey Beavers, Executive Assistant
Office of the Governor
State Capitol Building, Room 245
Atlanta, GA 30334
(404) 656–1794

The **Governor's Conference on Small and Minority Business** is held annually in various locations. The conference gives small business owners an opportunity to meet with the heads of state departments and agencies and discuss small business concerns. Attenders participate in "how-to" seminars and discuss issues of importance to small and minority business in Georgia and present them in report form to the governor and state legislature.

Hawaii

Small Business Offices, Programs, and Activities

Department of Business, Economic Development, and Tourism

Contact:
Mr. Thomas J. Smyth, Administrator
Business Services Division
Department of Business, Economic
    Development, and Tourism
Grosvenor Center, Mauka Tower
737 Bishop Street, Suite 1900
Honolulu, HI 96804
(808) 586-2591

The state supports small business through the **Department of Business, Economic Development, and Tourism, Business Services Division**. A variety of assistance is available to small firms.

Contact:
Ms. Sandy Cirie, Business Advocate
Department of Business, Economic
    Development, and Tourism
Grosvenor Center, Mauka Tower
737 Bishop Street, Suite 1900
Honolulu, HI 96813
(808) 586–2594

The **Business Advocate** has responsibility to assist small businesses in directing their concerns and problems to the appropriate governmental agency; serve as liaison with the business community and make recommendations to improve Hawaii's business climate; and review current and proposed statutes and administrative rules that may affect business and recommend appropriate changes.

Business Loan Programs

Contact:
Ms. Doreen Shishido, Chief
Financial Assistance Branch
Department of Business, Economic
    Development, and Tourism
Grosvenor Center, Mauka Tower
737 Bishop Street, Suite 1900
Honolulu, HI 96813
(808) 586–2577

The **Financial Assistance Branch** provides loans to small businesses and the local commercial fishing industry. The branch administers various loan programs to stimulate the growth of new businesses, assists in the expansion of existing businesses, and helps businesses suffering setbacks caused by major natural disasters. The Business Loan Programs were established to help fill the shortage in commercial loans offered by financial institutions.

The **Hawaii Capital Loan Program**, in participation with local lenders, provides loans of up to $1 million to business owners unable to secure financing from conventional sources. Loans are made to purchase or build facilities or equipment or for working capital. The interest rate varies with the prime rate and is generally lower than conventional funding sources. As of January 1992, the rate is 5.5. percent. Loans can be made to a maximum term of 20 years. Since the program's inception in 1964, 447 loans have been made totaling $69 million, including the state's contribution of $27.2 million.

The **Hawaii Innovation Development Program** has funding available for the development of products and services that use new technologies. The loan terms include interest as of January 1992 of 5.5 percent, with a $100,000 ceiling and a maximum term of 10 years.

The **Small Business Information Service** (SBIS) functions as an information and referral service and brings together information derived from other agencies that are repackaged, organized, and delivered to business decisionmakers, government agencies, and other interested parties. SBIS has published a variety of material including *Starting a Business in Hawaii*; *Hawaii's Business Regulations*; *Checklist for Exporters*; and *Checklist for Employers*.

The **Business Action Center** is a one-stop permit and license center providing information and assistance to individuals and companies interested in starting a business in Hawaii. In addition to obtaining brochures and application forms, consumers are able to get general excise tax numbers and file business registration and labor reporting applications. The center is equipped with a toll-free number to accommodate neighbor island calls, and has hot lines to the Department of Taxation, Commerce, and Consumer Affairs, and Labor and Industrial Relations so that questions regarding those agencies can be answered quickly and accurately.

Contact:
Mr. Steven R. Lee, Coordinator
Business Information Service
Department of Business, Economic
    Development, and Tourism
Grosvenor Center, Mauka Tower
737 Bishop Street, Suite 1900
Honolulu, HI 96813
(808) 586–2600

Contact:
Mr. Milton Kwock, Manager
Business Action Center
1130 North Nimitz Highway, Suite A-254
Honolulu, HI 96817
(808) 586–2545
(800) 468–4644 (neighbor island calls)

Contact:
Mr. Larry G. Nelson, Coordinator
Government Marketing Assistance Program
Department of Business, Economic
   Development, and Tourism
Grosvenor Center, Mauka Tower
737 Bishop Street, Suite 1900
Honolulu, HI 96813
(808) 586–2600

The **Government Marketing Assistance Program** helps businesses understand the procurement laws and regulations of the federal, state, and county governments. Services include identifying government purchasing activities, obtaining information on bid opportunities, explaining government procurement policies, and encouraging government uses of local commodities and services.

Contact:
Mr. Robert Agres, Consultant
Community-Based Economic Development
   Program
Department of Business, Economic
   Development, and Tourism
Grosvenor Center, Mauka Tower
737 Bishop Street, Suite 1900
Honolulu, HI 96813
(808) 586–2583

The **Community-Based Economic Development Program** was established to support economic alternatives for specific communities. The program has a revolving fund that provides grants and loan assistance to community organizations in developing very small business enterprises.

Contact:
Mr. Thomas H. Brandt
Enterprise Zones Program
Department of Business, Economic
   Development, and Tourism
Grosvenor Center, Mauka Tower
737 Bishop Street, Suite 1900
Honolulu, HI 96813
(808) 586–2593

The **Enterprise Zones Program** was established to help stimulate business activity and create jobs in areas with higher than average unemployment or below average income levels. Businesses within a designated enterprise zone that qualify under the program are eligible for exemption from the General Excise Tax and for income tax credits. The zones themselves are designated by each county and may include additional incentives as determined by the county.

The International Business Center of Hawaii

Contact:
International Business Center of Hawaii
City Financial Tower
201 Merchant Street, Suite 1510
Honolulu, HI 96813
(808) 587–2797

The **International Business Center of Hawaii** (IBCH) is a state-funded program committed to the development of Hawaii as an international business center. The IBCH offers the international business community a comprehensive resource center, providing them with trade information and assistance; connections to business resources; business relationship development opportunities; and business training opportunities.

Agricultural Loan Division

Contact:
Mr. Toshio Nakamoto, Administrator
Agricultural Loan Division
Department of Agriculture
P.O. Box 22159
Honolulu, HI 96823–2159
(808) 973–9460

Within the Department of Agriculture is the **Agricultural Loan Division**, which directly promotes agricultural development by providing or facilitating loans to qualified farmers through a series of programs, including the Regular Agricultural Loan Program, the New Farmer Loan Program, the Emergency Loan Program, the Hawaii Agricultural Products Program, and the Aquaculture Loan Program.

Small Business Development Center

Contact:
Ms. Janet Nye, State Director
Hawaii Small Business Development Center
University of Hawaii at Hilo
523 West Lanikaula Street
Hilo, HI 96720
(808) 933–3515

The **Small Business Development Center** (SBDC) provides assistance to existing and new businesses, primarily through counseling, training programs, and seminars. The lead center is in Hilo at the University of Hawaii, with subcenters in Honolulu, Kahului, and Lihue.

Governor's Advisory Council or Task Force

Contact:
Dr. Joshua Agsalud, Administrator
Office of the Governor
State Office Tower
235 Beretania Street
Honolulu, HI 96813
(808) 586–0005

Much of the responsibility for liaison with small business remains in the governor's office, which works closely with the legislature and the Small Business Advisory Committee.

Contact:
Ms. Bette Tatum, Chair
Governor's Small Business Advisory
    Committee
1588 Piikea Street
Honolulu, HI 96818
(808) 422–2163

Established in 1982, the 13-member **Governor's Small Business Advisory Committee** (GSBAC) is made up of department directors, small business organization representatives, and business owners, and serves as a communication link between government and small business.

Legislative Committees and Subcommittees

Legislative committees that deal regularly with small business and related issues include the Senate Business Development and Pacific Relations Committee, and Consumer Protection and Commerce Committee; and the House Consumer Protection and Commerce Committee, Labor and Public Employment Committee, and Water and Land Use Committee.

Contacts:

Senator Norman Mizuguchi
Chairman
Senate Labor and Employment Committee
State Capitol
235 South Bretania
Honolulu, HI 96813
(808) 548–2246

Senator Donna R. Ikeda
Chairperson, Senate Consumer Protection
    and Business Regulation
State Capitol
Honolulu, HI 96813
(808) 548–7553

Representative Dwight Y. Takamine
Chairperson, House Labor and Public
    Employment Committee
State Capitol
Honolulu, HI 96813
(808) 548–7506

Representative Mazie Hirono
Chairperson, House Consumer Protection
    and Commerce Committee
State Capitol
Honolulu, HI 96813
(808) 548–4187

Representative David Hagino
Chairperson, House Water and Land Use
    Committee
State Capitol
Honolulu, HI 96813
(808) 548–7560

Legislation

The Hawaii Legislature enacted the following in 1991:

- Unemployment insurance (UI) reform, signed into law by the governor on April 3, 1991, would provide a one-year reduction in unemployment insurance taxes for Hawaii businesses. The wage base, upon which taxes are paid, was reduced to $7,000 from $21,400. The impetus came from small business, prompted by the fact that the state has $400 million in the UI trust fund to pay unemployment benefits.

- Legislation was enacted to raise the state's minimum wage to $4.75 in April 1992, and then to $5.25 in January 1993. The 1992 increase was delayed until April to provide small businesses an opportunity to present amendments to create a "training wage" and a tip credit in the next legislative session.

- Legislation was enacted to provide a mandated family leave phase-in over several years. Beginning in 1992, all public employees who have been employed six months or longer are eligible for four weeks of unpaid leave each year. In 1994, the bill will apply to private employers with more than 100 employees.

- Between 1992 and 1994, the legislature will study the fiscal effects of the family leave bill, examine possible tax credits for employers, and require the Hawaii Department of Labor to draft rules and regulations governing family leave use.

State Small Business Conferences

No recent statewide small business conferences have been reported.

Idaho

Small Business Offices, Programs, and Activities

Department of Commerce

Contacts:
Mr. Jay Engstrom, Administrator
Economic Development Division
Idaho Department of Commerce
700 West State Street
Boise, ID 83720
(208) 334–2470

Mr. Brad Trost, Economic Development
  Specialist
Idaho Department of Commerce
700 West State Street
Boise, ID 83720
(208) 334–2470

Contact:
Mr. David Christensen, Administrator
International Trade Division
Idaho Department of Commerce
700 West State Street
Boise, ID 83720
(208) 334–2470

Contact:
Administrator
Division of Science and Technology
Idaho Department of Commerce
700 West State Street
Boise, ID 83720
(208) 334–2470

The **Idaho Department of Commerce** offers a variety of services to small firms, including site location; information on state and private financial assistance; Community Development Block Grants; Industrial Revenue Bonds; Idaho Travel Council grants; information on regulations, permits, and licensing; international trade assistance; travel and tourism promotion; and management and technical assistance programs.

The **Idaho Business Network** offers assistance to Idaho businesses in obtaining federal contracts and meeting federal bidding requirements.

The **International Trade Division** helps Idaho businesses make international trade contacts and deal with trade restrictions, protocol, and international trade financing.

The **Division of Science and Technology** cooperates with several high technology firms in Idaho in an effort to attract more high tech companies to the state and to obtain venture capital.

Small Business Development Centers

Contacts:
Mr. Ron Hall, State Director
Idaho Small Business Development Center
Boise State University
1910 University Drive
Boise, ID 83725
(208) 385–1640
(800) 225–3815 (toll-free, in-state)

Ms. Renee LeMoyne
Coordinator, SBIR Support Services
Idaho Small Business Development Center
(208) 385–3870

Idaho's **Small Business Development Center** (SBDC) is headquartered at Boise State University with affiliate centers in Boise, Hayden, Idaho Falls, Lewiston, Pocatello, Sandpoint, and Twin Falls. Services include business feasibility and planning seminars, counseling, and information research. A listing of all Small Business Development Centers and subcenters in Idaho is in Appendix A of this directory.

SBIR support services are coordinated with the Idaho Small Business Development Center, the U.S. Small Business Administration, the Idaho State Department of Commerce, and US West Foundation. SBIR support services are committed to increasing Idaho's SBIR proposal submission rate. This is achieved by providing information and assistance to the Idaho small business community through: SBIR regional resource libraries, electronic data base searching, solicitation matching, technical writing assistance, and business counseling and planning. Funding of up to $2,500 is available to assist in the background research and technical writing process necessary in compiling a SBIR proposal.

Small Business Incubators

Contacts:
Mr. Jim Deffenbaugh, Executive Director
Business Center for Innovation and
    Development
11100 Airport Drive
Hayden Lake, ID 83835
(208) 772–0584

Mr. Joe Pehrson, Manager
Idaho Innovation Center
2300 North Yellowstone
Idaho Falls, ID 83401
(208) 523–1026

Mr. Ron Millick, Director
Idaho State University Research and
    Business Park
Campus Box 8044
Idaho State University
Pocatello, ID 83209

Small Business Incubators are designed to encourage start-ups and help new firms survive their early years. Incubators provide services such as multitenant office space, business network assistance, and shared office services.

Permits and Licensing

Contact:
Mr. Dale Sharp, Senior Management Analyst
Operations Division
Idaho Department of Employment
317 Main Street
Boise, ID 83735
(208) 334–6398

The **Idaho Department of Employment's Clearinghouse Program** assists businesses in identifying required permits and licenses. The program is offered through the state's 24 job service centers.

Rural Development

Contact:
Mr. Dick Gardner
State of Idaho
Division of Financial Management
Room 122, Statehouse
Boise, ID 83720

The **Idaho Rural Development Council** was designated as one of the state councils to participate in the President's Initiative on Rural Development. Members of the steering committee attended a Rural Development Academy workshop in Utah to work on a strategic plan for rural development in Idaho. The council analyzes the strengths and weaknesses of the state in promoting rural development in Idaho.

Disadvantaged Business Emphasis

Contact:
Ms. Adrianne Saucerman
110 N. 27th Street
Boise, ID 83702
(208) 344–2531

185 S. Capital
Idaho Falls, ID 83402
(208) 529–2320

124 Blue Lakes Boulevard, #6
Twin Falls, ID 83301
(208) 734–7526

The state of Idaho works with the Idaho branch of the Associated Contractors of America to certify women- and minority-owned businesses as well as provide counseling and training services.

Governor's Advisory Council or Task Force

Contact:
Mr. William Hellar, Chairman
Economic Advisory Council
East 5225 Seltice Boulevard
Post Falls, ID 83854
(208) 756–1434

The **Economic Advisory Council** appointed by the governor consists of six members who represent both business and government from each of Idaho's six planning regions. The council provides guidance to the governor and the Department of Commerce director and approves implementation of plans, projects, and programs by the Department of Commerce.

Legislative Committees and Subcommittees

In the Idaho House of Representatives, small business concerns are addressed by the Commerce, Industry, and Tourism Committee. In the Senate, the Committee on Commerce and Labor addresses small business issues.

Contacts:
Representative Dorothy Reynolds
Chairman
House Committee on Commerce, Industry
    and Tourism
House of Representatives Chamber
Capitol Building
Boise, ID 83702
(208) 334–2000

Senator Ann Rydalch
Chairman
Senate Committee on Commerce
    and Labor
Senate Chamber, Capitol Building
Boise, ID 83720
(208) 334–2400

Legislation

Contact:
Honorable Steve Antone, Chairman
House Revenue and Taxation Committee
Room 404A, Statehouse
Boise, ID 83720

The most significant recent legislation affecting small businesses in Idaho was in the area of revenue and taxation. H.597 provides that the retailer, rather than the purchaser, shall have burden of proof for sales made that are excluded from the imposition of the states sales tax. H.805, a development impact fee law, is a program for the financing of public facilities to serve new growth and development. H.497 amends the Unclaimed Property Act. It shortens the holding period for certain unclaimed property, imposes a 10-year statute of limitations, changes the penalty provisions, and requires holders of unclaimed property to remit such property in the estate of a deceased within 5 years after the date of death of appointment of a representative.

State Small Business Conferences

Contact:
Mr. Jim Brandt, President
Western Power Sports
5272 Irving Street
Boise, ID 83706
(208) 376–8400

The **Idaho Conference on Small Business** was held in Boise on January 20, 1987. Approximately 60 small business issues were addressed. The issues were condensed into 27 recommendations and submitted to the governor and legislature. Many of the organizers were delegates to the 1986 White House Conference on Small Business. An informal task force formed during the conference is still in existence. On a quarterly basis, the task force conducts a survey of several hundred small business owners, the findings of which are forwarded to the governor, and in turn, to the legislature.

Illinois

Small Business Offices, Programs, and Activities

Department of Commerce and Community Affairs

Contact:
Mr. Jeff Mitchell, State Director
Illinois SBDC Program
Illinois Department of Commerce and
    Community Affairs
620 East Adams Street, 5th Floor
Springfield, IL 62701
(217) 524–5856

The **Department of Commerce and Community Affairs** provides management, technical, and financial assistance to the state's small businesses through a variety of programs and services. Governmental problems affecting significant numbers of businesses are analyzed, referred, and resolved through legislative and administrative processes to improve the overall climate for businesses in Illinois. The agency's small business activities are carried out under the umbrella of the Illinois Small Business Development Center Network. In addition, the Department of Commerce and Community Affairs represents the interests of small, minority- and women-owned businesses and various advocacy groups. Programs focus on resolving problems faced by small business in dealing with federal, state, and local governments.

The **Illinois Small Business Development Center Network** provides services and assistance to small businesseses and entrepreneurs in many areas, including technology commercialization, procurement, and export development. The network also encompasses small business incubator facilities.

Under the SBDC program, technology commercialization centers (TCCs) offer entrepreneurs and small businesses the services necessary for success in product sales. TCCs provide fledgling entrepreneurs direct research assistance, feasibility studies of new product or service ideas, technical resources, technology adaptation assistance, and product testing. SBDC subcenter offices provide business management assistance, counseling, and training in areas such as preparing business and marketing plans, securing capital, improving business skills, and accessing international trade opportunities. Specialized SBDCs assist minority- and women-owned business concerns. The centers serve Illinois' 102 counties. A complete listing of these centers in Illinois is in Appendix A of this directory.

The **Procurement Assistance Program** provides highly specialized assistance to Illinois companies interested in selling their products and services to federal, state, and local governments. During Fiscal Year 1991, the program assisted more than 8,300 businesses. Since Fiscal Year 1988, clients of the Procurement Assistance Program have received contracts totaling more than $337 million.

The **Illinois Product and Services Exchange** (IPSE) Program, operated in concert with the Procurement Assistance Program, encourages in-state purchasing by connecting large firms with smaller local suppliers of goods and services. The program uses a strategy called "import substitution" to keep investments and expenditures within the local or state economy rather than outside of Illinois. In the IPSE program, large businesses are requested to review their out-of-state purchases of products and services. The program then locates Illinois companies that can supply those products or services at the same or better quality and price and encourages the use of these in-state suppliers.

The **International Trade Centers Program** provides assistance to small businesses interested in exporting goods or services. Small business owners throughout the state are informed of overseas trade missions, meetings, training seminars, and other international activities. Small business export development centers (SBEDCs) serve the entire state and work closely with the Illinois SBDC program. "CORE" software—Company's Readiness to Export—is used in pre-screening clients for international trade opportunities.

The **Small Business Innovation Research** (SBIR) program stimulates technology innovation, encourages small innovative firms to participate in government research, and provides for the conversion of research results into commercial applications. SBIR money is awarded in three phases. In Fiscal Year 1991, Phase I grants totaled more than $1.3 million, and Phase II awards, over $4.1 million. Phase III involves private funds for commercial marketing of Phase II projects.

Loan Administration Division

Contact:
Mr. Richard LeGrand, Manager
Loan Administration Division
Illinois Department of Commerce and
    Community Affairs
620 East Adams
Springfield, IL 62701
(217) 524–4615

The **Loan Administration Division** contributes to economic development in the state by promoting and assisting in the growth and development of small business concerns. The principal objectives of the division are to foster increased employment opportunities, expand business and industry, and reduce energy costs by providing free energy audits. The division offers financial assistance through a variety of programs.

The **Build Illinois Small Business Development Loan Program** provides direct financing to small businesses at below-market interest rates in cooperation with private-sector lenders. Funds can be used for working capital, the lease or purchase of land and buildings, construction or renovation of fixed assets, and the lease, purchase, or installation of machinery and equipment. Debt refinancing or contingency funding is not allowed. Loans cannot exceed 25 percent of the cost of the business expansion. The maximum loan amount for any one project is $750,000.

The **Build Illinois Small Business Development Micro Loan Program** provides direct financing to small businesses at a below-market interest rate in cooperation with private-sector lenders. The purpose of the program is to help small businesses create or retain jobs and assist with business expansion. The Micro Loan Program may provide up to 25 percent of the total project cost, or a maximum of $100,000. Debt refinancing is not permitted.

The **Minority and Women Business Loan Program** provides direct financing to small businesses at below-market interest rates in cooperation with private-sector lenders. The purpose of the program is to help minority and women business owners create or retain jobs. Principal and interest repayments for the loans are used to maintain a state revolving-loan fund for use by other minority and women-owned businesses.

The **Disabled Business Owner Loan Program** provides direct financing to small businesses at below-market interest rates in cooperation with private-sector lenders. The program helps disabled business owners create or retain jobs. Principal and interest repayments for the loans are used to maintain a state revolving-loan fund for use by other disabled-owned businesses.

The **DBE/WBE Contractor Finance Program** is designed to increase participation of disadvantaged business enterprises (DBE) and woman business enterprises (WBE) in Illinois Department of Transportation (IDOT) contracting opportunities by offering short-term working capital. The Department of Commerce and Community Affairs (DCCA) participates with private banks to help secure loans these business owners might not otherwise obtain. The DBE/WBE must be IDOT certified to participate in the program. The term of the loan generally will be tied to the length of the contract being performed for IDOT. DCCA's participation level is 25 percent of the total loan, up to $100,000. The minimum loan considered by DCCA is $40,000.

The **Minority and Female Business Assistance Program** provides management, technical, and financial assistance. With an emphasis on the needs of minority and women business owners, activities include business skills workshops, start-up assistance, and assistance in bidding on government contracts.

Illinois Rural Affairs Council

Contact:
Mr. Lou DiFonso, Executive Director
Rural Affairs Council
Illinois Department of Commerce and
    Community Affairs
Wm. G. Stratton Building, Room 612
Springfield, IL 62706
(217) 782–7514

The **Illinois Rural Affairs Council** includes the directors of the following state agencies: Agriculture, Commerce and Community Affairs, Mines and Minerals, Transportation, Conservation, Energy and Natural Resources, Environmental Protection, the Housing Development Authority, Illinois Institute for Rural Affairs/Western Illinois University, the Farm Development Authority, the Finance Development Authority, and the University of Illinois. The council develops and supports programs that will strengthen the rural economy, maintain a rural emphasis in Illinois government, increase the viability of local governments, and improve education and human services in rural areas.

The **Illinois Rural Bond Bank** lends money at a reasonable cost to local units of government for financing improvements and development projects in communities.

Regulatory Assistance

Contact:
Mr. Rich Funderburk, Manager
Office of Small Business Regulatory
    Assistance
Illinois Department of Commerce and
    Community Affairs
620 East Adams
Springfield, IL 62701
(217) 782–7500

The **Office of Regulatory Assistance** provides targeted assistance to companies with regulatory problems and monitors state agencies' compliance with the Small Business Regulatory Flexibility Act. The goal of the Regulatory Flexibility Act is to increase small business participation and input in the rulemaking process. Under the act, state agencies are required to: (1) consider specific methods of reducing the impact of proposed rules on small business; (2) notify the small business community of regulatory proposals; and (3) provide analyses of proposed rules describing their possible effects on small business. Legislative research involves monitoring activities in other states to ensure that Illinois is keeping pace with legislative developments affecting small businesses.

In 1985, Illinois became the first state in the nation to create a **Small Business Utility Advocate**. Affiliated with the Department of Commerce and Community Affairs, but a separate entity, the advocate has wide-ranging authority to represent small businesses in all utility-related matters. Most significantly, the advocate can intervene in the rate-setting process for electric, gas, or telephone utilities. The advocate can also act as the ombudsman for small business in overbilling or deposit disputes with a public utility and can assist in financing energy conservation.

Office of Agency Outreach

Contact:
Ms. Luanne S. O'Shea, Manager
Office of Agency Outreach
Illinois Department of Commerce and
    Community Affairs
100 West Randolph, Suite 3–400
Chicago, IL 60601
(312) 814–4120
HOT LINE: (800) 252–2923
(toll-free, in-state)
(217) 785–7546 (out-of-state)

The **Office of Agency Outreach** coordinates small business information and publications distribution. Housed within the office are the following services:

- The **One-Stop Permit Center** is a clearinghouse through which new and established businesses receive information on licenses, permits, and other requirements necessary to conduct business in Illinois. The center acts as a problem resolution office for small businesses that encounter difficulties with state licensing or regulatory agencies. More than 5,000 one-stop permit kits have been mailed each year since 1985.

- The **Illinois Business Hotline** facilitates getting through government "red tape," providing quick responses to questions from the state's small firms. The hot line receives thousands of calls each year from all types of businesses.

Division of Industry Development

Contact:
Mr. Clint Bybee, Manager
Small Business Incubator Program
Illinois Department of Commerce and
    Community Affairs
100 West Randolph
Chicago, IL 60601
(312) 814–3540

Contact:
Mr. Sanford Morganstein, Manager
Division of Industry Development
Illinois Department of Commerce and
    Community Affairs
100 West Randolph Street
Chicago, IL 60601
(312) 814–5246

The **Small Business Incubator Program** provides management support, pooled office services, and affordable rents for start-up and existing small businesses. Firms share overhead expenses and are linked with financial, management, and other business assistance resources available through state and local governments. More than 1,500 jobs were created or retained in Fiscal Year 1991.

The **Technology Venture Investment Program** provides seed/early stage funding to Illinois companies to stimulate the development of new, advanced/high technology-based businesses. The program seeks to invest in firms that can demonstrate the potential to be economically and technically viable companies with products or services capable of being commercialized and creating employment. The highly competitive program will accept business plans from companies in a number of advanced/high technology fields, including computer hardware, software, and peripherals; biomedicine and biotechnology; chemicals and chemical products; agritechnology; automated manufacturing; and materials, including plastics, ceramics, and metals.

The Division of Industry Development manages Illinois' **Technology Challenge Grant Program**. The grant program responds to unique advanced technology projects for which no other source of funding is available; assists in leveraging major federal and private-sector research and development efforts to promote commercialization and technology transfer; and funds technology partnerships, consortia, and research centers.

The **Illinois Coalition** assesses the potential for economic development and commercialization of proposed state-funded research and development projects; advocates bringing major federal projects to Illinois; and organizes business input into the state's technology agenda.

Governor's Advisory Council or Task Force

Contact:
Mr. Matt Davidson, Executive Assistant
Governmental Relations
Illinois Department of Commerce and
    Community Affairs
620 Adams Street
Springfield, IL 62701
(217) 785–6315

The **Illinois Governor's Advisory Committee** evaluates the scientific and technical merits of state-funded technology challenge grant projects and shapes the science and technology base for the state's agenda.

The **Illinois Governor's Business Advisory Council** was created to assist in the establishment, survival, and growth of Illinois small business.

Legislative Committees

The Economic and Urban Development Committee handles business concerns in the House; the Commerce and Economic Development Committee handles small business matters in the Senate.

Contacts:
Senator Ted Leverenz, Chairman
Commerce and Economic Development
    Committee
201 North Stratton Building
Springfield, IL 62706
(217)782–5976

Representative Charles Morrow, Chairman
Economic and Urban Development
    Committee
2094 Stratton Building
Springfield, IL 62706
(217) 782–1702

Legislation

The following legislation affecting small business was enacted during the 87th Illinois General Assembly in 1990–1991.

- The Act Concerning Business Assistance. Amended to allow the Department of Commerce and Community Affairs to contract with units of local government, associations, chambers, and development organizations in efforts to enhance the delivery system to small businesses (P.A. 87–235).

- The Civil Administrative Code. Amended to designate special female and minority business advocates in efforts to assist such businesses in obtaining state and federal contracts (P.A. 86–0808).

- Disabled-owned businesses. Added to minority- and women-owned businesses regarding state government contracting (P.A. 87–0701).

- The Administrative Procedure Act. Amended to strengthen regulatory flexibility and the rulemaking process (P.A. 87–0823).

The following legislation affecting small business was passed during the 86th Illinois General Assembly.

- The Small Employer Group Health Insurance Law. Allows employers of 25 or fewer to provide "no frills" coverage. Plans will be at least 10 percent cheaper than previous policies, in some cases 40 percent less, allowing small businesses to offer health benefits to thousands of currently uninsured workers.

- The Underground Storage Tank Financial Responsibility Act. Amended to eliminate a $100 fee per tank; reduce the deductible from $100,000 to $10,000; add third party liability coverage; and levy a petroleum product storage fee to create a fund to assist in clean-up activity. Small gasoline stations benefit, especially those in rural areas.

- The Workers' Compensation Act. In part, the Industrial Commission experienced an increase in budget by nearly $2 million to fulfill a number of goals, including timely payment of benefits to injured workers and the potential to decrease costs for employers.

- The Illinois Tax Policy Act. Requires the governor to report annually to the General Assembly with a tax policy plan to help improve the business climate for small, minority-, and women-owned businesses.

- The Civil Administrative Code. Amended to require the Department of Commerce and Community Affairs to review the economic impact of legislation affecting small business and make recommendations in cooperation with the department or agency administering the law being studied.

- The Small Business Development Act. Amended to permit the Department of Commerce and Community Affairs to make grants available to small businesses that are awaiting federal Phase I Small Business Innovation Research grants while awaiting Phase II approval.

- The Civil Administrative Code. Amended to designate female and minority business advocates in efforts to assist such businesses in obtaining state and federal contracts.

State Small Business Conferences

Contact:
Mr. Jeff Mitchell, State Director
SBDC Program
Illinois Department of Commerce and
    Community Affairs
620 East Adams, 6th Floor
Springfield, IL 62701
(217) 524–5856

The **Illinois State House Conference on Small Business** taps the entrepreneurial experience of the state's small business community to develop recommendations for strengthening the environment for small business in Illinois and improving the overall economic climate and vitality of the state.

Indiana

Small Business Offices, Programs, and Activities

Indiana Department of Commerce

Contact:
Mr. John Humes, State Regulatory
  Ombudsman
Office of Business Regulatory Ombudsman
Indiana Department of Commerce
One North Capitol Avenue, Suite 700
Indianapolis, IN 46204
(317) 232–7304
Hot Line: (800) 824–2476
  (toll-free, in-state)

The **Indiana Department of Commerce** provides services to small businesses through various divisions and departments including the Community Development Division, the Office of Business Regulatory Ombudsman, the Business Development Division, the Business Marketing and Support Groups, the Government Marketing Assistance Group, the Tourism and Film Development Division, and the Financial and Administrative Services Division. Specific financing of business ventures is not offered through the Department of Commerce. Other state-regulated agencies provide venture and seed capital and technical assistance to new and existing businesses.

The **Office of Business Regulatory Ombudsman** was established to assist businesses, especially small businesses, in obtaining answers from federal, state, and local regulatory agencies. The ombudsman represents the lieutenant governor as a voting member of many of the state's major regulatory agencies. All state agencies are required to submit proposed rules and regulations to the ombudsman for review and comment about their effect on the small business community. Other services performed by the ombudsman include permit application assistance and the operation of a regulatory information network, including a toll-free hot line.

Contact:
Ms. Lynette Corey, Secretary
Permit Assistance Center
Office of Business Regulatory Ombudsman
Indiana Department of Commerce
One North Capitol Avenue, Suite 700
Indianapolis, IN 46204
(317) 232–7304

The **Permit Assistance Center** was established in the Office of Business Regulatory Ombudsman by the 1986 Indiana General Assembly. Through the center, businesses access information on the permit application process, including fee information and common reasons for permit denial.

The **Business Development Marketing Group** was created in 1989 to coordinate and market business services available from the Department of Commerce and other agencies. The group also works to promote new business from outside the state and coordinates Indiana's export programs. The Business Support Group serves as a switchboard for access to business services throughout the state, including business retention and expansion efforts. The group assists in export development and organizes local existing industry activities.

Contacts:

Mr. Frank Sabatine, Director
Business Development Marketing Group
Indiana Department of Commerce
One North Capitol Avenue, Suite 700
Indianapolis, IN 46204
(317) 232–0159

Mr. Bob Joseph, Director
Corporate Services, Business Development
Indiana Department of Commerce
One North Capitol Avenue, Suite 700
Indianapolis, IN 46204
(317) 232–8894

Ms. Deborah Coons, Director
Marketing, Business Development
Indiana Department of Commerce
One North Capitol Avenue, Suite 700
Indianapolis, IN 46204
(317) 232–4950

Contact:

Mr. John Goss, Director
Tourism and Film Development Division
Indiana Department of Commerce
One North Capitol Avenue, Suite 700
Indianapolis, IN 46204
(317) 232–8864

The **Tourism and Film Development Division** was created in 1989 to develop and assist Indiana's growing tourism and film industry. Technical assistance is offered throughout the state to small firms that have tourist-related business potential. The division also assists film and commercial production firms with site location and on-site logistics.

Contact:

Ms. Betty Cockrum, Director
Administrative Services
Indiana Department of Commerce
One North Capitol Avenue, Suite 700
Indianapolis, IN 46204
(317) 232–8780

The **Administrative Services Division** assists all the other divisions in the administration of various grant programs and research projects. Because the state of Indiana has established a network of business financial and technical support organizations, the Department of Commerce only grants dollars to communities for economic development, and not to specific businesses. Most recent is the **Strategic Development Fund**, which assists communities in developing cooperative efforts between the public and private sectors that are vital to the state's economy.

Indiana Commission for Agriculture and Rural Development

Contact:
Mr. Cresswell A. Hizer, Assistant
    Commissioner
Indiana Commission for Agriculture and
    Rural Development
Suite 414, ISTA Center
150 West Market
Indianapolis, IN 46204
(317) 232–8770

The **Indiana Commission for Agriculture and Rural Development** (ICARD) is the state's lead agency for agriculture and rural economic development. The office provides assistance in domestic and international marketing, funding for adding value to targeted basic products, publications on various aspects of agriculture, and expertise on technical and policy issues facing either the state's agricultural sector or rural population. In addition, the agency has been charged with the responsibility of examining the current condition and needs of rural Indiana, including infrastructure, education, economic development, access to capital, local leadership, and many other factors that affect the quality of life in rural Indiana.

Indiana Development Finance Authority

Contact:
Ms. Peggy Boehm, Executive Director
Indiana Development Finance Authority
One North Capitol Avenue, Suite 320
Indianapolis, IN 46204
(317) 233–4332

The **Indiana Development Finance Authority** provides services to small business through various programs, including export financing, rural development, domestic loan guarantees, and economic development bonding. The export finance program offers post-shipping financing and insurance to small and medium-size businesses. The rural development program offers loan guarantees to the agribusiness community. The domestic loan guarantee program supports expansion and job creation efforts of small and medium-size businesses. The economic development bonding program offers financing to the private sector through the use of industrial revenue bonds.

Indiana Statewide Certified Development Corporation

Contact:
Ms. Jean Wojtowicz, Executive Director
Indiana Statewide Certified Development
   Corporation
8440 Woodfield Crossing, Suite 315
Indianapolis, IN 46240
(317) 469–6166

The **Indiana Statewide Certified Development Corporation** offers small businesses fixed-rate loans through the SBA 504 program for the purchase of land and buildings (including new construction), machinery and equipment, and renovation/leasehold improvements. To be eligible, a small business must be located in Indiana; be a for-profit corporation, partnership, or proprietorship; have a net worth of under $6 million; and have an average net profit, after taxes, of less than $2 million per year for the preceding two years. The maximum loan is $750,000 at a rate of approximately 1 percent over Treasury bonds, issued in maturities of 10 and 20 years.

Indiana Community Business Credit Corporation

Contact:
Ms. Jean Wojtowicz
Indiana Community Business Credit
   Corporation
8440 Woodfield Crossing, Suite 315
Indianapolis, IN 46240
(317) 469–9704

The **Indiana Community Business Credit Corporation** is a privately owned company into which Indiana financial institutions pool funds for use by Indiana businesses unable to secure complete financing from conventional sources. The minimum size project is $200,000 and a participating lender must provide at least 50 percent of the financing.

Indiana Business Modernization and Technology Corporation

Contact:
Mr. Robert S. Fryer, Manager
Marketing and Outreach Promotions
Indiana Business Modernization and
   Technology Corporation
One North Capitol Avenue, Suite 925
Indianapolis, IN 46204
(317) 635–3058

The **Indiana Business Modernization and Technology Corporation** is a partnership of industry, academia, and government. This innovative organization was created by the Indiana General Assembly to strengthen the state's economy through the development and application of science and technology. The financial and technical resources of the corporation provide support for many enterprises vital to Indiana's economic future.

Contact:
Mr. William B. Glennon
Indiana Business Modernization and
   Technology Corporation
One North Capitol, Suite 925
Indianapolis, IN 46204
(317) 635–3058

Small Business Innovation Research (SBIR) Bridge Funding is a recent initiative of the Business Modernization and Technology Corporation (BMT) to assist Indiana companies intending to commercialize technologies developed as a result of SBIR funding. The funds are used to "bridge" the gap between the end of an SBIR Phase I award and the startup of a Phase II contract. BMT will make conditional loans available to Indiana companies that are SBIR Phase I recipients and that satisfy certain criteria. Awards are limited to a maximum of $50,000. Priority in the awarding of funds will be given to proposals considered by BMT to have the greatest commercial potential. The criteria established by BMT for companies requesting SBIR bridge funding include that: the company be an Indiana company that has a signed contract for an SBIR Phase I award; the company submit a Phase II proposal following up on the Phase I award; the SBIR project be scientific or technical in nature; and the company possess the potential and the intent to develop a viable business in Indiana utilizing the technology being developed.

The Indiana Small Business Development Corporation

Contact:
Mr. Bruce Kidd, Director, Business
   Assistance
Indiana Small Business Development
   Corporation
One North Capitol Avenue, Suite 1275
Indianapolis, IN 46204
(317) 264–2820

The **Indiana Small Business Development Corporation**, created by the Indiana General Assembly in 1991, is a not-for-profit corporation that combines the resources of the Institute for New Business Ventures, the Government Marketing Assistance Group, and the Women and Minority Business Assistance Program. This corporation supports the development and growth of small and emerging business enterprises by serving as a catalyst, linking entrepreneurs with the management, technical, and financial resources necessary for companies to succeed. Services are facilitated through the state's network of Small Business Development Centers. The Small Business Development Corporation also conducts conferences and workshops that focus on the challenges of managing and financing successful companies.

Contact:
Ms. Ann Neal-Winston, Executive Director
Women and Minority Business Assistance
    Program
Indiana Small Business Development
    Corporation
One North Capitol Avenue, Suite 1275
Indianapolis, IN 46204
(317) 264–2820

The **Women and Minority Business Assistance Program** is a counseling service that provides technical and management assistance, and, whenever possible, helps to identify sources of financing. The program also provides workshops and seminars.

Contact:
Mr. A. David Schaaf, Executive Director
Government Marketing Assistance Group
Indiana Small Business Development
    Corporation
One North Capitol Avenue, Suite 1275
Indianapolis, IN 46204
(317) 264–2820

The **Government Marketing and Assistance Group** is a counseling service for businesses interested in obtaining federal and/or state government contracts. Marketing assistance and data base information are available free of charge. The Government Marketing and Assistance Group also sponsors seminars on specific subjects related to government marketing strategies. This service currently assists more than 1,700 companies throughout Indiana in marketing to the government.

Small Business Development Centers

Contact:
Mr. Stephen Thrash, State Director
Indiana Small Business Development Center
One North Capitol, Suite 420
Indianapolis, IN 46204–2248
(317) 264–6871

Small Business Development Centers (SBDCs) provide practical and technical assistance to existing and prospective business owners. SBDCs are partially funded by the U.S. Small Business Administration and are usually affiliated with a college or university. In Indiana, a lead center is located in Indianapolis. A complete listing of all Small Business Development Centers and subcenters in Indiana is in Appendix A of this directory.

Governor's Advisory Council or Task Force

The **Governor's Commission on Minority Business Development** was established to foster the growth of Indiana's minority business community through increased participation in government procurement programs. The commission, consisting of 14 government and minority business members, identifies minority businesses in the state and encourages state and local governmental agencies to purchase from them. The commission's goal is for at least 5 percent of all state contracts to be awarded to minority business enterprises. The position of deputy commissioner for minority business development has been established in the State Department of Administration to implement programs developed by the commission and to encourage state contract awards to minority enterprises.

Contact:

Mr. Gary Alan Gibson, Deputy
   Commissioner
Minority Business Development
Department of Administration
Indiana Government Center South
402 West Washington Street
Indianapolis, IN 46204
(317) 232–3061

Legislative Committees and Subcommittees

The Senate Committee on Agriculture and Small Business examines small business issues. Small business issues in the House are handled by the House Committee on Insurance and Corporations or the House Committee on Commerce.

Contacts:

Senator Johnny Nugent
Chairman
Senate Committee on Agriculture
   and Small Business
State House
200 West Washington
Indianapolis, IN 46204
(317) 232–9541

Representative Craig Fry
Chairman
House Committee on Insurance
   and Corporations
State House
Indianapolis, IN 46204
(219) 233–2138

Representative Jeff Hays
Chairman
House Committee on Commerce
State House
Indianapolis, IN 46204
(812) 464–1850

Legislation

Recent legislation enacted in Indiana that affects small business follows.

- Mandated Benefits. S.B. 191 mandates that all businesses that purchase health care insurance in Indiana include unlimited coverage for chiropractic care.

- Unemployment Compensation. H.E.A. 1594 provides benefit increases, lowers eligibility requirements, and modifies the tax schedules.

- Workers' Compensation Reform. H.E.A. 1517 includes significant benefit increases over the next four years and numerous other changes, including a seven-fold increase in Indiana's OSHA fines.

- Mandated Mammography Offering. S.E.A. 295 requires that insurers offer mammography screening to employers purchasing an insured health care product. The employer may reject the coverage.

State Small Business Conferences

No state small business conferences were reported.

Iowa

Small Business Offices, Programs, and Activities

Iowa Department of Economic Development

Contact:
Mr. Allan T. Thoms, Director
Iowa Department of Economic Development
200 East Grand Avenue
Des Moines, IA 50309
(515) 242–4814

The reorganization of state government in 1986 improved the coordination of Iowa's economic development efforts through the creation of the **Iowa Department of Economic Development** (IDED). The IDED is working with the private sector to promote policies and implement programs to expand the economy and increase job opportunities for Iowans. Greater per capita income, increased output of goods and services, less out-migration, and a lower unemployment rate are some of the indicators used to measure the effectiveness of these policies and programs. The Department of Economic Development has six main divisions: Administration, Business Development, Community and Rural Development, International, Tourism, and Workforce Development.

Contact:
Ms. Toni Hawley, New Business
    Development Manager
Iowa Department of Economic Development
200 East Grand Avenue
Des Moines, IA 50309
(515) 242–4758
(800) 532–1216 (toll-free, in-state)

The mission of the **Small Business Bureau** is to further the economic well-being of Iowa's small businesses and provide them with growth opportunities by offering services and coordinating efforts with existing programs.

The **Iowa Small Business Vendor Programs** aid Iowa's small businesses competing for state government contracts. Application forms are available to vendors interested in having their names placed on lists for state agencies for soliciting bids.

The state of Iowa has developed a computerized **Business License Information Center**. The one-stop shop advises business owners on licenses they need and provides specific information on state licenses and regulations. The major objective of the center is to reduce the time and paperwork involved in establishing a business in Iowa.

"Small Business Helpline" is a toll-free number for small business information on licenses, permits, and other requirements to operate a business in Iowa.

Contact:
Mr. Burt Powley, SELF Manager
Bureau of Business Finance
Iowa Department of Economic Development
200 East Grand Avenue
Des Moines, IA 50309
(515) 242–4793

Contact:
Mr. Gregg Barcus, President
Iowa Product Development Corporation
200 East Grand Avenue
Des Moines, IA 50309
(515) 242–4860

Contact:
Mr. Timothy Wood, Small Business Liaison
Iowa Department of Economic Development
Bureau of Small Business Development
200 East Grand Avenue
Des Moines, IA 50309
(515) 242–4909
(800) 532–1216 (toll-free, in-state)

Contact:
Mr. Muhammad Y. Abdullah, Targeted Small
  Business Specialist
Iowa Department of Economic Development
200 East Grand Avenue
Des Moines, IA 50309
(515) 242–4721

The **Self-Employment Loan Program** assists low-income entrepreneurs by providing low-interest loans for new or expanding small businesses. The loans may not exceed $5,000 and the rate of interest may not exceed 5 percent simple interest per annum.

The **Iowa Product Development Corporation** (IPDC) is a state-funded seed capital fund that invests in start-up and emerging Iowa companies that are bringing new products and processes to the marketplace. Since its creation in 1983, the IPDC has invested over $8 million in more than 50 Iowa companies. The IPDC program invests in companies rather than offering loans or grants. IPDC investments can be structured in many ways, including royalty agreements, equity positions, or some form of debt instrument.

The office of the **Iowa Small Business Liaison** assists small businesses, women- and minority-owned businesses, and economic development service providers by being an accessible hands-on resource for economic development issues and an advocate for their problems and concerns with state government. The office can provide direct technical assistance, or can place the business with appropriate specialized technical assistance through Iowa's existing technical service provider network, the Iowa Network for Business Assistance (INBA). The office also administers state funds for the support of business incubators, rural technical assistance centers, and regional economic development centers.

The **Targeted Small Business Program** was established in 1986 to enhance business opportunities for minority- and women-owned businesses. This program implements the legislated targeted small business procurement goal program, works with state purchasing agencies to increase the number of contracts awarded to targeted small businesses, and develops legislation to increase procurement opportunities for these targeted businesses.

The **Iowa Satisfaction Performance Bond Program** requires all state government agencies to waive the requirement of satisfaction of performance bonds for targeted small businesses that demonstrate the inability to acquire such a bond because of lack of experience. This waiver applies only to projects amounting to $50,000 or less, and the business must be certified as a targeted small business.

Contact:

Ms. Donna Lowery
Targeted Small Business Financial
   Assistance Program
200 East Grand Avenue
Des Moines, IA 50309
(515) 242–4813

Contact:

Ms. Mary Kay Baker, Finance Specialist
Iowa Department of Economic Development
200 East Grand Avenue
Des Moines, IA 50309
(515) 242–4839

Contact:

Mr. Kenneth Boyd, CEBA Program
   Administrator
Bureau of Business Finance
Iowa Department of Economic Development
200 East Grand Avenue
Des Moines, IA 50309
(515) 242–4810

Contacts:

Mr. Lane Palmer, Chief
Bureau of Community Financing
Iowa Department of Economic Development
200 East Grand Avenue
Des Moines, IA 50309
(515) 242–4837

Mr. Michael Fastenau
Bureau of Business Finance
Iowa Department of Economic Development
200 East Grand Avenue
Des Moines, IA 50309
(515) 242–4831

The **Targeted Small Business Financial Assistance Program** was created by the legislature in 1987. The purpose of the program is to assist in the creation and expansion of minority and women-owned businesses in Iowa. Eligible applicants must meet criteria established for targeted small businesses. The program provides for loans, loan guarantees, or equity grants for eligible small businesses. Applications are reviewed monthly and are awarded on a competitive basis as funds allow.

The **National Rural Development Loan Program** (NRDLP) is designed to improve business, industry, and employment, specifically the direct retention and creation of jobs in rural areas of Iowa. A joint effort between the state of Iowa, the U.S. Department of Agriculture, and the National Rural Development Finance Corporation, the funds generated by this program are intended to stimulate innovative business and entrepreneurial practices and to assist in the diversification and revitalization of Iowa's rural economy.

The **Community Economic Betterment Account** (CEBA) uses state financial assistance to encourage local economic development projects. The program has resulted in more than 25,000 pledged jobs, with an investment of approximately $39 million since 1986. All cities, counties, or merged area schools are eligible to apply on behalf of local business enterprises that are starting up, expanding, or relocating to Iowa. Key criteria for approval of requests for assistance are the number of jobs created, the cost per job for the CEBA funds involved in the project, and significant community interest and involvement. The funds are used to acquire land or buildings for construction or reconstruction, to purchase machinery or equipment, inventory, working capital, and other business needs.

Iowa's **Community Development Block Grant** (CDBG) from the U.S. Department of Housing and Urban Development (HUD) is divided among three programs: (1) the regular CDBG program, which receives the majority of the annual federal dollars; (2) the Economic Development Set-Aside (EDSA); and (3) the Public Facilities Set-Aside. Community improvements—public works projects, housing rehabilitation, and job-generating business expansions, start-ups, and relocations to Iowa—are financed by the CDBG program in all counties and cities, except the nine largest Iowa cities, which receive funds directly from HUD. CDBG funds are awarded on a competitive basis.

Contact:
Ms. Kathy Beery, Division Administrator
Community and Rural Development
Iowa Department of Economic Development
200 East Grand Avenue
Des Moines, IA 50309
(515) 242–4807

Contact:
Mr. Thom Guzman, Coordinator
Main Street Program
Iowa Department of Economic Development
200 East Grand Avenue
Des Moines, IA 50309
(515) 242–4733

Contacts:
Mr. Michael Doyle, Acting Administrator
Ms. Kathy Hill-Crees, Marketing Manager
International Division
Iowa Department of Economic Development
200 East Grand Avenue
Des Moines, IA 50309
(515) 242–4743

The **Rural Community Leadership Development Program** is designed to prepare new volunteers to participate in community and economic development organizations. Goals of the program are to develop individual leadership skills, develop team skills, and encourage multi-community development initiatives and cooperation. The programs begin in the fall and are conducted by merged area schools, Iowa State University Extension, and independent colleges.

The purpose of the **Rural Enterprise Fund** is to provide support to rural communities through seed money, technical assistance, and training. The program encourages coalition building and pooling of resources within communities and across jurisdictional boundaries. Projects are locally determined with communities, businesses, and other groups providing a match to the state's grant money.

The **Iowa Main Street Program** is designed to encourage downtown economic revitalization using historic preservation as a tool to attract new investments to the community. It focuses on the organization, promotion, design, and business improvement of selected Iowa downtown areas.

The **International Division** performs many functions, all of which are designed to strengthen Iowa's presence in the international marketplace. The division has offices located in Des Moines; Tokyo, Japan; Hong Kong; and Frankfurt, Germany. The offices work together to promote Iowa products overseas, attract foreign investment into the state, and educate Iowa business people on topics related to exporting and doing business in other countries. The International Division also administers the Export Trade Assistance Program, which provides financial reimbursement for Iowa companies participating in overseas trade shows and trade missions. Trained staff in each of the offices are available to consult with Iowa companies on an individual basis.

Contact:
Mr. Bob Lipman
Workforce Development
Iowa Department of Economic Development
200 East Grand Avenue
Des Moines, IA 50309
(515) 242–4797

The **Iowa Small Business New Jobs Training Program** fosters the creation of new jobs in Iowa by helping businesses lower the cost of expanding or establishing a new work force. The program funds education and training services to enable new employees to perform their jobs. Services are designed to meet a business' specific training needs and may include skill assessment, orientation, skill training, re-employment training, and on-the-job training. On-the-job training services can provide up to 50 percent of an employee's wages and fringe benefits during the training period. Also, loans up to $50,000 are available and are repayable over a 10-year period. A percentage of incremental property taxes, machinery and equipment taxes, and payroll withholding taxes that an employer would otherwise pay are diverted to repay the loan. Income from the business is not used for repayment.

Contact:
Mr. William P. Angrick II
Citizen's Aide Ombudsman
215 East 7th Street
Capitol Complex
Des Moines, IA 50309
(515) 281–3592

The **Iowa Office of Ombudsman** formally investigates complaints against a department or official of the state and refers these inquiries to the appropriate state offices. The ombudsman cannot investigate federal agencies or actions between private parties not involving state or local government agencies.

Iowa Procurement Outreach Center

Contact:
Mr. Allen Williams, Director
Iowa Procurement Outreach Center
Kirkwood Community College
6301 Kirkwood Boulevard, Building 9
Cedar Rapids, IA 52406
(319) 898–5665
(800) 458–4465 (toll-free, in-state)

The **Iowa Procurement Outreach Center** (IPOC) is a service center for Iowa small businesses interested in selling goods and services to the federal government. Based in Cedar Rapids, IPOC uses existing resources and programs to identify interested businesses and assist them in bidding for government contracts.

Linked Investments for Tomorrow Program

Contact:
Ms. Lynn Muehlenthaler Bedford, Treasury
    Investment Officer
State Treasurer's Office
Hoover Building
Des Moines, IA 50319
(515) 281–3287

The **Linked Investments for Tomorrow Program** was established in 1988 to encourage economic growth by providing below-market financing to women- and minority-owned small businesses. Funds are available for lending through Iowa financial institutions by the office of the state treasurer. Loan applications from certified targeted small businesses may be for any small business purpose.

Iowa Small Business Loan Program

Contact:
Mr. Ted Chapler, Executive Director
Iowa Finance Authority
100 East Grand Avenue, Suite 250
Des Moines, IA 50309
(515) 242–4990

The purpose of the **Iowa Small Business/Economic Development Loan Program** is to assist in the development and expansion of business in Iowa. The Iowa Finance Authority issues bonds exempt from federal tax and distributes the proceeds to qualifying businesses in the form of low interest loans for the acquisition, construction, improvement, or equipping of facilities. Typically, these loans are one to two percentage points below conventional rates. Manufacturing-based businesses, multi-family residential rental projects benefiting low income residents, solid waste disposal facilities, and nonprofit organizations are eligible for financing through the Economic Development Loan Program. The Small Business Loan Program specifically serves the financial assistance needs of qualifying businesses with 20 or fewer full-time employees, or with less than $3 million in annual gross revenues during the past fiscal year or as an average of the three preceding years. Funds cannot be used for working capital or inventory. The maximum loan amount for either program is $10 million. The Iowa Finance Authority also issues taxable bonds for a wider range of business projects.

Iowa Business Development Credit Corporation

Contact:
Mr. Don Albertson, Executive Vice President
Iowa Business Development Credit
    Corporation
901 Insurance Exchange Building
505 Fifth Avenue
Des Moines, IA 50309
(515) 282–2164

The **Iowa Business Development Credit Corporation** (IBDCC) stimulates economic development through loans to new or established firms in conjunction with banks, insurance companies, savings and loan associations, and other financial institutions. Counseling is available in finance, marketing, and management. Loan proceeds may be used to purchase land; purchase or construct buildings, machinery, equipment, and inventory; or as working capital. A portion also may be used to retire debt. Nonprofit enterprises, lending or financial institutions, and firms able to acquire funds at reasonable rates from other sources are ineligible.

Iowa Business Growth Company

Contact:
Mr. Don Albertson, Executive Vice President
Iowa Business Growth Company
901 Insurance Exchange Building
505 Fifth Avenue
Des Moines, IA 50309
(515) 282–2164

The **Iowa Business Growth Company** (IBGC) received U.S. Small Business Administration certification in May 1981, thereby becoming the nation's first statewide Certified Development Company. This certification allows IBGC to offer the SBA 504 loan program to businesses in every Iowa community. The IBGC provides long-term, fixed-asset financing at a fixed rate of interest, slightly below market rate. The 504 program allows a company to receive up to 90 percent financing for a fixed-asset project.

Small Business Development Centers

Contact:
Mr. Ron Manning, State Director
Iowa Small Business Development Center
Chamberlynn Building
137 Lynn Avenue
Ames, IA 50010
(515) 292–6351

The Iowa **Small Business Development Center** (SBDC) comprises 15 resource centers that provide comprehensive confidential counseling, information, and educational opportunities to small business owners and prospective entrepreneurs. Most services are provided free or at a minimal cost.

The state office is located in Ames, at Iowa State University. Subcenters are located in Des Moines, Dubuque, Davenport, Ottumwa, Spencer, Council Bluffs, Mason City, Creston, Iowa City, Cedar Falls, Sioux City, Ames, Audubon, Cedar Rapids, and Burlington. A complete listing of Small Business Development Centers and subcenters in Iowa is in Appendix A of this directory.

Small Business Innovative Research Program

Contact:
Mr. Daniel Dittemore, Deputy Director
Wallace Technology Transfer Foundation
317 Sixth Avenue, Suite 840
Des Moines, IA 50309
(515) 243–1487

Iowa supports **Small Business Innovative Research** (SBIR) activity through funds appropriated to the Wallace Technology Transfer Foundation. The foundation may furnish financial assistance of up to $30,000 to firms in the "bridge" period between completion of a Phase I project and approval of a Phase II application. The foundation decides award of funds on a merit review basis. Funds for the program are allocated each year by the foundation's board of directors from appropriations provided by the state.

122

Center for Industrial Research and Service

Contact:
Mr. Lloyd Anderson, Interim Director
Center for Industrial Research and Service
ISU Research Park
2501 North Loop Drive, Suite 500
Ames, IA 50010–8286
(515) 294–3420

The **Center for Industrial Research and Service** (CIRAS), a part of the Iowa State University Extension program, provides management and technical assistance to manufacturing businesses in Iowa. The CIRAS strategy is to guide clients to solution activities rather than implement the solutions for them. The staff members average 20 years of industrial experience in fields of management, engineering, human resources, production, purchasing, and planning.

Iowa Department of Education

Contact:
Dr. William L. Lepley, Director
Iowa Department of Education
Grimes State Office Building
Des Moines, IA 50319–0146
(515) 281–5294

Since 1967, Iowa has helped individuals with low basic skills through the 15 community colleges' **Adult Basic Education programs**. These colleges have the qualified personnel and the ability to provide quality literacy programs for business and industry. The colleges work with business and industry to assess the need, design a program to meet the need, and provide materials and instructors to conduct the program. Programs are provided on-site or at other locations convenient to all parties involved. Other offerings are also available for business and industry through the community college system in Iowa.

Governor's Advisory Council or Task Force

Contact:
Ms. Toni Hawley, Manager of New Business
   Development
Iowa Department of Economic Development
200 East Grand Avenue
Des Moines, IA 50309
(515) 242–4758

The **Iowa Small Business Advisory Council** is a nine-member council of small business owners from across the state, appointed by the governor. The council makes recommendations on legislative matters affecting small business and serves as an advocate for small business in the state. The council's goal is to stimulate job creation and to encourage growth and expansion of Iowa small business.

Legislative Committees and Subcommittees

Small business issues in Iowa are handled by the Senate Committee on Small Business and Economic Development.

Contact:
Senator James Riordan, Chairman
Senate Committee on Small Business and
    Economic Development
State Capitol
Des Moines, IA 50319
(515) 281–3917 (during the session)
(515) 281–5307 (Clerk of the Senate,
    for period of adjournment)

Legislation

Major legislation passed during the 1991 session affecting small business accomplished the following:

- Established a nine-member Small Business Advisory Council (SBAC) to be appointed by the governor subject to Senate confirmation. The SBAC is charged with advising and consulting with the IED Board on matters of concern to small business. The SBAC is also authorized to review and monitor small business programs within the state to determine their effectiveness and to coordinate the delivery of programs and services aimed at small businesses (H.F. 322).

- Amended provisions of the state's targeted small business laws to revise the definition of a targeted small business. The new provision states that the size standard to be used shall be that the business has an annual gross income of less than $3 million, computed as an average of the three preceding fiscal years. The number of full-time equivalent employees would no longer be part of the consideration for participation in TSB programs (S.F. 257).

- Made several nonsubstantive changes to Chapter 280C, the Iowa Small Business New Jobs Training Act, including striking obsolete references relating to repayments to the permanent school fund (S.F. 90).

- Created an Office of Renewable Fuels within the Farm Commodity/Agricultural Marketing Division of the Department of Agriculture and Land Stewardship. Funds of $65,000 were appropriated for alternative fuel and Iowa-grown crop promotion. The purpose of the office is to further research, development, and promotion of renewable fuels and related technologies (S.F. 545).

- Updated references in the Iowa Tax Code to coordinate with changes in the Internal Revenue Code (IRC). Included was a provision to update Iowa's current 6.5 percent Research and Development Tax Credit to comply with updated federal eligibility guidelines. This provision also "decouples" Iowa's credit from the federal statute so that Iowa's credit will stand even if the federal credit expires (S.F. 83).

- Revised provisions of the Iowa Retraining Program to streamline the review process and provide for the request of information important to informed decisionmaking. The changes will eliminate a bias inherent in the original criteria toward larger firms and simplify the application process for small business (H.F. 498).

- Extended urban renewal and urban revitalization authority to counties. This bill allows unincorporated areas of counties to be declared eligible for development incentives such as tax increment financing and tax abatement programs currently available to cities (H.F. 704).

- Increased the solid waste tonnage fees collected for the waste volume reduction and recycling fund and provides for additional programs to be funded by these funds. Among the variety of new programs to be funded annually are a By-Products and Waste Exchange Service to assist Iowa companies to find alternative uses for waste by-products (H.F. 706).

- Created a voluntary shared work program for employers facing a decline in business activity. The legislation provides that an employer may elect to reduce the hours and wages of all or a particular group of employees rather than lay off workers when experiencing a temporary decline in business activity. The employees whose hours and wages are reduced would be eligible for partial unemployment compensation benefits to supplement lost wages (H.F. 589).

- Incorporated changes in the statutes relating to petroleum underground and aboveground storage tanks. One provision expands the eligibility for and amount of benefits offered under the Remedial Account for certain small businesses, including retroactive eligibility and benefits (S.F. 362).

- Enacted legislation that provides a premium credit and other incentives to small businesses that provide health insurance for their employees. The legislation effectively requires insurers to treat all Iowa small businesses as one large group for rate-setting purposes. It authorizes "basic benefit coverage" which includes primary, preventive hospital care for covered individuals based on certain minimum coverages (H.F. 688).

State Small Business Conferences

No recent statewide small business conferences have been reported.

Kansas

Small Business Offices, Programs, and Activities

Kansas Department of Commerce

Contact:
Secretary of Commerce
Kansas Department of Commerce
400 S.W. 8th Street, 5th Floor
Topeka, KS 66603–3957
(913) 296–3480

Contact:
Mr. Jerry Lonergan, Director
Division of Existing Industry Development
Kansas Department of Commerce
400 S.W. 8th Street, 5th Floor
Topeka, KS 66603–3957
(913) 296–5298

Contact:
Ms. Deana Beardmore
First Stop Clearinghouse
Division of Existing Industry Development
Kansas Department of Commerce
400 S.W. 8th Street, 5th Floor
Topeka, KS 66603–3957
(913) 296–5298

The **Kansas Department of Commerce** is the lead agency for economic development in Kansas. Through its six divisions, the department is responsible for fostering economic development through the promotion of business, commerce, and industry. This is accomplished through the department's six divisions, along with a network of business assistance providers throughout the state.

The **Division of Existing Industry Development** promotes the growth, diversification, and retention of business and industry in Kansas. Because the vast majority of Kansas businesses are small, much of the division's activity centers around small business assistance. The small business assistance staff identifies and addresses the needs of existing and start-up businesses. The division staff then provides the necessary assistance—both directly and through a statewide business assistance network— channeling appropriate resources for business planning, technical assistance, financing, or other business problems.

The Division of Existing Industry Development operates a clearinghouse for anyone wishing to do business in Kansas. The **First Stop Clearinghouse** keeps on file all state forms, applications, permits, and tax forms related to conducting business in Kansas. The clearinghouse is also responsible for providing advocacy services to Kansas' small businesses.

Contact:

Mr. Steve Kelly
Kansas Venture Capital Program
Division of Existing Industry Development
Kansas Department of Commerce
400 S.W. 8th Street, 5th Floor
Topeka, KS 66603–3957
(913) 296–5298

Contacts:

Mr. Antonio Augusto, Director
Office of Minority Business
Division of Existing Industry Development
Kansas Department of Commerce
400 S.W. 8th Street, 5th Floor
Topeka, KS 66603–3957
(913) 296–5298

Mr. Leo Vogel
Division of Purchases
Department of Administration
900 S.W. Jackson, 1st Floor
Topeka, KS 66612
(913) 296–2376

Contact:

Mr. Mikel Filter
Kansas Business Retention and Expansion
    Program
Division of Existing Industry Development
Kansas Department of Commerce
400 S.W. 8th Street, 5th Floor
Topeka, KS 66603–3957
(913) 296–5298

To increase the availability of risk capital in Kansas, the state has instituted the **Kansas Venture Capital Program** and seed capital programs that make use of income tax credits to encourage investment in venture and seed capital pools as a source of early stage financing for small businesses. Businesses demonstrating strong growth potential but lacking the financial strength to obtain conventional financing are the most likely candidates for risk capital funding. The Division of Existing Industry Development within the Kansas Department of Commerce has in operation—and continues to develop—a network of venture capital resources to assist a qualified small business in locating potential sources of venture capital financing.

As a part of the Division of Existing Industry Development, the **Office of Minority Business** promotes and assists in the development of minority-owned and women-owned businesses in Kansas. The program provides assistance in procurement and contracting, financing, business planning, and identification of business opportunities. A directory of minority-owned and women-owned businesses in Kansas is published annually.

In addition, the Office of Minority Business, in cooperation with the Kansas Department of Administration, provides assistance to businesses seeking procurement opportunities with the state. The Department of Commerce also provides information to potential vendors about contracting opportunities with the private sector and federal government.

Within the Division of Existing Industry Development is the **Kansas Business Retention and Expansion Program**. This program is offered to Kansas communities and counties who wish to sustain existing industry, support its modernization and competitiveness, foster its expansion, and provide an environment that encourages new industry creation and recruitment. The department works with community leaders and volunteers to conduct on-site surveys of local businesses. The information gathered is then analyzed and the results are used to solve immediate short-term problems, as well as to develop long-term local retention and expansion strategies.

Contact:
Mr. Cal Lantis, Director
Division of Community Development
Kansas Department of Commerce
400 S.W. 8th Street, 5th Floor
Topeka, KS 66603–3957
(913) 296–3485

Contact:
Mr. Bill Montgomery
Community Development Block Grant
    Program
Division of Community Development
Kansas Department of Commerce
400 S.W. 8th Street, 5th Floor
Topeka, KS 66603–3957
(913) 296–3485

Contact:
Mr. David Ross
Kansas Enterprise Zone Program
Division of Community Development
Kansas Department of Commerce
400 S.W. 8th Street, 5th Floor
Topeka, KS 66603–3957
(913) 296–3485

Contact:
Mr. David Ross
Kansas Partnership Fund
Division of Community Development
Kansas Department of Commerce
400 S.W. 8th Street, 5th Floor
Topeka, KS 66603–3957
(913) 296–3485

Contact:
Mr. Jim Beckley, Director
Division of Trade Development
Kansas Department of Commerce
400 S.W. 8th Street, 5th Floor
Topeka, KS 66603–3957
(913) 296–4027

Programs within the **Division of Community Development** that benefit small businesses include the Community Development Block Grant (CDBG) Program, the Kansas Partnership Fund, and the Kansas Enterprise Zone Program. Within the division, three regional field offices are established to provide technical assistance to businesses, communities, and other economic development organizations.

The **Community Development Block Grant** (CDBG) program, administered by the Division of Community Development, provides financing to businesses in cities with populations under 50,000. The funds are granted by the state to the local unit of government. The local government, in turn, loans the CDBG funds to the business entity. The loan between the local government is individually structured to meet the company's needs and available cash flow.

The **Kansas Enterprise Zone Act** allows for the establishment of enterprise zones in eligible counties and cities. Special incentives are provided to qualified businesses located in designated zones and existing companies that make qualified business facility investments in the zones. The businesses receive expanded tax credits under the Job Expansion and Investment Credit Act, which include $350 for each qualified business facility employee; $350 for each $100,000 of qualified investment; $500 for each employee who qualifies the employer for the federal Targeted Jobs Tax Credit; and sales tax reimbursement for machinery, equipment, materials, and services used in construction.

The **Kansas Partnership Fund** is a program providing low interest loans to cities and counties for public infrastructure improvements that support Kansas basic enterprises. The Kansas Partnership Fund is designed to assist city and county governments in their efforts to attract new businesses and to assist in the expansion of existing businesses.

The **Trade Development Division** of the Kansas Department of Commerce is responsible for both the promotion of Kansas products and services on a domestic and international scale, and the attraction of foreign direct investment into Kansas. The staff conducts domestic and foreign trade shows, solicits and disseminates trade inquiries, hosts foreign trade and investment delegations, conducts seminars, distributes directories of Kansas products and services, and maintains and improves international relationships.

The **Kansas Export Financing Program** is a program that allows the state to enter into agreements with Kansas exporters and financial institutions, and other public and private agencies to provide guarantees, insurance, reinsurance, and coinsurance for commercial pre-export and post-export credit risks.

The **Trade Fair Assistance Program** allows a Kansas company to receive a reimbursement of up to 50 percent of their overseas trade show expenses up to a maximum of $3,500 per show and $7,000 per state fiscal year.

The **Industrial Development Division** is responsible for the recruitment of new business to Kansas and the creation of new job opportunities for Kansans. The division is made up of two sections: (1) National Marketing, and (2) Work Force Training. National Marketing works with companies based in the United States that are considering the state for new business facilities. Work Force Training coordinates training programs for new and expanding companies.

The **Kansas Industrial Training** (KIT) program provides training assistance primarily to manufacturing, distribution, and regional or national service firms in the process of adding 10 or more new jobs to a new or existing Kansas facility. KIT will pay the negotiated cost of pre-employment, on-the-job, and classroom training expenses that include instructor salaries, travel expenses, minor equipment, training aids, supplies and materials, and curriculum planning and development.

The **Kansas Industrial Retraining** (KIR) program provides retraining assistance to employees of restructuring industries who are likely to be displaced because of obsolete or inadequate job skills and knowledge. Eligible industries include those restructuring their operations through incorporation of existing technology, development and incorporation of new technology, diversification of production or the development and implementation of new production activities. KIR training occurs on a shared-cost basis with the industry.

Contact:
Mr. Steve Jack
Kansas Industrial Training Program
Division of Industrial Development
Kansas Department of Commerce
400 S.W. 8th Street, 5th Floor
Topeka, KS 66603–3957
(913) 296–3338

Contact:
Mr. Claud Shelor, Coordinator
Waste Reduction, Recycling, and Marketing
Kansas Department of Commerce
400 S.W. 8th Street, 5th Floor
Topeka, KS 66603–3957
(913) 296–3481

Contact:
Mr. Greg Gilstrap, Director
Travel and Tourism Development Division
Kansas Department of Commerce
400 S.W. 8th Street, 5th Floor
Topeka, KS 66603–3957
(913) 296–7091

Contact:
Ms. Carole Morgan, Deputy Secretary
Kansas Department of Commerce
400 S.W. 8th Street, 5th Floor
Topeka, KS 66603–3957
(913) 296–3481

The **State of Kansas Investments in Lifelong Learning** (SKILL) program allows employers to enter into agreements to establish training projects for new employees. Training project costs are financed through tax exempt, public purpose bonds issued on an "as needed" basis by the Kansas Development Finance Authority. The SKILL program is primarily targeted to large firms and projects involving several smaller firms which have forced training consortiums to address common skill requirements.

The **Kansas Office of Waste Reduction, Recycling, and Market Development** was established in 1990 by the Kansas State Legislature to actively work with industry and public entities to establish and implement waste reduction, recycling programs, and act as a statewide clearinghouse regarding solid waste management.

The **Travel and Tourism Development Division** is charged with encouraging the traveling public to visit the state by promoting the recreational, historic, and natural advantages of the state and its facilities. The division's efforts include promotion to travel writers, motor coach tour operators, individual travelers, and the international travel community. The division also develops strategies and methods of promoting Kansas as a location for film production.

The **Administration Division** provides support services for all programs within the Department of Commerce, including policy analysis, economic research, information systems, and public information.

Kansas Development Finance Authority

Contact:
Mr. W.M.F. Caton, President
Kansas Development Finance Authority
400 S.W. 8th Street, Suite 100
Topeka, KS 66603
(913) 296–6747

The **Kansas Development Finance Authority** was created in 1987 by the Kansas Legislature and is dedicated to improving access to capital financing for state agencies, political subdivisions, public and private organizations, beginning farmers, and business enterprises through the issuance of bonds.

Certified Development Companies

Contact:
Mr. Jack Alumbaugh, President
Kansas Association of Certified
  Development Companies
151 North Volutsia
Wichita, KS 67214
(316) 683–4422

Kansas is served by a network of local and regional **Certified Development Companies** (CDCs) throughout the state that provide financial packaging services to businesses using state, U.S. Small Business Administration, and private financial sources. Although these organizations were certified by the SBA to package loans for the SBA 504 program, most CDCs are familiar with available financing sources and have experience utilizing a variety and mix of financing tools. The state provides supplemental funding to these organizations in recognition of the service they provide.

Economic Development Information Network

Contact:
Mr. Duane Johnson, State Librarian
Kansas State Library
Statehouse, 3rd Floor
Topeka, KS 66612
(913) 296–3296
(800) 432–3919

The **Economic Development Information Network** provides information to entrepreneurs, established businesses, elected officials, and a variety of other users associated with economic development. The network calls on resources of academic, public, and special libraries to provide user specific information.

Small Business Development Centers

Contact:
Mr. Thomas Hull, State Director
Kansas Small Business Development Center
Wichita State University
Campus Box 148
Wichita, KS 67208
(316) 689–3193

The **Kansas Small Business Development Centers** (SBDCs) provide support to help small businesses succeed through free professional consultation services and low-cost seminars. The centers provide assistance in a variety of business management areas including accounting, business planning, market analysis, personnel, and procurement. The lead SBDC in Kansas is located in Wichita, at Wichita State University. There are 20 SBDCs located throughout the state. Appendix A of this directory contains a complete listing of all Small Business Development Centers and subcenters in Kansas.

Kansas Venture Capital, Inc.

Contacts:
Mr. Rex E. Wiggins, President
Mr. Thomas C. Blackburn, Vice President
Mr. Marshall D. Parker, Vice President
Overland Park Office
6700 Antioch Plaza, Suite 460
Overland Park, KS 66204
(913) 262–7117

Topeka Office
500 South Kansas Avenue, Suite J
Topeka, KS 66603
(913) 233–1368

Wichita Office
One Main Plaza
100 North Main, Suite 806
Wichita, KS 67202
(316) 262–1221

Kansas Venture Capital, Inc. (KVCI), is a licensed small business investment company capitalized through a combination of private investment and state funds. This venture capital company was created to focus on investments in qualified Kansas-based businesses. KVCI will consider investments in most industries, with the exceptions of retail, natural resources, real estate, or financial institutions. Investments are primarily in companies with an operating history and an established market for their product.

Kansas Technology Enterprise Corporation

Contact:
Mr. Kevin Carr, Vice President
Kansas Technology Enterprise Corp.
112 S.W. 6th Street, Suite 400
Topeka, KS 66603–3957
(913) 296–5272

The **Kansas Technology Enterprise Corporation** (KTEC) is a nonprofit public organization established in 1987 to foster innovation in existing and developing Kansas enterprises. KTEC programs have several functions:

- Financing collaborative research and technology transfer between academic institutions in order to move innovations toward commercialization;

- Financing Centers of Excellence for basic and applied research and technology transfer;

- Engaging in seed capital financing for the development and implementation of innovations for new and emerging technology-based Kansas industry;

- Providing technical information and referral services to new, emerging, or mature businesses;

- Providing funds to industrial liaison offices at academic institutions;

- Providing matching grants for the federal Small Business Innovation Research (SBIR) program; and

- Working to attract research and development facilities and programs to Kansas.

Agricultural Value-Added Processing Center

Contact:
Dr. Richard Hahn, Director
Agricultural Value-Added Processing Center
306 Umberger Hall
Kansas State University
Manhattan, KS 66505
(913) 532–7033

The **Agricultural Value-Added Processing Center** at Kansas State University promotes the growth of agricultural value-added processing (both food and nonfood) facilities in Kansas. The center identifies new technologies and assists Kansas companies in commercialization efforts. It also provides a facility and skilled technicians to conduct developmental and problem-solving work on specific industrial problems.

Advanced Technology Programs

Contact:
Dr. Farhad Azadivar, Director
Advanced Manufacturing Institute
158 Durland Hall
Kansas State University
Manhattan, KS 66506
(913) 532–6329

The goal of the **Advanced Manufacturing Institute** (AMI) is to perform research and technology transfer that will help companies expand their services, manufacture new products, and increase productivity. AMI focuses on research in the area of automated design and manufacturing systems, drawing upon multiple disciplines, with faculty members involved in computer-aided design and manufacturing, knowledge-based systems, and intelligent materials processing.

Contact:
Dr. Julian C. Holtzman, Director
CECASE
Nichols Hall
University of Kansas
Lawrence, KS 66045
(913) 864–4896

The **Center for Excellence in Computer-Aided Systems Engineering** (CECASE), located at the University of Kansas, was established to aid companies in designing and tailoring software to meet their individual needs. CECASE supports all facets of computer-aided analysis and design (CAAD); develops CAAD tools and related technologies in direct support of sponsors; and fosters the development of spin-off companies. Further support is provided by the transfer of technology in fields of engineering and computer science for product development and marketing.

134

Contact:
Dr. Harvey Dean, Director
Center for Technology Transfer
Shirk Hall
Pittsburg State University
Pittsburg, KS 66762
(316) 235–4114

The goal of the **Center for Technology Transfer** (CTT), housed on the campus of Pittsburg State University, is to assist businesses in solving technology-related problems, developing prototypes, and expanding their technical capabilities. In addition, the center attempts to improve businesses' productivity by linking them with expertise available at Pittsburg State University. CTT provides consulting services including needs analysis and recommendations, and training and education services. Areas of faculty expertise include production printing, materials handling, coatings applications, mold design, plastics testing, kinematics, application design, and machine tool processes.

Contact:
Dr. Charles Decedue, Director
Higuchi Biosciences Center
2099 Constant Avenue
Lawrence, KS 66045
(913) 864–5183

The goal of the **Higuchi Biosciences Center** (HBC), located at the University of Kansas, is to establish a world-renowned pharmaceutical research hub in Kansas. It currently is a complex of three research centers: (1) the Center for Bioanalytical Research develops methods to detect, identify, and analyze trace amounts of biologically active compounds in living systems and environmental contaminants; (2) the Center for Drug Delivery Research develops chemically driven drug delivery systems such as prodrugs and focuses on the efficient delivery of proteins, and complex carbohydrates throughout the body; and (3) the Center for Molecular Engineering and Immunology focuses on genetic engineering, including the design of catalytic antibodies.

Technology, Innovation, and Internship Program

Contacts:
Mr. Tom Moore, State Director
Kansas State Board of Education
120 East 10th
Topeka, KS 66612–1182
(913) 296–3952

Mr. Richard Russell, Technical Education
Kansas State Board of Education
120 East 10th
Topeka, KS 66612–1182
(913) 296–4921

A new program established recently under the Kansas Board of Education is the Kansas **Technology, Innovation, and Internship Program**, which allows area vocational-technical schools and community colleges to apply for: (1) start-up support for innovative technical courses/programs in "emerging technologies," manufacturing, or areas of skill shortages; and (2) staff internships to enable faculty of vocational education institutions to work in an industrial setting, or to enable industrial employees to work in an educational setting. This new program will be beneficial not only to the educational needs of the state, but also to business and industry.

Kansas Department of Human Resources

Contact:
Mr. Joe Dick
Office of the Secretary
Kansas Department of Human Resources
401 S.W. Topeka Boulevard
Topeka, KS 66603–3182
(913) 296–7474
fax: (913) 296–0179

The **Kansas Job Training Partnership Act** (JTPA) program is administered by the Kansas Department of Human Resources. JTPA forges a public/private partnership to conduct job training programs. It enlists business leaders, representatives of labor, education, rehabilitation, and nonprofit community groups to find the best way to use public funds for the greatest local benefit. The JTPA is designed to meet the specific labor skill needs of Kansas employers, while serving economically disadvantaged workers, dislocated workers, and workers facing serious barriers to employment.

A work force literacy initiative developed in conjunction with JTPA is the **Kansas Competency System: Basic Skills for Employment**, which is a basic skills curriculum management system made up of three parts: (1) criterion-referenced basic skills assessment tools that measure levels of functional literacy; (2) learning objectives—reading and math competencies identified by Kansas employers as being necessary for their entry-level jobs; and (3) curriculum resources for teachers to use to teach the functional basic skills in a competency-based manner.

Governor's Advisory Council or Task Force

Contact:
Mr. Steve Bittel, Rural Development
    Specialist
Division of Community Development
Kansas Department of Commerce
400 S.W. 8th Street, 5th Floor
Topeka, KS 66603
(913) 296–1847

The **Kansas Rural Development Council's** mission is to help identify long-term solutions to the challenges facing rural Kansas. Council members fulfill this mission by seeking to:

- Promote better interdepartmental and intergovernmental relations. Improved relationships between all rural service providers, both public and private, will translate into increased efficiency and effectiveness of existing rural efforts at all levels.

- Inventory rural economic development problems and the resources available to address revitalization.

- Develop a strategy for applying available resources to achieve long-term rural revitalization.

- Implement the strategy.

The council provides a focal point for the use of federal, state, local, and private sector resources, all targeted toward the fulfillment of the top priorities as identified within the strategy.

Kansas Inc. is a public-private partnership that oversees the formulation of economic development policy for Kansas by recommending legislative action. Kansas Inc. is governed by a 15-member board of directors consisting of representatives from state government, major Kansas industries, and organized labor.

Contact:
Mr. Charles Warren, President
Kansas Inc.
400 S.W. 8th Street, Suite 113
Topeka, KS 66603
(913) 296–1460

Legislative Committees and Subcommittees

Small business and economic development legislation are handled by the Senate Committee on Economic Development, the House Committee on Economic Development, and a Joint Committee on Economic Development.

Contacts:
Senator Dave Kerr
Chairman
Senate Committee on Economic
   Development
State Capitol
Topeka, KS 66612
(913) 296–7368

Representative Diane Gjerstad
Chairperson
House Committee on Economic
   Development
Joint Committee on Economic Development
State Capitol
Topeka, KS 66612
(913) 296–7616

Legislation

Legislation passed in 1990 that benefits small business in Kansas includes the following:

- Legislation was passed establishing a program of Statewide Waste Reduction, Recycling, and Market Development within the Department of Commerce. This bill put reporting and disposal requirements on waste tire facilities and established an 11-member Commission on Waste Reduction, Recycling, and Market Development.

- Legislation was approved that established the Community Strategic Planning Assistance Program, which authorizes the Kansas Department of Commerce to award grants to counties or multi-county units to be used in the development of comprehensive strategic plans for local economic development. The bill also provides for action grants to be awarded to implement existing and newly developed strategic plans.

- The Kansas Senate passed a bill reducing the number of years a certified Kansas venture capital company has to invest its original capitalization before losing its certification.

- The Senate also approved a bill authorizing the establishment of a patent depository library by the Kansas Technology Enterprise Corporation (KTEC). Funding for the establishment of the library will come from KTEC and/or the private sector.

- The House passed a bill authorizing the formation of limited liability companies in Kansas.

- Legislation was passed imposing strict disclosure regulations on invention promoters who develop or offer to develop or promote an invention for a consumer.

Major legislation passed during the 1991 session affecting small business is as follows:

- Legislation was passed to establish the State of Kansas Investments in Lifelong Learning (SKILL) Program, to be administered by the Department of Commerce.

- A bill was approved that regulates the telemarketing of consumer goods to provide that a verbal agreement is not binding unless the consumer signs a written contract. The bill does not apply where there has been prior negotiation between parties or where the consumer initiated the sale.

- The House enacted legislation that removes impediments to the acquisition of banks or bank holding companies in Kansas by bank holding companies located in states contiguous to Kansas or in the states of Arkansas or Iowa.

- The Senate passed a bill permitting the creation of credit card banks in the state of Kansas. Prior law prohibited the creation of any bank that did not accept demand deposits and make commercial loans.

- The House amended the Kansas Act Against Discrimination to bring it into compliance with the Americans With Disabilities Act. The Kansas law has two significant differences in that it took effect July 1, and it applies to employers with four or more employees. The act also covers not only disabled, but those perceived as disabled.

State Small Business Conferences

No recent statewide small business conferences were reported.

Kentucky

Small Business Offices, Programs, and Activities

Kentucky Cabinet for Economic Development

Contact:
Mr. Norris Christian, Director
Division of Small Business
2300 Capital Plaza Tower
Frankfort, KY 40601
(502) 564–7140

The **Kentucky Cabinet for Economic Development** is the lead agency for small and minority business activities in Kentucky.

The **Division of Small Business** was created in December 1983. The primary mission of the division is to serve as an advocate for small businesses in Kentucky by coordinating and initiating economic development activities between private and public resources. The division's services include working with the Legislative Small Business Task Force to initiate legislation beneficial to small businesses; serving as ombudsman to Kentucky small businesses to provide assistance in dealing with state agencies; providing information on specific programs of interest and benefit to small businesses; directing potential and existing entrepreneurs to resources that can provide specialized assistance; and serving as an information center for Kentucky's Small Business Development Centers.

Contact:
Mr. Floyd C. Taylor, Director
Division of Minority Business
Department of Existing Business and
  Industry
2201 Capital Plaza Tower
Frankfort, KY 40601
(502) 564–2064

The **Division of Minority Business** coordinates minority enterprise activities throughout the state's administrative structure and acts as an advocate for minority businesses. The division's programs include mobilizing educational and business-related resources and information; developing procurement opportunities; and developing the financial, technical management, and marketing resources of the minority business community. The programs also provide individual guidance to clients seeking financial assistance, marketing resources, and other specialized programs, as well as assisting minority firms in obtaining bonding and encouraging the waiver of bonds whenever feasible.

The division also administers a public-sector purchasing assistance program that serves as a clearinghouse for the business and public sectors. The staff assists minority firms by including them on state and federal bid mailing lists, disseminating information on contracting and subcontracting opportunities on state projects, assisting prime contractors of state construction projects to identify and utilize minority entrepreneurs, and maintaining the *Kentucky Minority Purchasing Guide*.

Contact:
Ms. Patti Kirk, Manager
Business Information Clearinghouse
2200 Capital Plaza Tower
Frankfort, KY 40601
(502) 564–4252
(800) 626–2250 (toll-free, in-state)

Contact:
International Trade Specialist
Office of International Marketing
Kentucky Cabinet for Economic
    Development
2400 Capital Plaza Tower
Frankfort, KY 40601
(502) 564–2170

Contact:
Ms. Debbie Kimbrough, Executive Director
Office of Business and Technology
Kentucky Cabinet for Economic
    Development
2400 Capital Plaza Tower
Frankfort, KY 40601
(502) 564–7670

The **Business Information Clearinghouse** offers new and existing businesses a centralized information source on business regulations, assists businesses in securing necessary licenses, permits, and other endorsements; provides an ombudsman service with regulatory agencies; and acts as a referral service for government financial and management assistance programs. Clients are provided with customized application and information packets that will assist them in complying with regulations.

The **Office of International Marketing** provides exporting assistance to Kentucky's small manufacturers.

The **Office of Business and Technology** serves as a link between businesses and the technological resources and research capabilities of the state universities, provides coordination of technology transfer to the private sector, and provides a state focus on technology. This office works with the federal **Small Business Innovation Research** (SBIR) program.

Financing Programs

Contact:
Mr. Jeff Noel, Executive Director
Kentucky Development Finance Authority
2400 Capital Plaza Tower
Frankfort, KY 40601
(502) 564–4554

Contact:
Ms. Theresa Middleton, President
Commonwealth Small Business
    Development Corporation
2400 Capital Plaza Tower
Frankfort, KY 40601
(502) 564–4320

The **Kentucky Development Finance Authority** makes low-interest state loans available to partially finance manufacturing and certain nonmanufacturing projects, as defined by statute. The authority, a state government agency within the Cabinet for Economic Development, provides these loans in conjunction with other programs and private financing sources.

Loans for up to 40 percent of the fixed-asset expansion costs for qualifying Kentucky small businesses are available through the **Commonwealth Small Business Development Corporation**, a nonprofit corporation operated by the Kentucky Cabinet for Economic Development. The loans assist qualified small businesses unable to obtain long-term, fixed interest rate financing.

Contact:
Ms. Theresa Middleton, Small Business
Branch Manager
Kentucky Development Finance Authority
2400 Capital Plaza Tower
Frankfort, KY 40601
(502) 564–4554

Contact:
Mr. R. Stephen Jones, Executive Director
Kentucky Rural Economic Development
Authority
2400 Capital Plaza Tower
Frankfort, KY 40601
(502) 564–7670

Contact:
Ms. Sheila White, Program Coordinator
Division of Small Business
2300 Capital Plaza Tower
Frankfort, KY 40601
(502) 564–7140

Contact:
Ms. Marilyn Eaton
Kentucky Infrastructure Authority
Finance and Administration Cabinet
Room 075, New Capitol Annex
Frankfort, KY 40601
(502) 564–2090

Contact:
Ms. Beth Hilliard
Finance and Administration Cabinet
Room 301, New Capitol Annex
Frankfort, KY 40601
(502) 564–2924

Contact:
Ms. Lisa Payne, Financial and Investment
Program Analyst
Office for Financial Management and
Economic Analysis
Kentucky Agricultural Finance Corporation
261 New Capitol Annex
Frankfort, KY 40601
(502) 564–2924

The **Kentucky Crafts Guaranteed Loan Program** provides loans up to $20,000 to qualified craftspersons.

The **Kentucky Rural Development Authority** issues revenue bonds on behalf of manufacturing companies for land acquisition, building construction and renovation, and fixtures within the facility. Security and placement of the bonds are the responsibility of the company. The company is allowed to recapture the debt service payments through a state corporate income tax credit and job development assessment fee made in lieu of the employee's state and local income taxes.

The **Kentucky Investment Capital Network** (ICN) is a computerized matching system for entrepreneurs and investors. ICN allows them to match up according to interests and financing, and is primarily used for start-up capital in medium to high-risk ventures.

The **Kentucky Infrastructure Authority** provides financing programs for local communities in need of waste water treatment, distribution, storage and source facilities, and solid waste collection, disposal, and recycling facilities. Funding is based on such concerns as environmental or economic development impact and ability to repay. Project needs are matched with the appropriate program.

The 1988 Kentucky General Assembly passed legislation establishing the **Commonwealth Venture Capital Program**, designed to encourage the establishment or expansion of small business and industry, provide additional jobs, and encourage the development of new products and technologies in the state.

The **Kentucky Agricultural Finance Corporation's** bond program is designed to help lenders aid eligible farmers in obtaining low-interest loans through the issuance of tax-exempt agricultural revenue bonds.

Kentucky Small Business Development Center

Contact:
Ms. Janet Holloway, State Director
Kentucky Small Business Development
  Center
University of Kentucky
Center for Business Development
205 Business and Economics Building
Lexington, KY 40506–0341
(606) 257–7668

The 15 **Small Business Development Centers** (SBDCs) located around the state of Kentucky offer counseling and training programs to potential entrepreneurs and existing small businesses. The centers are funded by the U.S. Small Business Administration, the Kentucky Cabinet for Economic Development, and the university system. A complete listing of these centers, including their addresses and telephone numbers, is in Appendix A of this directory.

Kentucky Procurement Assistance Program

Contact:
Mr. Jim Kurz, Branch Manager
Kentucky Procurement Assistance Program
Division of Small Business
Cabinet for Economic Development
2200 Capital Plaza Tower
Frankfort, KY 40601
(502) 564–4252

The **Kentucky Procurement Assistance Program** (KPAP) is designed to help Kentucky businesses tap the federal procurement market. Program services include market research, identifying bid opportunities, assistance with bid package preparation, copies of specifications and standard price history information, and training programs on selected topics. The program is funded by the U.S. Department of Defense, the Kentucky Cabinet for Economic Development, and the Appalachian Regional Commission.

University of Kentucky's Management Center

Contact:
Mr. Ronald L. Sanders, Director
Management Center
Business and Economics Building
University of Kentucky
Lexington, KY 40506–0034
(606) 257–8746

The **University of Kentucky's Management Center** provides business-related training and continuing education programs to Kentucky's small business community. In addition to public programs, the management center assists in identifying potential training needs and provides company-specific seminars and training programs for individual organizations. Quality education provided by faculty and continuing education instructors offers successful training programs at the management center.

Governor's Advisory Council or Task Force

The **liaison office** assists the governor in formulating small business policies.

Contact:
Mr. David Lovelace, Administrative Assistant
Office of the Governor
Room 157, New Capitol Building
Frankfort, KY 40601
(502) 564–2611

Legislative Committees and Subcommittees

The Kentucky Legislative Research Commission created the Small Business Task Force and its Subcommittee on Issue Development to study the problems of small business, including the adverse effects of government and government regulations, and develop legislation to address these problems. The Task Force has 46 members: 9 senators, and 37 representatives.

Contact:
Mr. Michael Greer, Committee Staff
    Administrator
Small Business Task Force
Legislative Research Commission
Fourth Floor, New Capitol Building
Frankfort, KY 40601
(502) 564–8100, Ext. 358

Legislation

Some examples of recent significant small business legislation in Kentucky are as follows:

- The 1988 Kentucky General Assembly approved legislation creating the Commonwealth Venture Fund. The fund is authorized to invest in the state's small businesses, providing loans of up to $500,000.

- Legislation enacted in 1988 removed a seller's responsibility to collect sales and use taxes when the seller exercises certain good faith provisions and when the purchaser presents a resale or exemption certificate, or when the purchase is from out-of-state.

- A new liability law provided that a corporate director is not personally liable for a discretionary act unless it is shown clearly that he or she was acting deliberately to injure the company.

- In 1990, the Kentucky Agricultural Finance Corporation was authorized to create a lending pool for small farmers and business enterprises related to agricultural products. This program may loan up to $50,000 to small entrepreneurs.

State Small Business Conferences

Contact:
Mr. Michael Greer, Committee Staff
    Administrator
Small Business Task Force
Legislative Research Commission
Fourth Floor, New Capitol Building
Frankfort, KY 40601
(502) 564–8100, Ext. 358

The Legislative Research Commission and Small Business Task Force, in cooperation with the University of Kentucky, held a conference on **Small Business Development in Rural Kentucky** in October 1991. The conference addressed rural development issues including school-based enterprise development, management assistance and work force development, building community leadership, telecommunications, capital formation, secondary wood industry, tourism, and value-added agriculture.

Louisiana

Small Business Offices, Programs, and Activities

Louisiana Department of Economic Development

Contact:
Secretary
Office of Commerce
Department of Economic Development
P.O. Box 94185
Baton Rouge, LA 70804
(504) 342–5388

The **Department of Economic Development** creates employment for Louisiana citizens by attracting new industry to the state, helping resident industry to expand, and aiding in the start-up of new business enterprises. The department offers a wide array of programs and incentives, including marketing, advertising promotions, financial and managerial assistance, and various tax incentives. The department also offers publications, including the *Directory of Louisiana Manufacturers*, a source book on Louisiana manufacturers that includes information on products and companies by geographic location, Standard Industrial Classification code, and company name.

The Department of Economic Development underwent major reorganization during the 1991 regular session of the Louisiana Legislature. Among the major offices of the restructured department are the Office of the Secretary; the Office of Management and Finance; the Office of Commerce; the Office of Business Development Services; the Office of Policy and Research; the Office of Technology, Innovation, and Modernization; and the Louisiana Development Finance Corporation.

The **Office of the Secretary** provides overall direction to all of the department's activities and monitors the performance of the department's **Legal Division**. It also provides state government procurement assistance for minority and women's business development.

The **Office of Management and Finance** provides the balance of the support services to the department, including personnel, purchasing, and fiscal services.

The **Office of Commerce** markets Louisiana as a business location to U.S. and international companies through direct contacts and other marketing techniques.

The **Finance Division** administers state economic development incentives and provides administrative support services to the Board of Commerce and Industry, which is responsible for approving applications for most state development incentives. The division also conducts on-site inspections of facilities that receive benefits under incentive programs to ensure that regulations are followed. The tax abatement programs administered by the division include the 10-year industrial tax exemption enterprise zones, the corporate headquarters tax equalization program, the industrial tax equalization program, the jobs tax credit program, warehousing and distribution facilities tax equalization program, and the Louisiana Capital Companies tax credit.

The **National Market and International Marketing Division** promote Louisiana's advantages as a business and industrial location to executives throughout the United States and the world. Staff members prepare sales presentations, conduct site inspection tours, and organize joint marketing ventures with local development agencies and other economic development experts from private industry.

The **International Trade Division** assists firms in opening new overseas markets for Louisiana products, services, and equipment. It also seeks to attract foreign business and other commercial enterprises to Louisiana. The office coordinates its export-import trade efforts with Louisiana chambers of commerce, the World Trade Center, and the U.S. Department of Commerce's International Trade Administration.

To increase exports, expand joint ventures, and encourage foreign investments, the office has established field representatives in Asia and has developed business contacts in Europe and Africa. The office has formed business information referral networks with several financial institutions and private industry trade groups in Japan, Korea, and Taiwan. Services provided by the Office of International Trade, Finance and Development, include export counseling, matching exporters to foreign markets, sponsoring foreign trade shows and exhibits, promoting foreign investment, assisting with export financing, identifying international trade opportunities, organizing export seminars, and providing information on export programs.

Contact:
Ms. Janis Burbank, Assistant Secretary
Office of Business Development Services
Department of Economic Development
P.O. Box 94185
Baton Rouge, LA 70804–9185
(504) 342–3000

The **Office of Business Development, Services Division,** provides economic development services to communities, resident industries, and small businesses operating within the state. The division works with community and civic leaders, elected officials, and representatives of private and economic development groups to facilitate the start-up of new businesses and the expansion of existing ones.

The office also houses the **Regional Economic Development Alliance** (REDA) program. This program allows the department to strengthen and expand its partnerships with sub-state economic development agencies for the purpose of delivering new and enhanced initiatives to promote the retention and growth of Louisiana firms, promote small business development, and encourage multi-parish and public-private cooperation in job creation and business development.

Contact:
Director
Office of Policy and Research
Department of Economic Development
P.O. Box 94185
Baton Rouge, LA 70804–9185
(504) 342–5385

The new **Office of Policy and Research** will expand and enhance the ability of the Department of Economic Development to maintain and analyze economic development data and conduct high-quality analyses of policies and programs pertaining to jobs and the Louisiana economy.

Contact:
Mr. Kevin Reilly, Secretary
Department of Economic Development
Office of Technology, Innovation, and
    Modernization
P.O. Box 94185
Baton Rouge, LA 70804–9185
(504) 342–5388

The new **Office of Technology, Innovation, and Modernization** will allow the Department of Economic Development to develop a state strategy to promote economic growth, job creation, and industrial diversification through the start-up of new growth-oriented and technology-based enterprises, as well as strengthen existing manufacturing operations through appropriate applications of new technologies.

The reorganization of this office also includes the establishment of a one-stop shop for information and referrals on doing business in Louisiana, and a regulatory assistance section. This section will promote a cooperative state strategy focused on achieving both economic growth and environmental quality objectives—with emphasis on clear policy articulation, stabilization of the regulatory climate, and assistance with compliance.

Louisiana Development Finance Corporation

Contact:
Mr. Tracy J. Mandart, Jr., Executive Director
Louisiana Development Finance Corporation
P.O. Box 94185
Baton Rouge, LA 70804–9185
(504) 342–5675

The old Louisiana Economic Development Corporation became the **Louisiana Development Finance Corporation** (LDFC)—a revolving public-private fund—on January 1, 1992. The Louisiana Legislature authorized several new financing programs including: Capital Access, Seed Capital Incentive Micro Enterprise, and Business and Industrial Development Corporations. These programs are in addition to the current Small Business Innovation Research (SBIR) Matching Grant Program, Venture Capital Coinvestment Program, Venture Capital Match Program, Minority Venture Capital Match Program, Minority and Women's Business Development Program, and Small Business Equity Program.

The **Small Business Innovation Research** (SBIR) program supports innovative private sector research and development activities that are intended to generate commercial products, processes, or services. Through its SBIR program, the state matches Phase I grants or contracts awarded by the federal government. Eligibility is based upon receipt of a federal SBIR Phase I Award and Louisiana residency (or agreement by an out-of-state firm to relocate headquarters, research, and development operations to Louisiana).

Small Business Development Centers

Contact:
Dr. John P. Baker, State Director
Louisiana Small Business Development Center
Northeast Louisiana University
College of Business Administration, Room 2057
Monroe, LA 71209–6435
(318) 342–5506

The **Louisiana Small Business Development Center** (LSBDC) is a consortium of state universities working with the Louisiana Department of Economic Development. The LSBDC provides management and technical assistance to existing and potential Louisiana businesses through local, state, and federal programs; private sector assets; and resources available at member organizations.

The lead Small Business Development Center is in Monroe at Northeast Louisiana University. Subcenters are located in Alexandria, Baton Rouge, Hammond, Lafayette, Lake Charles, Natchitoches, New Orleans, Ruston, Shreveport, and Thibodaux. A complete listing of Small Business Development Centers and subcenters is in Appendix A of this directory.

Business and Technology Center, Entrepreneurship Institute

Louisiana State University coordinates the state's **Business and Technology Center** and the **Entrepreneurship Institute**.

Contacts:

Dr. Robert T. Justis, Director
Business and Technology Center
South Stadium Drive
Louisiana State University
Baton Rouge, LA 70803–6100
(504) 334–5555

Dr. Robert T. Justis, Director
Entrepreneurship Institute
3139 CEBA
College of Business Administration
Louisiana State University
Baton Rouge, LA 70803–6333
(504) 388–6645

Governor's Advisory Council or Task Force

Contacts:

Ms. Janis Burbank, Assistant Secretary
Louisiana Department of Economic
    Development
P.O. Box 94185
Baton Rouge, LA 70804
(504) 342–2907

Dr. John Baker, State Director
Louisiana Small Business Development
    Center
ADM. 2–57
Northeast Louisiana University
Monroe, LA 71209
(318) 342–5506

The development of a comprehensive and unified small business assistance program in Louisiana is provided by the **Louisiana Small Business Development Center Consortium**. This consortium consists of the 12 universities that participate in the Louisiana Small Business Development Center (LSBDC), in addition to the Louisiana Economic Development Department and the LSBDC Advisory Council. The LSBDC Advisory Council consists of seven small business owners from throughout Louisiana. This consortium reviews problems and challenges facing small businesses and advises the Secretary of Economic Development and the governor on small business issues.

Legislative Committees and Subcommittees

The House and Senate Commerce Committees address small business issues and economic development.

Contacts:

Senator J.E. Jumonville, Jr.
Chairman
Senate Commerce Committee
State Capitol
Baton Rouge, LA 70804
(504) 342–2040

Representative Dale Sittig
Chairman
House Commerce Committee
P.O. Box 44186, Capitol Station
Baton Rouge, LA 70804
(504) 342–6151

Legislation

Major legislation passed in the 1991 regular session of the Louisiana Legislature included the following:

- Act 13 permits employers who are members of professional associations or engaged in similar businesses to self-insure their common workers' liabilities.

- Act 359 provided tax credits for the purchase of equipment used to process post-consumer waste and manufacture goods containing recycled materials.

- Act 396 provided for the creation of a rural development fund and program.

- Act 506 enacted the Louisiana Business and Industrial Development Corporation Act (BIDCO).

- Act 845 changed the definition within the Louisiana Small Business Procurement Act of "dominant in its field of operation."

- Act 1052 provided for a phased-in credit against income tax and corporate franchise taxes for the purchase of qualifying recycling equipment.

The Louisiana legislature also passed an act requiring that a minimum of 10 percent of all goods and services purchased in the construction of Louisiana's roads and highways be set aside for socially or economically disadvantaged individuals or women-owned business.

State Small Business Conferences

Several U.S. representatives from Louisiana have recently sponsored procurement meetings for small business owners.

Maine

Small Business Offices, Programs, and Activities

Office of Business Development

Contact:
Ms. Joan Anderson Cook, Acting Deputy
    Commissioner
Office of Business Development
Department of Economic and Community
    Development
State House Station #59
Augusta, ME 04333
(207) 289–3153

Contact:
Ms. Dora M. Dostie, Business Answers
    Program
Office of Business Development
Department of Economic and Community
    Development
State House Station #59
Augusta, ME 04333–0949
(207) 289–3153
(800) 872–3838 (toll-free, in-state)
(800) 541–5872 (toll-free, out-of-state)

The **Office of Business Development** encourages investment in new Maine businesses and provides technical assistance to businesses in labor training, financing, site selection, and state licenses and permits. It also assists firms with facility and work force expansions. The office publishes and distributes data on business development in Maine.

The **Maine Products Marketing Program** promotes national and international awareness of Maine's consumer products and enhances the ability of Maine value-added manufacturers to reach new markets.

Business Answers is a toll-free telephone referral service for individuals with questions about doing business in Maine. A publication, *Answers: A Guide to Doing Business in Maine*, and a business start-up kit are available.

Finance Authority of Maine

Contacts:

Mr. David Markovchick, Director of Business
  Development
Finance Authority of Maine
83 Western Avenue
P.O. Box 949
Augusta, ME 04332–0949
(207) 623–3263

Mr. Charles Spies, Director of Natural
  Resources
Finance Authority of Maine
83 Western Avenue
P.O. Box 949
Augusta, ME 04332–0949
(207) 623–3263

Contact:

Mr. Carl Flora, Deputy Commissioner
Department of Agriculture, Food and Rural
  Resources
State House Station #28
Augusta, ME 04333
(207) 623–3263

Contacts:

Mr. Charles Spies, Director of Natural
  Resources
Finance Authority of Maine
83 Western Avenue
P.O. Box 949
Augusta, ME 04332–0949
(207) 623–3263

Mr. Samuel Shapiro
State House of Maine
State House Station #39
Augusta, ME 04333
(207) 289–2771

The **Finance Authority of Maine** (FAME) assists business development and job creation by administering a variety of direct loan and loan guarantee programs for small and larger businesses, as well as state tax credits for investments in eligible seed capital stage companies. FAME programs include commercial loan insurance, tax-exempt and taxable bonds for commercial activities, and targeted lending programs such as loans for underground oil tank removal, waste reduction and recycling, low income borrowers, and occupational safety improvements. Loan insurance can be provided for loans for fixed assets, working capital, asset based lines of credit, and export financing.

The **Potato Marketing Improvement Fund** provides direct loans to potato growers and packers to improve the quality and marketing of Maine potatoes. Funds can be used for new storage facilities or retrofits, and grants are available for water systems to increase the washing of tablestock potatoes. The Finance Authority of Maine assists the Department of Agriculture, Food and Rural Resources division, in the administration of the program.

The purpose of the **Linked Investment Program** is to reduce the interest cost on eligible borrowings by 2 percent per year for up to two years. The program can reduce the interest rate on up to $8 million in loans each year—half for farm loans and half for commercial enterprises. For farmers, eligible uses include operating funds for purchases of seed, chemicals, fertilizer, feed, veterinary services, labor, and other production inputs. For other commercial enterprises, the borrower must be a manufacturer or must sell at least 70 percent of products or services out of the state of Maine. The state treasurer will deposit an amount equal to the loan with the lending bank and will accept a deposit rate 2 percent below what the deposit would otherwise have earned. The lender in turn reduces the rate on the loan by 2 percent. The Finance Authority of Maine assists the treasurer in the administration of the program.

Technical Assistance for International Business

Contact:
Mr. Daniel W. Marra, President
Maine World Trade Association
77 Sewall Street
Augusta, ME 04330
(207) 622–0234

The **Maine World Trade Association** is a private, nonprofit organization offering extensive export services to Maine businesses, including one-to-one counseling, a mentoring program, training courses, international telex services, translation services, a referral program of Maine-based services, hosting of international visitors, marketing assistance, a "Network" international trade lead service, trade show participation assistance, numerous publications, international venture and licensing assistance, export statistical information, and an international research library.

Small Business Development Centers

Contact:
Ms. Diane Branscomb, Acting State Director
Maine Small Business Development Center
University of Southern Maine
15 Surrenden Street
Portland, ME 04101
(207) 780–4420

Small Business Development Centers (SBDCs) provide practical management and technical assistance to present and prospective small business owners. They offer courses, seminars, and one-on-one counseling as well as access to information on marketing, managing, and financing a small business. SBDCs are partially funded by the U.S. Small Business Administration, and are usually affiliated with a state college or university. In Maine, a lead SBDC is located in Portland, at the University of Southern Maine. There are seven subcenters, located in Auburn, Bangor, Caribou, Machias, Sanford, Wicasset, and Winslow. A complete listing of all Small Business Centers and subcenters is in Appendix A of this directory.

Governor's Advisory Council or Task Force

There is no specific council to advise the governor on small business issues.

Legislative Committees and Subcommittees

The Maine Legislature has no committee or subcommittee focusing on small business. Many small business issues are considered by the Joint Committee on State Government. The legislature meets January through June in odd-numbered years and January through mid April in even-numbered years.

Contacts:
Senator Georgette Berube
Representative Ruth Joseph
Joint Committee on State and Local
  Government
State House, Room 121B
Augusta, ME 04333
(207) 289–1330

The Joint Standing Committee on Housing and Economic Development has primary jurisdiction over legislation dealing with small business promotion and support. Related issues—including labor, taxation, and business regulation—are handled by other legislative committees. The legislature is in session from January until June in odd-numbered years and from January until April in even-numbered years.

Contacts:
Senator Zachary Matthews, Co-Chairperson
Representative Rita Melandy,
  Co-Chairperson
Joint Standing Committee on Housing and
  Economic Development
State House Station #115
Augusta, ME 04333
(207) 289–3123

Legislation

The 115th Maine Legislature enacted several measures that affect small business.

- P.L. 826 created a permitting center within the Department of Economic and Community Development (DECD). The center will make life easier for small businesses, who often need as many as 17 permits to run a single business entity. The DECD will build a data base of applications and time tables from all state departments and agencies. When an entrepreneur calls the DECD, they will be supplied with a list of required permits, applications, and forms.

- P.L. 811 amends the underground oil storage facilities and groundwater protection laws and the uncontrolled hazardous substance sites laws. The new law begins the process of properly assessing liability for environmental cleanup by looking to responsible parties, and not to financial institutions who have not actively participated in the management of a particular property.

- P.L. 861 adopts community rating for small group health care policies. The law includes lower cost policies provisions for small businesses. Community rating contrasts with experience rating where rates are based on the actual experience of a group with respect to the cost of paying claims.

- P.L. 1991 Ch. 123, an act concerning nighttime business operation, prohibits a convenience store from operating 24 hours a day unless the store has a drop safe, carries no more than $50 cash available and accessible to employees, and posts a sign stating that between 9 p.m. and 5 a.m. the cash register contains $50 or less.

- P.L. 1991 Ch. 237 authorizes recovery of certain collection costs. With respect to consumer credit transactions, this bill restricts changes as a result of default by a consumer but permits reasonable charges incurred in realizing on a security interest in personal property.

- P.L. 1991 Ch. 261 amends the Maine Consumer Credit Code to prohibit the provider of a travel service from imposing a surcharge on or reducing the commission of a travel agent whose customer uses a credit card to purchase travel services.

- L.D. 17699, creates a tax increment financing plan similar to those used by municipalities in Maine to stimulate private investment. The law creates the Maine Street Investment Program to provide loans to businesses for investments in downtown areas and business districts.

State Small Business Conferences

Contact:
Mr. Derek Langhauser
Office of the Governor
State House Station #1
Augusta, ME 04333
(207) 289–3531

The **Governor's Annual Economic Development Conference** was held on March 7, 1990.

Maryland

Small Business Offices, Programs, and Activities

Department of Economic and Employment Development

Contact:
Mr. James Peiffer, Assistant Secretary
Division of Business Development
Maryland Department of Economic and
 Employment Development
Redwood Towers, 10th Floor
217 East Redwood Street
Baltimore, MD 21202
(410) 333–6985

Contact:
Mr. Len Elenowitz
Department of Economic and Employment
 Development
Division of Business Resources
Office of Technology Development
217 East Redwood Street
Baltimore, MD 21202
(410) 333–6975

Established in 1987, the **Department of Economic and Employment Development** brings into a single administrative structure the activities of the former Department of Economic and Community Development and promotes Maryland in six major areas: business development, retention, and expansion; marketing and tourism development; international trade; employment security and training services; financing for businesses; and technology development.

The Department of Economic and Employment Development also provides technical assistance and information on the **Small Business Innovation Research** (SBIR) program to interested Maryland businesses. Although Maryland does not offer a financial program similar to the federal SBIR or add on funds to SBIR awardees, the state operates a Challenge Grant Program, which provides early stage financing to commercialize innovative technology. Funds are available on a competitive basis, but are not available for basic research and development. The program is currently being revised.

Small Business Assistance Center

Contact:
Mr. Alan Kutz, Director
Office of Business Assistance
Department of Economic and Employment
 Development
Redwood Towers, 10th Floor
217 East Redwood Street
Baltimore, MD 21202
(410) 333–6975

The **Maryland Business Assistance Center** was established in 1984 by the Department of Economic and Employment Development to assist businesses in dealing with state agencies, participating in government procurement, and in promoting economic growth.

158

Procurement Program

Contact:
Mr. Len Elenowitz, Senior Business
   Assistance Representative
Department of Economic and Employment
   Development
Redwood Towers, 10th Floor
217 East Redwood Street
Baltimore, MD 21202
(410) 333–6975

Maryland's **Procurement Program** provides a 5-percent preferential advantage to small businesses for all state agency commodity purchases. The state's minority business program has a 10-percent goal for certified minority-owned business. Criteria include gender and handicaps, as well as racial and ethnic factors. Maryland also has established a Minority Business Enterprise Certification Program.

Loans and Capital Formation

Contact:
Mr. Stanley W. Tucker, Executive Director
Maryland Small Business Financing
   Authority
Redwood Towers, 22nd Floor
217 East Redwood Street
Baltimore, MD 21202
(410) 333–4270

Maryland's **Small Business Development Financing Authority**, established in 1978, provides loans to small and minority businesses. The authority provides short-term financing for government contracts and long-term guarantees on financing for equipment and working capital. It also operates a surety bond guarantee program for small businesses and an equity participation investment program for potential minority franchises.

Office of Minority Affairs

Contact:
Mr. Mitchell Smith, Director
Office of Minority Affairs
301 West Preston Street
Room 1008E
Baltimore, MD 21201
(410) 225–1843

The **Office of Minority Affairs**, established in the governor's office, promotes the growth of minority firms by providing technical and management assistance. It advises the governor on minority unemployment problems and makes recommendations for employment and procurement opportunities.

Small Business Development Centers

Contact:
Mr. Michael Long, State Director
Small Business Development Center
217 East Redwood Street, 10th Floor
Baltimore, MD 21202
(410) 333–6996
(800) USE–SBDC
(800) 873–7232 (toll-free, in-state)

Small Business Development Centers (SBDCs) provide practical management and technical assistance to present and prospective small business owners. They offer courses, seminars, and one-on-one counseling, as well as access to information on marketing, managing, and financing a small business. SBDCs are partially funded by the U.S. Small Business Administration, and are usually affiliated with a state college or university. A complete listing of all the Small Business Development Centers and sub-centers in Maryland, including addresses and telephone numbers, is in Appendix A of this directory.

Governor's Advisory Council or Task Force

Maryland has no formal small business advisory council. The governor has established regional business advisory task forces.

Legislative Committees and Subcommittees

Neither Maryland chamber has a small business committee. Small business matters and legislation are handled by the following standing committees:

Contacts:

Senator Clarence W. Blount
Chairman
Senate Economic and Environmental Affairs
    Committee
Senate Office Building, Room S201
Annapolis, MD 21401
(301) 841–3697

Representative Casper R. Taylor, Jr.
Chairman
House Economic Matters Committee
House Office Building, Room 151
Annapolis, MD 21401
(301) 841–3519

Legislation

The Basic Benefits Act (H.B. 1120) was passed into statute law in April 1991. The law, which became effective in July 1991, gives small businesses the opportunity to buy health insurance policies at substantial savings. Aimed exclusively at firms with 25 or fewer employees, the legislation waives expensive mandates that are required in commercial policies in the state.

State Small Business Conferences

Contact:
Mr. Miles Cole, Director of Business Affairs
Maryland State Chamber of Commerce
275 West Street, Suite 400
Annapolis, MD 21401–3480
(301) 269–0642

As a direct follow-up to the 1986 White House Conference on Small Business, the White House Planning Group established a Small Business Conference Program at which small businesses identify issues of immediate and direct concern, and elect advocates with the responsibility of pursuing those issues with the Maryland General Assembly. Conferences have been held annually since 1985. Participating organizations include the Maryland Department of Economic and Employment Development; the Baltimore County Chamber of Commerce, the SBA, and a representative from the elected small business advocates. A broad array of private companies provide volunteer logistical support, as well as contributions.

Massachusetts

Small Business Offices, Programs, and Activities

Small Business Purchasing Program

Contact:
Ms. Maureen E. Fritz, Coordinator
Small Business Purchasing Program
Massachusetts Office of Business
    Development
100 Cambridge Street, 13th Floor
Boston, MA 02202
(617) 727–3206

The office of the **Small Business Purchasing Program** compiles and maintains a bidder's list of small businesses, makes recommendations for simplification of procurement specifications and terms, and encourages certified firms to participate in other state economic development programs. To be eligible to partici- pate in this program, companies must be independently owned and operated, have Massachusetts as their principal place of business, and meet certain industry size standards.

State Office of Minority and Women Business Assistance

Contact:
Ms. Sunny Brent-Harding, Executive
    Director
State Office of Minority and Women
    Business Assistance
100 Cambridge Street, Room 1305
Boston, MA 02202
(617) 727–8692

The **State Office of Minority and Women Business Assistance** helps minority- and women-owned business enter- prises in obtaining public contracts for goods and services. The office provides information, referral, education, training, and advo- cacy services. It reviews companies to determine whether or not they are certifiable as minority- or women-owned businesses and publishes a directory of certified firms. The directory is circulated widely to purchasing agents, awarding authorities, and cities and towns, and is used by buyers to identify eligible companies. A firm may apply for certification if it is actively in business, is not a broker, middleman, or manufacturer's representative, and is at least 51-percent owned and controlled by minorities or women.

Office of International Trade and Investment

Contact:
Ms. Abbe Goodman, Executive Director
Office of International Trade and Investment
100 Cambridge Street, Room 902
Boston, MA 02202
(617) 367–1830

The **Office of International Trade and Investment**, located in the Executive Office of Economic Affairs, oversees the state's international trade activities, primarily through the development of a Massachusetts export promotion program and continuation of Massachusetts reverse investment efforts. The office provides corporate counseling and maintains an organized trade commission.

Trade Development Unit, Massachusetts Port Authority

Contact:
Mr. Andrew W. Bendheim, Director
Trade Development Unit
Massachusetts Port Authority
World Trade Center, Suite 321
Boston, MA 02210
(617) 439–5560

The **Massachusetts Port Authority** (Massport), in conjunction with the Smaller Business Association of New England, operates the Small Business Export Program (SBEP) for small business manufacturers with assistance in market analysis, training, and advice on export practices and financing for participation in foreign trade missions.

By expanding the scope of the program, Massport's **Trade Development Unit** introduces small and medium-sized companies to new markets. Targeted for special attention are developing world markets in Europe, the Far East, and Latin America. The program provides export counseling and market research, and identifies foreign contacts for exporting firms in the areas of information technology, health care and biomedical supplies and equipment, electronic components, and electronic industrial production equipment. The program organizes and conducts trade events and prepares technical assistance materials for the targeted industries and markets.

Community Development Finance Corporation

Contact:
Mr. Milton Benjamin, President
Communities and Development Finance
  Corporation
10 Post Office Square, Suite 1090
Boston, MA 02109
(617) 482–9141

The **Community Development Finance Corporation** is a public corporation that invests in business enterprises sponsored by community development corporations (CDCs) in economically depressed areas of Massachusetts. New and existing businesses are selected through review of business plans and community impact evaluations. To qualify, businesses should show that they will increase full-time employment in the CDC target area; that they are unable to meet their capital needs from traditional sources; and that they have a reasonable expectation of success. Eligible activities for these businesses include commercial, industrial, or real estate ventures or other economic development activity undertaken in the target area.

Massachusetts Industrial Finance Authority

Contact:
Mr. Joseph D. Blair, Executive Director
Massachusetts Industrial Finance Authority
75 Federal Street
Boston, MA 02110
(617) 451–2477

The **Massachusetts Industrial Finance Authority** (MIFA) is a state agency that promotes the expansion of small businesses in Massachusetts through the use of investment incentives. The MIFA issues tax-exempt industrial revenue bonds for industrial development projects involving land acquisition; plant construction, expansion, or renovation; or equipment purchase. The MIFA also may approve the industrial development financing authorities. Industrial revenue bonds may finance up to a $10 million capital expenditure limit. Pollution projects and qualified solid waste disposal facilities are exempt from the $10 million ceiling.

Massachusetts Technology Development Corporation

Contact:
Mr. John F. Hodgman, President
Massachusetts Technology Development
  Corporation
131 State Street, Suite 215
Boston, MA 02109
(617) 723–4920

The **Massachusetts Technology Development Corporation** (MTDC) is an independent, publicly funded venture capital organization that makes investments in new and expanding technology-based companies in Massachusetts. The MTDC finances companies that have the capacity to expand and generate new jobs, but have been unable to obtain conventional financing for expansion.

The corporation works with private sector investors such as venture capital firms, banks, and SBICs, which often invest two to four times the amount of capital MTDC provides. Initial investments typically total $100,000 to $250,000, and are made as debt, equity, or a combination of these. The debt portion of the financing is usually a long-term, unsecured, subordinated note at a favorable interest rate with a partial moratorium on principle repayment. Typical equity participation is through the purchase of common or preferred stock.

While the investment program has been MTDC's principle activity, its management assistance program also aids emerging companies by referring them to appropriate alternative sources of funding. A written business plan is the only required form of application.

Massachusetts Business Development Corporation

Contact:
Mr. Kenneth J. Smith, President
Massachusetts Business Development
  Corporation
One Liberty Square
Boston, MA 02109
(617) 350–8877

The **Massachusetts Business Development Corporation** (MBDC) is a private corporation under state charter that provides loans to private for-profit and nonprofit firms. Loans may be used for the purchase or construction of fixed business assets (land, plant, or equipment) and for working capital. Loan terms are similar to those for conventional loans, although MBDC allows for floating interest rates and longer terms (as long as 20 to 25 years) and can provide up to 100 percent of financing, depending on need.

Small Business Development Centers

Contact:
Mr. John Ciccarelli, State Director
Massachusetts Small Business Development
    Centers
University of Massachusetts
School of Management, Room 205
Amherst, MA 01003
(413) 545–6301

The objective of the **Massachusetts Small Business Development Centers** (MSBDCs) is to provide a high quality program of one-to-one management and technical assistance counseling and educational programs by effectively combining the resources of government, education, and the private sector. With a lead center at Amherst and a network of regional and specialty centers, the MSBDC provides free counseling to prospective and existing small businesses on topics such as business plan development, finance, cash flow management, human resources issues, marketing, and international trade. Training programs are offered for a nominal fee on a wide variety of management issues. Subcenters are located in Boston, Chestnut Hill, Fall River, Salem, Springfield, and Worcester. A complete listing of all Small Business Development Centers and subcenters is in Appendix A of this directory.

Contact:
Mr. Paul Van de Geer, Program Manager
Center for Manufacturing Assistance
Massachusetts Small Business Development
    Center
University of Massachusetts
School of Management, Room 201A
Amherst, MA 01003
(413) 545–3925

The MSBDC's **Manufacturers Assistance Program** provides small manufacturers with technical assistance in production, quality control, new technology, plant layout, and cost control. The program also conducts training programs for manufacturers.

Governor's Advisory Council or Task Force

There is no specific council that advises the governor on small business issues in Massachusetts.

Legislative Committees and Subcommittees

Small business issues in Massachusetts are addressed by the Joint Committee on Commerce and Labor.

Contacts:

Representative Suzanne Bump
Chairman
Joint Committee on Commerce and Labor
State House, Room 43
Boston, MA 02133
(617) 722–2030

Senator Lois G. Pines
Senate Chairman
Joint Committee on Commerce and Labor
State House, Room 518
Boston, MA 02133
(617) 722–1639

Legislation

The recently enacted Research and Development Tax Credit Law of 1991 is a corporate tax credit for incremental research and development expenditures incurred on or after January 1, 1991. Under the provisions, the research credit is:

- 10 percent of the excess of the qualified research expenses for the income year over the base amount, and

- 15 percent of the basic research payments.

State Small Business Conferences

No recent statewide small business conferences have been reported.

Michigan

Small Business Offices, Programs, and Activities

Michigan Department of Commerce

Contact:
Mr. Arthur Ellis, Director
Michigan Department of Commerce
P.O. Box 30004
Lansing, MI 48909
(517) 373–7230

The **Michigan Department of Commerce** provides a variety of services to small firms through its Business Ombudsman Office, Technical Business Services Bureau, and various other programs.

Michigan Business Ombudsman

Contact:
Ms. Judith Miller, Director
Business Ombudsman Office
Michigan Department of Commerce
P.O. Box 30107
Lansing, MI 48909
(517) 373–6241
(800) 232–2727 (toll-free, in-state)

The **Michigan Business Ombudsman** negotiates and advocates various regulatory issues for small business throughout state government, and initiates corrective actions on policy matters. The office also researches and lobbies on business-related issues.

Michigan Development Services Bureau

Contact:
Mr. William Lontz, Director
Michigan Development Services Bureau
Michigan Department of Commerce
P.O. Box 30004
Lansing, MI 48909
(517) 373–0601

The **Michigan Development Services Bureau** provides full location, expansion, and retention services to manufacturing and manufacturing-related service firms. The bureau also provides economic development assistance to local communities.

Location Services

Contact:
Mr. John B. Czarnecki, Director
Development Services Division
Michigan Department of Commerce
P.O. Box 30004
Lansing, MI 48909
(517) 373–9135

The **Development Services Division** provides firms with information on available industrial properties, including land and vacant buildings. Site recommendations are based on criteria submitted by firms.

Michigan Small Business Development Center

Contact:
Dr. Norman J. Schlafmann, State Director
Michigan Small Business Development
  Center
Wayne State University
2727 Second Avenue
Detroit, MI 48201
(313) 577–4848

The **Michigan Small Business Development Center** (MI–SBDC) is a network of counseling and service centers that provides practical management and technical assistance to small business owners and prospective entrepreneurs. Counseling is available at no charge and a variety of educational programs are offered at a nominal fee. Specialty centers provide assistance to businesses interested in exporting, acquiring markets for forestry products, or obtaining funds for research and development. Focused programs for women, minorities, veterans, and the handicapped are offered throughout the state network. The program is a partnership between the U.S. Small Business Administration and Wayne State University. Several of the local SBDC centers are jointly funded by the Michigan Department of Commerce and the Small Business Development Center Program. Together, the Department of Commerce and the MI–SBDC sponsor 50 centers, which are listed with addresses and telephone numbers in Appendix A of this directory.

Technology Services Office

Contact:
Ms. Sharon Woollard, Manager
Technology Services Office
Technical Business Services
Michigan Department of Commerce
P.O. Box 30004
Lansing, MI 48909
(517) 335–2139

The **Technology Services Office** supports several technical programs for small business: technological assistance/problem solving; research and development (R&D) funding and technical assistance; new product development/commercialization funding; and technical assistance and new technologies/products available for licensing. Technical Services works in partnership with programs such as state and federal R&D grants, including the State Research Fund and the federal Small Business Innovation Research (SBIR) grants program; and the Michigan Energy and Resource Research Association (MERRA). MERRA Technology Services is the policy and program development office for state government regarding the SBIR program and other small business R&D/technology transfer programs. It also serves as a program manager for the State Research Fund.

Through a network of five technology transfer centers, the **Technology Transfer Network** (TTN) gives Michigan firms access to research and development resources available in Michigan's state-supported research universities and colleges. The TTN links the knowledge, expertise, and facilities of Michigan research universities with state and local business assistance programs. Each center's staff assesses the needs of firms and the technical assistance required, and provides referrals to appropriate resources. The technology transfer centers are located at:

University of Michigan   (313) 763–900
Wayne State University   (313) 577–2788
Michigan Technological University   (906) 487–2470
Michigan State University   (517) 355–1660
Western Michigan University   (616) 387–2714

MERRA Small Business Development Center

Contact:
Mr. Mark Clevey, Vice President
Small Business R&D
MERRA SBDC
2200 Commonwealth Boulevard, Suite 230
Ann Arbor, MI 48105
(313) 930–0033

The **Michigan Energy and Resource Research Association Small Business Development Center** (MERRA–SBDC) is operated by MERRA, a statewide organization dedicated to stimulating economic development in Michigan through increased research and development (R&D) and commercialization activities. The center provides executive business counseling services to Michigan's small technology-based R&D firms, sponsors conferences and workshops, and serves as an official secondary distribution and matching center in Michigan for the federal **Small Business Innovation Research** (SBIR) program. The MERRA–SBDC is funded by the U.S. Small Business Administration, the Michigan Strategic Fund, the Michigan Department of Commerce, and MERRA. The center coordinates the Michigan SBIR program called the **State Research Fund**. More than 125 of Michigan's small technology-based firms have been awarded roughly $45 million through the federal SBIR and State Research Fund in Michigan.

Metropolitan Center for High Technology

Contact:
Mr. Charles Henderson, President
Metropolitan Center for High Technology
2727 Second Avenue
Detroit, MI 48201
(313) 963–0616

The **Metropolitan Center for High Technology** operates a small business incubator for companies that produce technological products and services. The center also develops technology-based products for the market, especially in the biomedical field. The center leases space to research institutes involved in information technology, chemical toxicology, and molecular biology.

Industrial Development Division

Contact:
Mr. J. Downs Herold, Director of Liaison
Industrial Development Division
University of Michigan
2200 Bonisteel Boulevard, Room 2117
Ann Arbor, MI 48109–2099
(313) 764–5260

The **Innovation Center** uses the resources of the University of Michigan to help Michigan firms develop and use new products. Specific programs assist manufacturers in managing technology and understanding the use of licensing as a means of obtaining new products and processes. The program assists the **Inventor's Council of Michigan** by stimulating and evaluating new product ideas from the state's independent product developers.

Michigan International Office

Contact:
Mr. Field Reichardt, Director
Michigan International Office
Michigan Department of Commerce
P.O. Box 30225
Lansing, MI 48909
(517) 373–6390

The **Michigan International Office** (MIO) is divided into four divisions: (1) Export; (2) Direct Investment; (3) Michigan Export Development Authority; and (4) International Liaison. The major responsibilities of the MIO are promoting the export of the goods and services of small and medium-size Michigan enterprises in world markets; encouraging investment by foreign firms in Michigan and assisting Michigan firms as they seek joint venture opportunities abroad; assisting small and medium-size exporters through a proprietary working capital guarantee program and through cooperative programs with the federal Export Import Bank of the United States and private sector Michigan banks; and performing as an international liaison for the state. In addition to its staff in Michigan, the bureau has offices in Europe, Canada, Asia, and Africa.

Michigan Strategic Fund/Capital Resources Group

Contacts:
Mr. Mark Morante, Acting Director of
   Operations
Capital Resources Group
Michigan Department of Commerce
P.O. Box 30234
Lansing, MI 48909
(517) 373–7550

Ms. Karen Ammarman, Program Manager
Capital Access Program
Capital Resources Group
Michigan Department of Commerce
P.O. Box 30234
Lansing, MI 48909
(517) 373–7551

Mr. James Paquet, Program Manager
BIDCO Investment Program
P.O. Box 30234
Lansing, MI 48909
(517) 373–7551

The **Michigan Strategic Fund/Capital Resources Group** is designed to address the financing needs of entrepreneurs and small and medium-size businesses in Michigan. The fund consolidates and streamlines existing state programs and adds new, more flexible programs to meet the needs of Michigan's changing business environment. The private-sector institutional approach of the fund is embodied in several programs, including Capital Access, BIDCO Investment, Seed Capital, Minority BIDCO, and Technology Development.

Under the **Capital Access Program**, bank financing is possible for small businesses that might otherwise not be able to obtain such assistance.

Under the **BIDCO Investment Program**, commitments have been made to help capitalize seven specific BIDCOs (privately-operated financial institutions designed to address moderate-risk growth capital needs of businesses that cannot be met by banks or venture capital funds). It is estimated that these first seven BIDCOs, with $14.9 million in Michigan Strategic Fund investment, can provide almost $500 million in business financing during their first 10 years of operation.

Contact:
Mr. Lawrence Schrauben, Manager
Public Finance Division
Michigan Department of Commerce
P.O. Box 30234
Lansing, MI 48909
(517) 373–6213

Newly available is a $12.4 million pool of **Seed Capital**. Managed by three private seed capital funds, the pool is to be used for start-ups with rapid growth potential as well as potential for becoming major companies and attracting substantial additional private investment.

Minority business support is administered by the Michigan Strategic Fund. The fund also administers state support for three nonprofit research and development institutes.

In November 1982, the **Michigan Certified Development Company** (MCDC) was formally approved by the U.S. Small Business Administration to operate statewide as a Section 504 Certified Development Company. Working with local economic development professionals, the MCDC assists small businesses with preparation of loan packages before the packages are submitted to the MCDC for approval. The Michigan Strategic Fund provides staff support.

The **Community Development Block Grant Program** provides funds for financing infrastructure and businesses by making grants to eligible communities. Business loans for working capital and fixed assets are available for up to 20 percent of project costs at market interest rates for three to seven years. The loan maximum is $1,000,000.

Pension Fund/Venture Capital

Contact:
Mr. Paul E. Rice, Administrator
Alternative Investments Division
Department of Treasury
Treasury Building
Lansing, MI 48922
(517) 373–4330

It is now possible for **Michigan's Public Pension Funds** to invest 2 to 5 percent of their portfolios as venture capital in small businesses demonstrating excellent potential for growth, profitability, and equity appreciation. Joint investments with other institutions are also considered. Firms looking for venture capital support should have a unique product, service, or market position that gives the business a competitive edge.

Governor's Advisory Council or Task Force

Michigan has no specific advisory council to make recommendations on small business.

Legislative Committees and Subcommittees

The Michigan House of Representatives' Committee on Economic Development and Energy focuses on small business issues. In the Senate, small business issues are handled by the Commerce and Technology Committee. The legislature meets annually from January through December.

Contacts:

Rep. Teola Hunter
Chair
House Committee on Economic
    Development and Energy
P.O. Box 30014
Lansing, MI 48909
(517) 373–0587

Sen. Doug Cruce
Chair
Senate Committee on Commerce
P.O. Box 30036
Lansing, MI 48909
(517) 373–2523

Legislation

Recently enacted legislation affecting small businesses includes retention of the capital acquisition deduction, which allows businesses to deduct the full value of depreciable capital purchases from a firm's single business tax.

State Small Business Conferences

Contact:
Ms. Donna Wegryn
Technical Business Services Bureau
Michigan Department of Commerce
P.O. Box 30225
Lansing, MI 48909
(517) 373–74850

The primary small business associations in Michigan, in cooperation with the Department of Commerce and the U.S. Small Business Administration District Office, hold a statewide spring conference. The annual conference offers workshops, honors small
business award winners, and provides an opportunity for owners
of small businesses to meet with legislative leaders.

Minnesota

Small Business Offices, Programs, and Activities

Minnesota Small Business Assistance Office

Contact:
Dr. Charles Schaffer, Director
Minnesota Small Business Assistance Office
900 American Center Building
150 East Kellogg Boulevard
St. Paul, MN 55101
(612) 296–3871

The **Minnesota Small Business Assistance Office** provides accurate, timely, and comprehensive information in all areas of start-up, operation, and expansion. Services are provided through the Bureau of Business Licenses and the Bureau of Small Business. The Assistance Office also administers the state's Small Business Development Center network.

The **Bureau of Business Licenses** provides information on the requirements for doing business in Minnesota and helps applicants fulfill these requirements through a master application and preapplication conference procedure.

The **Bureau of Small Business** provides a single point of access for small businesses for information on requirements for organization, regulation, taxation, and employer issues. The office responds to direct requests for assistance, produces assistance publications, and conducts workshops on small business issues.

A number of publications are available, free of charge, through the Assistance Office, including *A Guide to Starting a Business in Minnesota; Buying and Selling a Business in Minnesota; Environmental Issues in Business Operations and Commercial Transactions; A Guide to Intellectual Property Protection; A Legal Guide for the Software Developer; Introduction to Franchising; An Employer's Guide to Employment Law Issues in Minnesota; State of Minnesota Directory of Licenses and Permits; Mini-Directory of Licenses; Licenses and Permits: Starting a Food Business in Minnesota; Government Procurement in Minnesota;* and *Small Business Notes.*

Small Business Development Centers

Contact:
Mr. Randall Olsen, Director
Minnesota Small Business Development
    Centers
Minnesota Department of Trade and
    Economic Development
900 American Center Building
150 East Kellogg Boulevard
St. Paul, MN 55101
(612) 297–5770

Through small business workshops/seminars, in-depth counseling, referrals to other small business assistance organizations, and the Small Business Institute program, **Small Business Development Centers** (SBDCs) provide start-up and existing businesses and women and minority entrepreneurs with information and assistance in areas such as business plan preparation and loan packaging. Services are provided free of charge. A complete listing of the SBDCs in Minnesota can be found in Appendix A of this directory.

Minnesota Department of Trade and Economic Development

Contact:
Mr. Robert Benner, Deputy Commissioner
Community Development Division
Minnesota Department of Trade and
    Economic Development
900 American Center Building
150 East Kellogg Boulevard
St. Paul, MN 55101
(612) 297–2515

The **Community Development Division** provides information concerning a variety of programs that assist Minnesota communities and small businesses.

- *Minnesota Development Program.* This program provides funds for agricultural and economic development in the state. Funds may be used for the acquisition of land, buildings, machinery, equipment, building construction and renovation, and development costs. Working capital is not an eligible use of funds. The Minnesota Agricultural and Economic Development Board issues revenue bonds backed by a state reserve.

- *Rural Development Board.* The board can award up to $1 million in challenge grants to six designated regional organizations around the state. These regional organizations use the challenge grants, matched with private funds, to provide loans to new and expanding businesses. Loans cannot be less than $5,000 or more than $100,000.

- *Small Cities Development Program (SCDP).* The purpose of the competitive SCDP is to assist communities in financing housing rehabilitation, public facility construction, and business and industrial development.

- *OMNI.* A private financing corporation, OMNI provides subordinated mortgage financing to industry and manufacturing enterprises. Funds may be used for the acquisition of land, buildings, machinery and equipment, building renovations and other fixed-asset purchases. Proceeds from the sale of OMNI debentures are used to provide fixed-rate financing for up to 40 percent of any project or $750,000, whichever is less. A local lending institution is required to provide 50 percent of the financing for the project. The remaining 10 percent of a project is financed in the form of equity by the company.

- *Minnesota Enterprise Zone Program.* This program uses state and local tax credits to reduce businesses' costs of operating in Minnesota. It consists of two parts: the Border Cities Program, which helps retain existing businesses, and the Competitive Zone Program, which helps municipalities attract new and expanding businesses.

The **Office of Marketing and Development** administers the Star City, Community Profile, Industrial Profile, and Available Building Locator programs. In addition, this office has field staff to provide direct technical assistance to communities on achieving Star City designation, needs assessment, leadership development, and special projects. Emphasis is on development of projects that lead to permanent job creation.

The **Business Development and Analysis Division** provides industrial site selection assistance to help businesses considering relocation to Minnesota. Information on existing buildings is collected and coordinated with the physical and locational needs of a business.

Contact:
Mr. David M. Jennings, Director
Office of Marketing and Development
Minnesota Department of Trade and
   Economic Development
900 American Center Building
150 East Kellogg Boulevard
St. Paul, MN 55101
(612) 296–3976

Contact:
Mr. Terrell Towers, Industry Recruiter
Business Development and Analysis Division
Minnesota Department of Trade and
   Economic Development
900 American Center Building
150 East Kellogg Boulevard
St. Paul, MN 55101
(612) 296–4039

Mr. David Leckey, Deputy Commissioner
Business Development and Analysis Division
Minnesota Department of Trade and
    Economic Development
900 American Center Building
150 East Kellogg Boulevard
St. Paul, MN 55101
(612) 296–8341

Contact:

Mr. George Crolick, Jr., Executive Director
Minnesota Trade Office
Minnesota Department of Trade and
    Economic Development
1000 Minnesota World Trade Center
30 East Seventh Street
St. Paul, MN 55101–4902
(612) 297–4227

A **"locational fit analysis"** identifies and compares Minnesota business location factors for specific industries to those in other geographical areas. Analyses may examine markets, labor, taxes, and inputs.

The primary mission of the **Minnesota Trade Office** is to encourage export development and reverse investments that can have a positive effect on the Minnesota economy. The office's efforts are concentrated on small business—which creates 80 percent of new jobs but less than 10 percent of total exports. The trade office has several divisions including the following:

- The **Export Outreach and Education Division** conducts export training workshops and seminars; hosts educational programs on foreign markets and technical trade issues; and provides trade leads and information on export financing, shipping, packaging, international advertising, travel, and translation.

- The **International Marketing and Investment Division** arranges and leads trade missions; promotes Minnesota products and services at trade shows; assists foreign companies locating in Minnesota; helps foreign trade delegations find appropriate Minnesota companies; provides market intelligence and personalized export consulting; and refers Minnesota firms to other international trade services and resources within and outside of government.

- The **Minnesota Export Finance Authority** provides information on a variety of financing programs, individual counseling, insurance coverage, and guaranteed loans.

Contact:
Mr. Gil Young, Executive Director
Minnesota Technology, Inc.
Minnesota Department of Trade and
   Economic Development
111 3rd Avenue South, Suite 400
Minneapolis, MN 55401
(612) 338–7722

Minnesota Technology, Inc., is a nonprofit corporation established to help Minnesota companies improve productivity, reduce costs, enhance product quality, increase profitability, and overall become more competitive. The corporation assists small and medium-size businesses in applying appropriate technology; supports the commercialization of advanced technology; and increases the awareness of and exposure to manufacturing technology. Minnesota Technology also serves as the focus for the state's technology development initiatives. It is responsible for developing priorities and policies for the state in relation to science and technology. During 1992, its recommendations for a science and technology policy were adopted into law by the state legislature. The corporation also is facilitating the development of the state's youth apprenticeship initiatives; working to enhance supplier development; and establishing an equity investment fund for small technology-related Minnesota companies.

Minnesota Project Innovation, Inc.

Contact:
Mr. James S. Hayes, Executive Director
Minnesota Project Innovation, Inc.
111 Third Avenue South, Suite 410
Minneapolis, MN 55401–2554
(612) 338–3280

Created by the state of Minnesota, **Minnesota Project Innovation, Inc.**, (MPI), helps bring the discoveries of the laboratory to the marketplace. MPI is a private nonprofit organization that assists small technology and manufacturing companies with federal funding, procurement, and technology transfer opportunities. It is a program that is designed to stimulate the development of innovative technologies, new products and services, advanced technology research, and competitive bids for federal contracts.

To help Minnesota businesses access federal funding opportunities, MPI developed a data base that indexes the thousands of technology solicitation topics available at participating **Small Business Innovative Research** (SBIR) agencies. Innovative technologies are easily matched with SBIR opportunities.

Minnesota Inventors' Congress

Contact:
Ms. Penny Becker, Executive Director
Minnesota Inventors' Congress, Inc.
P.O. Box 71
Redwood Falls, MN 56283
(507) 637–2344
(800) INVENT–1 (toll-free, in-state)

The **Minnesota Inventors' Congress** (MIC) is the focal point for Minnesota's invention support system. The MIC provides information and assistance for inventors through a year-round Inventors' Resource Center and also sponsors the longest continuously running inventors' congress, which provides inventors an opportunity to display their inventions, obtain a test market, attend educational seminars, gain publicity, receive networking opportunities, and compete for awards. The MIC also hosts the Minnesota Student Inventors' Congress State Event (for kindergarten through 12th grade students) and the Minnesota Inventors' Hall of Fame induction ceremony, which takes place during the annual convention held in Redwood Falls the second weekend in June.

Minnesota Technical Assistance Program

Contact:
Ms. Cindy McComas, Director
Minnesota Technical Assistance Program
1313 5th Street, S.E., Suite 207
Minneapolis, MN 55414
(612) 627–4646
(800) 247–0015 (toll-free, in-state)

The **Minnesota Technical Assistance Program** (MnTAP), a program of the Minnesota Waste Management Board, assists small companies that generate hazardous waste. MnTAP provides information and referrals on the regulatory process and information on how small businesses can reduce or improve the management of their hazardous wastes.

Small Business Procurement Program

Contact:
Helpline, Materials Management Division
Minnesota Department of Administration
112 Administration Building
50 Sherburne Avenue
St. Paul, MN 55155
(612) 296–2600

The **Small Business Procurement Program** helps small businesses sell their goods or services to the state of Minnesota. Each fiscal year, the commissioner of administration must ensure that small businesses receive at least 25 percent of the value of anticipated total state procurements of goods and services. The commissioner must also ensure proportionate purchasing from Minnesota-based small businesses owned and operated by women and minorities through set-asides or purchasing preference. In addition, small businesses in Minnesota's economically disadvantaged counties may be eligible for purchasing preferences.

Small Business Management Program

Contact:
Mr. John Murray, Program Manager
Small Business Management Program
Minnesota State Board of Technical
  Colleges
550 Cedar Street
St. Paul, MN 55101
(612) 297–3792

The **Small Business Management Program** provides business management education to Minnesota's small business owners at many technical colleges. Instruction is provided in individualized sessions at the business site and in group sessions. Business planning, record systems, financial analysis, marketing, inventory management, payroll, negotiating for money, computer applications, and other areas are covered as needed by the business owner. Technical colleges also offer many short courses, workshops, and seminars in small business management and entrepreneurship.

Governor's Advisory Council or Task Force

Contact:
Mr. Robert A. Schroeder, Assistant
  Commissioner
Minnesota Department of Administration
200 Administration Building
50 Sherburne Avenue
St. Paul, MN 55155
(612) 297–4261

The **Small Business Procurement Advisory Council** consists of 13 members appointed by the commissioner of administration. The council advises the commissioner on small business procurement matters; reviews small business vendor and contractor complaints or grievances; and reviews the report of the commissioners of administration and trade and economic development to ensure compliance with the goals of the program.

Legislative Committees and Subcommittees

The Senate and House Commerce and Economic Development and Housing Committees and the House Subcommittee on Small Business handle most of the legislation pertaining to small business.

Contacts:

Senator Sam G. Solon
Chairman
Senate Commerce Committee
State Capitol, Room 303
St. Paul, MN 55155
(612) 296–4158

Senator James Metzen
Chairman
Senate Economic Development and
    Housing Committee
State Capitol, Room G–10
St. Paul, MN 55155
(612) 296–8864

Representative John Sarna
Chairman
House Commerce Committee
State Capitol, Room 563
St. Paul, MN 55155
(612) 296–4219

Representative Gloria Segal
Chair
Economic Development Committee
State Office Building, Room 417
St. Paul, MN 55155
(612) 296–9889

Representative Jerry Janezich
Chairman
House Subcommittee on Small Business,
    Energy and Real Estate
State Capitol, Room 597
St. Paul, MN 55155
(612) 296–0172

Legislation

Recent Minnesota legislation affecting small business includes the following:

• Mandatory licensing of residential building contractors and remodelers.

• Under the Omnibus Finance Bill, the Supreme Court will study the need for a business court in Minnesota.

• An international partnership pilot program is created between Minnesota and Israel and other potential trade partners to enhance economic development.

- Research and development qualifying expenses are deductible on the Minnesota tax return even though they are not allowed under federal law.

- Expenses for making property accessible to the disabled are deductible even if they are not fully deductible under federal law.

State Small Business Conferences

No statewide small business conferences were scheduled for 1992.

Mississippi

Small Business Offices, Programs, and Activities

Mississippi Department of Economic and Community Development

Contact:
Mr. Bill Barry, Director
Mississippi Business Finance Corporation
Mississippi Department of Economic and
　　Community Development
P.O. Box 849
Jackson, MS 39205
(601) 359–3552

The role of the **Mississippi Department of Economic and Community Development** (MDECD) is to create wealth and jobs within the state. During Fiscal Year 1991, MDECD was restructured into three groups: (1) Economic Development, (2) Community Development, and (3) Support Services. The Economic Development group is composed of the following offices: Business Services, Minority Business Enterprise, National Development, International Development, and Tourism Development. The Community Development group is composed of the following offices: Community Assistance, Labor Assistance, Employment Training, Energy and Transportation, and Aeronautics. Each of these divisions addresses a vital component of the economic development process. MDECD's strategies are comprehensive, involving all economic sectors and geographic areas—MDECD is committed to all Mississippians.

The **Mississippi Business Finance Corporation** is a statewide certified development company established by MDECD with a $4 million state fund allocation. MDECD administers financing programs that are applicable to Mississippi small businesses: the SBA 504 Loan, the Small Business Loan Guarantee program, the Minority Loan program, the Small Enterprise Development Bond program, and the Emerging Crops Finance program.

Contact:
Mr. Van A. Evans, Manager
Business Assistance Division
Mississippi Department of Economic and
　　Community Development
P.O. Box 849
Jackson, MS 39205
(601) 359–3552

The **Business Assistance Division** of MDECD provides assistance to businesses locating or expanding in Mississippi. The Division has consultants in Jackson and in five regional offices located in Tupelo, Greenwood, Meridian, Summit, and Hattiesburg.

Contact:
Mr. Elliott Travis, Director
Office of Minority Business Enterprise
Mississippi Department of Economic and
   Community Development
P.O. Box 849
Jackson, MS 39205
(601) 359–3449

Contact:
Mr. David DeBlanc, Director
Mississippi Technology Transfer Office
Mississippi Department of Economic and
   Community Development
John C. Stennis Space Center,
   Building 1103
Stennis Space Center, MS 39525–6000
(601) 688–3144

Contact:
Mr. Bob Gray
Regional Operations Division
Mississippi Department of Economic and
   Community Development
P.O. Box 894
Jackson, MS 39205
(601) 359–3552

Contact:
Ms. Alice Lusk, Assistant Director
Enterprise Development Division
Mississippi Department of Economic and
   Community Development
P.O. Box 849
Jackson, MS 39205
(601) 359–3179

The **Office of Minority Business Enterprise** was created by the Mississippi Legislature to promote the development of minority and women-owned businesses. This legislation, effective July 1, 1988, established three goals for this branch of the Mississippi Department of Economic and Community Development: (1) to foster economic activities that increase the availability of resources to the minority business community; (2) to promote the growth and development of minority-owned businesses in Mississippi; and (3) to advocate that an equitable portion of state procurement contracts be awarded to minority businesses.

The **Mississippi Technology Transfer Office** (MTTO) is located at the John C. Stennis Space Center. MTTO serves as Mississippi industry's link with federal laboratories at the Space Center and more than 600 other federal laboratories nationwide. The center offers guidance on contact persons; technical consultation; information on **Small Business Innovation Research** grants; access to federal government standards and calibration services; access to MTTO, NASA, and Navy libraries; links to venture capital groups; and participation in technology transfer projects to develop new products, improve productivity, and increase profitability.

The **Regional Operations Division** of the Mississippi Department of Economic and Community Development provides assistance to businesses locating or expanding in Mississippi. It acts as a link between community economic development efforts and the state's resources and overall goals, and assists communities in analyzing their strengths and weaknesses. In addition, this division is responsible for rural development in the state and operates five regional offices throughout the state.

The **Enterprise Development Division** assists the growth of new enterprises within the state. Divided into two branches— New Business Assistance and Entrepreneurial Development—the Division provides support to entrepreneurs and local business support groups such as chambers of commerce and Planning and Development Districts. The new Business Assistance Branch provides counseling to individuals interested in starting their own business; the Entrepreneurial Development Branch concentrates on developing programs designed to promote and support entrepreneurship at the local level.

Business Incubator

Contact:
Mr. Jeff Dukes, Manager
Community Initiatives Division
Mississippi Department of Economic and
    Community Development
P.O. Box 849
Jackson, MS 39205
(601) 359–3179

The **Business Incubator** aims to create jobs and reduce small business failures by providing services to businesses and entrepreneurs during the critical early stages of development. The incubator is a multi-tenant building in which new and fledgling businesses can locate and operate at lower overhead rates than in conventional space. Incubator facilities are characterized by (1) affordable rental rates; (2) access to shared, centralized services such as clerical and administrative help, shipping and receiving facilities, and conference rooms; and (3) counseling on various business operations.

The Mississippi Department of Economic and Community Development works with local economic professionals to develop a statewide system of incubators. The department also sponsors the Mississippi Incubator Network, which consists of a diversified group of individuals who share a common interest in small business incubators as an economic development tool. The Mississippi Incubator Network meets quarterly and encourages anyone interested in acquiring or sharing information on the subject to attend.

Operating Incubators

Gulf Coast Business Technology Center
Ms. Adele Lyons, Director
1636 Popps Ferry Road
Biloxi, MS 39532
(601) 392–9741

Kemper County Industrial Incubator
Mr. Lance LaCour, Director
P.O. Box 280
DeKalb, MS 39328
(601) 743–2755

Jackson Enterprise Center
Mr. Dick Acker, Director
Battlefield Park Industrial Complex
931 Highway 80 West
Jackson, MS 39205
(601) 352–0957

Meridian Community College Incubator
Mr. Bill Lang, Director
5500 Highway 19 North
Meridian, MS 39305
(601) 482–7445

Incubators Under Construction

Coahoma County Incubator
c/o Mr. Ron Hudson
P.O. Box 160
Clarksdale, MS 38614
(601) 627–7338

Columbus/Lowndes Business Development
    Center
Mr. Bob Fouchard, Director
118 McCrary Road
Columbus, MS 39702
(601) 328–4491

Vicksburg Business Development Center
Mr. Tom Wilson, Jr., Director
P.O. Box 709
Vicksburg, MS 39181
(601) 636–1012

Inventors' Workshops

Contact:
Society of Mississippi Inventors
P.O. Box 5111
Jackson, MS 39296–5111
(601) 984–6047

The staff of the Mississippi Department of Economic and Community Development assisted in establishing the **Society of Mississippi Inventors**, which meets monthly in Jackson. The counseling that is provided in these meetings is designed to assist inventors in developing their projects. Some of the topics discussed are design, manufacturing, marketing, and patent information.

Mississippi Seed Capital Corporation

Contact:
Ms. Alice Lusk, Assistant Director
Enterprise Development Division
Mississippi Department of Economic and
   Community Development
P.O. Box 849
Jackson, MS 39205
(601) 359–3179

Created by the Economic Development Reform Act, the **Mississippi Seed Capital Corporation** is a private sector, for-profit fund offering an income tax credit to investors of 30 percent of their investment in the fund and raises funds to provide start-up capital to high-growth-oriented businesses.

Businesses eligible for financing through the Seed Capital Corporation include corporations, general and limited partnerships, joint ventures, trusts, proprietorships, or other entities or organizations expected to experience significant sales growth over a five-year period. The ceiling on allowed tax credits for investors is $3 million, allowing the fund to be as large as $10 million. Financing through the Seed Capital program will be made available as soon as the minimum capital reserves have been raised.

Procurement Programs

Contact:
Mr. C.W. Rayland, Director
Mississippi Contract Procurement Center
3015 12th Street
P.O. Box 610
Gulfport, MS 39502
(601) 864–2961

In 1986, a nonprofit procurement assistance system was established to provide direct assistance and information to firms wanting to do business with the federal government. Known as the **Mississippi Contract Procurement Center** (MCPC) and operating five service centers, this statewide project is jointly sponsored by many public and private sector organizations. Interested small businesses are provided copies of current bid summaries that match their capabilities. The MCPC counselors review bid packets for bidding consideration, as well as offer specialized counseling on bid, performance, and payment bonds. A reference library is maintained at the MCPC office and is available to all Mississippi businesses.

Jackson Minority Business Development Center

Contact:
Mr. Robert G. Funches, Director
Jackson Minority Business Development
  Center
5285 Galaxy Drive, Suite A
Jackson, MS 39206
(601) 362–2260

The **Jackson Minority Business Development Center** assists the development of minority entrepreneurs. The center helps minority-owned firms create new jobs by providing comprehensive assistance services through a network of local business development centers.

Mississippi Small Business Development Center

Contact:
Mr. Raleigh H. Byars, Statewide Director
Mississippi Small Business Development
  Center
Suite 216, Old Chemistry Building
University, MS 38677
(601) 232–5001

The **Mississippi Small Business Development Center** subcenters, located throughout the state, offer assistance to the state's small business community. They provide technical services and training to small business owners and managers. A complete list of all Small Business Development Centers and subcenters is in Appendix A of this directory.

Governor's Advisory Council or Task Force

Contact:
Ms. Alice Lusk, Assistant Director
Small Business Consortium
Enterprise Development Division
Mississippi Department of Economic and
  Community Development
P.O. Box 849
Jackson, MS 39205
(601) 359–3179

The **Small Business Consortium** is the policymaking body for Mississippi's small business assistance programs. It is composed of agencies and universities providing technical assistance and research services to Mississippi small businesses. The consortium oversees the delivery of assistance to small businesses to ensure that its members and other small business support offices do not duplicate services.

Legislative Committees and Subcommittees

In Mississippi, the Senate Committee on Finance, the Senate Subcommittee on Economic Development, and the House Select Committee on Economic Development handle small business legislation.

Contacts:

Senator Rick Lambert
Chairman
Finance Committee
Mississippi State Senate
P.O. Box 1018
Jackson, MS 39215–1018
(601) 359–3246

Senator John Keeton
Chairman
Subcommittee on Economic Development
Mississippi State Senate
P.O. Box 1018
Jackson, MS 39215–1018
(601) 359–3240

Representative H. L. Meridith, Jr.
Chairman
House Select Committee on Economic
   Development
Mississippi House of Representatives
P.O. Box 1018
Jackson, MS 39215–1018
(601) 359–3343

Legislation

The Mississippi Legislature passed several bills during the 1990 regular session that revised and expanded the landmark economic development reform bills passed in 1989 and addressed new economic development needs of the state. Senate Bills 2576, 3042, and 2503, and House Bill 1190—all of which were signed into law by Governor Mabus—addressed the refinancing of many economic development programs as well as tax credit programs, property tax exemptions, small business incubators, and other economic development issues.

- Several revisions in the area of finance were developed in the new legislation. The Major Economic Impact Authority (MEIA) was provided with an additional $10 million, bringing the MEIA's total bonding authority to $30 million. The MEIA, designed to assist in the development of communities within 50 miles of the location of a major project of $300 million or more, has granted $20 million in bonds for projects associated with the NASA Advanced Solid Rocket Motor (ASRM) plant in northeast Mississippi. The additional funds were provided in the event other major projects locate in the state. None of the additional $10 million will be eligible for projects considered in conjunction with the NASA ASRM plant.

- The legislation also provided $5 million in Mississippi Business Investment Act (MBI) funds for the purchase by the MEIA of approximately 5,000 acres surrounding the NASA ASRM plant to be used as a buffer zone. The property will be available for future expansions of the NASA project site, but the title to the property will remain in the name of the MEIA.

- The Department of Economic and Community Development was provided $3 million in MBI funds to establish small business incubator centers across the state. Previous application restrictions were eliminated that limited the business incubator centers to only those enterprises filing applications with the National Space Technology Laboratory.

- New legislation lifted the $10 million taxable bond issue cap on the Mississippi Business Finance Corporation (MBFC). The self-imposed $10 million limit was established to follow the federal tax exemption statute.

- A minority loan program was established through the MBFC. The law provides the MDECD with a maximum of $2 million in bonding authority to make grants to qualified Planning and Development Districts (PDD) to set up minority loan revolving funds. The PDDs can borrow up to $250,000, which must be matched on a one-to-one basis.

- The bond issuance authorization for Small Enterprise Development programs was increased from $20 million to $30 million. The Small Enterprise Development Finance Act provides tax exempt general obligation bonds on qualified projects up to $1 million. By using the state's backing on the bonds, smaller Mississippi banks' letters of credit can be used to sell the bonds in the bond market, thus saving the large issuance costs charged by larger lending institutions. This allows smaller projects, from $200,000 to $1 million, the advantage of a general obligation bond umbrella and reduced rates while relying on the security of the state of Mississippi's credit in the marketplace.

- Excise taxes on aviation fuel and oil, not currently used to support the Mississippi Aeronautics Commission, may now be matched with federal funds and diverted to a special fund to make loans and grants to state airports for facility renovation and expansion.

- The Emerging Crop Loan program was established to encourage lenders to provide loans to agribusinesses that are developing alternative or "emerging" crops. The 1990 legislation redefined "emerging crops," removing the minimum time requirement for harvest of an emerging crop. The alteration was required because of the many technological advances in hydroponics and aquaculture, which made the previous minimal harvest requirement of 18 months obsolete. The new legislation will also allow the MDECD to make loans to certain agribusinesses. Up to 20 percent of the total cost of a project or $200,000, whichever is less, is now available.

- The MDECD may now purchase the state's overseas offices allocation, in part or whole, in appropriate foreign currencies, at the beginning of the fiscal year to protect against currency fluctuations against the dollar.

- An additional $18 million in bonding authority was added to the Economic Development Highway Fund for building highways or sections of highways for adequate access to economic development projects. The legislation broadens the scope to economic development projects to include large resort hotels (150 rooms or more), movie industry studios, and air and transportation maintenance facilities. This legislation also allows counties or municipalities to construct sections of roads with MDECD approval. The new road must meet State Highway Department standards including a minimum 80,000 pound capacity.

- Other sections of the new legislation provide job tax credits to large regional malls, resort hotels, movie industry studios, air and transportation facilities, and other development projects serving as catalysts for economic activity and growth. The legislation also lowers from 30 to 20 the created jobs in developed counties required to be eligible for job tax credits.

- The carry-forward provision of the Child Care/Retraining tax credits was increased from three to five years. State retraining tax credits were limited to 50 percent of a taxpayer's liability and are only eligible for hourly employees. Retail businesses were excluded.

- New legislation provides an initial five-year property tax (ad valorem) exemption for certain enterprises, including air transportation and maintenance facilities, large hotels, and movie studios, with extensions of the exemptions not to exceed 10 years. The legislation requires a city or county to notify a company holding exemptions 90 days prior to expiration of the exemption.

State Small Business Conferences

Contact:
Ms. Alice Lusk, Assistant Director
Enterprise Development Division
Mississippi Department of Economic and
  Community Development
P.O. Box 849
Jackson, MS 39205
(601) 359–3179

Two **Small Business Resource Conferences** were planned for 1992, involving the U.S. Small Business Administration and the Mississippi Department of Economic and Community Development.

In 1991, the Enterprise Development Division of the Mississippi Department of Economic and Community Development held a statewide conference on women in business.

Missouri

Small Business Offices, Programs, and Activities

Missouri Department of Economic Development

Contact:
Mr. David C. Harrison, Director
Missouri Department of Economic
   Development
Truman State Office Building
301 West High Street
P.O. Box 1157
Jefferson City, MO 65102
(314) 751–4962

The **Missouri Department of Economic Development** is the lead agency for promoting job creation and capital investment in Missouri. The department houses the state's economic development programs; the business regulation divisions of finance, credit unions, savings and loan supervision, and transportation; the Public Service Commission; the Office of Public Counsel; the professional registration boards and commissions that license architects, nurses, barbers, and other licensed practitioners; the state divisions of tourism and job development and training; the Housing Development Commission; and the Council on the Arts.

Contact:
Mr. John Johnson, Assistant Director
Business Development Section
Missouri Department of Economic
   Development
Truman State Office Building
P.O. Box 118
Jefferson City, MO 65102
(314) 751–9055

The Small Business Office in the **Business Development Section** provides assistance and counseling to small businesses in their dealings with federal, state, and local governments. An ombudsman analyzes current legislation and regulations and their effect on small business, and determines ways to eliminate or simplify unnecessary regulatory requirements at the state level. The staff assists small businesses in obtaining technical and financial assistance. A small business coordinator initiates and encourages small business education programs in cooperation with public and private educational institutions. In addition, a procurement coordinator helps existing businesses become involved in both the federal and state marketplace. A minority business coordinator can assist minority companies within the state and act as their advocate on legislative issues.

Contact:
Mr. Ken Konchel, Program Coordinator of
    Procurement
Small Business Office
Missouri Department of Economic
    Development
Truman State Office Building
P.O. Box 118
Jefferson City, MO 65102
(314) 751–4982

The **Procurement Program** was established to assist existing businesses in Missouri to participate in the federal and state marketplace. To facilitate this effort, "Product Finder," an electronic product matching network, was established and is provided at no charge to the public. The Missouri Product Finder is a computerized registration system—offered free to Missouri companies—that allows easy access to information on products and services available from Missouri business, information on production process, raw materials used, and by-product or surplus materials. This valuable marketing tool markets Missouri products and services worldwide and encourages Missouri businesses to purchase needed products, materials, and services from other Missouri companies.

Contact:
Ms. Aleta Mitchell, Manager of Minority
    Business
Missouri Department of Economic
    Development
Truman State Office Building
P.O. Box 118
Jefferson City, MO 65102
(314) 751–3237

The **Minority Business Assistance Office** helps minority-owned businesses obtain technical and financial assistance, offers education programs, advocates on behalf of minority businesses, and works with other programs and agencies to promote development of a strong economic climate to benefit minority-owned firms.

Contact:
Ms. Sharon A. Gulick, Manager
Business Information Programs
Missouri Department of Economic
    Development
Truman State Office Building
P.O. Box 118
Jefferson City, MO 65102
(314) 751–4982

The **Business Information Programs** serve as a central point for access of critical demographic, comparative, and reference information for businesses. There are three programs: Missouri Economic Development Information System (MEDIS), Missouri Product Finder, and the Missouri Business Assistance Center.

The **Missouri Economic Development Information System** (MEDIS) is a computerized data base of 18 subsystems containing critical economic development reference and planning information. Subsystems include a listing of available industrial buildings and land sites, demographic information, utility rates, transportation costs, and market information.

Contacts:
Ms. Marilyn York, Business Specialist
Mr. Roy Thirtyacre, Business Specialist
Missouri Business Assistance Center
Missouri Department of Economic
   Development
Truman State Office Building
P.O. Box 118
Jefferson City, MO 65102
(314) 751–4982
(800) 523–1434 (toll-free)

Contact:
Mr. Tom Barry, Coordinator
High Technology Program
Missouri Department of Economic
   Development
Truman State Office Building
P.O. Box 118
Jefferson City, MO 65102
(314) 751–3906

Contact:
Mr. Mark Burgess, Manager
International Business Development
   Program
Missouri Department of Economic
   Development
Truman State Office Building
P.O. Box 118
Jefferson City, MO 65102
(314) 751–3607

The **Missouri Business Assistance Center** provides access to all state forms, regulations, requirements, permits, and other information necessary to do business in Missouri. The business assistance office offers a one-stop program that provides help on all aspects of running a small business. A toll-free hot line is available to answer small business questions regarding licenses, permits, and other concerns.

The Department of Economic Development works with several high technology initiatives in the state. The **Missouri Corporation for Science and Technology**, a private nonprofit corporation, advises the governor on science and technology-related economic development issues. Four innovation centers in the state provide facilities, equipment, and technical services to new advanced-technology businesses. New legislation will provide seed capital through these centers to innovative high technology companies. The Higher Education Research Assistance Act provides funding for challenge grants to state colleges and universities for research and applied projects likely to stimulate private investment. Centers for Advanced Technology encourage cooperation between universities and private business in research and development programs. The **Small Business Innovation Research** (SBIR) program has specialists to assist Missouri small businesses in obtaining SBIR grants by matching federal requirements with the capabilities of Missouri businesses.

The **Missouri Export Development Office** (EDO) is prepared to help Missouri business tap into world markets. The staff of the EDO can help Missouri companies initiate or increase international sales by helping them analyze the export potential of their products and identify growing export markets.

The EDO can help with marketing overseas by representing Missouri firms at international trade shows and by assisting them in finding overseas buyers, agents, representatives, licensing and/or joint venture partners, and by providing insurance and trade leads. The office utilizes the expertise of four overseas offices located in Japan, Korea, Taiwan, and Germany.

Contact:
Ms. Nancy Straub, Coordinator
Tax Benefit Programs
Missouri Department of Economic
  Development
Truman State Office Building
P.O. Box 118
Jefferson City, MO 65102
(314) 751–6835

The **Tax Benefit Programs** offer tax incentives to businesses that create jobs and investments in Missouri. The Enterprise Zone Act provides credits in economically distressed areas for new jobs, investment, employees, and employee training. A percentage of "special" and resident income is also sheltered from taxes, and improvements to property may be exempt from local property taxes for up to 25 years. The new business facility tax credits are offered to certain businesses creating jobs and investment outside enterprise zones.

Contacts:
Mr. Mike Downing, Manager
Finance Program
Missouri Department of Economic
  Development
Truman State Office Building
P.O. Box 118
Jefferson City, MO 65102
(314) 751–0717

Mr. Ken Lueckenotte, Executive Director
Rural Missouri, Inc.
1014 Northeast Drive
Jefferson City, MO 65101
(314) 635–0316

The **Finance Program** of the Missouri Department of Economic Development works with the Missouri Economic Development, Export, and Infrastructure Board (MEDEIB) to provide loan guarantees to selected businesses. The MEDEIB may use its development fund—consisting of state appropriations, contributions, and reserve participation fees—to guarantee loans made through a participating lender for qualified projects. Qualified projects include facilities, equipment, improvements to facilities, and certain export trade activities, such as consulting, advertising, marketing, product research, legal assistance, and warehousing.

Missouri Customized Training Program

Contact:
Mr. Larry Earley, Director
Division of Job Development and Training
Missouri Department of Economic
  Development
P.O. Box 118
Jefferson City, MO 65101
(314) 751–7796

Through a cooperative effort of the Division of Job Development and Training, the Department of Elementary and Secondary Education, and the state's Private Industry Councils, businesses have access to a wide range of training services designed for specific businesses and their employees through the **Missouri Customized Training Program**. Starting, expanding, or improving a business is not an easy task. It requires a search for qualified employees and teaching them new skills. The Missouri Customized Training Program assists firms in building a competent and skilled work force.

Missouri Agricultural and Small Business Development Authority

Contact:
Mr. Dale Angel, Executive Director
Missouri Agricultural and Small Business
  Development Authority
P.O. Box 630
Jefferson City, MO 65102–0630
(314) 751–2129

The **Missouri Agricultural and Small Business Development Authority** (MASBDA) was created by the legislature in 1981 with the power to participate in loans to small businesses through the issuance of industrial revenue bonds approved by the MASBDA board.

SBA 504 Certified Development Centers

Contact:
Mr. Ken Lueckenotte, Executive Director
Rural Missouri, Inc.
1014 Northeast Drive
Jefferson City, MO 65101
(314) 635–0136

Rural Missouri, Inc., is a statewide Certified Development Company that packages U.S. Small Business Administration 504 loans.

Small Business Development Centers

Contact:
Mr. Max Summers, State Director
Missouri Small Business Development
  Centers
300 University Place
Columbia, MO 65211
(314) 882–0344

In 1982, Missouri was authorized to establish **Small Business Development Centers** (SBDCs) in four schools. The lead SBDC is located at the University of Missouri at Columbia. There are now 15 subcenters located throughout the state. The centers provide management, pre-business seminars, and individual counseling to prospective business owners. A complete listing of all Small Business Development Centers and subcenters in Missouri is in Appendix A of this directory.

Governor's Advisory Council or Task Force

The **Missouri Small Business Advisory Council** was established January 7, 1986, by executive order. The council works to identify and solve problems specific to small business. It reports annually to the governor, the General Assembly, and the Department of Economic Development.

Contact:
Mr. John Johnson, Assistant Director
Business Development Programs
Missouri Department of Economic
    Development
Truman State Office Building
P.O. Box 118
Jefferson City, MO 65102
(314) 751–3906

Legislative Committees and Subcommittees

Small business and economic development legislation are handled by the Senate Local Government and Economic Development Committee and the House Commerce Committee.

Contacts:
Senator Norman L. Merrell
Chairman
Senate Local Government and Economic
    Development Committee
State Capitol Building, Room 403
Jefferson City, MO 65101
(314) 751–4200

Representative Joe Driskill
Chairman
House Commerce Committee
State Capitol Building, Room 403 B
Jefferson City, MO 65101
(314) 751–2363

Legislation

Major legislation passed during the 1991 session affecting small business includes the following:

- S.B. 148, the Durable Power of Attorney for Health Care Act, adds the authorization for an attorney to consent or prohibit health care in accordance with provisions to existing law.

- Under S.B. 87, manufacturers of meat or poultry food products can receive credit for state sales taxes paid on the purchase of flexible cellulose casing manufactured from cotton linters if the material is recycled.

- S.B. 185 authorizes issuing up to $35 million dollars in bonds for waste water control and water pollution control projects.

- S.B. 241 covers written or oral contracts between any persons, firms, or corporations that are in the business of selling or repairing industrial, maintenance, and construction power equipment, including cancellation or discontinuation of a contract.

- S.B. 45 authorizes the Department of Natural Resources to impose administrative penalties for major violations of laws pertaining to solid waste, hazardous waste, air quality, water quality, and other environmental concerns.

- S.B. 438 is legislation whereby any handicapped child can receive services from school districts upon reaching their third birthday.

- S.B. 353, entitled the Economic Survival Act of 1991, provides a tax increase to enhance funding for elementary and secondary education, and for higher education.

- Under H.B. 294, the House enacted numerous changes in the provisions of the new and expanded business facility tax credits and enterprise zone tax credits.

- H.B. 219 amends income, sales, and franchise tax law to comply with changes in Missouri law with respect to corporations.

- H.B. 422 makes several changes in the employment security law regarding unemployment benefits and workers' compensation.

State Small Business Conferences

No recent statewide small business conferences have been reported.

Montana

Small Business Offices, Programs and Activities

Department of Commerce, Business Development Division

Contacts:
Ms. Delrene Rasmussen
Ms. Karen Elliott
Business Division
Department of Commerce
1424 Ninth Avenue
Helena, MT 59620
(406) 444–3923
fax: (406) 444–2808

The **Business Development Division** of the Department of Commerce provides services that constitute the direct technical assistance component of Montana's economic development effort, including consulting, training, and providing information in the area of finance, marketing, exporting, data management, government contracting, local development, and business licensing. The Business Development Division incorporates the Small Business Development Center (SBDC) program, a cooperative project jointly funded by the Montana Department of Commerce and the U.S. Small Business Administration. SBDC offices are located in Helena, Glendive, Kalispell, Bozeman, and Billings.

The division also publishes and distributes the *Montana Exporter's Guide*, the *Montana Consumer Products Buyer's Directory*, and the *Montana Manufacturer's Directory*.

Contact:
Mr. David Elenbaas
Business Division
Department of Commerce
1424 Ninth Avenue
Helena, MT 59620
(406) 444–4780
fax: (406) 444–2808
BIS data line: (406) 444–4457
BIS voice line: (406) 444–2463

The **Small Business Development Center's Business Information System** (BIS) is a computerized information and communication tool designed to assist Montana's economic and business community. BIS is accessible, free of charge, to anyone with a personal computer, communications software, and modem. Individual or group training is available upon request. The BIS posts a variety of economic, demographic and business data, including state government bid solicitations; export trade opportunity leads from the U.S. Department of Commerce; population, income, and employment statistics for Montana cities and counties; and federal procurement in the six-state region.

Contact:
Mr. Gary Morehouse
Business Division
Department of Commerce
1424 Ninth Avenue
Helena, MT 59620
(406) 444–2787
fax: (406) 444–2808

Contact:
Mr. Jerry Tavegia
Business Division
Department of Commerce
1424 Ninth Avenue
Helena, MT 59620
(406) 444–4378
fax: (406) 444–2808

Contacts:
Ms. Delrene Rasmussen
(406) 444–4153
Mr. Jim Burns
(406) 444–4127
Mr. Gary Faulkner
(406) 444–4780
Business Division
Department of Commerce
1424 Ninth Avenue
Helena, MT 59620
fax: (406) 444–2808

Mr. Al Jones
(406) 245–9989
(SBDC/Billings)

Mr. Darryl Berger
(406) 587–3113
(SBDC/Bozeman)

The division administers **Community Development Block Grant** funding for economic development projects. This federally funded grant program awards approximately $1.3 million annually to Montana cities, towns, and counties for re-lending by the local government to private business projects. Applications are made to the division by the local government sponsoring the project. Projects are selected for funding based on a number of criteria, including project feasibility, economic impact, and job creation for low- to moderate-income persons.

The **Certified Communities Program** is a statewide economic development effort designed to educate and stimulate local development organizations, including economic development corporations and chambers of commerce, to exercise optimal influence over their economic environment. The long-term objective of the certified communities program is to establish an active network of local development organizations statewide that will respond professionally and consistently to local economic development concerns and opportunities. The network of certified communities receives out-of-state location inquiries forwarded by the Montana Department of Commerce and serves as the initial intake mechanism for referral of new business clients to the state's Small Business Development Center program.

The **Finance Technical Assistance Program** provides consulting and training to businesses in the areas of financial analysis, financial planning, loan packaging, industrial revenue bonding, state and private capital sources, and business tax incentives. The program is also designed to work with communities, businesses, and financial institutions to encourage the use of various public sector programs, including Community Development Block Grants (CDBG), Economic Development Administration (EDA) loans and grants, U.S. Small Business Administration loan guarantees, the Montana Board of Investments' (BOI) in-state investment funds, Montana Science and Technology Alliance (MSTA), and the Montana Growth through Agriculture Program.

Mr. Daniel Manning
(406) 752–5222
(SBDC/Kalispell)

Mr. Gary Mariegard
(406) 365–2377
(SBDC/Glendive)

Contact:
Mr. Greg DePuy
Business Division
Department of Commerce
1424 Ninth Avenue
Helena, MT 59620
(406) 444–2750
fax: (406) 444–2808

Contacts:
Mr. Matthew Cohn, Director of International
  Trade
(406) 444–4112
Mr. Moe Wosepka, Canadian Trade Officer
(406) 444–4780
Ms. Tami Lanning, International Promotions
  Specialist
(406) 444–4780
Business Division
Department of Commerce
1424 Ninth Avenue
Helena, MT 59620
fax: (406) 444–2808

Contact:
Ms. Becky Baumann
Business Division
Department of Commerce
1424 Ninth Avenue
Helena, MT 59620
(406) 444–4109
(800) 221–8015 (toll-free, in-state)
fax: (406) 444–2808

Contact:
Mr. Rick Jones
Business Division
Department of Commerce
1424 Ninth Avenue
Helena, MT 59620
(406) 444–4323
fax: (406) 444–2808

Through the **Government Procurement Assistance Program**, the division disseminates current government procurement information to small businesses interested in contracting to state and federal government agencies. It also provides technical assistance, either directly or through cooperating university system units, to assist small businesses in market identification, production management, quality control, cost accounting, and payment procedures for government procurement contracting.

The **International Trade Program** is designed to increase the international sales of Montana manufacturers and service providers. In addition, tourism promotion and reverse investment opportunities are pursued by the international trade staff. One-stop technical assistance to businesses wishing to enter foreign markets is available. Trade shows and foreign buyers are matched to exporters, and special training programs are conducted throughout the year to prepare more firms for export activity. The division maintains a product showroom in the Taipei World Trade Center in Taiwan, and Pacific Rim Trade Offices in Tokyo and Kumamoto, Japan.

The Business Development Division also distributes information concerning **state licensing requirements** for starting and operating a business in Montana and provides assistance to businesses in applying for licenses and permits. The division also serves as an advocate for small businesses in their dealings with government. An in-state, toll-free telephone number is available for licensing and advocacy information. (Calls cannot be transferred to other departments of government.)

The **Business Location Program** publicizes and advertises Montana firms planning relocations or expansions. The program initiates and develops relations with target industries and individual firms, and prepares and presents location data in response to inquiries received by the department. The program also works closely with local development organizations in their efforts to locate new firms to their communities.

Contacts:
Mr. Gene Marcille
(406) 444–4392
Mr. Jim Burns
(406) 444–4127
Business Division
Department of Commerce
1424 Ninth Avenue
Helena, MT 59620
fax: (406) 444–2808

Mr. Gary Mariegard
(406) 365–2377
(SBDC/Glendive)

Contact:
Ms. Becky Baumann
Business Division
Department of Commerce
1424 Ninth Avenue
Helena, MT 59620
(406) 444–4109
fax: (406) 444–2808

Contacts:
Mr. Evan McKinney, State Director
Ms. Delrene Rasmussen, Deputy Director
Montana Small Business Development
    Center
Department of Commerce
1424 Ninth Avenue
Helena, MT 59620
(406) 444–4780

Marketing Assistance staff members work with individual small businesses and trade associations to develop and expand outlets for products manufactured or processed in Montana. Products of Montana manufacturers are represented at selected trade shows both in the United States and foreign countries.

The **Montana Product Promotion Program** is designed to elevate the status of Montana-made products in the marketplace, and also serves to educate Montanans about the diversity of products manufactured in their state. As part of this program, a full-color "Made in Montana" logo is available to manufacturers of products that have a minimum of 50 percent of their value added in Montana. The department operates an extensive public awareness campaign using television, newspaper, outdoor, and radio advertising to encourage Montanans to "Look for the Label."

In response to a private sector recommendation, the state has implemented the **Montana Ambassador Program** to complement the department's business location, retention, marketing, and Montana promotion efforts. The program is made up of approximately 200 business and university leaders from throughout the state. Members familiarize out-of-state business executives and tour operators with Montana as a place in which to do business and as a travel destination. Additionally, ambassadors work with Montana manufacturers to help them market their products outside the state, and they assist the state in hosting foreign visitors and trade delegations. The program is funded by its members and staffed by the Department of Commerce.

The **Small Business Development Center** (SBDC), with headquarters at the Department of Commerce in Helena and subcenters across the state, acts as the outreach arm of the Business Division, providing counseling and training to businesses in the areas of finance, marketing, data management, and government contracting. SBDC officers travel the state to bring direct technical assistance to small businesses in their own communities. The SBDC program is jointly funded by the Montana Department of Commerce and the U.S. Small Business Administration. A listing of all Montana Small Business Development Centers and subcenters is in Appendix A of this directory.

Board of Investments

Contact:
Mr. Robert M. Pancich, Assistant Investment
  Officer
Board of Investments
Capitol Station
Helena, MT 59620–0125
(406) 442–1970
fax: (406) 449–6579

The **Board of Investments' Office of Development Finance** manages a series of small business loan programs. The board's responsibility is to strengthen and diversify the state's economy through prudent investments in qualifying Montana businesses. The board's programs are designed to make available long-term, fixed-rate financing to businesses for a variety of needs.

Coal Tax Loans are limited to investments in businesses that will bring long-term benefits to the Montana economy. Priority is given to businesses that will create jobs without displacing existing jobs in other Montana businesses. While a minimum or maximum loan limit has not been established, loans of $500,000 to $3 million are targeted.

Through the **Interest Rate Reduction Program**, the board will provide an interest rate reduction based on the number of jobs created over a two-year period from the time the loan is delivered to the board. Full credit will be allowed for each job created that pays at least 100 percent of the average wage as determined by the quarterly statistical report published by the Montana Department of Labor. Partial credit will be allowed for each 25-percent increment above or below the average wage. No partial credit will be given unless one whole job is created. The interest rate reduction shall be calculated as .05 percent reduction for each job created up to a maximum of 2.50 percent.

Through the **Federal Guaranteed Loan Program**, the board may fund a small business loan by purchasing the guaranteed portion of any federally backed loan, such as those guaranteed through the U.S. Small Business Administration, the Farmer's Home Administration, and the Economic Development Administration. The financing can be used toward working capital, inventory, equipment, real property, or similar items. The interest rate to the board is set at 110 percent of the rate for U.S. Treasury bonds of a like or similar maturity for monthly payment loans, and 115 percent for annual payment loans.

Through the **Business Loan Participation Program**, the board may fund a small business loan by purchasing from the originating lender up to 80 percent of the loan amount. Unencumbered land, buildings, and equipment may be financed through this program. The financial institutions service the entire loan and receive a servicing fee in addition to the board's quoted interest rate. The board participates in the security for the loan proportionally to the board's share of the loan. The interest rate to the board is set at 120 percent of the rate for U.S. Treasury bonds of a like or similar maturity for monthly payment loans.

The **Economic Development Linked Deposit** (EDLD) program offers businesses extended-term, fixed-rate financing for working capital, inventory, or real property. The board places a long-term deposit, at the pre-established rate, with the financial institution originating the qualifying business loan. The proceeds of the deposit must be used to finance a long-term fixed rate loan to the applicant business. The rate and terms to the borrower are linked to the rate and terms of the EDLD. The interest rate to the board is set at 105 percent of the rate for U.S. Treasury bonds of like or similar maturity for monthly payment loans.

Under the **"Stand Alone" Industrial Revenue Bond Program**, the Board of Investments issues bonds on a "stand alone" basis to Montana borrowers. The board acts as an issuing authority to allow exemption of interest on a qualifying loan. The originating business assumes total risk on the financed project. The project owner is required to pay the bond counsel fees and the board's administrative and financing fees. Program eligibility is restricted primarily to manufacturing enterprises.

The **Conservation Reserve Enhancement Program** offers Montana farmers the opportunity to obtain a lump sum amount from their federal Conservation Reserve Program (CRP) payments. Through the board's program, a farmer can receive a loan against future CRP payments. This loan is then repaid by the CRP contract, which the farmer pledges to the board. The proceeds of the loan must be used for direct agricultural purposes in the state such as debt reduction, working capital, or equipment. The board requires a first mortgage on the CRP acres.

Department of Agriculture

Contact:
Mr. Clyve Rooney, Marketing Program
    Manager
Montana Department of Agriculture
Agricultural Development Division
Agricultural/Livestock Building
Capitol Station
Helena, MT 59620
(406) 444–2402
fax: (406) 444–5409

The **Montana Department of Agriculture Marketing Program** provides market enhancement and development assistance to Montana's agricultural producers, agribusiness, and value-added processors. The marketing program seeks to develop and enhance domestic and foreign markets for Montana's agricultural products. Transportation and product movement through the state are also areas of focus and research assistance. Crop, livestock, and grain movement data are summarized for market information purposes.

Contact:
Mr. Michael E. Murphy, Administrator
Agricultural Development Division
Montana Department of Agriculture
Agriculture/Livestock Building
Capitol Station
Helena, MT 59620
(406) 444–2402
fax: (406) 444–5409

The **Agriculture Development Council** manages a portion of the coal severance tax funds to strengthen and diversify the agriculture industry by investing in innovations in agricultural production, processing, and marketing. These investments aim at expanding business opportunities and creating new jobs. The **Montana Growth through Agriculture Program** allows the state to leverage coal tax funds with private capital to improve the agricultural business climate in Montana. The council is authorized to fund the following activities: foreign and domestic market development activities, agricultural business incubators in towns with a population of 15,000 or less, agricultural technological research and transfer, seed capital loans for development and commercialization of new products and processes, and foreign trade office activities.

SBA 504 Certified Development Companies

Contact:
Ms. Robyn Young, Chief Executive Officer
Montana Community Development Finance
    Corporation
P.O. Box 916
Helena, MT 59624
(406) 442–3261
fax: (406) 443–0429

The **Montana Community Finance Corporation** is certified under the U.S. Small Business Administration's 504 Program, and lends to small and medium-size businesses at fixed rates for terms of 10 to 20 years. Companies must create one job for every $15,000 they receive in financing. A 504 loan is funded through the sale of a debenture that is guaranteed by the SBA for up to $750,000 or 40 percent of the total cost of land, buildings, and equipment.

Contact:
Mr. Jeffrey D. Leuthold, Executive Director
Economic Development Corporation of
Yellowstone County
490 North 31st, TW II #107
Billings, MT 59101
(406) 245–0415
(406) 245–5555

The **Economic Development Corporation** is certified under the SBA 504 program, which combines first and second mortgage positions to provide long-term financing for equipment or land and buildings, either new or existing construction. Projects range from $125,000 to $1,875,000. The program allows a 10-percent equity position with a 20-year term and a fixed rate.

Disadvantaged Business and Women Business Procurement Assistance

Contact:
Mr. Raymond Brown, Chief
Civil Rights Bureau
Montana Department of Transportation
2701 Prospect Avenue
Helena MT 59620
(406) 444–6331
fax: (406) 444–6363

The **Montana Department of Transportation, Civil Rights Bureau**, was developed to assist disadvantaged business enterprises (DBEs) and women business enterprises (WBEs) obtain federally funded state highway contracts. The bureau also publishes a civil rights newsletter and a DBE *Directory of Area Highway Contractors*.

Census and Economic Development Center

Contact:
Ms. Patricia Roberts, Program Manager
Census and Economic Information Center
Department of Commerce
1424 Ninth Avenue
Helena, MT 59620
(406) 444–2896
fax: (406) 444–2808

The **Census and Economic Information Center** (CEIC) serves as a central location for businesses, government agencies, and the general public to obtain demographic, economic, and business information for research, planning, and decisionmaking purposes. CEIC prepares *County Profiles*, which contain data on health, education, housing, and other economic statistics on Montana counties.

Community Development Block Grant Program

Contact:
Mr. Gus Byrom, Program Manager
CDBG, Local Government Assistance
Division
Department of Commerce
Cogswell Building, Room C–211
Helena, MT 59620
(406) 444–3757
fax: (406) 444–2606

The **Montana Community Development Block Program** (CDBG) is a federally funded competitive grant program that assists Montana cities, towns, and counties in meeting their greatest community development needs. All projects must be designed to principally benefit low and moderate income persons or families. The program awards approximately $5 million annually in grants to local governments for a variety of economic development, housing, and public facility projects. At least 10 percent of funds awarded are set aside for economic development projects.

Port of Montana

Contact:
Mr. Ed Morris, Business Manager
Port of Montana
P.O. Box 3641
Butte, MT 59702
(406) 723–4321
fax: (406) 782–8510

The **Port of Montana Port Authority** provides access to major overseas shippers and provides transloading of materials from rail to truck, truck to rail, and into containers for overseas shipment. The Port offers U.S. Customs Service and general warehouse storage.

Institute for Tourism and Recreation Research

Contact:
Dr. Stephen F. McCool, Director
Institute for Tourism and Recreation
   Research
School of Forestry, University of Montana
Missoula, MT 59812
(406) 243–5406
fax: (406) 243–4510

The **Institute for Tourism and Recreation Research** serves as the research arm for the state's tourism and recreation industry. Its overall mission is to provide information that will help the industry make informed decisions about promotion and management. It is administered by the Montana Forest and Conservation Experiment Station at the University of Montana's School of Forestry, and is funded by a portion of the state's accommodations tax. The research program of the institute is developed in cooperation with the Governor's Tourism Advisory Council.

Governor's Advisory Council or Task Force

Contact:
Mr. Evan McKinney, Director of Business
   Assistance
Department of Commerce
1424 Ninth Avenue
Helena, MT 59620
(406) 444–4780

The governor does not have a small business advisory council or task force, but has designated Evan McKinney as the state's small business advocate.

Legislative Committees and Subcommittees

Small business concerns are handled by the House Committee on Business and Economic Development and by the Senate Committee on Business and Industry.

Contacts:

Representative Robert J. Pavlovich
Chairman
House Committee on Business and
Economic Development
State Capitol, Room 138
Helena, MT 59620
(406) 444–3064

Senator Gene Thayer
Chairman
Senate Committee on Business
and Industry
State Capitol, Room 138
Helena, MT 59620
(406) 444–3064

Legislation

Legislation adopted by the 1989 legislature of importance to small business includes the following:

- H.B. 649 increases from $1,500 to $2,500 the maximum amount of a claim that could be heard in small claims court. This increase allows small business owners to resolve more small dollar disputes quickly and with less expense than going to county court.

- H.B. 603 establishes a petroleum storage tank cleanup fee, to be paid by gasoline distributors. It further provides for the use of such fees to reimburse owners and operators of petroleum storage tanks for expenses incurred when cleaning up property damaged by leaking petroleum storage tanks.

- H.B. 20 reduces personal property taxes on certain classes of business equipment.

- The Montana Supreme Court upheld the two-year-old Montana Wrongful Discharge from Employment Act. The act protects workers from arbitrary dismissal but also limits their court awards if they win lawsuits against a former employer. Under the act, employees who do not belong to a union or have individual contracts gain broad protection from arbitrary dismissals. The law forbids firing without showing "good cause." In exchange for these benefits, recovery for emotional distress is excluded. Punitive damages are barred except in cases where the employer demonstrates fraud or malice.

No regular legislative session was held in 1990.

Legislation of importance to small businesses enacted by the 1991 Montana Legislature includes the following:

- H.B. 693 allows insurance companies to write a "bare-bones" health insurance policy for small businesses. Such a policy will drastically reduce mandatory benefits and should substantially reduce premium costs. To qualify for this plan, firms must have 20 or fewer employees who work at least 20 hours per week; have been in business in Montana for at least 12 months; and have made no contribution to any employee health coverage during the past 12 months. Employers adopting this health program will be allowed a tax credit of up to $25 per month per employee.

- H.B. 477 provides $3.2 million of in-state investment money, which will be packaged into $20,000 loans for businesses with fewer than 10 employees and less than $500,000 in gross revenues. These loans can be matched with local economic development money in order to provide increased funding.

- H.B. 703 allows the Science and Technology Alliance to fund up to $2.5 million in venture capital deals (but not necessarily involving high technology businesses).

- S.B. 242 allows the Science and Technology Alliance to provide $5.5 million in long-term research and development loans. Such funds will supply seed money for new ideas that could develop into new Montana businesses.

- S.B. 26 increases the size of the coal-tax loan program for in-state small businesses by nearly $50 million.

- H.B. 452 allows local governments, which can give up to 50 percent in property tax reductions to new, expanding industries, to lower the threshold for eligible investments of real property or equipment from $250,000 to $50,000.

- H.B. 970 enhances H.B. 452 by allowing the 50-percent tax break to businesses that earn at least 50 percent of their income from out-of-state, rather than requiring a manufacturing base.

- S.B. 420 mandates that the State Fund and any private insurance company offering workers' compensation insurance policies in Montana must offer a deductible policy by July 1991.

State Small Business Conferences

Contact:
Mr. Jerry Christison, Director
Business Development
U.S. Small Business Administration
528 Federal Building
301 South Park Street
Helena, MT 59626
(406) 449–5381

The **Governor's Business Growth and Development Conference** was held in Billings from September 19–20, 1991. The conference featured Montana manufacturers and offered workshops on assistance available to business from state and federal agencies.

The **Governor's Conference on Tourism** was held May 21–22, 1990, in Missoula, Montana. This conference was designed to provide tourist-based businesses with training and information about the tourism industry in Montana.

Nebraska

Small Business Offices, Programs, and Activities

Nebraska Department of Economic Development

Contact:
Mr. Steve Buttress, C.E.D., Director
Nebraska Department of Economic
  Development
P.O. Box 94666
301 Centennial Mall South
Lincoln, NE 68509–4666
(402) 471-3747
(800) 426-6505 (toll-free)

Contact:
Mr. Jack Ruff, Director
Existing Business Assistance Division
Nebraska Department of Economic
  Development
P.O. Box 94666
301 Centennial Mall South
Lincoln, NE 68509–4666
(402) 471-3769
(800) 426-6505 (toll-free)

Contact:
Mr. Steve Williams, Business Assistance
  Manager
Existing Business Assistance Division
Nebraska Department of Economic
  Development
P.O. Box 94666
301 Centennial Mall South
Lincoln, NE 68509–4666
(402) 471-3782
(800) 426-6505 (toll-free)

The **Nebraska Department of Economic Development's** primary mission is to support the creation, expansion, and retention of businesses and to provide leadership and direction in enterprise development. Its divisions include Existing Business Assistance, Business Recruitment, Research, Community and Rural Development, Travel and Tourism, and Field Service.

The **Existing Business Assistance Division** provides a referral service to business owners and others seeking information or assistance in several areas, including exporting, procurement, job training, and general information on starting a business. The division also has financial packagers who help businesses understand a variety of public finance programs and who prepare applications for financial assistance under the department's economic development finance programs.

The **One-Stop Business Assistance Center** offers information on economic development programs and on regulations, licenses, fees, patents, trademarks, and state requirements for operating a business in Nebraska.

The **Community Development Block Grant Program** (CDBG) is a federal program administered by the state to help small cities address economic development issues—such as chronic unemployment—through business development initiatives. Some job creation activities for low- and middle-income residents must be a part of each CDBG project. The state awards CDBG funds to local governments, who in turn provide the money to eligible businesses.

Assistance in designing and implementing **Industrial Training Programs** is available from the Department of Economic Development, in cooperation with various training entities throughout the state. Programs are designed to provide short-term training for new hires and for upgrading skills of existing employees.

Nebraska companies interested in selling to the federal government can obtain procurement assistance from the Department of Economic Development's **Existing Business Assistance Division**. The agency can help identify business opportunities as well as aid in understanding bidding procedures and project requirements. Post-award assistance is also available in areas of quality control and inspection procedures.

Contact:
Mr. David Gilfillan, Development Finance
    Manager
Existing Business Assistance Division
Nebraska Department of Economic
    Development
P.O. Box 94666
301 Centennial Mall South
Lincoln, NE 68509–4666
(402) 471–3765
(800) 426–6505 (toll-free)

Contact:
Ms. Pat Prieb, Job Training Liaison
Existing Business Assistance Division
Nebraska Department of Economic
    Development
P.O. Box 94666
301 Centennial Mall South
Lincoln, NE 68509–4666
(402) 471–3780
(800) 426–6505 (toll-free)

Contacts:
Mr. Jack Ruff, Director
Existing Business Assistance Division
Nebraska Department of Economic
    Development
P.O. Box 94666
301 Centennial Mall South
Lincoln, NE 68509–4666
(402) 471–3769
(800) 426–6505 (toll-free)

Mr. Michael Reeves, Government Marketing
    Specialist
Existing Business Assistance Division
Nebraska Department of Economic
    Development
200 South Silber
North Platte, NE 69101
(308) 535–8213

Contact:
Ms. Susan Rouch, Export Promotion
  Manager
Existing Business Assistance Division
Nebraska Department of Economic
  Development
P.O. Box 94666
301 Centennial Mall South
Lincoln, NE 68509–4666
(402) 471–4668
(800) 426–6505 (toll-free)

Exporters and potential exporters can learn about **international trade** by contacting the Existing Business Assistance Division, whose staff works closely with the U.S. and Foreign Commercial Service Office and the U.S. Small Business Administration office in Omaha. A variety of services are available, including the following:

- Publications, such as *The International Commerce Guide* and *International Trade Directory*, to help business owners understand the export process, assess their company and product potential, research markets, identify local resources for export assistance, and successfully market their products abroad.

- Workshops on various aspects of international trade.

- Help in reaching foreign audiences through trade missions and trade shows.

- Trade leads updated on a daily basis and made available to Nebraska firms on hard copy, as well as through the Existing Business Assistance Division's Electronic Bulletin Board. This information is provided free of charge to Nebraska firms.

- Consulting services to help organize export programs.

Contact:
Ms. Jenne Garvey Rodriguez, Director
Community and Rural Development Division
Nebraska Department of Economic
  Development
P.O. Box 94666
301 Centennial Mall South
Lincoln, NE 68509–4666
(402) 471–4388
(800) 426–6505 (toll-free)

The **Community and Rural Development Division** offers financial assistance for rural infrastructure and technical assistance for local rural development programs.

Small Business Development Centers

Contact:
Mr. Robert Bernier, State Director
Nebraska Business Development Center
University of Nebraska-Omaha
1313 Farnam-on-the-Mall, Suite 132
Omaha, NE 68182–0248
(402) 595–2381

The **Nebraska Business Development Center** (NBDC) is a cooperative program of the U.S. Small Business Administration and the University of Nebraska at Omaha. Providing management assistance to small businesses, NBDC offers individual management consulting, workshops and seminars, business and financial planning analysis, feasibility studies, monthly business reports, special studies, studies on selected rural communities, market research, and identification of sources of capital.

The lead Small Business Development Center is located in Omaha at the University of Nebraska. Subcenters are located in Chadron, Kearney, Lincoln, North Platte, Peru, Scottsbluff, and Wayne. A listing of all Small Business Development Centers and subcenters in Nebraska is in Appendix A of this directory.

Nebraska Investment Finance Authority

Contact:
Mr. Larry Bare, Executive Director
Nebraska Investment Finance Authority
1033 "O" Street, Suite 218
Lincoln, NE 68508
(402) 434–3900

The **Nebraska Investment Finance Authority** (NIFA) is an independent, nonprofit, quasi-state agency that provides lower cost financing for manufacturing facilities, certain farm property, health care, and residential developments. NIFA seeks to encourage private financing to stimulate economic activity in Nebraska. NIFA has no taxing authority and receives no state appropriations; it borrows money by issuing notes and bonds.

NIFA established a **Small Industrial Development Bond Program** to help small Nebraska-based companies. Industrial Development Revenue Bonds are available to provide financing for industrial or manufacturing projects. Bond proceeds can buy land, plants, equipment, and on-site utilities. Issuance of bonds can be made through local units of government and NIFA, and are tax exempt with a maximum of $10 million.

SBA 504 Certified Development Companies

Contact:
Mr. Alan Eastman, Program Director
Nebraska Economic Development
    Corporation (NEDCO)
2631 "O" Street
Lincoln, NE 68510
(402) 475–2795

The **Nebraska Economic Development Corporation** (NEDCO) is a statewide Certified Development Agency certified by the U.S. Small Business Administration. Through the SBA 504 program, NEDCO helps to provide small businesses with long-term, low-interest, fixed-asset financing. A private lending institution provides up to 50 percent of total project costs. The SBA provides up to 40 percent (not to exceed $750,000). The term of the SBA portion is 10 or 20 years, based upon life of the asset; private lenders set their own terms.

Advanced Technology Programs

Contact:
Mr. Thomas Spilker, Director
Nebraska Technical Assistance Center
W191 Nebraska Hall—UNL
Lincoln, NE 68588–0535
(402) 471–5600
(800) 742–8000 (toll-free, in-state)

The **Nebraska Technical Assistance Center** (NTAC) is an engineering and technical outreach service established to provide assistance for engineering, technical, and scientific problems faced by small business. The NTAC was established through the cooperative efforts of the Nebraska Department of Economic Development and the University of Nebraska at Lincoln. Its primary objectives are to improve productivity and to promote technology transfer.

State Small Business Ombudsman

Contact:
Mr. Marshall Lux, Ombudsman
State Capitol, Room 807
P.O. Box 94712
Lincoln, NE 68509–4712
(402) 471–2035
(800) 742–7690 (toll-free, in-state)

Nebraska's Ombudsman receives complaints from small businesses on matters concerning state regulations, laws, and agencies.

Nebraska Department of Education

Contact:
Mr. Gregg Christensen
Entrepreneurship Projects
P.O. Box 94987
301 Centennial Mall South
Lincoln, NE 68509–4987
(402) 471–4803

The Nebraska Department of Education, Division of Education Services, is an active member of the **International Entrepreneurship Education Consortium**, with more than 30 other departments of education, private industry members, and four-year institutions. The purpose of the consortium is to infuse entrepreneurship education into vocational programs. Accomplishments have included a Model Programs Synopsis; Entrepreneurship Education Database; Resource Guide; Successful Entrepreneurs Videotape; a newsletter, *Entreprenews and Views*; and sponsorship of annual forums on entrepreneurship. The PACE (Program for Acquiring Competence in Entrepreneurship) curriculum was revised in 1990–91; the three levels of student modules and teacher's modules were published in 1991.

An **Entrepreneurship Education Curriculum Assistance Program** and related Nebraska materials have been disseminated to more than 300 Nebraska vocational education teachers in a series of workshops since 1988. These vocational education teachers were provided curriculum materials during one-hour workshops; the response of the workshop participants was overwhelmingly positive. Participants included teachers of agricultural education, business, home economics, industrial education, and marketing.

In addition, a newsletter, **The Highlighter**, is published four times a year to update marketing and entrepreneurship teachers on trends in national and international entrepreneurship.

Department personnel are available to provide assistance to individual school districts and teachers as they enhance current course offerings and update curriculum.

Governor's Advisory Council or Task Force

Nebraska does not have a governor's small business advisory council or task force.

Legislative Committees and Subcommittees

Questions concerning small business legislation can be directed to the Business and Labor Committee; Banking, Commerce, and Insurance Committee; or the Research Division of the Department of Economic Development.

Contacts:
Mr. Stu Miller, Deputy Director
Nebraska Department of Economic
  Development
P.O. Box 94666
301 Centennial Mall South
Lincoln, NE 68509–4666
(402) 471–3783
(800) 426–6505 (toll-free)

Senator George Coordsen
Chairman
Business and Labor Committee
State Capitol, Room 1406
Lincoln, NE 68509

Senator David Landis
Chairman
Banking, Commerce and Insurance
  Committee
State Capitol, Room 1116
Lincoln, NE 68509

Legislation

Recently enacted Nebraska legislation that affects small business includes the following:

- L.B. 297, which changes the minimum wage rate and provides for a training wage rate. The Nebraska minimum wage would be increased by this bill—currently, Nebraska's minimum wage is $4.25 per hour, and $2.13 per hour for tipped employees. Section three of the bill allows for a training wage (sub-minimum wage) to be paid, similar to federal law. Both the state and the federal training wage provision expire on March 31, 1993. From July 1, 1991, to March 31, 1993, this wage will be $3.61 per hour (both under this bill and the federal law).

- L.B. 840, the Municipal Economic Development Act, is a constitutional amendment allowing the use of municipal general tax revenues for local economic development. Only general property and general sales tax revenues may be used.

- L.B. 829, which eliminates certain items from the personal property tax exemption. This bill removes business machinery and equipment from personal property taxation and establishes new taxes and fees on business and agriculture amounting to $39.2 million. The provisions of this legislation are as follows:

(1) Removes all personal property (business machinery and equipment) from the tax rolls for tax year 1991 only. This property was scheduled to return to the tax rolls for tax year 1992, unless the legislature acted to change the law before then.

(2) Imposes a 2-percent surcharge on depreciation.

(3) Imposes a 15-percent corporate income tax surcharge on taxable incomes in excess of $200,000.

(4) Reduces the retailers' sales tax collection fee from 3 percent to 1.5 percent.

(5) Imposes the 5 percent state sales tax on utility energy purchases by generators. This sales tax also applies to manufacturers, processors, and hospitals, with a $100,000 cap per facility.

(6) Imposes a corporate filing fee of $150 on every corporation.

State Small Business Conferences

Several conferences are held each year in Nebraska pertaining to small business in the areas of exporting, government procurement, finance, and management.

Nevada

Small Business Offices, Programs, and Activities

Statewide Certified Development Company

Contact:
Mr. Harry H. Weinberg, President
Nevada State Development Corporation
350 South Center Street, Suite 310
Reno, NV 89501
(702) 323-3625

The **Nevada State Development Corporation** (NSDC) assists businesses in financing their expansion in order to create permanent full-time jobs throughout the state. NSDC offers three programs to businesses: SBA 504 fixed asset loans, SBA 7(a) loans, and Export-Import Bank loans for international trade.

SBA 504 Fixed Asset Loans are long-term, fixed rate, low down payment, second-mortgage financing for real estate and fixed assets to owner-operated businesses. As a Certified Development Company, the NSDC is authorized by the U.S. Small Business Administration to offer and package loans and obtain private sector, first-mortgage financing and SBA second-mortgage approval on a statewide basis.

SBA 7(a) Loans provide SBA guarantees for up to 90 percent of loans made by banks to businesses for a wide range of financing purposes. The program provides assistance to borrowers in packaging their loan requests and in locating a bank to make the loan.

The **Export-Import Bank Loan Program** provides loan guarantees to firms seeking to become involved in international trade. The NSDC is certified by the Export-Import Bank of the United States to market and package loans to individuals who wish to export. The programs include working capital guarantees to assist in the production of the export item, medium and long-term financing to finance foreign buyers of American goods, and providing insurance for foreign accounts receivable.

Department of Commerce

Contact:
Ms. Jolene B. Rose, Deputy Director
Department of Commerce
1665 Hot Springs Road
Carson City, NV 89710
(702) 687–4250

The **Industrial Revenue Bond Program** was introduced through the Department of Commerce in 1981 as a mechanism to help companies expand or build new facilities through the use of tax-exempt financing. In 1987, the focus of the program was narrowed by the U.S. Congress to allow only manufacturing concerns to use composite tax-exempt bonds for their programs. The program offers low cost, long-term tax-exempt financing of up to $10 million to encourage new facilities or expansion that is compatible with Nevada's plan for economic development and diversification.

The **Venture Capital Bond Program**, established in 1987, enables the Department of Commerce to issue up to $100 million in bonds to fund venture capital projects in Nevada. Studies are under way to determine what needs exist in this area and whether the bonds can be marketed.

Nevada Small Business Development Center

Contact:
Mr. Sam Males, State Director
Nevada Small Business Development
   Center
University of Nevada-Reno
College of Business Administration
Business Building, Room 411
Reno, NV 89557–0100
(702) 784–1717

The **Nevada Small Business Development Center** (NSBDC) is a joint effort by the University of Nevada-Reno and the U.S. Small Business Administration to provide business development and marketing assistance to small business. The NSBDC provides free services such as planning, counseling, strategy formulation, and education programs. The NSBDC is headquartered on the University of Nevada-Reno campus and has several subcenters throughout the state. A complete listing of Small Business Development Centers and subcenters in Nevada is in Appendix A of this directory.

Commission on Economic Development

Contact:
Ms. Lori Martin, Small Business
   Representative
Commission on Economic Development
Capitol Complex
Carson City, NV 89710
(702) 687–4325

Nevada aids small businesses through its Small Business Revitalization Program and Procurement Outreach Program.

The **Small Business Revitalization** (SBR) program was introduced in January 1983. SBR encourages private lender participation on creative loan packaging, drawing on a variety of public programs. Among these are the U.S. Small Business Administration's 504 loan and 7(a) loan guarantee programs and the Nevada Revolving Fund. SBR also gives Nevada small businesses access to low-cost, long-term financing to encourage their expansion and diversification into job creating activities. One hundred and five loans totaling more than $50 million have stimulated the creation of over 1,500 jobs.

Contacts:
Mr. Ray Horner, Program Director
Procurement Outreach Program
Commission on Economic Development
Capitol Complex
Carson City, NV 89710
(702) 687–4325

Mr. Jerry Tactagan, Southern Nevada
   Regional Manager
Procurement Outreach Program
Commission on Economic Development
3770 Howard Hughes Parkway, Suite 295
Las Vegas, NV 89158
(702) 486–7282

The **Procurement Outreach Program** (POP) was established in October 1985 through a cooperative agreement with the Defense Logistics Agency of the U.S. Department of Defense. POP is designed to assist small and disadvantaged businesses in Nevada to obtain and complete federal government contracts. POP has offices in Carson City and Las Vegas. Information and technical assistance is provided for firms seeking to bid on government contracts. POP is staffed by former procurement officials from the U.S. Department of Defense. Since the inception of the program, POP has assisted small businesses in obtaining 254 government contracts totaling more than $24 million dollars. POP's activities add to Nevada's economic diversification by encouraging expansion of the manufacturing and service sectors into government contracting, thereby creating jobs for Nevada workers.

POP also provides **Small Business Innovation Research** (SBIR) assistance to Nevada firms. The office helps firms obtain copies of the SBIR Program Solicitation from federal agencies, and offers briefings on the SBIR program and suggestions regarding proposal preparation. Proposal critique, seminars, and workshops on the SBIR program are also available to prospective applicants.

Contacts:
Ms. Sarah Mesereau
Mr. John Meder
Rural Action Program
Commission on Economic Development
Capitol Complex
Carson City, NV 89710
(702) 687–4325

Contact:
Ms. Helen Myers, Director
State of Nevada Office of Small Business
Commission on Economic Development
3770 Howard Hughes Parkway, Suite 295
Las Vegas, NV 89158
(702) 486–7282

The **Rural Action Program** consists of intensive local training programs, data base and references assistance, local economic development plans, community assessments, and advertising and public relations cooperative programs.

Governor's Advisory Council or Task Force

The **Office of Small Business** was created by the governor in 1989 and is part of Nevada's Commission on Economic Development. The mission of the Office of Small Business is to "encourage, assist, and support the survival, expansion and diversification of new, emerging and established Nevada small businesses." These goals are accomplished though a variety of programs and activities, under the supervision of its director. The office is charged with serving as an advocate for the development and coordination of programs to enhance the economic climate for small firms in the state. Additionally, the office acts as a liaison between small firms and other state agencies if problems arise. Information and assistance on financing and procurement is also available.

The **Governor's Small Business Council** was created to assist in the accomplishment of these goals. The board is composed of 33 individuals, appointed by the governor, representing all industry sectors and geographic areas of the state. The council's activities include advising the governor and the legislature on issues affecting small firms in Nevada; recommending regulatory and statutory changes to support small business development and expansion; addressing the special needs of women- and minority-owned businesses; and enhancing export opportunities for small businesses.

Legislative Committees and Subcommittees

The following committees handle small business legislation: the Senate Commerce and Labor Committee; the Assembly Commerce Committee; and the Assembly Economic Development, Small Business, and Tourism Committee.

Contacts:

Senator John M. Vergiels
Chairman
Senate Commerce and Labor Committee
Legislative Building, Capitol Complex
Carson City, NV 89710
(702) 687–3557

Assemblyman Gene T. Porter
Chairman
Assembly Commerce Committee
Legislative Building, Capitol Complex
Carson City, NV 89710
(702) 687–3627

Legislation

There was no recent legislation in Nevada specifically targeting small business.

State Small Business Conferences

No recent statewide small business conferences have been reported.

New Hampshire

Small Business Offices, Programs, and Activities

New Hampshire Industrial Development Authority

Contact:
Mr. Clark Chandler, Executive Director
Industrial Development Authority
Four Park Street
Concord, NH 03301
(603) 271–2391

The **New Hampshire Industrial Development Authority** (IDA) assists businesses in all areas of finance, including guaranteeing mortgages, establishing credit, and securing loans. Up to $18 million is available to the authority to carry out its various programs. With the permission of the governor and council, the authority may borrow up to an additional $1 million to protect the interests of the state in any project previously financed. The IDA provides several programs for service to the business community.

Industrial Development Revenue Bond Financing is a vehicle for tax-free development revenue bonds that provide 100-percent financing for eligible projects. Bond proceeds may be used to finance manufacturing facilities or to acquire machinery or equipment. They may also be used to construct facilities for the disposal of waste material, small scale power facilities for producing electric energy, water-powered electric generating facilities, or facilities for the collection, purification, storage, or distribution of water for use by the general public.

Guaranteed Loans are secured by the company pledge of payment and full faith and credit of the state of New Hampshire for partial payment. The IDA may guarantee up to 50 percent of first mortgage loans made by financial institutions to manufacturing or recreational industries that acquire, construct, or reconstruct facilities. There is a guaranty limit of $5 million for any single project, and the loan term may not exceed 25 years.

The **Guarantee Plan for Machinery and Equipment** can guarantee up to 35 percent of a loan for machinery and equipment, with 10 year maximum repayment terms.

Office of Business and Industrial Development

Contact:
Mr. William Pillsbury, Director
Office of Business and Industrial
  Development
172 Pembroke Road
Concord, NH 03302–0856
(603) 271–2591
fax: (603) 271–2629

The **Office of Business and Industrial Development** helps existing New Hampshire businesses as well as companies considering locating in New Hampshire. The office helps businesses review manpower and facility requirements, marketing considerations, support services, and other criteria. Included in these confidential commercial services are location recommendations based on a detailed examination of project requirements; assistance with private and public financial institutions and with the New Hampshire Industrial Development Authority in locating financing for real estate, machinery, and equipment; information on transportation; marketing assistance programs; and assistance in the acquisition and disposal of plant facilities, in mergers and acquisitions, in capital formation, and in product diversification and development.

Corporate Division

Contact:
Corporate Division
New Hampshire Department of State
State House Annex
Concord, NH 03301
(603) 271–3244
fax: (603) 271–2361

The **Corporate Division** of the New Hampshire Department of State is responsible for recording and effecting the commencement of business in New Hampshire by private concerns. Under New Hampshire law, there are four basic business organizations: (1) proprietorship, (2) general partnership, (3) limited partnerships, and (4) corporation. The Corporate Division is responsible for recording business identities and administering state legislation affecting the commencement of business.

New Hampshire Department of Revenue Administration

Contact:
Mr. Stanley R. Arnold, Jr., Commissioner
New Hampshire Department of Revenue
  Administration
61 South Spring Street
Concord, NH 03301
(603) 271–2191
fax: (603) 271–2361

The **New Hampshire Department of Revenue Administration** is the tax collection agency for New Hampshire state government and is responsible for processing all tax returns, handling compliance and collection of delinquent taxes, and directing audits of individuals and business organizations required to submit New Hampshire state tax returns. An 8-percent tax on income from conducting business activity within the state of New Hampshire is known as the Business Profits Tax.

228

New Hampshire Department of Labor

Contact:
Ms. Katherine Barger, Director
New Hampshire Department of Labor
State Office Park South
95 Pleasant Street
Concord, NH 03301
(603) 271–3176
fax: (603) 271–2361

The **New Hampshire Department of Labor** administers the state Workers' Compensation Law (RSA 281) and related administrative rules. If an employee is injured on the job, the employee's medical treatment costs will be paid by the workers' compensation policy. All employers in New Hampshire must obtain this coverage by purchasing an insurance policy through the insurance agent or company of their choice.

Public Information and Permitting Unit

Contact:
Mr. Timothy W. Drew, Administrator
Public Information and Permitting Unit
New Hampshire Department of
    Environmental Services
6 Hazen Drive
Concord, NH 03301
(603) 271–2975
fax: (603) 271–2867

The **Public Information and Permitting (PIP) Unit** was created to help citizens obtain a permit or license from the New Hampshire Department of Environmental Services. The PIP unit's role is to serve as a one-stop contact point for all permit applications; coordinate and streamline the permitting process; track all permits; and provide informational materials to the general public, organizations, government officials, and the media.

Export Assistance

Contact:
Mr. Bill Herman, Program Information
    Officer
Office of Business and Industrial
    Development
172 Pembroke Road
Concord, NH 03302
(603) 271–2591

The **Export Promotion Program**, in cooperation with the U.S. Small Business Administration and the U.S. Department of Commerce, promotes international trade by answering inquiries, making business referrals, and sponsoring foreign trade shows overseas and informational seminars in the state.

New Hampshire State Port Authority

Contact:
Ms. Arlene Cohn, Marketing Director
555 Market Street, Box 506
Portsmouth, NH 03801
(603) 436–8500
fax: (603) 427–0771

The **New Hampshire State Port Authority** is responsible for the management and development of the Port of New Hampshire-Portsmouth and its terminal facilities. The U.S. Department of Commerce has designed the New Hampshire Port Authority as the grantee/operator of Foreign Trade Zone 81, where foreign traders can store, mix, blend, repack, and assemble various commodities with an exemption from normal custom duties and federal excise taxes.

New Hampshire Department of Resources and Economic Development

Contact:
Ms. Dawn Wivell, Trade Specialist
New Hampshire Department of Resources
   and Economic Development
P.O. Box 856
Concord, NH 03302–0856
(603) 271–2591

The **New Hampshire Department of Resources and Economic Development** (DRED) annually publishes *Made in New Hampshire*, a directory of manufacturers and exporters. DRED also negotiates "sister state" and "sister port" agreements, sponsors foreign trade shows and trade missions, manages the visits of foreign trade delegations, and jointly cosponsors seminars with, and partially funds, the New Hampshire International Trade Association.

Small Business Development Centers

Contact:
Ms. Helen Goodman, State Director
Small Business Development Center
University of New Hampshire
108 McConnell Hall
Durham, NH 03824
(603) 862–2200

Small Business Development Centers (SBDCs) provide practical management and technical assistance to present and prospective small business owners. They offer free business counseling and provide analysis, advice, education, and referral services. SBDCs are partially funded by the U.S. Small Business Administration, and are usually affiliated with a state college or university. In New Hampshire, a lead SBDC is located in Durham, at the University of New Hampshire. Subcenters are located in Durham, Keene, Littleton, Manchester, and Plymouth. A complete listing of these centers, including addresses and telephone numbers, is in Appendix A of this directory.

Training and Education

Contact:
Mr. H. Jeffrey Rafin, Director
New Hampshire Department of
   Postsecondary Technical Education
State House Annex, Room 401
Concord, NH 03301
(603) 271–2722
(800) 247–3420 (toll-free, in-state)

Contact:
Mr. Ray O. Worden, Executive Director
New Hampshire Job Training Council, Inc.
64 Old Suncook Road
Concord, NH 03301
(603) 228–9500
(800) 772–7001 (toll-free, in-state)

Contact:
Mr. Jack Jarvis, Director
State Apprenticeship Program
New Hampshire Department of Labor
State Office Park South
95 Pleasant Street
Concord, NH 03301
(603) 271–3176

Contact:
Mr. John J. Ratoff, Commissioner
New Hampshire Department of Employment
   Security
32 South Main Street
Concord, NH 03301–4857
(603) 224–3311
fax: (603) 228–4145

The **New Hampshire Department of Postsecondary Technical Education** administers the New Hampshire Technical Institute at Concord and the six New Hampshire Technical Colleges at Berlin, Claremont, Laconia, Manchester, Nashua, and Stratham. The technical colleges and the institute offer collegiate education preparing students for direct employment in business, industry, health, and service related fields.

The **New Hampshire Job Training Council, Inc.**, (NHJTC), is dedicated to the employment and training needs of the state. NHJTC is run by New Hampshire business leaders, and administers the Job Training Partnership Act to provide businesses with skilled and qualified workers.

The **State Apprenticeship Program** provides for the promotion and development of skilled work force training through coordination of full-time on-the-job training and part-time related instruction. The combination of training and instruction provides the apprentice with an opportunity to learn a skill while earning a living, and also provides the employer with an established development and training program at no cost.

The **Department of Employment Security** (DES) provides training programs to veterans seeking permanent career-oriented employment, as well as to individuals displaced as a result of foreign competition.

Community Development Block Grant Program

Contact:
Mr. Jeffrey Taylor, Director
Office of State Planning
2 1/2 Beacon Street
Concord, NH 03301
(603) 271–2155
fax: (603) 271–1728

The **Community Development Block Grant Program** is administered by the Office of State Planning, part of the governor's office. Grant funds must be requested by a municipality, but may be passed through as a loan to private business. Economic development funding is based on job creation and retention by projects that will generate business activity that will benefit low or moderate income individuals.

Venture Capital Network, Inc.

Contact:
Mr. B.J. Hulen, Acting Director
Venture Capital Network, Inc.
MIT Enterprise Forum of Cambridge, Inc.
201 Vassar Street
Cambridge, NH 02139
(617) 253–7163
fax: (617) 258–7264

Venture Capital Network, Inc., (VCN), was founded as a not-for-profit corporation. VCN provides a formal market where entrepreneurs and other growing concerns needing financing can be linked with individuals of means and other sources of capital.

New Hampshire Business Development Corporation

Contact:
Mr. Jeffrey Pollock
New Hampshire Business Development
   Corporation
1001 Elm Street
Manchester, NH 03103
(603) 623–5500

The **New Hampshire Business Development Corporation** (NHBDC) is a nonprofit, state-chartered lender that is guaranteed by the U.S. Small Business Administration. NHBDC was recently funded by the state through an industrial development bond issue of $2 million.

Governor's Advisory Council or Task Force

Contact:
Office of the Governor
State House
Concord, NH 03301
(603) 271–2121

Small business issues should be addressed directly to the office of the governor.

232

Legislative Committees and Subcommittees

New Hampshire has committees focusing on small business issues in both chambers of the legislature. In the Senate, the Executive Departments Committee acts on small business issues. In the House, the Commerce and Consumer Affairs Committee considers small business matters. The legislature meets annually from January through June. Committees are appointed in December following a November election.

Contacts:

Senator Edward C. Dupont, Jr.
Chairman
Executive Departments Committee
Senate Office, Room 301
State House
Concord, NH 03301
(603) 271–2708

Representative Patricia Foss
Chairman
Commerce and Consumer Affairs
  Committee
State House
Concord, NH 03301
(603) 271–3369

Legislation

In 1990, New Hampshire approved landmark legislation to ensure the consistent, affordable, and equitable operation of the state's workers' compensation system. The time-consuming and expensive litigation process has been replaced with an administrative appeals procedure. In addition, medical reimbursement levels have been established, and worker safety programs have been re-emphasized.

State Small Business Conferences

No recent statewide small business conferences have been reported.

New Jersey

Small Business Offices, Programs, and Activities

Department of Commerce and Economic Development

Contact:
Mr. Charles A. Jones III, Director
Division of Development for Small
   Businesses and Women and Minority
   Businesses
New Jersey Department of Commerce and
   Economic Development
20 West State Street, CN 835
Trenton, NJ 08625
(609) 292–3860

Contact:
Mr. Patrick J. Guidotti, Administrator
Office of Technical Assistance
New Jersey Department of Commerce and
   Economic Development
20 West State Street, CN 835
Trenton, NJ 08625
(609) 292–3860

Contact:
Mr. Hank Diaz, Administrator
Contract Services Unit
Division of Development for Small
   Businesses and Women and Minority
   Businesses
New Jersey Department of Commerce and
   Economic Development
20 West State Street, CN 835
Trenton, NJ 08625
(609) 984–9835
(609) 292–2103 (SAVI–II)

Many of New Jersey's programs that assist small businesses are administered by the **Division of Development for Small Businesses and Women and Minority Businesses**. The mission of this division is to function as an advocate and to provide a central resource for small, women-owned, and minority-owned businesses in dealing with federal, state, and local governments; to provide financial, marketing, procurement, technical, and managerial assistance; and to initiate and encourage training programs for procurement and business development. This division includes the Office of Technical Assistance and the Contract Services Unit.

The **Office of Technical Assistance** offers business expansion and start-up counseling, financial advice, business referrals, and information about franchising and entrepreneurship to New Jersey's small, women, and minority business owners. Additionally, it provides technical assistance regarding management, procurement, operations, acquisitions, joint ventures, and government assistance programs and regulations. Services also include business seminars, workshops and conferences, networking resources, and guest speakers.

Procurement programs are administered by the **Contract Services Unit**. The Department of Commerce and Economic Development and the Department of the Treasury are jointly responsible for implementing the Set-Aside Act for Small, Urban Development, and Micro Business Enterprises. The act requires the 19 departments of the state government and 44 quasi-state agencies (such as commissions and authorities) to establish goals to set aside at least 15 percent of their contracts and purchases for small businesses, 7 percent for Urban Development Enterprises, and 3 percent for Micro Businesses.

The state has compiled a computerized listing of Small, Urban Development Enterprises and Micro Businesses eligible to participate in the set-aside program. The Selective Assistance Vendor Information System (SAVI–II) lists businesses registered to bid on state contracts as well as those wishing to participate in future procurement programs. The state's purchasing officials can access vendors by state commodity code, status (i.e., Urban Development Enterprise or Micro Business), and county.

The **New Jersey Unified Certification Program** for women-owned and minority-owned businesses was established in June 1987. The Contract Services Unit serves as the sole certifying agency, verifying vendors' claims of ownership and control by minorities or women.

Contact:
Chief
Office of Business Advocacy
New Jersey Department of Commerce and
   Economic Development
20 West State Street, CN 829
Trenton, NJ 08625
(609) 292–0700

Contact:
Mr. S. Charles Garofolo, Administrator
Urban Enterprise Zone Program
New Jersey Department of Commerce and
   Economic Development
20 West State Street, CN 829
Trenton, NJ 08625–0829
(609) 292–1912

The **Office of Business Advocacy** acts as an ombudsman, handling complaints and problems of business owners. The office advises companies of necessary permits required for construction and operations. It also monitors—and in many cases expedites—permit applications through the regulatory process. The office also serves as an information source on license, certification, and registration for businesses and individuals.

The **Urban Enterprise Zone Program** was created in 1983 to stimulate economic revitalization in 10 urban cities: Bridgeton, Camden, Newark, Plainfield, Trenton, Elizabeth, Jersey City, Kearny, Orange, and Millville/Vineland, which, among other circumstances, suffered high unemployment and deterioration.

All qualified Urban Enterprise Zone businesses will receive two New Jersey sales benefits: one for the purchase of personal property and services, (other than motor vehicles and telecommunication services); the other exemption is on building materials. Other benefits could include a $500 or $1,500 corporation business tax credit and/or an unemployment tax award for hiring certain employees, and priority for certain financial and/or training assistance. In addition, qualified retailers in certain Urban Enterprise Zones can charge a 50-percent sales tax reduction on live purchases.

Contact:

Mr. A. Philip Ferzan, Director
Division of International Trade
New Jersey Department of Commerce and
   Economic Development
153 Halsey Street, 5th Floor
Newark, NJ 07101
(201) 648–3518

The **Division of International Trade** is a catalyst for all activities relating to New Jersey's role in international trade. The division is responsible for the development and implementation of trade policy and programs to promote the state and its products and services. The division assists New Jersey companies in export development and expansion by providing technical assistance and guidance on country- and industry-specific topics as well as the mechanics of international trade. A variety of services are offered including counseling, hosting foreign trading missions, and organizing international trade shows and missions.

The programs and activities are targeted to a diverse constituency: small, medium, and large firms; manufacturing and service businesses; and industrial, consumer, and agricultural sectors.

To accomplish its overall goals, the division is expanding its partnerships with other government agencies, the private sector, and academia. Successful implementation of this partnership will lead to the development of a long-term comprehensive export trade policy in New Jersey.

The New Jersey Economic Development Authority

Contacts:

Bond Financing
Mr. Frank T. Mancini, Jr., Director of Bond
   Finance
New Jersey Economic Development
   Authority
Capital Place One, CN 990
200 South Warren Street
Trenton, NJ 08625
(609) 292–0192

Loans or Guarantees
Mr. Eugene J. Bukowski, Director of Finance
New Jersey Economic Development
   Authority
Capital Place One, CN 990
200 South Warren Street
Trenton, NJ 08625
(609) 292–0187

The **New Jersey Economic Development Authority** (NJEDA) is a state business financing and development authority that uses tax-exempt private activity bonds to provide below-market-rate financing to manufacturers, (501(c)(3)) nonprofit organizations, and certain other specified borrowers for facilities, land acquisition, and machinery purchases. It also issues taxable bonds to provide financing for manufacturing, distribution, research, commercial, services, and other business uses. In addition, NJEDA has a guaranteed loan program, a direct loan program, an exporting line of credit that can be used for reshipment and post-shipment working capital, and a loan program directed to small retail and commercial businesses in urban centers and other targeted distressed communities. NJEDA targets its loan and guarantee programs to such industries as manufacturing, distribution, agriculture, and the like. The authority also operates a real estate development program to stimulate economic development and administers a federally funded Trade Adjustment Assistance Center for manufacturing companies hurt by foreign imports.

Contact:
Mr. Eugene J. Bukowski, Director of
  Finance
New Jersey Economic Development
  Authority
Capital Place One, CN 990
200 South Warren Street
Trenton, NJ 08625
(609) 292–0187

The **Local Development Financing Fund** (LDFF) was established to provide long-term, fixed-asset financing to commercial and industrial projects on a competitive basis.

The primary objectives of the program are to assist businesses that are located in urban aid cities and that meet the mandated competitive criteria: (1) to create and preserve employment; (2) to increase the municipality's tax base; and (3) to promote economic and physical revitalization to the qualifying municipalities.

SBA 504 Certified Development Company

Contact:
Mr. Eugene J. Bukowski, Secretary
Corporation for Business Assistance in New
  Jersey
Capital Place One, CN 990
200 South Warren Street
Trenton, NJ 08625
(609) 633–7737

The **Corporation for Business Assistance** (CBA) in New Jersey is designated by the U.S. Small Business Administration as a Section 504 Certified Development Company, with authority to operate statewide. The Division of Development for Small Businesses and Women and Minority Businesses works with CBA by advising small business owners on how to participate in the program of 504 loan packages. Loan applications are reviewed, processed, and recommended by the New Jersey Economic Development Authority.

Division of Rural Resources

Contact:
Ms. Karen M. Kritz
Agribusiness Development Representative
New Jersey Department of Agriculture
John Fitch Plaza, CN 330
Trenton, NJ 08625
(609) 292–5511

The **Division of Rural Resources** fosters the agricultural economic development of rural areas in New Jersey through such services as financial assistance for farmers and agribusinesses.

The **Agricultural Economic Development Program** of the New Jersey Department of Agriculture provides technical assistance in initiating agricultural economic development projects as well as directly assisting established farm and agribusiness operations in resolving regulatory, environmental, and growth conflicts.

New Jersey Commission on Science and Technology

Contact:
Mr. Joseph Montemarano, Associate
  Director
New Jersey Commission on Science and
  Technology
20 West State Street, CN 832
Trenton, NJ 08625–0832
(609) 984–1671

The **New Jersey Commission on Science and Technology** was established by legislation in 1985 to implement the recommendations of the Governor's Commission on Science and Technology. The permanent statutory commission is composed of 18 members from industry, academia, and state government. The commission works closely with the Department of Higher Education to improve the scientific and technical capabilities within the state, encourage existing and new high technology business, and support the preparation of a technology-literate work force. The long-term objective is to create an environment in New Jersey that is conducive to accelerated economic development.

The commission has sponsored the formation of a network of advanced technology centers and technology transfer stations, and funds partnerships that support innovative research projects. To small, technology-oriented companies, it provides such services as management and technical assistance, funding for new business incubators, and referrals to private and public sector financing sources.

The states's **Small Business Innovation Research** (SBIR) program is handled through the Venture Development Office. An enhancement office makes SBIR information available to New Jersey companies, provides representation in Washington, D.C., and assists companies seeking grants and contracts. The office has initiated conferences to increase SBIR participation and to teach successful proposal writing techniques. The Bridge Loan Program funds (with loans of up to $50,000) companies that have completed Phase I and are awaiting results on a Phase II proposal. Companies winning SBIRs receive management and technical assistance from the Venture Development Office and its network of Advanced Technology Centers. The commission's SBIR-related budget includes $20 million for bridge loans.

Small Business Development Centers

Contact:
Ms. Brenda B. Hopper, State Director
New Jersey Small Business Development
  Center
Rutgers University
Graduate School of Management
University Heights
180 University Avenue
Newark, NJ 07102
(201) 648–5950

The **New Jersey Small Business Development Center** (NJSBDC) network is a part of a national partnership between state and federal governments, the private sector, and colleges and universities. The program is designed to provide the highest quality of business assistance services to established enterprises and promising new starts, with the objective of increased employment and increased contributions to the state and federal treasuries.

In 1988, the NJSBDC was established as one of the first national SBDC pilot projects resulting from the passage of Public Law 96–302 by Congress. At present, the NJSBDC network is composed of the headquarters located at Rutgers Graduate School of Management and seven full-service regional centers at Brookdale Community College, Kean College, Mercer County Community College, Rutgers-Camden, Rutgers-Newark, Warren Community College, and Greater Atlantic City Chamber of Commerce. A complete listing of these centers, including addresses and telephone numbers, is in Appendix A of this directory.

A variety of educational and business resources are used to counsel and train small business owners as they deal with financing, marketing, and managing their companies. Clients are assisted in determining the feasibility of their business ideas and plans, developing business plans, cash flow projections, financial statements, and marketing strategies. Specialty programs are coordinated from NJSBDC headquarters and include international trade, government procurement, the Air Services Development Office, and technology resources.

The NJSBDC network also provides opportunities for students to participate and to apply educational theory to actual practice under the supervision of faculty and business professionals. In addition, NJSBDC benefits from both cash and in-kind contributions from the host institutions and an allocation from the Port Authority of New York and New Jersey. In CY 1990, these dollars combined to form an NJSBDC budget of more than $2.5 million.

Governor's Advisory Council or Task Force

The **Governor's Advisory Council on Minority Business Development** is chaired by the commissioner of the Department of Commerce and Economic Development and consists of 33 members—26 of whom are minority entrepreneurs. The other members represent the governor's office, cabinet members, and officials of state government.

The council meets every two months and provides recommendations on federal, state, and local policies and programs and on executive and legislative measures affecting minority business development.

The **Division of Development for Small Businesses and Women and Minority Businesses** has three advisory groups: the Small Business Advisory Council, the Women Business Advisory Council, and the Minority Business Advisory Council. Each council member is appointed by the governor and is confirmed by the Senate.

Contact:
Mr. James N. Albers, Chief of Staff
New Jersey Department of Commerce and
    Economic Development
20 West State Street, CN 820
Trenton, NJ 08625
(609) 984–2324

Contact:
Mr. Charles A. Jones, III, Director
Division of Development for Small
    Businesses and Women and Minority
    Businesses
New Jersey Department of Commerce and
    Economic Development
20 West State Street, CN 835
Trenton, NJ 08625
(609) 292–3860

Legislative Committees and Subcommittees

The New Jersey Legislature has no small business committees or subcommittees. Legislation concerning small business may be referred to several committees.

Contacts:
Senator Raymond Lesniak, Chairman
Senate Labor, Industry, and Professions
    Committee
24–52 Rahway Avenue
Elizabeth, NJ 07202
(908) 353–7722

Senator Wynona M. Lipman, Chairman
Senate State Government, Federal and
    Interstate Relations
50 Park Place, Suite 1035
Newark, NJ 07102
(201) 622–0090
(201) 622–0007

Assemblyman Anthony Impreveduto, Chairman
Assembly Commerce and Regulated
    Professions Committee
100 Route 153
Secaucus, NJ 07094
(201) 864–3232

Assemblyman Byron M. Baer, Chairman
Assembly State Government Committee
80 West Street
Englewood, NJ 07631
(201) 569–9700

Legislation

During the present legislative session, no bills of significant impact on the small business community have been signed into law.

State Small Business Conferences

No statewide small business conferences were planned for 1992.

New Mexico

Small Business Offices, Programs, and Activities

Economic Development Department

New Mexico's **Economic Development Department** is now organized into six divisions: Administrative Services, Economic Development, Film, Housing, Technology Enterprises, and Trade.

The **Administrative Services Division** provides managerial services for the department and ensures that the department complies with legislative and statutory mandates on fiscal control, accountability, and reporting. The division also supervises contracting, purchasing, warehousing, personnel, and computer services.

The **Economic Development Division** conducts a wide variety of programs aimed at assisting existing New Mexico businesses, recruiting new businesses to New Mexico, and assisting local and regional economic development efforts in the state. The division is divided into the areas of business and community finance, community development, existing industry, industrial recruitment, regional planning, and research and statistics.

The **New Mexico Film Commission** promotes and facilitates film making activity in New Mexico. The division is organized to provide definitive service in the areas of features and television; commercials, music videos, and print; and marketing/publications and advertising.

The division has more than 50 communities and pueblos involved in a volunteer liaison program to assist in the promotion and coordination of production work in the respective communities.

Contact:
Mr. Joe J. Ruiz, Director
Administrative Services Division
Joseph Montoya Building
1100 St. Francis Drive
Santa Fe, NM 87503
(505) 827–0380

Contact:
Mr. Stanley G. Lane, Director
Economic Development Division
Joseph Montoya Building
1100 St. Francis Drive
Santa Fe, NM 87503
(505) 827–0380

Contact:
Ms. Linda Taylor Hutchinson, Director
New Mexico Film Commission
Joseph Montoya Building
1100 St. Francis Drive
Santa Fe, NM 87503
(505) 827–0380

Contact:
Mr. Porfirio Perez, Director
New Mexico State Housing Authority
Joseph Montoya Building
1100 St. Francis Drive
Santa Fe, NM 87503
(505) 827–0380

Contact:
Mr. Ponziano Ferraraccio, Director
Technology Enterprises Division
Joseph Montoya Building
1100 St. Francis Drive
Santa Fe, NM 87503
(505) 827–0265

Contacts:
Mr. Roberto Castillo, Director
Trade Division
Joseph Montoya Building
1100 St. Francis Drive
Santa Fe, NM 87503
(505) 827–0309

Mr. Michael Cerletti
Tourism Division
Joseph Montoya Building
1100 St. Francis Drive
Santa Fe, NM 87503
(505) 827–0293

The **New Mexico State Housing Authority** works in partnership with public and private entities to assure that every citizen of New Mexico has the right to and opportunity for affordable, safe, decent, and sanitary housing. The division plans and coordinates housing renovations and new developments and establishes policies, guidelines, regulations, and distribution formulas for mandated programs. Technical assistance and training is provided to local and regional housing authorities, and information is distributed on statewide housing needs and available resources.

The **Technology Enterprise Division**, formerly the New Mexico Research and Development Institute, works to develop a strong statewide technology-driven private sector through leveraging public institutional and financial resources with private business initiatives to produce economic growth from New Mexico's technology base.

The **Trade Division** has programs to identify trade opportunities for New Mexico businesses and to promote and market New Mexico products and services to potential domestic and international consumers. The division assists individual businesses and community organizations with marketing and advertising strategies, and develops promotional materials to increase New Mexico's national and international prominence.

New Mexico Procurement Assistance Program

Contact:
Mr. J. Steve Griego, Director
New Mexico Procurement Assistance
   Program
1100 St. Francis Drive, Room 2150
Santa Fe, NM 87503
(505) 827–0425

The **New Mexico Procurement Assistance Program's** goals are (1) to make the business community aware of contract opportunities that originate in the public sector, ensuring that more New Mexico businesses compete for public sector contracts; (2) to increase public sector contracts awarded to New Mexico business; and (3) to increase public procurement dollars that remain and are recycled back into New Mexico's economy. These missions are accomplished by educating business owners in all phases of government contracting and by providing the comprehensive technical procurement counseling necessary to compete for defense, federal, state, and local government contracts.

The program offers training seminars in the practical requirements of contracting, business basics for the emerging contractor, and on-going technical procurement assistance and guidance to help secure and maintain government contracts. All services are provided at no cost to the client.

Assistance is provided on obtaining bid information from federal, state, and local government agencies; applying for placement on bidders' lists; reading and understanding bid packets; identifying and locating referenced standards and specifications; understanding the importance of the Federal Acquisition Regulations; coding products and services into government terms; completing the SF 129; completing the U.S. Department of Commerce Minority Business Profile form; getting entered into the U.S. Small Business Administration's Procurement Automated Source System (PASS); and using the *Commerce Business Daily* for locating bid opportunities, market research, and award information.

Regulation and Licensing Department

Contact:
Mr. Jerry Monzagol, Superintendent
Regulation and Licensing Department
725 St. Michael's Drive
P.O. Box 25101
Santa Fe, NM 87504
(505) 825–7004

The **Regulation and Licensing Department** is a regulatory agency with six divisions: Administrative Services, Alcohol and Gaming, Construction Industries, Manufactured Housing, Financial Institutions, and Securities. In addition, 26 professional licensing boards are administratively attached to this department. The department mission is to enforce applicable laws, rules, regulations, and codes, and to administer them in a manner that effects a balanced approach to public safety, financial welfare, and the development of the regulated industries. Small business can get help in securing licenses required by the state or information about regulations.

New Mexico Business Development Corporation

Contact:
Ms. Irene Catanach, Administrative Officer
New Mexico Business Development
    Corporation
6001 Marbel, N.E., Suite 6
Albuquerque, NM 87110
(505) 268–1316

The **New Mexico Business Development Corporation** (BDC) is a state-chartered, privately owned corporation that provides risk capital for sound business ventures. Funding is available for new product and market development or for the purchase of equipment needed to expand or modernize. The BDC works with local and regional banks, savings and loan associations, and credit unions.

Small Business Development Centers

Contact:
Mr. Randy Grisson, State Director
New Mexico Small Business Development
    Center
Santa Fe Community College
P.O. Box 4187
Santa Fe, NM 87502–4187
(505) 438–1362

The **New Mexico Small Business Development Center** (SBDC) provides assistance to existing and new businesses, primarily through counseling, training programs, and seminars. The lead SBDC is located at Santa Fe Community College, and there are centers and subcenters throughout the state. A complete listing of all Small Business Development Centers and subcenters is in Appendix A of this directory.

Contact:
Mr. Jim Greenwood, Executive Director
Los Alamos Economic Development
  Corporation
P.O. Box 715
Los Alamos, NM 87544
(505) 662–0001

The federal **Small Business Innovation Research** (SBIR) program is promoted in New Mexico through the state's SBDC network. The SBDC located at the Los Alamos Campus of the University of New Mexico manages the program, which is jointly funded by the New Mexico SBDC Network, US West Foundation, and the Los Alamos National Laboratory. The SBDC's promotional program consists of a series of workshops, presented across the state, to familiarize small business with the SBIR program; an annual conference to give New Mexico businesses training in writing SBIR proposals; a directory of SBIR-winning companies in the state to allow networking among winners and other proposal writers; resource centers at all 17 New Mexico SBDC subcenters consisting of SBIR solicitations, proposal writing guides, video tapes, and other materials; and assistance in preparing SBIR proposals. New Mexico has one of the highest per capita award ratios for SBIR contracts among the 50 states, and this program is designed to increase participation among other small businesses in the state to make the award rate even greater.

Governor's Advisory Council or Task Force

Contact:
Ms. Jane E. Powdell-Culbert, Executive
  Director
Governor's Commission on the Status of
  Women
4001 Indian School Road, N.E., Suite 220
Albuquerque, NM 87110
(505) 841–4662

The governor has established the **Governor's Commission on the Status of Women** to assess the needs of women in business in the state and to formulate plans to meet those needs.

Legislative Committees and Subcommittees

The Economic Development Committee is an interim committee created by the New Mexico Legislative Council to focus on legislation for the enhancement of economic development and diversification in New Mexico. The committee consists of 16 members from the House of Representatives and the Senate and eight advisory members.

Legislation

There was no recent legislation in New Mexico specifically targeting small business.

State Small Business Conferences

No recent statewide small business conferences have been reported.

New York

Small Business Offices, Programs, and Activities

Division for Small Business

Contact:
Mr. Manuel Saenz, Deputy Commissioner
Division for Small Business
New York State Department of Economic
    Development
1515 Broadway, 51st Floor
New York, NY 10036
(212) 827–6140

Contact:
Mr. Richard Drucker, Assistant Deputy
    Commissioner
Division for Small Business
New York State Department of Economic
    Development
1515 Broadway, 51st Floor
New York, NY 10036
(212) 827–6147

Contact:
Mr. Richard Drucker, Assistant Deputy
    Commissioner
Division for Small Business
New York State Department of Economic
    Development
1515 Broadway, 51st floor
New York, NY 10036
(212) 827–6142

The **Division for Small Business** of the **New York Department of Economic Development** is responsible for developing programs, providing services, and undertaking other initiatives that are responsive to the special needs of the state's small businesses.

The mission of the **Small Business Advocacy Program** is to make the general public, the business community, and government agencies aware of the special needs of the state's small businesses. Advocacy services are coordinated through the New York State Small Business Advisory Board and the Interagency Small Business Task Force. (For information on the Small Business Advisory Board and the Interagency Small Business Task Force, see section entitled "Governor's Advisory Committee or Task Force" below.)

Responsibilities of the advocacy program also include maintaining communications with business organizations on the state and federal level on behalf of small business. Publications include the *New York State Small Business Advisory Board Brochure*.

The **New York State Small Business Advisory Board** advises the governor, the state legislature, and the commissioner of economic development on policies, programs, and legislation affecting small business in the state.

Contact:
Ms. Kaye Kelly, Liaison
Small Business Awards Program
Division for Small Business
New York State Department of Economic
  Development
1515 Broadway, 51st floor
New York, NY 10036
(212) 827–6147

Created by legislation and signed into law by the governor in 1986, the **Small Business Awards Program** recognizes the contributions of the small business community to the economy of the state. The program honors the Small Business Person of the Year, the Small Business Advocate of the Year and honorable mentions in both categories.

The **Procurement Assistance Program** helps businesses obtain contracts and subcontracts from federal and state agencies, departments, and authorities, and from prime contractors in the private sector. The program assists the state's small businesses in obtaining a larger share of the billions of dollars that government agencies spend annually on goods and services. The program monitors government agency purchasing programs and mails notices of upcoming contract opportunities.

The Procurement Assistance Program offers training seminars, workshops, and trade shows to help companies get on bidders' lists, receive bid packages, understand qualifications, and complete bid documents. Through the program, specialists also help New York's small businesses locate subcontracting opportunities with large firms that provide goods and services to government.

The state's **P.L. 99–661 Program** takes advantage of the federal government's Fiscal Year 1987 Defense Authorization Act (Public Law 99–661), which directs the U.S. Department of Defense to place 5 percent of its contract awards with small disadvantaged businesses. The New York Department of Economic Development has drawn up a 10-point program to attract P.L. 99–661 contracts to New York State. This outreach and technical assistance program was assembled in cooperation with leaders of the state's minority business community, the Economic Development Subcabinet on Minority Business Enterprises, the Department of Economic Development's Division for Small Business, and the Minority and Women's Business Division.

Contact:
Mr. Raymond Gillen, Director
Procurement Assistance Unit
Division for Small Business
New York State Department of Economic
    Development
One Commerce Plaza
Albany, NY 12245
(518) 474–7756

The **Procurement Assistance Unit** makes available a publication entitled *Selling to Government: Finding New Customers for New York's Businesses*.

Contact:
Mr. Richard Drucker, Assistant Deputy
    Commissioner
Division for Small Business
New York State Department of Economic
    Development
1515 Broadway, 51st Floor
New York, NY 10036
(212) 827–6142

The **Business Service Ombudsman** helps firms resolve "red tape" difficulties with all levels of government. Ombudsmen work as advocates for the business community by recommending new laws and regulations and working with government agencies and businesses to coordinate resolutions to problems.

New York State Contract Reporter

Contact:
Mr. Michael Riggi
Division for Small Business
New York State Department of Economic
    Development
One Commerce Plaza
Albany, NY 12245
(518) 486–4141

The **New York State Contract Reporter** was authorized by Chapter 564 of the Laws of 1988. The first issue was launched in July of 1989. Roughly 200 state agencies, divisions of agencies, and authorities have used this weekly publication to promote state government opportunities. The *Contract Reporter* registered 5,630 active subscribers as of July 18, 1991. Minority- and women-owned businesses constitute approximately 25 percent of the subscription base.

Currently beginning its third year of publication, the *Contract Reporter* listed 15,800 contract opportunities in Fiscal Year 1990–91, enabling businesses to bid on—and win—state government contracts.

The *Contract Reporter* has been successful in increasing the number of small, minority, and women-owned businesses bidding on state contracts. As a result of the increased competition many agencies reported a lowering of the price they are paying for goods and services.

Contact:
Mr. Milton Elis, Director
Training and Technical Assistance Unit
Division for Small Business
New York State Department of Economic
    Development
1515 Broadway, 51st Floor
New York, NY 10036
(212) 827–6145

Contact:
Mr. Milton Elis, Director
Training and Technical Assistance Unit
Division for Small Business
New York State Department of Economic
    Development
1515 Broadway, 51st Floor
New York, NY 10036
(212) 827–6145
(800) STATE NY (toll-free hot line)
or (800) 782–8369

The purpose of the **Training and Technical Assistance Program** of the Division for Small Business is to provide small businesses with training on a variety of topics of interest and value to them. The program alerts small businesses to new market opportunities for their products and services and offers technical assistance in obtaining a share of these markets. Workshops and training sessions cover such topics as federal and state procurement opportunities, export and investment opportunities, state tax policy and investment incentives, and New York State services available to them through the federal Small Business Innovation Research (SBIR) program. These services are provided for a nominal fee.

The **Training and Technical Assistance Hot Line** is a telephone screening and referral service using a toll-free number (1–800–STATE NY) to market the state's business assistance programs. Calls are generated by radio and television ads, newspaper print ads, and direct mail targeted to the state's business community.

The hot line staff provides direct access to state economic development offering financing, job training, technical assistance, and general information. The staff determines the specific needs of each caller and responds with information and assistance. An integral component of the program is response to calls within 24 hours.

The Division for Small Business was chosen to receive an **Immigration Grant** to be the lead agency to educate business owners about the federal Immigration Reform and Control Act (IRCA). The agency's goal in administering the grant is to help employers avoid unintentional discrimination resulting from a misunderstanding or misinterpretation of the employer sanction provisions of the law. Services provided include training seminars and workshops, distribution of literature, toll-free telephone assistance, and media spots.

These efforts aim to reduce the unintentional hiring discrimination against the foreign born, thereby reducing the risk of sanctions against New York State firms who might otherwise be fined for failing to comply with the provisions of the IRCA. Funding for these efforts comes from the U.S. Immigration and Naturalization Service through the New York State Department of Social Services.

New York State Urban Development Corporation

Contact:
Mr. Vincent Tese, Chairman and Chief
  Executive Officer
New York State Urban Development
  Corporation
1515 Broadway, 52nd Floor
New York, NY 10036
(212) 930–0200

The **New York State Urban Development Corporation** (UDC) is a public finance and development authority that participates in a broad range of initiatives. The UDC's goal is to create and retain jobs, particularly in economically distressed areas. The corporation addresses the needs of the state in six areas, including downtown development, industrial development, minority business development, university research and development, and planning and special projects. The UDC has the authority to condemn real property, to invest in property at below-market interest rates, to issue both tax-exempt and taxable bonds, to offer tax benefits to developments, and to provide flexibility in the application of local codes.

Since 1968, the UDC has created more than 100,000 permanent jobs and has been involved in projects valued at $6 billion. Programs operated by the UDC include a minority revolving loan fund, a commercial revitalization program, a targeted investment program, and a regional economic development loan program.

New York State Job Development Authority

Contact:
Ms. Audrey Bynoe, Acting President
Job Development Authority
605 Third Avenue
New York, NY 10158
(212) 818–1700

The **New York State Job Development Authority** (JDA) is the state's economic development bank. The JDA assists companies wishing to expand or build new facilities, thereby retaining existing jobs or creating new employment opportunities. Nearly every type of business is eligible for JDA assistance. (Loans or loan guarantees to retail establishments, hotels, or apartment buildings are not made under this program.) Under the direct loan program, JDA may lend up to 40 percent of a project's costs for construction, acquisition, rehabilitation, or improvement of industrial or manufacturing plants and research and development facilities. The authority also provides loan guarantees of up to 80 percent of a project's costs for a maximum of 20 years. Other programs offered by JDA include a rural development loan fund, a long-term economic development fund, an export program, and a regional economic development partnership program.

The **Bonding Assistance Experimental Program** (BAX) reflects the policy of the state of New York to assist minority, women, and small business owners to participate fully in the economic activity of the state and, more specifically, to do business with the state itself. The program has been expanded to include contracts for public projects of any state agency, authority, or public benefit corporation, and by cities, towns, and villages.

Office of Business Permits and Regulatory Assistance

Contact:
Ms. Ruth Walters, Director
Office of Business Permits and Regulatory
   Assistance
A.E. Smith Office Building, 17th Floor
Albany, NY 12225
(518) 473–8197

The **Office of Business Permits and Regulatory Assistance** provides a wide spectrum of services to small business owners. Through its master application procedure, the office identifies, consolidates, and expedites all the permits a business person will need for a new business or expansion. As part of the office's long-term goals, it reviews the licensing process and regulatory programs in New York State to ensure that regulations are clearly written, do not duplicate existing state or federal requirements, and are necessary to achieve a specific legislative purpose.

Rural Development

Contact:
Ms. June O'Neil, Director Designate
Office of Rural Affairs
State Capitol, Executive Chamber
Albany, NY 12224
(212) 474–9003

Contact:
Ms. Roberta Boatti, Director
Special Programs
New York Job Development Authority
605 Third Avenue
New York, NY 10158
(518) 818–1700

The **Office of Rural Affairs** serves as an advocate for rural needs and seeks to improve the integration and structure of state programs as they relate to rural areas. The office also works to strengthen communications between state and local governments, serving as an ombudsman for rural communities.

The **Rural Development Loan Fund** was designed to meet the special financial needs of small businesses located in rural areas. The program aims to stimulate the growth and expansion of private sector employment in the state's distressed rural communities.

Contact:
Mr. Steven Morello
New York Department of Commerce
1 Commerce Plaza
Albany, NY 12245
(518) 474–7910

The **Agricultural Product Promotion** program encourages producers to form industry supported cooperative marketing agreements and to build consumer awareness of New York grown products.

SBA 504 Certified Development Corporations

Contact:
Mr. Gerald Demers, Senior Loan Officer
Empire State Certified Development
   Corporation
41 State Street
Albany, NY 12205
(518) 463–2268

The **Empire State Certified Development Corporation** is formally approved by the U.S. Small Business Administration as a Section 504 Certified Development Company, with authority to operate on a statewide basis.

New York Business Development Corporation

Contact:
Mr. Robert W. Lazar, President and Chief
   Executive Officer
New York Business Development
   Corporation
41 State Street
Albany, NY 12207
(518) 463–2268

The **New York Business Development Corporation** (NYBDC) is a private corporation that makes term loans available to small businesses. The NYBDC coordinates both the SBA Section 504 Certified Development Corporation and a new loan program, the New York State/U.S. Small Business Administration Initiative. With an initial capitalization of $100 million coming from New York State employee pension funds, the initiative program is a revolving loan fund for small business. In order to safeguard the pension funds, the initiative is required to have guarantees attached to at least 50 percent of the loans it makes. The SBA will provide these guarantees as each loan package is processed and approved.

New York Science and Technology Foundation

Contact:
Mr. Graham Jones, Executive Director
New York State Science and Technology
    Foundation
99 Washington Avenue, Suite 1730
Albany, NY 12210
(518) 474–4349

The **New York Science and Technology Foundation** is a state-funded organization that was set up to stimulate research and development (R&D), strengthen the state's leadership position as an R&D center, disseminate benefits from new developments in science and technology, and encourage innovation. The foundation provides several major resources: it conducts special training programs, awards R&D grants for university-based research that has commercial applications, encourages local high technology, and provides grants and other services to the Centers for Advanced Technology. It also created the Corporation for Innovation Development program.

The **Centers for Advanced Technology** are designed to support linkages between industry and universities. The foundation has designated several areas of advanced technology: automation and robotics, biotechnology, medical instruments and devices, optics, semiconductors, integrated circuits, advanced materials, and telecommunications. By 1988, a total of 10 centers were funded by the foundation.

The **Corporation for Innovation Development** (CID) program is a venture capital fund for technology-based start-ups and young, growing business ventures in New York State. The corporation is partly funded by the U.S. Department of Commerce and was recently recapitalized by the state. The corporation focuses on ventures with innovative products or services ready for introduction to a rapid growth market. The CID program will invest up to $250,000 in a business, but any investments must be matched by loans or investments from other sources.

Contact:
Mr. Owen Goldfarb
New York Science and Technology
    Foundation
99 Washington Avenue, Suite 1730
Albany, NY 12210
(518) 473–9746

Through its 10 Regional Technology Development Organizations, the Science and Technology Foundation also provides seminars, workshops, and direct technical assistance to state firms interested in using the federal **Small Business Innovation Research** (SBIR) program.

Minority and Women's Business Division

Contact:
Mr. Heyward Davenport, Deputy
   Commissioner
Minority and Women's Business Division
1515 Broadway, 51st Floor
New York, NY 10036
(212) 827–6180

The **Minority and Women's Business Division** is the point of access for minority- and women-owned businesses looking for referrals and assistance in solving problems. The division assists in obtaining statewide certification, financing, business development and technical assistance, permit and regulatory assistance, market and sales expansion, and employment and training.

Small Business Development Centers

Contact:
Mr. James L. King, State Director
New York Small Business Development
   Center
State University of New York
SUNY Plaza, S–523
Albany, NY 12246
(518) 443–5398
(800) 732–SBDC (toll-free, in-state)

Small Business Development Centers (SBDCs) provide practical management and technical assistance to present and prospective small business owners. They offer courses, seminars, and one-on-one counseling as well as access to information on marketing, managing, and financing a small business. SBDCs are partially funded by the U.S. Small Business Administration, and are usually affiliated with a state college or university. In New York, a lead SBDC is located in Albany at the State University of New York. There are 18 subcenters located throughout the state. A complete listing of all these centers, including addresses and telephone numbers, is in Appendix A of this directory.

Governor's Advisory Council or Task Force

Contact:
Mr. Ron Neufeld, Liaison
Interagency Small Business Task Force
Division for Small Business
New York State Department of Economic
   Development
One Commerce Plaza
Albany, NY 12245
(518) 486–4141

The **New York State Small Business Advisory Board** advises the governor, the state legislature, and the commissioner of economic development on policies, programs, and legislation affecting small business in the state.

The **Interagency Small Business Task Force** is made up of subcabinet-level representatives from 29 state agencies, departments, and authorities with functions that directly or indirectly affect small businesses in the state. These agency representatives act as small business advocates in their respective government units. The task force encourages programmatic and administrative actions to improve the economic climate for small businesses in New York. The deputy commissioner of the Small Business Division presides as chairperson of the task force. The director of the Office of Business Permits serves as cochairperson.

Legislative Committees and Subcommittees

The New York State Assembly and the New York State Senate each have a subcommittee on small business.

Contacts:

Senator John McHugh
Chairman
Senate Standing Committee on Commerce,
   Economic Development and Small
   Business
Legislative Office Building, Room 814
Albany, NY 12247
(518) 455–2346

Assemblyman Robin Schimminger
Chairman
Assembly Committee on Small Business
Legislative Office Building, Room 847
Albany, NY 12248
(518) 455–4767

Legislation

The following measures have recently been signed into law in New York State:

- To end spring borrowing, the March sales tax prepayment was eliminated, and a cap was placed on future state spending.

- The International Trade and Industrial Competitiveness Act of 1990 created and expanded the number of export trade programs within the State Department of Economic Development, helping New York industries to meet the challenge of a global economy. New York small and medium-sized firms will now get a hand to increase exports and stay competitive.

- The Industrial Technology Extension Service was established within the Science and Technology Foundation. This program will send field agents to manufacturing firms to help them improve management and production processes through technology improvements.

- The Equal Access to Justice Act will provide businesses that believe they have been unjustly ruled against by an agency the ability to recover for court and related expenses if prevailing in an agency appeal.

- Two or more employees are now able to sponsor a credit union.

- A reimbursement bill was passed to give hospitals money to recruit more health care workers, pay current workers more, and relieve emergency room overcrowding. This bill also has a low cost health insurance program for poor children. For $25, participating parents under a certain income level could have free doctor check-ups, laboratory tests, and prescription drugs for their children.

- An act was passed establishing a unified, comprehensive system for day care regulation in New York State.

- In the new workers' compensation agreement, the weekly maximum compensation rate for partially disabled New Yorkers would increase from $150 to $280. The maximum rate for totally disabled persons would rise from $300 to $340. On July 1, 1991, the state eliminated the distinction between partial and total disability.

- Legislation that expands the Office of Business Permits and Regulatory Assistance (OBRA) authority in the rule-making process was passed. The legislation broadened OBRA's oversight responsibilities to include Notices of Revised Rule Making and also extends OBRA's sunset to 1995.

- The small claims action limit by a business will be raised from $1,500 to $2,000 to conform with the same increase adopted for small claims court. Businesses will be able to have a claim of up to $2,000 resolved for a filing fee of $20 plus postage without incurring the cost of the attorney. A court clerk will send out the summons.

- The legislature passed an act to establish a Minority and Women Business Development and Revolving Loan Fund program to improve the delivery of small loans to minority and women-owned firms and encourage the creation of incubator programs serving these enterprises.

- The New York State budget includes the following small business programs:

Small and Medium-Sized Business Assistance Program is a fund to provide low interest loans for small and medium-sized manufacturers.

Entrepreneurial Assistance Program provides money to support management training and technical assistance for entrepreneurs.

Export Trade Development Projects Program aids regional efforts to help more small firms enter the export field.

Small Business Innovation Research (SBIR) provides matching grants to the federal SBIR award winners.

State Small Business Conferences

A **State Small Business Presentation** is held in Albany each year. Its purpose is to bring together small business leaders and state elected officials and decisionmakers throughout New York. The presentation emphasizes the importance of small business to the New York economy and informs lawmakers about the issues that are important to small business owners.

Contacts:
Mr. Chris Pugliese, Manager
Government Relations Business Council of
  New York State, Inc.
152 Washington Avenue
Albany, NY 12210
(518) 465–7511

Mr. Mark Alesse, Director
Governmental Relations
National Federation of Independent
  Business
134 State Street
Albany, NY 12207
(518) 434–1262

North Carolina

Small Business Offices, Programs, and Activities

North Carolina Technological Development Authority

Contact:
Mr. E. Brent Lane, Director
North Carolina Technological Development
   Authority
P.O. Box 13169
Research Triangle Park, NC 27709–3169
(919) 990–8558

The **North Carolina Technological Development Authority, Inc.,** (NCTDA), was established by the New Technology Jobs Act of 1983, and was authorized to become a private non-profit corporation as of September 1991. The NCTDA oversees the North Carolina Innovation Research Fund, providing seed capital financing for new products and technologies. The NCTDA also is expected to establish an incubator facility in Research Triangle Park and will manage a statewide system of business incubators. The NCTDA also provides information on the federal **Small Business Innovation Research** (SBIR) program.

Business License Information Office

Contact:
Mr. Charles W. Moore, Director
Business License Information Office
301 West Jones Street
Raleigh, NC 27611
(919) 733–0641
(800) 228–8443 (toll-free, in-state)

Established by the Department of the Secretary of State, the **Business License Information Office** provides information on regulations and licenses, permits, or authorizations necessary for North Carolina businesses.

Procurement Program

Contacts:
Mr. Harry Payne, Small Business
   Coordinator
Division of Purchase and Contract
116 West Jones Street, 4th Floor
Raleigh, NC 27611
(919) 733–8965

Although the state does not mandate set-asides to small business, an effort is made to make it easy to sell to the state. For example, small and minority businesses are easily placed on vendors' lists because the state waives the usual requirements for this listing. In addition, the state will often waive the requirement for performance bonds. A biweekly purchase directory is published that lists public works, as well as goods and services contract offerings by the state government. The subscription price is $40 per year.

Federal Government Procurement Technical Assistance Program

Contact:
Ms. Susan Kinney, Director
PROTAP
Small Business and Technology
   Development Center
4509 Creedmoor Road, Suite 201
Raleigh, NC 27612
(919) 571–4154

The **Federal Government Procurement Technical Assistance Program** (PROTAP) is operated by the Small Business and Technology Development Center with support of the U.S. Department of Defense. Services include computer-based matching, counseling and seminars, and workshops.

Small Business Centers

Contact:
Dr. R. Jean Overton, Director for Small
   Business
Department of Community Colleges
200 West Jones Street
Raleigh, NC 27603–1337
(919) 733–7051

Small Business Centers are located at 53 community college campuses throughout the state. Classes and seminars are held to meet the needs of small businesses and potential small business owners. Topics include international trade, business basics, record keeping, advertising, and business plans.

Small Business Development Centers

Contact:
Mr. Scott R. Daugherty, State Director
North Carolina Small Business Development
   Center
University of North Carolina
4509 Creedmoor Road, Suite 201
Raleigh, NC 27612
(919) 571–4154

Small Business Development Centers (SBDCs) provide practical management and technical assistance to present and prospective small business owners. They offer courses, seminars, and one-on-one counseling as well as access to information on marketing, managing, and financing a small business. SBDCs are partially financed by the U.S. Small Business Administration, and are usually affiliated with a state college or university. In North Carolina, SBDCs operate through the University of North Carolina system.

In addition to general counseling and training, the SBDCs offer specialized assistance in three areas: (1) international trade, (2) product and technology development, and (3) procurement. Offices are located in Raleigh, Greenville, Elizabeth City, Charlotte, Wilmington, Cullowhee, Fayetteville, Greensboro, Boone, Hickory, and Winston-Salem. A complete listing of all these centers, including addresses and telephone numbers, is in Appendix A of this directory.

High Technology

Contact:
Dr. Matt Kuhn, President
Microelectronics Center of North Carolina
P.O. Box 12889
Research Triangle Park, NC 27709
(919) 248–1800

Incorporated in 1980, the **Microelectronics Center of North Carolina** (MCNC) is a private nonprofit corporation that provides technological support for North Carolina businesses and universities.

The primary mission of MCNC is to manage advanced research programs in microelectronics, communications, and superconducting that do the following:

- Build technology resources in North Carolina to attract, retain, and increase the growth of science-based industry;

- Support North Carolina universities and industry with state-of-the-art research facilities and contribute in research, teaching, and technology development;

- Involve leading industry in collaborative research; and

- Support North Carolina economic development agencies in their industrial development programs.

The MCNC computer network includes more than 70 industrial supporters in the areas of microelectronics, supercomputing, and communications, as well as all of the state's universities.

North Carolina Biotechnology Center

Contact:
Dr. Charles Hamner, President
North Carolina Biotechnology Center
Box 13547
Research Triangle Park, NC 27709
(919) 541–9366

The **North Carolina Biotechnology Center** was established in 1981 to support biotechnology research and development statewide through research, programmatic activities, faculty recruitment, new facilities, meetings, and commercial ventures. The center supports activities in all phases from basic research to product development. It encourages technology transfer among universities and industries. The center is a private, non-profit corporation that works with all parties involved in development of the technology. Currently, the center receives $8.2 million biannually from the state for its activities.

The **Product and Technology Innovation Network** (PATIN) is a cooperative venture of the Small Business Technology Development Center (SBTDC) and virtually all of North Carolina's technology-based resources. This network creates a structure that brings together experts from a wide variety of technological fields to help the smaller business community, faculty researchers, private researchers, and independent inventors as they evaluate, protect, and commercialize their new products or technologies.

The SBTDC functions as the coordinator and entry point for PATIN clients. At any of the SBTDC's regional offices across the state, businesses and inventors can receive help with intellectual property issues, product or technology feasibility assessments, prototype development, testing and funding source identification to help them understand and develop specific commercialization or transfer strategies.

Members of PATIN include the North Carolina Biotechnology Center, North Carolina Alternative Energy Corporation; University of North Carolina-Chapel Hill; East Carolina University School of Medicine; North Carolina A&T University School of Engineering; University of North Carolina-Charlotte Applied Research Facility; and the North Carolina State University Industrial Extension Service.

Research Triangle Institute

Contact:
Dr. S. Thomas Wooten, President
Research Triangle Institute
P.O. Box 12194
Research Triangle Park, NC 27709
(919) 541–6000

The **Research Triangle Institute** is a nonprofit consulting R&D firm with approximately 900 employees. The institute conducts contract research involving physical, life, and social sciences. The work is done for federal, state, and local governments as well as the private sector. This nonprofit corporation was created and incorporated by the University of North Carolina, Duke University, and North Carolina State University and operates under separate management.

Institute for Private Enterprise

Contact:
Mr. Jack Kasarda, Director
Institute for Private Enterprise
University of North Carolina at Chapel Hill
Frank H. Kenan Institute of Private
Enterprise, CB 3440
Chapel Hill, NC 27599–3440
(919) 962–8201

The **Frank H. Kenan Institute for Private Enterprise** was established in 1985 at the University of North Carolina at Chapel Hill. The institute is a national center for private enterprise research, focusing on entrepreneurial development, new venture management, and development of coursework for use in business schools across the country.

Rural Economic Development Center

Contact:
Mr. Billy Ray Hall, President
Rural Economic Development Center
4 Blount Street
Raleigh, NC 27601
(919) 821–1154

The **Rural Economic Development Center** is a nonprofit corporation involved in research and demonstration efforts to identify new ideas, strategies, or programs that will generate economic development in rural North Carolina. The center also helps to facilitate job creation in rural areas of the state and helps several small communities.

Governor's Advisory Council or Task Force

Contact:
Mr. Scott Daugherty, State Director
North Carolina Small Business and
Technology Development Center
4509 Creedmoor Road
Raleigh, NC 27612
(919) 571–4154

The governor has had an appointed **Small Business Advisory Council** since 1980. This 23-member council meets at least quarterly in formal session and has conducted a series of forums throughout the state.

Legislative Committees and Subcommittees

North Carolina does not have small business committees in either the Senate or the House.

Legislation

Sales, individual income, and corporate income tax rates were increased in the 1991 legislative session. A bill was also passed that may facilitate small business access to group health insurance.

State Small Business Conferences

No recent statewide small business conferences have been reported.

North Dakota

Small Business Offices, Programs, and Activities

Department of Economic Development and Finance

Contact:
Mr. Mitchell D. Bohn, Director
Department of Economic Development &
  Finance
1833 East Bismarck Expressway
Bismarck, ND 58504
(701) 224–2810

The 1991 State Legislature adopted "Growing North Dakota" legislation to revamp the state's economic and business development programs. The legislation created the **Department of Economic Development and Finance** (ED&F). Under the plan, four new programs were established:

- A new women's business development program will provide services to women in the primary sector businesses.

- A new position calls for a professional development administrator to work with the university system to develop a curriculum for economic development professionals.

- The department will have a native American business development coordinator, who will be responsible for assisting in the development of private native American-owned businesses and in providing new jobs for native Americans.

- The department will have a marketing coordinator to better assist North Dakota businesses develop marketing strategies.

In the future, federal procurement assistance will be contracted from the U.S. Small Business Administration. The SBA will pay the salary of the procurement specialist, and the state of North Dakota will provide office space and secretarial support. International trade services will be provided under contract by North Dakota World Trade, Inc., a nonprofit organization.

The ED&F will continue to promote economic development to enhance the general welfare of the state through the establishment of new business and industry, the development of new markets for agricultural and other products, the encouragement of international trade, the development of tourism, and the attraction of new residents, business, and industry.

The ED&F will assist start-up and expanding businesses by providing information to prospective small business ventures and assisting in location decisions. The ED&F will maintain a library of business, demographic, and economic information and will provide prospective small business owners with information on current labor practices, transportation facilities, taxation, finance and legal structures, and geographic factors. The department will provide small business ombudsman, information, and referral services and publish *Business Reports, Forms, and Licenses Required in the State of North Dakota*, as well as statistical reports and financial referrals.

Two other programs directly administered by the ED&F include the Community Development Loan Fund and the North Dakota Future Fund.

Under the **Community Development Loan Fund,** businesses that will create jobs for low- or moderate-income people may qualify for loans of up to $300,000 per project in the primary sector or up to $50,000 per project in the retail sector. Businesses located in Bismarck, Grand Forks, and Fargo may not qualify. The interest rate is based on need and averages 6 percent. Funds may be used for fixed assets and infrastructure.

The **North Dakota Future Fund** provides "gap" financing not available from other, more conventional, sources. Innovative financing options are available to provide both long- and short-term capital to new, expanding, or relocating businesses. Primary sector businesses may qualify for up to $300,000 or 50 percent of required capital, whichever is less, for debt or equity financing. The maximum for grants is $100,000.

Robert Perkins Engineering Computer Center

Contact:
Robert Perkins Engineering Computer
  Center
College of Engineering and Architecture
North Dakota State University
Fargo, ND 58105
(701) 237–7975

The **Robert Perkins Engineering Computer Center** was established at North Dakota State University, Fargo, to enable North Dakota firms to use the most advanced technologies. A Cyber 180 Control Data Corporation (CDC) mainframe minicomputer provides North Dakota businesses access to CDC's worldwide computer software. The computer was purchased by the state and placed at NDSU through a successful cooperative effort of the private sector, academia, and state government.

Bank of North Dakota

Contact:
Mr. Eric Hardmeyer, Commercial Loan
  Officer
Bank of North Dakota
700 East Main Avenue, Box 5509
Bismarck, ND 58502
(701) 224–5674
(800) 472–2166, Ext. 5674

The **Bank of North Dakota** is the nation's only state-authorized and operated bank. The bank offers several unique lending programs for promoting agriculture, commerce, and industry within the state.

The **Small Business Loan Program** is designed to assist new and existing businesses in securing competitive financing on reasonable terms and conditions. Loans are restricted to non-farming small businesses located within the state. The maximum loan is $250,000 and applications must be made by a lead financial institution. The lead institution may charge the borrower an interest rate of up to 2 percent above the bank's floating rate.

The **Risk Loan Program** is designed to assist new and existing businesses in obtaining loans that would have a higher degree of risk than would normally be acceptable to a lending institution. The bank's participation percentage will be negotiated on a loan-by-loan basis, up to $500,000. A lead lender must apply for and service the loan, and may not charge more than 2 percent above the bank's base rate.

The Bank of North Dakota's **Export Loan Program** makes low-interest loans available to foreign buyers who want to purchase North Dakota products.

Pace Program loans provide interest buy-down financing for businesses in manufacturing, processing, value-added processing, and targeted service industries (such as data processing, data communications, and telecommunications). The purpose of the Pace Program is to create jobs. The borrower must show evidence that within the first year there will be a minimum of one job created for every $75,000 borrowed.

The **Match Program** provides low-interest loans of up to $25 million to companies with an "A" or better credit rating. The interest for Match Program loans is set at .25 percent above the U.S. Treasury note rate, with a life of up to 15 years. The program targets North Dakota's businesses involved in manufacturing, processing, and value-added industries.

Through **Business Development Loans**, North Dakota businesses may qualify for loans of up to $500,000 to finance working capital, equipment, and real property. The interest rate is set to the Bank of North Dakota's base rate for the portion held by the bank and up to 3 percent over that base rate for the portion held by the lead lender. **Small Business Development Loans** are available to some businesses. Small businesses may qualify for loans up to $250,000 at Bank of North Dakota's base for the bank's portion, and that base rate plus 3 percent for the local lender's share of the loan. The funds can be used for working capital, equipment, and real property.

The **Tourism and Recreation Investment Program** (TRIP) provides loans of up to $10,000 to tourism-related businesses. The interest rate is held to 1 percent below the Bank of North Dakota's base rate for the portion of the loan held by the bank and 4 percent above that base rate on the portion held by a local lender.

Under the **Micro Business Loan Program**, businesses with a net worth of less than $150,000 may qualify for loans of not more than $10,000. The interest rate is held to 1 percent below the Bank of North Dakota's base rate for the portion of the loan held by the bank and 4 percent above that base on the portion held by the local lender.

Agricultural Product Utilization Commission

Contact:
Mr. Jerry Rustand, Chairman
Agricultural Products Utilization Commission
State Capital Building
600 Boulevard Avenue
Bismarck, ND 58501
(701) 224–4760

The **Agricultural Product Utilization Grant** provides funding and technical assistance to private industry for establishment of processing plants for the manufacture and marketing of agriculturally derived fuels, chemicals, and value-added processing.

Contact:
Mr. David Nelson, Vice President
Capital Dimensions, Inc.
400 East Broadway Avenue, Suite 420
Bismarck, ND 58501
(701) 222–0995

The **Myron G. Nelson Fund**, created as a venture capital fund, provides assistance to businesses based on growth potential, management abilities, objectives, plans, and personal goals of the business's principals. Fund participation is limited to 40 percent of equity.

Tax Incentives

Contact:
Mr. Mitchell D. Bohn, Director
Department of Economic Development and
    Finance
1833 East Bismarck Expressway
Bismarck, ND 58504
(701) 224–2810

There are several tax incentives available to small businesses in North Dakota:

- Income and property tax incentives include property tax exemptions for new or expanding business projects; income tax exemptions for new or expanding business projects; income tax deductions for selling or renting a business to a beginning businessperson; and wage and salary income tax credits for new businesses.

- Research and development incentives include income tax credits for research expenditures; and income tax credits for the cost of installing geothermal, solar, and wind energy devices.

- Sales tax incentives include a sales and tax exemption for a new or expanding business project for equipment used for manufacturing or agricultural processing.

Work Force Incentives

Contact:
Mr. James J. Hirsch, Director of Job
  Training Division
Job Service
P.O. Box 1537
Bismarck, ND 58502
(701) 224–2825

Contacts:
Mr. Al Austad, Executive Director
North Dakota Counsel on Vocational
  Education
P.O. Box 1373
Bismarck, ND 58502
(701) 224–2080

Mr. Carrol Burchinal, State Director
Department of Vocational Education
Capital Building, 15th floor
Bismarck, ND 58505–0610
(701) 224–2259

Contact:
Mr. Edward Straus
Coordinator of Related Study
North Dakota State College of Science
800 North 6th Street
Wapton, ND 58076
(701) 671–1130

North Dakota's **Customized Training Programs** offer on-site classes, in-plant training, open ended/open exit enrollment in state-run technical schools, multiple scheduling of classroom training, coupled on-the-job training, noncredit adult education programs at the state's universities, and access to multi-district vocational centers and community college programs.

The **Vocational Instructional Program** (VIP) provides financial and technical assistance for developing a business' training program. Administered by the Department of Vocational Education, VIP can allocate funds for trainers' salaries, instructional materials and supplies, equipment leases, and contractual services. Also, if needed, the Department of Vocational Education can draw from its own staff and network of education and industry advisors to offer technical assistance in developing curricula and training plans, and performing job analysis.

The **North Dakota State College of Science** has mobile training laboratories that can provide short-term training in 12 program areas. The mobile labs are fully equipped, comprehensive training facilities.

Disadvantaged Business Assistance

Contact:
Mr. James Laducer
Laducer & Associates, Inc.
919 South 7th Street, Suite 202
Bismarck, ND 58504
(701) 255–3002

The **North Dakota Department of Highways** offers assistance to disadvantaged business enterprises (DBEs). Through a contract with a private consulting firm, DBEs receive a full range of business assistance, from competitive bid preparation to financial consulting to contract management.

NDSU Institute for Business and Industry Development

Contact:
Mr. Wally Eide, Director
NDSU IBID
North Dakota State University
P.O. Box 5437
Fargo, ND 58105
(701) 237–7867

The **Institute for Business and Industry Development** at North Dakota State University in Fargo is a technology transfer system dedicated to promoting economic development in North Dakota through application of appropriate technical, engineering, business, and scientific technologies. This assistance is aimed primarily at manufacturers.

Assistance for Rural Small Businesses

Contact:
Mr. Dale Zetocha, Small Business
  Management Specialist
NDSU Extension Center for Rural
  Revitalization
North Dakota State University
P.O Box 5437
Fargo, ND 58105
(701) 237–7502
fax: (701) 237–7044

The **NDSU Extension Service** has a program specifically designed to assist rural small businesses. Funding is primarily through the U.S. Department of Agriculture. Business management publications and bi-monthly business management newsletters are available.

SBA 504 Certified Development Company

Contact:
Mr. Warren Litten, Executive Director
Fargo Cass County Economic Development
  Corporation
417 Main Avenue
Fargo, ND 58103
(701) 237–6132
fax: (701) 235–6706

The **Fargo Cass County Economic Development Corporation**, the only certified development company in North Dakota, has been expanded to cover the entire state. This certified development company lends to small and medium-size businesses at fixed rates for terms of 10 or 20 years. Small businesses must create or save one job for every $15,000 they receive in financing. A 504 loan is funded through the sale of a debenture that is guaranteed by the U.S Small Business Administration up to $750,000 or 40 percent of the total cost of land, buildings, and equipment.

Small Business Development Centers

Contact:
Mr. Walter Kearns, State Director
North Dakota Small Business Development
   Center
University of North Dakota
Gamble Hall, University Station
Grand Forks, ND 58202–7308
(701) 777–3700
fax: (701) 777–5099

The **Small Business Development Center** (SBDC) is located at the University of North Dakota in Grand Forks. The center provides assistance to existing and new businesses, primarily through one-on-one consulting and specific training programs and seminars. The Small Business Development Center has subcenters located in Bismarck, Dickinson, Jamestown, Grand Forks, and Minot. A listing of all Small Business Centers and subcenters in North Dakota is provided in Appendix A of this directory.

Center for Innovation and Business Development

Contact:
Mr. Bruce Gjovig, Director
Center for Innovation and Business
   Development
University of North Dakota
Box 8103, University Station
Grand Forks, ND 58202
(701) 777–3132
fax: (701) 777–2339

The **Center for Innovation and Business Development** (CIBD) provides business and technical support services to entrepreneurs, inventors, and small manufacturers. It specifically assists with the product evaluation process, the patenting process, technology commercialization, market feasibility studies, marketing plans, and business plans. The center also operates a **Rural Manufacturing Assistance Program**.

Contact:
Mr. Kevin Cooper, SBIR Coordinator
Center for Innovation and Business
   Development
University of North Dakota
Box 8103, University Station
Grand Forks, ND 58202
(701) 777–3132
fax: (701) 777–2339

Information on the **Small Business Innovation Research** (SBIR) program is also available through CIBD. CIBD supplies up to $1,000 in matching funds for proposal preparation assistance, and accesses personnel from within the North Dakota University system to serve as principal investigators or consultants for SBIR applicants.

Governor's Advisory Council or Task Force

Contact:
Mr. Chuck Fleming, Chief of Staff
Office of the Governor
600 East Boulevard
Bismarck, ND 58505–0001
(701) 224–2200

The governor does not have an advisory board focused exclusively on small business issues and concerns, but the Governor's Roundtable advises the governor on all business in North Dakota. The governor serves as chairperson of the Roundtable, which is composed of 12 clusters of economic development professionals representing many different industries, and including a cluster devoted to small business development.

Legislative Committees and Subcommittees

Contact:
Senator Jayson Greba
Chairman
Committee on Industry, Business, and Labor
Legislative Council
State Capitol
Bismarck, ND 58505
(701) 224–2916
fax: (701) 224–3615

Most small business matters are referred to the Joint Committee on Industry, Business, and Labor. North Dakota uses joint House/Senate committees during the interim. The Joint Committee on Industry, Business, and Labor will be active until the 1993 general session.

Legislation

Legislation affecting small business that was adopted by the 1989 state legislature follows.

- S.B. 2043 streamlines securities regulations to help launch new businesses by reducing the costs involved in raising capital under certain circumstances. Qualifying businesses can raise up to $500,000 in capital by selling securities without having to register them, as long as they comply with other requirements. Funds raised are place in an escrow account.

- H.B. 1025 appropriates $5.5 million to the state economic development commission for the 1989 and 1990 biennium. H.B. 1025 spells out the functions of the commission, which include promoting economic development generally, assisting the establishment of new businesses and industries, promoting the expansion of existing businesses and industries, developing new markets for agricultural and other products, encouraging international trade, developing tourism, and attracting new residents, business, and industry. The economic development commission co-locates small business development centers, regional economic development offices, and agricultural extension offices. A grant of $100,000 was appropriated for small business innovation research.

- S.B. 2354 establishes an "Economic Feasibility Institute." The purpose of this institute is to initiate, encourage, and enhance the commercial development of agricultural and nonagricultural products, processes, commodities, and services in North Dakota. The institute will benefit small businesses engaged in supplying ancillary services to agriculture.

- S.B. 2234 establishes a statewide nonprofit equity corporation, which is authorized to take equity positions in new and existing businesses in North Dakota. The corporation's primary goal is the economic development and expansion of North Dakota. It may participate with other states or other state organizations in projects that clearly benefit North Dakota residents by creating jobs or secondary business.

No regular legislative session was held in North Dakota in 1990.

Legislation affecting small business that was adopted by the 1991 state legislature includes the following:

- S.B. 2058, commonly known as "Growing North Dakota," disbands the Economic Development Commission, restructuring the agency as the Department of Economic Development and Finance and creating new financing programs for primary sector businesses in agriculture, manufacturing, and exported services industries. The bill requires any business receiving monies from the primary sector development fund to pay all full-time workers a wage that is at least equal to the federal poverty level for a family of four for the life of the transaction.

Another major section of S.B. 2058 set up a $6.7 million primary sector development fund. The fund is designed to provide "gap" financing not available from other, more conventional sources. Monies from the fund can be made available to primary sector business through innovative financing mechanisms to provide long-term capital to new, expanding, or relocating businesses. A primary sector business is defined as one that "through the employment of knowledge or labor, adds value to a product, process, or service that results in the creation of new wealth." Primary business does not include production agriculture.

- S.B. 2206 provides for the merger of the Workers Compensation Bureau and Job Service North Dakota by 1993. The Workers Compensation Bureau was directed to create a schedule of fees for payment of medical costs. Under S.B. 2206, employers will pay the first $250 of the cost of each employee's injuries (i.e., cover each employee's $250 deductible). The bureau, however, will make all compensation decisions and track all paperwork. This reform measure also adds binding arbitration as an optional dispute resolution process. If used, a three-person panel will hear a case, and the panel's decision is binding and nonreviewable in a district court. Finally, a third party administrator and managed-care program is created by S.B. 2206 to ensure claimants receive appropriate medical treatment in a cost-effective manner. This change allows the bureau to require claimants to begin treatment with different doctors to better direct their medical care.

- H.B. 1321 revises workers' compensation premiums. Effective July 1, 1992, the base against which premiums are charged will change from $3,600 to 70 percent of the state's average wage (about $11,800). Effective in 1993, the legislation rewards employers for a "good experience" rating. The resulting system will assess premiums in a manner similar to the unemployment compensation system.

- H.B. 1042 allows health insurance carriers to market a no-frills group health insurance policy. A no-frills health policy will have lower premiums because it does not include certain state-mandated coverages.

- H.B. 1539 permits insurance carriers to provide coverage for small employers by charging a base premium for each class of business according to a rating period. Small employers—those having 25 or fewer employees—are eligible.

- H.B. 1272 keeps tort reform provisions in state law from expiring in 1993. In past years, increasingly higher claim awards caused insurance to be virtually out of reach of small businesses. Several tort reform bills were adopted in the 1980s to limit court settlements. These reforms sought to bring greater predictability into the judicial process and to stabilize liability insurance premiums.

- H.B. 1439 funds the EPA's required $1 million in pollution liability on tank owners by imposing a $75 fee per above ground tank and $125 fee per below ground tank, and increasing the fuel tax to one cent per gallon. This legislation is effective until June 30, 1993.

- H.B. 1048 exempts manufacturing equipment purchased for new or expanding businesses from state sales and use taxes. This change improves the state's ability to retain existing business as well as to recruit new businesses.

- S.B. 2554 repeals the minimal income tax for corporations, leaving only the regular tax formula for corporations.

State Small Business Conferences

Contact:
Ms. Kim Stenehjem, Public Information
  Specialist
Department of Economic Development and
  Finance
1833 East Bismarck Expressway
Bismarck, ND 58504
(701) 224–2810

The Governor's Economic Development Roundtable was held on November 20–21, 1991, in Jamestown, North Dakota.

Ohio

Small Business Offices, Programs, and Activities

Ohio Department of Development

The **Ohio Department of Development**, the lead agency providing business assistance in the state, offers business services through many programs and offices, including the Small Business Development Center Program, the Business Permit Center, the Women's Business Resource Program, and the Minority Business Development Program.

Small Business Development Centers

Contact:
Ms. Holly Schick, Director
Ohio Small Business Development Center
   Program
Ohio Department of Development
30 East Broad Street
P.O. Box 1001
Columbus, OH 43266
(614) 466–27110
(800) 848–1300 (toll-free)

The **Small Business Development Center** (SBDC) program is a major management assistance delivery program of the U.S. Small Business Administration, administered in partnership with the Ohio Department of Development. The program's mission is to provide leadership that strengthens the Ohio SBDC network, thereby furthering the growth and stability of Ohio's small businesses. SBDCs offer in-depth assistance in business planning, development, and problem solving to pre-venture and existing small businesses. Through a statewide network of service providers, SBDCs provide free and confidential business counseling, training, and other customized support services.

The SBDC program also offers specialized business services in the areas of federal procurement (through partnerships established with the U.S. Defense Logistics Agency), international trade, women's business ownership, and child day care. A list of all the Small Business Development Centers and subcenters in Ohio is in Appendix A of this directory.

Contact:
Mr. Dick Ising, Manager
One-Stop Business Permit Center
Ohio Small Business Development Center
Ohio Department of Development
P.O. Box 1001
Columbus, OH 43266–0101
(614) 466–4232
(800) 848–1300 (toll-free)

Contact:
Ms. Melody Borchers, Manager
Women's Business Resource Program
Ohio Small Business Development Center
Ohio Department of Development
P.O. Box 1001
Columbus, OH 43266–0101
(614) 466–4945
(800) 848–1300 (toll-free)

Contact:
Mr. Patrick Valente, Manager
Child Day Care Grant and Loan Program
Ohio Small Business Development Center
Ohio Department of Development
P.O. Box 1001
Columbus, OH 43266–0101
(614) 752–9221
(800) 848–1300 (toll-free)

Contact:
Ms. Renee Higgins, Manager
Office of Management and Technical
    Assistance/Contract Procurement
    Assistance
Ohio Department of Development
P.O. Box 1001
Columbus, OH 43266–0101
(614) 466–5700
(800) 848–1300 (toll-free)

The **One-Stop Business Permit Center** was established in August 1983 to facilitate obtaining state permit and application forms needed to open a business. The center provides tailored start-up business assistance kits for many types of enterprises and serves as an ombudsman for individuals experiencing delays in obtaining state license and permit approvals. The unit also publishes a weekly listing of all proposed Ohio agency rules and regulations that may have an impact on the small business community.

Women seeking assistance in starting, managing, or expanding a business in Ohio find the help they need through the **Women's Business Resource Program**. The program serves as an information clearinghouse for business resources, is an advocate on behalf of female entrepreneurs, and ensures women equal access to state business assistance programs. The program publishes *Ohio Women Business Leaders* (a directory of women business owners), sponsors seminars and workshops, and identifies purchasing opportunities. It also coordinates the Ohio Women Business Resource Network, a statewide consortium that provides counseling, training, and local financing to women business owners.

The **Child Day Care Grant and Loan Program** is a new initiative operated in conjunction with the Ohio Department of Human Services. It's purpose is to improve the quality of child day care in the state and to make it more accessible to low income families. Through a development block grant from the U.S. Department of Health and Human Services, the program awards grants for both start-up and expansion of day care programs throughout the state.

Minority Business Development Program

The **Minority Business Development Program** provides a variety of services designed to meet the needs of minority business enterprises. Services include the following:

- Management and Technical Services. Staff works closely with the client to develop ideas for expanding a business and provides technical, management analysis, and educational assistance for various business ventures. Financial consulting staff compiles and reviews loan packages from minority businesses and assists in capital formation through identified public- and private-sector funding sources, whether debt or equity financing.

- Procurement Services. The Procurement Service Office provides support services for construction and goods and services contractors. Compiled information on local, state, federal, and corporate purchasing programs that are available to minority businesses can be obtained through this office. The office also helps public- and private-sector managers and purchasing officials locate minority firms by providing pertinent information on minority businesses.

Minority Business Development Center

Contact:
Ms. Margie A. Montgomery, Program
   Manager
Minority Contractors and Business
   Assistance Program
Ohio Department of Development
P.O. Box 1001
Columbus, OH 43266–0101
(614) 466–2691
(800) 848–1300 (toll-free)

The **Minority Business Development Center** coordinates the nine-agency statewide Minority Contractors and Business Assistance Program, which provides management and technical assistance, counseling, and training to minority business enterprises. In addition, statewide and local conferences, workshops, and seminars are held.

Small Business Innovation Research

Contact:
Mr. G. Mark Skinner, Manager
SBIR Program
77 S. High Street, 25th Floor
Columbus, OH 43215
(614) 466–5867

Ohio's **Small Business Innovation Research** (SBIR) program is designed to introduce more of Ohio's technology-oriented small businesses to the federal R&D market, to assist companies in applying for SBIR awards, and to serve as an aide and mentor to the community of SBIR winners in the state. Pursuant to these goals, Ohio's SBIR program offers technical, educational, and promotional assistance through its office in Columbus. Sponsored programs and activities include workshops and seminars designed to increase awareness and understanding of SBIR; one-on-one technical assistance to help individuals writing SBIR proposals; and customized assistance designed to assist SBIR winners in taking their projects through to commercialization.

Construction Contract Bond Assistance Program

Contact:
Mr. Philip G. Shotwell, Executive Director
Minority Development Financing
  Commission
Ohio Department of Development
P.O. Box 1001
Columbus, OH 43266–0101
(614) 644–7708
(800) 848–1300 (toll-free)

The **Construction Contract Bond Assistance Program** has a $10-million bonding capacity for minority contractors. State-certified minority contractors may apply if they have been refused bonds by two surety companies within the contractor's current fiscal year.

Under the **Mini-Loan Program**, loans are directed to businesses with fewer than 25 employees for fixed-asset expansion projects of less than $100,000. The state has targeted 50 percent of the funds for allocation to businesses owned by minorities and women. Ohio's participation is in the form of a loan guarantee.

Minority Development Loan Program

Contact:
Ms. Carolyn Seward, Credit Manager/Loan
  Officer
Ohio Department of Development
P.O. Box 1001
Columbus, OH 43266–0101
(614) 644–7708
(800) 848–1300 (toll-free)

The **Minority Development Loan Program** offers qualified minority businesses below-market financing for fixed assets, land, buildings, and equipment. Eligible enterprises must engage in manufacturing, distribution, commerce, or research.

Governor's Advisory Council or Task Force

Contact:
Ms. Karen B. Conrad, Manager
Office of Small and Minority Business
Ohio Department of Development
P.O. Box 1001
Columbus, OH 43266–0101
(614) 466–2718
(800) 848–1300 (toll-free)

The **Ohio Small Business and Entrepreneurship Council** was created to help the state government formulate policies that aid small business development. The council comprises private-sector representatives who own or manage small businesses or have substantial business expertise, state legislators, and the director of the Ohio Department of Development.

Contact:

Ms. Mary Raines, Acting Director
Women's Policy and Research Commission
Women's Policy and Research Center
30 East Broad Street, B–1 Level
Columbus, OH 43266
(614) 466–5580
(800) 282–3040

The purpose of the **Women's Policy and Research Commission** is to promote the advancement of women and remove barriers to women's equality. It is required by law to provide an annual report of its activities by February of each year to the governor, the president of the state Senate, and the speaker of the Ohio House of Representatives.

The commission is also charged with the governance of the Women's Policy and Research Center (formerly the Women's Information Center). The center is required by law to: identify through research, data collection, and public hearings, barriers to women's equality; analyze current and proposed public policies to determine their impact on women; educate the public on the status of women and on the impact of public policy on women; issue reports and recommendations to the executive and legislative branches of government and to the general public regarding women's issues; maintain lists of persons qualified for positions in state government and make these lists available to appropriate appointment authorities; encourage collaboration between the center and other public agencies and institutions on issues of mutual interest; and help the public and private sectors develop programs and services for women. Services available through the center include a toll-free line for obtaining information on legal rights; a free legislative update; and a referral service that directs inquiries to appropriate state or federal agencies.

Legislative Committees and Subcommittees

Both houses of the Ohio Legislature have committees dealing with small business matters.

Contacts:

Senator Charles Horn, Chair
Senate Economic Development and Small
   Business Committee
State House
Columbus, OH 43266–0604
(614) 466–4538

Representative Troy James, Chair
House Economic Development and Small
   Business Committee
Vern Riffe Center
77 South High Street
Columbus, OH 43266–0603
(614) 466–1414

Legislation

The following legislation affecting small business was passed during the 1991 session:

- H.B. 142 requires group insurance policies to offer coverage for mammography screening and pap smears. Employers offering health insurance benefits would be required to provide coverage for mammography screening and pap smears, either through insurance or other arrangements.

- S.B. 272 revises definitions of real and personal property to clarify that "business fixtures" be treated and classified as personal property for property tax purposes.

- Am. Sub. S.B. 11 requires group health insurance policyholders (i.e., employers) to notify employees that a required premium payment or contribution has not been made. Notification must be given within five days after the employer receives notice from the insurer that the policy has been terminated.

State Small Business Conferences

Contact:
Ms. Sallie D. Gibson, Administrator
Special Projects
Ohio Department of Development
P.O. Box 1001
Columbus, OH 43266–0101
(614) 466–5700
(800) 848–1300 (toll-free)

An all-Ohio minority trade fair was held in May 1992 and attracted more than 2,000 potential small business contractors. The trade fair, a coordinated effort between the Ohio Department of Development and Ohio's five regional minority purchasing councils, created a statewide opportunity for large corporations to meet small minority-owned businesses. A 1991 trade fair resulted Kin contracts totaling $34 million for minority vendors.

Oklahoma

Small Business Offices, Programs, and Activities

Oklahoma Department of Commerce

Contact:
Mr. Glen Robards, Director of Programs
Department of Commerce
State Capitol, Room 210
Oklahoma City, OK 73105
(405) 521–3370

Contact:
Ms. Pam Bryan, State Director for Small
  Business
Department of Commerce
6601 Broadway Extension
Oklahoma City, OK 73116
(405) 843–9770

Contact:
Mr. Robert Heard, Director
Capital Resources Division
Department of Commerce
6601 Broadway Extension
Oklahoma City, OK 73116–8214
(405) 843–9770

The **Oklahoma Department of Commerce** includes nine divisions to assist businesses in the state. The department provides assistance in developing business plans and financial packages, industry-customized training, foreign and domestic market services, and small and minority business programs.

The specialized **Small Business Assistance Office** provides targeted assistance to Oklahoma's small business owners and entrepreneurs. The Small Business Office includes the following technical assistance programs: **General Small Business Assistance; Minority/Individual Indian/Women-Owned Business Assistance; Tribal Government Assistance;** and the **Main Street Program**. The office provides a wide range of business assistance publications, including *A Guide for Small Business*. The office also sponsors workshops and how-to seminars on topics pertinent to the small business owner.

The **Business Development Division** develops industrial prospects for the state and assists local communities in their industrial development efforts. The division has four area directors responsible for working with community leaders to match industrial assets with prospects. More than 200 community profiles provide information to prospective new industries on building and industrial sites, industrial foundations and trusts, local financing, utility and rail services, and other information. One-stop service is provided to businesses on tax information, required permits, available industrial revenue bonds, and other financing sources.

The **Capital Resources Division** is designed to help Oklahoma companies gain access to the capital they need to grow and prosper. The division's central program is the Capital Resources Network. This program provides financial specialists to help businesses analyze their financing needs and to work closely with local economic development staff to help them package proposals for their local companies. The division also administers several other programs, including the Oklahoma Innovation Network Public/Private Partnership Incentive and Jobs Development Incentive Program, the Inventor's Assistance Program, and programs authorized by Oklahoma's Small Business Incubator Incentives Act. In addition, the division assists in the development of new loan and investment programs, sponsored by both public and private organizations.

Teamwork Oklahoma is a one-stop statewide business referral service sponsored by the Department of Commerce in cooperation with various statewide economic development groups. The *Teamwork Oklahoma Guide to Services* is available to callers free of charge.

The **International Division** encourages foreign investment in Oklahoma by working with companies in the state to increase their exports. The Oklahoma International Export Services program is a cooperative effort of the U.S. Department of Commerce district office and the International Division of the Oklahoma Department of Commerce. Trade specialists are assigned to five areas of the state to work with Oklahoma firms in exporting. The International Division also works closely with the governor's International and Waterways teams to promote the use and development of the Arkansas River navigation system.

Contact:
Mr. John Reid, Director of Marketing
Department of Commerce
6601 Broadway Extension
Oklahoma City, OK 73116–8214
(405) 843–9770
(800) 443–OKLA (toll-free, out-of-state)
(800) 522–OKLA (toll-free, in-state)

Contact:
Mr. Gary Miller, Director of International
   Trade
Department of Commerce
6601 Broadway Extension
Oklahoma City, OK 73116–8214
(405) 521–2401

Training for Industry Program

Contact:
Ms. Dana Hieronymus, Economic
   Development Liaison
Oklahoma State Department of Vocational
   and Technical Education
6601 Broadway Extension
Oklahoma City, OK 73116–8214
(405) 843–9770

The **Training for Industry Program** provides customized needs assessment, pre-employment training, curriculum development, training facilities, equipment, and instructors at no cost to new or expanding companies in Oklahoma. Other services include customized retraining and upgraded training in existing companies (companies pay one-third of cost); a bid assistance network to help companies procure government contracts; management development training programs; a business development program for small and growing companies; entrepreneurship opportunities through self-employment training and business incubators; and training in Small Business Innovation Research (SBIR) and technology transfer to assist companies through the SBIR application process.

Small Business Innovation Research Program

Contact:
Ms. Sherilyn S. Stickley, Director
Technology Development
Oklahoma Center for the Advancement of
   Science and Technology (OCAST)
205 N.W. 63rd Street, Suite 305
Oklahoma City, OK 73116–8209
(405) 848–2633

Oklahoma's **Small Business Innovation Research** (SBIR) program is a Phase I Incentive Funding Program, which reimburses a company's federal SBIR proposal preparation costs at $0.50 per $1.00 with a Fiscal Year 1993 (July 1, 1992 through June 30, 1993) maximum award amount of $1,250. The state also has an SBIR Matching Funds Program. Oklahoma companies that have won a federal SBIR Phase I contract and have been encouraged by the federal agency to apply for Phase II funding are eligible for Oklahoma Center for the Advancement of Science and Technology (OCAST) Matching Funds. The OCAST Matching Funds Program will award up to one-half of the federal Phase I award amount. For FY93, the maximum OCAST/SBIR Matching Funds award is $10,000.

For FY93, OCAST has $95,000 in funding under the SBIR Programs described above. The Phase I Incentive Funding and Matching Fund awards are made on a first-come, first-served basis. The OCAST Board of Directors makes the final decision to grant reimbursement funds under the Phase I Incentive Funding and Matching Funds Program.

Finance Authorities

Contacts:
Mr. Carl Clark, Executive Vice President
Oklahoma Development Finance Authority
205 N.W. 63rd Street, Suite 270
Oklahoma City, OK 73115
(405) 848–9761

Mr. Jay Casey, President
Oklahoma Industrial Finance Authority
205 N.W. 63rd Street, Suite 260
Oklahoma City, OK 73116
(405) 521–2182

Two statewide entities dealing in business finance are the **Oklahoma Development Finance Authority** and the **Oklahoma Industrial Finance Authority**. Both issue notes and bonds to fund business projects. Interest earnings on the notes or bonds can be either taxable or tax-exempt.

Oklahoma Small Business Development Center

Contact:
Dr. Grady Pennington, State Director
Small Business Development Center
Southeastern State University
517 West University
Durant, OK 74701
(405) 924–0277
(800) 522–6154 (toll-free, in-state)

A consortium of Oklahoma universities forms a **Small Business Development Center** (SBDC) to serve small businesses in the state. Financial support is provided by the state, along with in-kind contributions from consortium members and assistance from the U.S. Small Business Administration. The Oklahoma SBDC provides management assistance to small and new business ventures. The center counsels potential entrepreneurs, promotes sound growth in existing businesses, and develops services to strengthen the small business community of Oklahoma. The lead center is located in Durant at Southeastern Oklahoma State University. Subcenters are located in Ada, Edmond, Enid, Langston, Lawton, Midwest City, Muskogee, Poteau, Tahlequah, Tulsa, and Weatherford. A complete listing of SBDCs and subcenters is in Appendix A of this directory.

Central Industrial Applications Center

Contact:
Dr. Dickie Deel, Director
Central Industrial Applications Center
P.O. Box 1335
Durant, OK 74702
(405) 924–5094
(800) 658–2823 (toll-free)

The **Central Industrial Applications Center** (CIAC) provides technology data searches to Oklahoma businesses by using more than 400 data bases, and makes available a library of word technology information with assistance from the National Aeronautics and Space Administration. Answers to technical questions are available from CIAC through use of computer banks holding more than 50 million references. Final reports come in a range of formats—from a personal visit by a CIAC technical advisor to a printed list of citations that open new possibilities for technology transfer by Oklahoma business and industry.

Rural Development

Contact:
Mr. Tom Seth Smith, Chief Executive Officer
Rural Enterprises, Inc.
Durant, OK 74702
(405)924–5094
(800) 633–0720 (toll-free, out-of-state)

Rural Enterprises, Inc., (REI), is a nonprofit industrial development corporation and national demonstration model headquartered in Durant. It provides financial services, technology transfer, incubators, new product evaluations, and other resources to rural businesses. It serves 25 counties in rural southeastern and south central Oklahoma, working to create new, long-term private-sector jobs in an area of chronic economic depression.

Contact:
Ms. Claudette Henry, State Treasurer
State Treasurer's Office
State Capitol, Room 217
Oklahoma City, OK 73105
(405) 521–3191

The **Agricultural Linked Deposit Program** provides low-interest money for distressed farmers and ranchers, as well as low-interest money for alternative agricultural production.

Contact:
Mr. Ron Stewart
Community Affairs and Development
    Division
Oklahoma Department of Commerce
6601 Broadway Extension
P.O. Box 26980
Oklahoma City, OK 73126–0980
(405) 843–9770

The mission of the **Rural Development** office is to enhance economic development and diversification of rural Oklahoma, acting in cooperation with various local, state, and national rural development agencies and the private sector.

Oklahoma Bid Assistance Centers

Contact:
Ms. Denise Agee, Coordinator
Oklahoma Bid Assistance Centers
Oklahoma Department of Vocational and
    Technical Education
1500 West Seventh Avenue
Stillwater, OK 74074
(405) 443–5574

The **Bid Assistance Centers Program** is a procurement technical assistance program designed to help Oklahoma businesses capture a larger share of contract opportunities available within both the government and private sector.

Direct Marketing Programs

Contact:
Mr. John David, Market Development
    Coordinator
Market Development Division
Oklahoma Department of Agriculture
2800 North Lincoln Boulevard
Oklahoma City, OK 73105–4298
(405) 521–3864

The **Direct Marketing Programs** develop direct marketing outlets for farmers by providing leadership, guidance, and direction to community leaders and others. The two major components of the program are: (1) promotion of direct retail sales through pick-your-own operations, mail order sales, mobile markets, flea markets, and shopping malls; and (2) promotion of direct wholesaling through commercial systems to grocery chains, restaurants, nutrition centers, and other wholesale buyers.

Governor's Advisory Council or Task Force

Small business and economic development issues are the responsibility of the governor's chief of staff, who also serves as liaison to the U.S. Small Business Administration, small business groups, and other economic development planning groups.

Contact:
Ms. Pam Bryan, State Director for Small
    Business
Business Development Division
Department of Commerce
6601 Broadway Extension
Oklahoma City, OK 73116–8214
(405) 843–9770

Contact:
Ms. Linda Sponsler, Liaison
Office of the Governor
440 South Houston, Room 304
Tulsa, OK 74127
(918) 581–2801

The **Governor's Committee on the Status of Women** monitors programs and benefits for women.

Legislative Committees and Subcommittees

Small business legislation is considered by the House and Senate Economic Development Committees.

Contacts:

Senator Ted Fisher
Chairman
Senate Committee on Economic
    Development
State Capitol
Oklahoma City, OK 73105
(405) 524–0126

Representative Don McCorkell
Chairman
House Committee on Economic
    Development
State Capitol
Oklahoma City, OK 73105
(405) 521–2011

Legislation

The following legislation was recently passed by the Oklahoma Legislature:

- The Oklahoma Small Business Surety Bond Guaranty Program Act establishes a program to assist those small contractors who bid on public works projects to obtain required surety bonds.

- A modification to the Oklahoma Capital Investment Act, which was enacted in 1987, removed provisions that impeded the development of an investment fund.

- Legislation authorizing the Department of Commerce to designate enterprise zones in the state.

- Provisions to allow public trust to qualify for low interest loans under the Small Business Linked Deposit Act.

State Small Business Conferences

Contact:
Mr. Randy Hogan, Chairman
Governor's Conference on Small Business
Journal Record
Oklahoma City, OK 73126–0370
(405) 278–6006

Oklahoma's third annual **Governor's Conference on Small Business** was attended by more than 2,000 people in Oklahoma City in June 1989. State and federal small business issues were discussed and business educations seminars were held. This forum has grown tremendously since its inaugural year in 1987, and it serves as a useful platform from which small business interests are highlighted and profiled.

Oregon

Small Business Offices, Programs, and Activities

Economic Development Department

Contact:
Mr. Mike Shadbolt, Small Business Program
    Manager
Office of Small Business Assistance
Oregon Economic Development Department
775 Summer Street, N.E.
Salem, OR 97310
(503) 373–1241
(800) 233–3306 (toll-free, in-state)

Oregon's economy has a strong small business base. A range of services, including small business advocacy, permit and regulatory assistance, and technical and financial assistance are provided through Oregon's Economic Development Department. The Economic Development Department works closely with the Commerce Department in responding to requests for information regarding regulated business activities. The objective is to provide quick, accurate information.

The **Office of Small Business Assistance** serves as an advocate, representing and promoting small business needs and activities to the legislature, state agencies, and the community at large. It also coordinates state, federal, local, and private small business resources, including the Small Business Development Centers, Oregon Marketplace, the Oregon Downtown Development Program, and the Government Contract Acquisition Program. In addition, it operates the First Stop Regulatory Information Center, which provides information on licenses and permits to new or expanding Oregon businesses.

Contact:
Mr. Greg Baker, Administrator
Business Development Division
Oregon Economic Development Department
775 Summer Street, N.E.
Salem, OR 97310
(503) 373–1225
(800) 233–3306 (toll-free, in-state)
(800) 547–7842 (toll-free, out-of-state)

The **Business Development Division** maintains a business retention and expansion program to identify business problems and opportunities, and offers a publications kit describing state government and other services available to Oregon businesses. These services include technical assistance, job training, education, financial incentives, regulatory assistance, and export marketing assistance, as well as local and federal programs.

Contact:
Ms. Kim Jackson, Secretary
The One-Stop Permit Center
Oregon Economic Development Department
775 Summer Street, N.E.
Salem, OR 97310
(503) 373–1241

Contacts:
Mr. Mark D. Huston, Manager
Mr. Barrett MacDougall, Senior Finance
    Officer
Business Finance Section
Oregon Economic Development Department
775 Summer Street, N.E.
Salem, OR 97310
(503) 373–1240, Ext. 371

Permit and regulatory assistance is provided by the department's one-stop permit information service. The **One-Stop Permit Center** assists thousands of Oregon businesses every year in beginning or expanding their operations. The program provides telephone numbers for obtaining permits for activities regulated by state agencies. For more complex questions, the service sets up conferences between the affected business and the appropriate regulatory agency. Most of the businesses using these services have fewer than 50 employees.

The **Oregon Business Development Fund** was created by legislation in 1983 to provide financing to small and medium-sized manufacturing, processing, and tourism-related firms expanding their operations or locating in the state. Loans of up to $250,000 are made for land, buildings, fixed assets, or working capital. The maximum term is 20 years, with the rate fixed at one percentage point below U.S. Treasury bond rates. The fund was capitalized at approximately $10 million in Economic Development Administration funds, state lottery, and general funds. The fund is administered by the state's Economic Development Department (EDD). The EDD also is the state coordinator for an industrial revenue bond program designed to help manufacturers expand.

Business Resources Division

Contact:
Mr. Tom Fuller, Administrator
Business Resources Division
Oregon Economic Development Department
775 Summer Street, N.E.
Salem, OR 97310
(503) 378–6310

The **Business Resources Division** coordinates business, financial, job training, and community development resources for individuals, businesses, and local jurisdictions.

Contact:
Ms. Paula Kaeb, Secretary
Business Resources Division
Oregon Economic Development Department
775 Summer Street, N.E.
Salem, OR 97310
(503) 378–6310

The following **publications** are available from the Business Resources Division: *Doing Business in Oregon*, *Starting a Business in Oregon*, *A Summary of Oregon Taxes*, *Services to Promote the Growth of Oregon Business*, *Oregon Economic Development Revenue Bonds*, and *Oregon Economic Trade and Investment Facts*.

Oregon Resource and Technology Development Corporation

Contact:
Mr. John Beaulieu, President
ORTDC
1934 N.E. Broadway
Portland, OR 977232–1502
(503) 282–4462

The **Oregon Resource and Technology Development Corporation** (ORTDC) was created by the Oregon legislature to provide investment capital for early-stage business finance (seed capital) and applied research and development projects that can lead to commercially viable products. Seed capital investments are limited to $500,000 per enterprise. Applied research investments are limited to $100,000 and must be matched through cash or in-kind services.

Minority- and Women-Owned Business Programs

Contact:
Mr. Barrett MacDougall, Senior Finance
   Officer
Business Finance
Oregon Economic Development Department
775 Summer Street, N.E.
Salem, OR 97310
(503) 378–6359

Fifteen percent of funds in the ORTDC are reserved for minority- and women-owned businesses. The Economic Development Department actively encourages applications from minority- and women-owned businesses.

Contact:
Ms. Marie McHone, Special Programs
   Coordinator
Purchasing Division
Department of General Services
1225 Ferry Street
Salem, OR 97310
(503) 373–1250

The **Department of General Services** has operated a Minority and Women's Business Enterprise (MWBE) program since 1976 and has had a set-aside program since 1981. Contracts under $50,000 may be considered for the MWBE set-aside. For public works contracts over $50,000, MWBE goals are set for individual projects.

Contact:
Mr. Harold Lasley, Civil Rights Manager
Oregon Department of Transportation
105 Transportation Building
Salem, OR 97310
(503) 378–8077

The **Oregon Department of Transportation** administers a goal program for minority, disadvantaged, and women-owned business participation in contracting. Contracting opportunities include highway and bridge construction consulting services. The department sets annual and individual project or contract goals.

Department of Agriculture

Contact:
Mr. Bruce Andrews, Director
Department of Agriculture
635 Capitol Street, N.E.
Salem, OR 97310–0110
(503) 378–4665

The **Department of Agriculture** runs a marketing program that assists in the development of new markets and expansion of existing markets for agricultural commodities produced or processed in Oregon. This effort is directed towards developing and improving overseas and domestic markets.

Small Business Development Centers

Contact:
Mr. Sandy Cutler, State Director
Oregon Small Business Development Center
Lane Community College
99 W. 10th, Suite 216
Eugene, OR 97401
(503) 726–2250

Small Business Development Centers (SBDCs) coordinate federal, state, university, and private resources to counsel and train owners of small businesses. SBDCs offer this assistance through courses, seminars, one-on-one counseling, and by making available research facilities. They are organized by the U.S. Small Business Administration and are usually affiliated with a state college or university. The lead SBDC in Oregon is located in Eugene at Lane Community College. Subcenters are located in Albany, Ashland, Bend, Coos Bay, Grants Pass, Gresham, Klamath Falls, LaGrande, Lincoln City, Medford, Ontario, Pendleton, Roseburg, Salem, Seaside, and Tillamook. A listing of all Small Business Development Centers and subcenters in Oregon is in Appendix A of this directory.

Governor's Advisory Council or Task Force

Contact:
Mr. Mike Shadbolt, Small Business Program
   Manager
775 Summer Street, N.E.
Salem, OR 97310
(503) 373–1241

The **Small Business Advisory Committee** promotes programs and legislation favorable to small business.

Legislative Committees and Subcommittees

The Committee on Business and Consumer Affairs and the Joint Committee on Trade and Economic Development handle small business issues. Oregon's legislative assembly meets once every two years. The House and Senate Committees on Business and Consumer Affairs can be reached only when the legislature is in session. The Trade and Economic Development Committee is a standing committee.

Contacts:

Representative Peg Jolin
Chairperson
House Committee on Business and
   Consumer Affairs
State Capitol
Salem, OR 97310
(503) 378–5952

Senator Jim Hill
Chairperson
Senate Committee on Business, Housing,
   and Finance
State Capitol
Salem, OR 97310
(503) 378–8117

Senator Joyce Cohen
Cochairperson
Representative Wayne Fawbush,
   Cochairperson
Joint Committee on Trade and Economic
   Development
State Capital
Salem, OR 97310
(503) 378–8811

Legislation

The Oregon Legislature enacted key pieces of legislation related to small business in 1991 including health insurance, wages, family leave, and the environment. Oregon expanded health insurance markets for small employers, allowed employers more flexibility in issuing final paychecks to employees who quit without final notice, and passed legislation requiring employers to provide 12 weeks of family leave every two years for workers with ill dependents. In the area of environmental legislation, the Oregon Department of Environmental Quality will now provide hazardous waste technical assistance without levying new fees on small business.

State Small Business Conferences

Contact:
Ms. Leann Griffith
U.S. Bank of Oregon
309 SW 6th Avenue, BB–10
Portland, OR 97204
(800) 422–8762 (toll-free)

In 1991, the **Oregon Small Business Consortium** held a series of conferences in 15 cities and towns throughout the state. More than 1,500 small businesspersons throughout the state participated. The conferences were held throughout the year and concluded in November 1991.

The first annual **U.S. Bank Small Business Conference and Expo** was held in September 1992. The conference featured more than 80 educational sessions for small business owners and managers. In conjunction with the conference, the event featured 150 exposition booths of products and services used by small businesses.

Pennsylvania

Small Business Offices, Programs, and Activities

Pennsylvania Department of Commerce

Contact:
Ms. Emily White, Acting Director
Office of Enterprise Development
Pennsylvania Department of Commerce
401 Forum Building
Harrisburg, PA 17120
(717) 783–8950

As the Commonwealth's advocate for small business, the Department of Commerce's **Office of Enterprise Development** is responsible for advocacy of the interests of small business in policy and legislative matters. The Business Resource Network within the office is responsible for providing referral services for small businesses dealing with state government and for coordinating technical assistance programs for small businesses.

Additionally, the **Pennsylvania Economic Development Partnership** was established in 1987 as a mechanism to bring together business, labor, education, and government leaders to address major economic concerns facing Pennsylvania. Within this partnership 15 task forces were established, including the Office of Enterprise Development. This task force developed numerous recommendations related to small businesses.

The Office of Enterprise Development administers the programs of the **Appalachian Regional Commission** (ARC) and the **Enterprise Development Program** (EDP) in Pennsylvania. The program goal is to accelerate the creation of jobs by helping small entrepreneurial enterprises capture new growing markets for Pennsylvania products.

Through the EDP, seven **Local Development Districts** (LDDs) serve Pennsylvania's 52 Appalachian counties and link resources to support local business expansion and job creation. Each LDD is active in finance, federal procurement assistance and export outreach, business incubators, job training, and advanced technology.

Contact:
Ms. Katherine Wilson, Director
Bureau of Small Business and Appalachian
  Development
Department of Commerce
461 Forum Building
Harrisburg, PA 17120
(717) 783–5700

Contact:
Mr. Gerald Kapp, Executive Director
Pennsylvania Industrial Development
  Authority
Department of Commerce
480 Forum Building
Harrisburg, PA 17120
(717) 787–6245

Contact:
Mr. Robert W. Coy, Executive Director
Ben Franklin Partnership
Pennsylvania Department of Commerce
352 Forum Building
Harrisburg, PA 17120
(717) 787–4147

The **Business Resource Network** serves as Pennsylvania's advocate for small business and provides prompt information on licenses and permits needed to start and operate businesses in the state. It can provide the necessary state forms for starting a business and will assist with difficulties involving state agencies. The network provides the following publications: *Small Business Planning Guide*, *Resource Directory for Small Business*, and *Starting A Small Business in Pennsylvania*.

The **Pennsylvania Industrial Development Authority** (PIDA) was established in 1956 to make long-term, low-interest business loans to firms engaged in manufacturing or industrial enterprises. PIDA funds may be used for purchases of land and buildings. Current policy targets PIDA funds to small and advanced technology businesses, enterprise zones, and minority- and women-owned businesses. A qualified business may receive up to $2 million with interest rates ranging from 3 percent to 9 percent, depending upon the unemployment rate in the critical economic area where the project is located. PIDA defines a small business as one employing fewer than 50 persons.

PIDA requires that at least one full-time job, or its equivalent, be created for every $15,000 of financing provided. This job creation target must be met within three years of occupancy of the project site.

The **Ben Franklin Partnership** (BFP) programs promote advanced technology in an effort to make traditional industry more competitive in the international marketplace and to spin off new small businesses on the leading edge of technological innovation.

The BFP's four **Advanced Technology Centers** represent consortia of private sector, labor, research universities and other higher education institutions, and economic development groups. Each center provides:

- Joint applied research and development efforts, in concert with the private sector, in specified areas such as robotics, biotechnology, and CAD–CAM. Each center emphasizes three or four research areas.

- Education and training, helping higher educational institutions to provide training and retraining in technical and other skill areas essential in assisting firm expansions and start-ups.

- Entrepreneurial assistance services, which include linking research and development, entrepreneurs, venture capitalists and other financial resources; assisting in preparation of business plans and feasibility studies; and providing small business incubator services and technology transfer activities.

Other services offered by the BFP include the **Small Business Incubator Program**, which funds the development of facilities that provide new manufacturing or product development companies with the space and business development services they can use for start-up and early years' growth. Five privately managed Seed Venture Capital Funds, established through a BFP challenge grant program, provide equity financing to new businesses during their earliest stages of growth. The BFP also awards Research Seed Grants of up to $35,000 to small businesses seeking to develop or introduce advanced technology into the marketplace.

The Ben Franklin Technology Centers also assist individuals and companies in locating and obtaining **Small Business Innovation Research** (SBIR) information. The center answers questions concerning preparation of proposals, including critiquing rough drafts and providing suggestions. Each of the Ben Franklin Technology Centers has current copies of agencies' solicitations that clients can use.

The **Bureau of International Development** offers specific assistance to Pennsylvania companies seeking the latest information on potential foreign markets for their products. The office also provides regional economic development organizations and companies with general assistance regarding all facets of international trade, and responds to numerous inquiries from foreign importers in search of new suppliers. Foreign offices are located in Frankfurt, Brussels, and Tokyo.

Contact:
Mr. David McClelland
Ben Franklin Technology Center
Northwest Satellite
The Behrend College
Station Road
Erie, PA 16563–0601
(814) 898–6114

Contact:
Mr. Joseph Burke, Acting Director
Office of International Development
Department of Commerce
486 Forum Building
Harrisburg, PA 17120
(717) 787–7190

The office frequently participates in international trade exhibitions or missions, which provide direct exposure for Pennsylvania companies to potential foreign buyers, agents, distributors, licensees, and joint venture partners. These trade activities are forums for immediate, personal contact and informal exchange of information invaluable to the establishment of international business relationships. In addition, the office cosponsors and participates in several international trade conferences and seminars throughout Pennsylvania. These events educate Pennsylvania firms as to the intricacies of the export process and inform them of the office's export assistance programs.

Contact:
Ms. Anne Brennan, Project Analyst
Revenue Bond and Mortgage Program
Department of Commerce
466 Forum Building
Harrisburg, PA 17120
(717) 783-1108

Financing for projects approved through the **Revenue Bond and Mortgage Program** is secured from private sector sources. These funds are borrowed through a local Industrial Development Authority (IDA). Because the authority is recognized as a political subdivision, the lender (except those affected by the Tax Reform Act of 1986) does not pay taxes on the interest earned from the loan, and the borrower has the benefit of an interest rate lower than conventional rates. Businesses can use the funds to acquire land, buildings, machinery, and equipment. Filing fees vary with the local IDAs.

Manufacturing projects must create or retain one job for every $50,000 within three years. All other projects must create or retain at least 10 jobs per loan.

Contact:
Ms. Patricia Habersberger, Administrator
Pennsylvania Capital Loan Fund
Department of Commerce
493 Forum Building
Harrisburg, PA 17120
(717) 783-1768

The **Pennsylvania Capital Loan Fund** (PCLF) provides low-interest loans to businesses for capital development projects that will result in long-term new employment opportunities. The PCLF is capitalized with federal funds from the Appalachian Regional Commission, the Economic Development Administration, and state appropriations. Recent legislative changes have expanded the program to provide assistance to manufacturers of apparel products, and assistance to small business enterprises that are increasing their penetration of foreign export markets. Eligibility criteria, terms, fees, and rates differ depending on funding source and class of loan.

Businesses applying for loans under Class I, II, or III must create at least one new full-time job (or its equivalent) for every $15,000 in loan proceeds within three years of the loan's disbursement. For apparel industry loans, businesses must create or preserve at least one job for every $10,000 in assistance. Applicants for export assistance loans for purposes other than working capital should present a plan for continued exporting that will create at least one new job for every $15,000 in loan proceeds within 5 years.

Loans of up to $100,000 or 50 percent of the total project cost (whichever is less) may be made to eligible businesses under Class I and II. Eligible businesses requesting apparel industry loans may receive up to $200,000 or 50 percent of the total pro-ject cost. Class III loans and export assistance loans of up to $200,000 or 50 percent of the total cost (whichever is less) may be made to eligible businesses. Processing time from date of application is an average of 90 days.

Contact:
Ms. Lisa Marshall, Director
Pennsylvania Economic Development
 Financing Authority
Department of Commerce
466 Forum Building
Harrisburg, PA 17120
(717) 783–1109

The **Pennsylvania Economic Development Financing Authority** (PEDFA) provides low-cost financing to growing busi-nesses in Pennsylvania by issuing both tax-exempt and taxable industrial revenue bonds. PEDFA issues and sells bonds, then lends the proceeds to eligible businesses to finance land, build-ings, renovations, equipment, and working capital. Loan terms are up to 30 years and interest costs are between 75 and 95 percent of the prime rate. Tax exempt eligible businesses include manufacturing facilities, nonprofit 501(c)(3) organizations, and exempt facilities such as solid waste disposal utilities plants. Tax-able eligible projects include all kinds of businesses.

Contact:
Mr. Aqil Sabur, Director
Pennsylvania Minority Business
 Development Authority
Department of Commerce
461 Forum Building
Harrisburg, PA 17120
(717) 783–1127

The **Pennsylvania Minority Business Development Authority** (PMBDA) provides low-interest, long-term loans and equity guarantees to assist in the start-up or expansion of minority-owned businesses. The maximum loan amount is $100,000 per applicant and is not to exceed 75 percent of the total required financing. The project must show that one job will be created or preserved for every $15,000 requested.

For advanced technology firms and manufacturing companies located in the state designated enterprise zones or redevelopment areas, loans may be made up to $200,000. Loans also are available for a maximum of 20 years. Interest rates are 50 percent of the prime lending rate as of the date approved by PMBDA. Projects must show that one job will be created for every $15,000 requested.

In 1985, PMBDA established the **Surety Bond and Working Capital Program** to guarantee up to 90 percent of bid and performance bonds needed by a minority business enterprise to obtain a contract with a state agency, and to provide short-term loans to minority contractors with the state for working capital. Also, a portion of the proceeds will be used for all forms of financial and technical assistance to aid in the start-up or expansion of minority-owned businesses.

The **Bureau of Women's Business Development** was established to address concerns of women business owners. Its mission is to function as the Commonwealth's single point of contact for fostering and promoting women-owned business in Pennsylvania. The staff provides information to women from the start-up phase of their business to and through expansion. Referrals are made to agencies within the state's Department of Commerce, other state, local, and federal agencies, and private entities regarding financing, contracting opportunities, management and financial skills, training, and networking.

The **Office of Small Business Advocate** was created to represent the interests of small business consumers of utility services in cases before the Pennsylvania Public Utility Commission (PUC), the courts, and those federal agencies that are involved with setting rates for utility services. Its activities include participating in cases involving rate increase requests made by Pennsylvania's utilities to the PUC and in other proceedings that will affect the cost of or the conditions applicable to utility service. In those cases, the office's lawyers and technical consultants speak on behalf of small commercial and industrial customers. Their primary objective is to ensure that only those rate increases that are reasonable and necessary are granted to the utilities, and that the burden of the increased rates is distributed among the main classes of customers (residential, commercial, and industrial) in proportion to the costs of providing service to each of those customer groups.

Contact:
Ms. Lenore Cameron, Director
Bureau of Women's Business Development
Department of Commerce
403 Forum Building
Harrisburg, PA 17120
(717) 787–3339

Contact:
Mr. Bernard Ryan, Jr., Small Business
    Advocate
Department of Commerce
301 Chestnut Street, Suite 500B
Harrisburg, PA 17101
(717) 783–2525

Bureau of Minority and Women Business Enterprise

Contact:
Mr. Theodore S. Clements, Director
Minority and Women Business Enterprise
  Office
Department of General Services
400 North Office Building
Harrisburg, PA 17125
(717) 787–7380

The **Bureau of Minority and Women Business Enterprise** actively pursues contracting and subcontracting opportunities for Minority Business Enterprises (MBEs) and Women Business Enterprises (WBEs) with state government and with firms that do business with state government. The bureau also serves as a clearinghouse for information, policies, and issues pertaining to MBEs and WBEs.

Penn-Ag Fund

Contact:
Mr. Christian Herr, Director
Bureau of Agricultural Development
2301 North Cameron Street
Harrisburg, PA 17110
(717) 783–8460

Under the **Penn-Ag Fund** program, loans of up to $100,000 are offered at 3 percent to small business persons for food and agriculture processors.

Small Business Development Centers

Contact:
Mr. Gregory Higgins, State Director
Pennsylvania Small Business Development
  Center
The Wharton School
University of Pennsylvania
444 Vance Hall
3733 Spruce Street
Philadelphia, PA 19104
(215) 898–1219

Small Business Development Centers (SBDCs) provide practical management and technical assistance to present and prospective small business owners. They offer courses, seminars, and one-on-one counseling as well as access to information on marketing, managing, and financing a small business. SBDCs are partially funded by the U.S. Small Business Administration, and are usually affiliated with a state college or university. In Pennsylvania, a lead SBDC is located in Philadelphia, at the Wharton School of the University of Pennsylvania. There are 14 subcenters located throughout the state. A complete listing of all these centers, including addresses and telephone numbers, is located in Appendix A of this directory.

Governor's Advisory Council or Task Force

Contact:
Ms. Kim Albright, Director
Governor's Response Team
Room 439 Forum Building
Harrisburg, PA 17120
(717) 787–6500

The **Governor's Response Team** economic development specialists work with individual companies on a confidential basis to help them find business locations that meet specifications for start-up or expansion projects. The team also packages state financial and technical assistance.

As part of the response team's continuing efforts to retain Pennsylvania's existing industrial base, its economic development professionals systematically call on Pennsylvania manufacturers. The purpose of these calls is to make the firm aware of the various financial and technical assistance programs available, to find out if the firm is experiencing any problems, and to learn if there are any plans for expansion or cutbacks. Information is coordinated with local economic development organizations when appropriate. If a problem exists with another state agency, the response team will intervene on behalf of the firm for a successful resolution.

Contact:
Mr. Andrew T. Greenberg, Acting Secretary
   of Commerce
   and Executive Director
Department of Commerce
The Pennsylvania Economic Development
   Partnership
433 Forum Building
Harrisburg, PA 17120
(717) 787–3003

The **Governor's Small Business Advisory Council** was formed in 1988 for the purpose of addressing issues of concern to the small business community. The group comprises small business leaders and state officials, and the secretary of commerce serves as chairman.

Legislative Committees and Subcommittees

Pennsylvania established a Small Business Subcommittee of the House Business and Commerce Committee in 1981. In the Senate, small business matters are handled by the Community and Economic Development Committee. In the House, small business matters are under the jurisdiction of the Business and Commerce Committee.

Contacts:

Honorable Tim Shaffer
Chairman
Senate Community and Economic
    Development Committee
Room 170, Main Capitol Building
Harrisburg, PA 17120
(717) 787–9684

Representative Fred Taylor
Business and Commerce Committee
Room 328, Main Capitol Building
Harrisburg, PA 17120
(717) 787–3055

Legislation

The following legislation was enacted by the Commonwealth of Pennsylvania in 1988 and 1989:

- The state's Business Corporation Law of 1988 makes it easier and more attractive for firms to incorporate in Pennsylvania. Forms and procedures have been simplified, and outmoded rules eliminated (such as the old requirement of keeping a dual set of books). Certain shareholder rights are strengthened also.

- Companies chartered in Pennsylvania have an edge in fighting off hostile takeovers, thanks to the Jobs, Community, and Shareholders Protection Act. Their assets, employees, and shareholders also are protected more fully from the consequences of a takeover.

- In 1988, the state repaid the balance on loans it had taken from the U.S. government to cover unemployment benefits during the recession of the late 1970s and early 1980s. S.B. 1534 also set up a "trigger mechanism," which will automatically adjust taxes to avoid future deficits in the unemployment compensation trust fund. This legislation could save businesses an estimated $1.6 billion in unemployment compensation costs through 1994.

State Small Business Conferences

No recent statewide small business conferences have been reported.

Puerto Rico

Small Business Offices, Programs, and Activities

Department of Commerce

Contact:
Mr. Jorge Santiago-Roman, Secretary
Puerto Rico Department of Commerce
P.O. Box S–4275
San Juan, PR 00905
(809) 724–3290

There is no office designated solely to assist small businesses in Puerto Rico, but the **Puerto Rico Department of Commerce**, created in 1960, serves the entire business community with information, assistance, promotions, and direct services. Within the department are two programs: Development of Local Commerce and International Trade.

Most of the business activities fall under the program for **Development of Local Commerce**, which offers assistance through five divisions responsible for (1) assistance services in finance and accounting, (2) registration and regulation of business, (3) management assistance, (4) commercial education, and (5) promotion and development. Each division offers several types of assistance.

Office of Ombudsman

Contact:
Lcdo. Adolfo De Castro
Office of Ombudsman
P.O. Box 41088
Estacion Minillas
San Juan, PR 00940–1088
(809) 724–7373

Puerto Rico offers a variety of services to businesses through its **Office of Ombudsman**.

Economic and Industrial Development

Contact:
Mr. Alfredo Salazar, Jr., Administrator
Economic Development Administration
GPO Box 2350
San Juan, PR 00936
(809) 758–4747

The **Economic Development Administration** (EDA) and the **Puerto Rico Industrial Development Agency** (PRIDCO) constitute the "Fomento," Puerto Rico's catalyst for economic and social progress. EDA attracts small and large manufacturers from around the world through a package of tax incentives and

307

other inducements, and assists Puerto Rican entrepreneurs on a day-to-day basis to start and operate businesses. PRIDCO provides industrial park sites and factories, constructed in advance, to private enterprises qualifying for tax exemptions under the island's comprehensive law.

Procurement Technical Assistance Center

Contact:
Mr. Pedro J. Acevedo, Program Manager
Procurement Technical Assistance Center
Economic Development Administration
GPO Box 2350
San Juan, PR 00936
(809) 758–4747 ext. 2220

The procurement responsibilities are also centered at the Economic Development Administration, under the **Procurement Technical Assistance Center**. The center's main objective is to provide direct technical and marketing assistance concerning the Department of Defense, federal civilian agencies, and commercial acquisition processes to business enterprises located throughout Puerto Rico.

The Government Development Bank for Puerto Rico

Contact:
Mr. Hiram Melendez, Senior Vice President
Government Development Bank for Puerto
   Rico
GPO Box 42001
San Juan, PR 00940
(809) 722–2525

One of the primary functions of the **Government Development Bank (GDB) for Puerto Rico** is to foster economic development in both the public and private sectors. Responsibility within the bank for private-sector economic development rests principally with the private financing department, which lends to commercial, industrial, and service firms that contribute to Puerto Rico's economy. The GDB's loan section consists of three divisions: (1) the Credit Administrative Division, (2) the Credit Analysis Division, and (3) the Special Loans Division.

Real estate, machinery, and equipment can be used as collateral for loans. Personal or corporate guarantees are required. In all cases, the bank seeks guarantees from the U.S. Small Business Administration, the Farmers Home Administration, or another agency of the federal government.

The Economic Development Bank for Puerto Rico

Contact:
Mr. Ramon Peña
Banco de Desarrollo Economico Para
    Puerto Rico
P.O. Box 5009
Hato Rey, PR 00919–5009
(809) 766–4300

The **Economic Development Bank for Puerto Rico** began operations in May 1986. The fund lends to manufacturing and commercial concerns under more flexible lending and collateral terms than the Government Development Bank. The maximum amount the fund may lend on direct loans is $1.5 million; on guaranty loans the amount is up to $1 million.

Innovation and Technology

Contact:
Diego F. Loinaz, Executive Director
Corporation for Technological
    Transformation
P.O. Box 41249, Minillas Station
San Juan, PR 00940–1249
(809) 722–7000

There are two entities dealing with Innovation and Technology: the **Corporation for Technological Transformation** and the **Innovation and Research Division of the Economic Development Administration**.

The **Corporation for Technological Transformation** (CTT) is an autonomous public corporation in the Commonwealth of Puerto Rico for catalyzing generation of advanced technology and invention and high performance industry. CTT invites strategic relationships and joint ventures with technology centers as well as individual inventors, investigators, and entrepreneurs. Its primary focus is to stimulate development of world-class technological capabilities for the modernization, innovation, and creation of manufacturing, agro-industrial, and service enterprises. CTT seeks outstanding, emerging technological developments for commercializing and creating centers of operation in Puerto Rico.

Contacts:
Mr. William Riefkohl
Deputy Administrator
Economic Development Administration
GPO Box 2350
San Juan, PR 00936
(809) 758–4747, Ext. 2127

Dr. John Stuart
Economic Development Administration
GPO Box 2350
San Juan, PR 00936
(809) 758–4747, Ext. 2350

Innovation and Technology is also handled—but with a more general scope—by the Economic Development Administration, under the **Innovation and Research (Technology) Division**.

Small Business Development Centers

Contact:
Mr. Jose M. Romaguera, Director
Small Business Development Center
University of Puerto Rico
Mayaguez Campus
Box 5253, College Station
Mayaguez, PR 00680
(809) 834–3590

Small Business Development Centers (SBDCs) provide practical management and technical assistance to present and prospective small business owners. They offer courses, seminars, and one-on-one counseling as well as access to information on marketing, managing, and financing a small business. SBDCs are partially funded by the U.S. Small Business Administration and are usually affiliated with a state college or university. In Puerto Rico, the lead SBDC is located in Mayaguez, at the University of Puerto Rico. There are subcenters located in Hato Rey, Humacao, Ponce, and Rio Piedras. A complete listing of all these centers, including addresses and telephone numbers, is in Appendix A of this directory.

Governor's Advisory Council or Task Force

Contact:
Mr. Amadeo Francis, Chairman
Economic Council for the Governor
La Fortaleza
GPO Box 82
San Juan, PR 00901
(809) 721–7000

The 20-member **Economic Council for the Governor** advises the governor on economic matters and legislation contributing to development and expansion of all businesses.

Contact:
Yolanda Zayas, Executive Director
Commission for Women Affairs
P.O. Box 11382
Fernandez Juncos Station
Santurce, PR 00910
(809) 722–2857

The **Commission for Women Affairs** was created by the legislature to report directly to the governor. The commission's main objective is to help women deal with the problems and obstacles that may, in any way, interfere with their personal and social-economic development.

Legislative Committees and Subcommittees

There is no committee in the Senate or House of Representatives that focuses entirely on small business issues. The committees that deal most frequently with legislation affecting small business are the Senate Committee on Industry, Commerce, and Industrial Development and the House Committee on Industry.

Contacts:

Senator Américo Martinez
Chairman
Senate Committee on Industry, Commerce,
   and Industrial Development
State Capitol
San Juan, PR 00901
(809) 722–4299
(809) 724–2030
(809) 722–0651

Representative Ramon Diaz
Chairman
House Committee on Industry
State Capitol
San Juan, PR 09901
(809) 721–6040

Legislation

Local products will have as much as a 15-percent preference margin over imports that are competing in government bids.

An act permitting stores to open Monday through Saturday from 5:00 am to midnight, and on Sundays from 11:00 am to 5:00 pm was passed. Family-owned and operated stores are exempt from this law, as well as large stores in the designated tourism zones.

State Small Business Conferences

No recent statewide small business conferences have been reported.

Rhode Island

Small Business Offices, Programs, and Activities

Department of Economic Development

Contact:
Mr. William J. Parsons, Associate Director
Business Development Division
Rhode Island Department of Economic
   Development
7 Jackson Walkway
Providence, RI 02903
(401) 277–2601
fax: (401) 277–2102

The **Department of Economic Development** offers a variety of incentive programs and support services to help companies—both those already in Rhode Island and those looking to relocate there. Assistance ranges from site location assistance to industrial revenue bond financing. Specifically, the department is an excellent resource in the areas of federal procurement opportunities, minority business counseling, export assistance, state-sponsored financing, insured bond and mortgage programs, economic data, job training, and real estate inventory.

The **Business Development Division** assists new and existing small businesses by providing management and technical assistance, site location assistance, minority business development, and federal procurement assistance.

Contact:
Mr. Daniel E. Lilly, Jr., Administrator
Rhode Island Department of Economic
   Development
7 Jackson Walkway
Providence, RI 02903
(401) 277–2601
fax: (401) 277–2102

The **Federal Procurement Program** offers assistance to companies interested in selling goods and services to the federal government. Companies may obtain procurement information, procurement policies, bidding procedures, and receive daily bid notices.

Contact:
Mr. Charles Newton, Coordinator
Office of Minority Business Assistance
Rhode Island Department of Economic
   Development
7 Jackson Walkway
Providence, RI 02903
(401) 277–2601
fax: (401) 277–2102

The **Office of Minority Business Assistance** helps minorities, women, and disadvantaged participants in preparing business plans and loan packages. The office certifies minority, women, or disadvantaged business owners as eligible to participate in state procurement and construction set-aside programs.

Contact:
Mr. Kurt Maksad, International Trade
  Coordinator
Rhode Island Department of Economic
  Development
7 Jackson Walkway
Providence, RI 02903
(401) 277–2601
fax: (401) 277–2102

The **International Trade Coordinator** provides export assistance to companies interested in marketing their goods overseas. The international trade coordinator attends foreign trade shows and assists companies wishing to be represented at these trade shows. The Export Assistance Center also offers consultation services, directs clients to appropriate sources of information, and processes 24,000 trade leads each year.

Department of Employment and Training

Contact:
Mr. John Robinson, Director
Rhode Island Department of Employment
  and Training
101 Friendship Street
Providence, RI 02903
(401) 277–2090

The **Employer Relations Unit** provides support to employers planning on expanding or opening operations by helping to develop strategies for meeting employer recruitment needs. The unit provides administrative support and coordinates activities for the State Job Service Employer Committee.

The **Dislocated Worker Program** is managed and coordinated as mandated by the Economic Dislocation and Worker Adjustment Assistance Act (EDWAA). It provides, in conjunction with the Employer Services office, a comprehensive strategy in meeting the needs of employees who have lost jobs because of plant closings or mass layoffs. The state's Rapid Response Team quickly intervenes, and the program provides technical assistance to employers and employees in petitioning for Trade Adjustment Assistance.

Employer Services manages and coordinates services to employers planning on expanding or opening operations. It assists companies with positive recruitment or Affirmative Action and provides technical assistance and logistical support. The office coordinates recruiting activities with local offices and employment and training entities, as well as supporting and coordinating Job Option Fairs. Employer Services provides administrative support and coordination for the State Job Service Employer Committee and works closely with local offices. It provides planning assistance to local communities and marketing assistance to communities and chambers of commerce through economic development commissions.

Individuals eligible for help include those who have been terminated or laid off or have received notice, are eligible for or have exhausted their unemployment compensation, and are unlikely to return to their previous industry or occupation; have been terminated as a result of any permanent closure of or substantial layoff at a plant, facility, or enterprise; are long-term unemployed and have limited opportunities, including older individuals who may have substantive barriers to employment by reason of age; or were self-employed—including farmers and ranchers—and are unemployed as a result of general economic conditions or natural disasters.

Rhode Island Work Force 2000 Council

Contact:
Mr. John M. Robinson, Chairman
Work Force 2000
Rhode Island Department of Employment
   and Training
101 Friendship Street
Providence, RI 02903
(401) 277–6700

The mission of the **Rhode Island Work Force 2000 Council** is to improve current and long-term employment and opportunities for all Rhode Islanders, as well as enhance the competitiveness of the state's employers in a global economy through independent and cooperative action. This is accomplished by providing leadership for the development of business/education/government partnerships and by funding innovative demonstration projects that test new ideas and approaches to problems.

Financing Programs

Contact:
Mr. Earl F. Queenan, Associate Director
Rhode Island Department of Economic
   Development
7 Jackson Walkway
Providence, RI 02903
(401) 277–2601
fax: (401) 277–2102

Several **financing programs** are offered through the Department of Economic Development. The agency serves as a one-stop clearinghouse for financing packages, assisting qualified companies with all steps from the initial contact with financial institutions to assembling the project in final form for approval.

Contact:
Mr. Earl F. Queenan, Treasurer
Rhode Island Industrial Facilities Corporation
Rhode Island Department of Economic
   Development
7 Jackson Walkway
Providence, RI 02903
(401) 277–2601
fax: (401) 277–2102

The **Rhode Island Industrial Facilities Corporation** provides financial aid through taxable and tax-exempt revenue bonds for construction, acquisition, or renovation of commercial and industrial projects.

Contact:
Mr. Robert E. Donovan, Manager
Rhode Island Industrial–Recreational
    Building Authority
Rhode Island Department of Economic
    Development
7 Jackson Walkway
Providence, RI 02903
(401) 277–2601
fax: (401) 277–2102

The **Rhode Island Industrial–Recreational Building Authority** issues insurance on mortgages, tax-free industrial revenue bonds, and taxable revenue bonds. Insured loans can be used for the construction of or renovation of manufacturing, office, retail, wholesale, and tourist travel facilities and for the acquisition of associated machinery and equipment.

Contact:
Mr. Robert E. Donovan, Administrator
Small Business Loan Fund
Rhode Island Department of Economic
    Development
7 Jackson Walkway
Providence, RI 02903
(401) 277–2601
fax: (401) 277–2102

The **Small Business Loan Fund** provides loans for portions of the project costs for manufacturing, processing, and marine resource development. These loans can be for either fixed assets or working capital, for new or existing businesses.

Contact:
Mr. Vincent K. Harrington, Research Analyst
Rhode Island Department of Economic
    Development
7 Jackson Walkway
Providence, RI 02903
(401) 277–2601

The following **publications** are available from the Rhode Island Department of Economic Development: *Starting a Business in Rhode Island*, *Rhode Island Basic Economic Statistics*, *Rhode Island Directory of Manufacturers*, and the *Rhode Island Export Directory*.

Ocean State Business Development Authority

Contacts:
Mr. Henry A. Violet, President
Ocean State Business Development
    Authority
7 Jackson Walkway
Providence, RI 02903
(401) 277–2601

Mr. Bruce Lang
Ocean State Business Development
    Corporation
3 Hammarlund Way
Aquidneck Industrial Park
Middletown, RI 02840
(401) 848–7790

The **Ocean State Business Development Authority** (OSBDA) is a Certified Development Company as designated by the U.S. Small Business Administration. The authority focuses on administering the SBA 504 program, which provides financing at favorable rates and terms to small businesses for expansion projects. By combining long-term bank debt with the sale of SBA-guaranteed debentures, OSBDA can offer terms and blended rates approaching those available to larger companies.

Small Business Development Centers

Contact:
Mr. Douglas Jobling, State Director
Rhode Island Small Business Development
  Center
Bryant College
1150 Douglas Pike
Smithfield, RI 02917–1284
(401) 232–6111

Rhode Island has a network of four **Small Business Development Centers** (SBDCs) that provide individual counseling, workshops, and seminars on small-business-related topics such as marketing, accounting, financing, and developing business plans. The SBDC lead office at Bryant College in Smithfield has the responsibility for the overall statewide management of the Rhode Island SBDC program. Funding is provided by the college, the U.S. Small Business Administration, and the Department of Economic Development Centers. Program development, management, public relations, financial accounting, contract administration, and management information activities of the SBDC are all conducted from this office. Consulting services and training programs are also available at the Smithfield SBDC. A listing of small business development centers and subcenters in Rhode Island, including addresses and telephone numbers, is in Appendix A of this directory.

Rhode Island Partnership for Science and Technology

Contact:
Ms. Claudia E. Terra, Executive Director
Rhode Island Partnership for Science and
  Technology
7 Jackson Walkway
Providence, RI 02903
(401) 277–2601

The **Rhode Island Partnership for Science and Technology** is a nonprofit organization founded with state monies that offers grants to businesses for applied research that is done in conjunction with universities, colleges, or hospitals in the state. The partnership seeks major innovative projects with a minimum research budget of $200,000 that offer potential for profitable commercialization. The partnership will fund up to 60 percent of a research project. The research funding must be spent at the universities, colleges, or hospitals working with the company.

A state-supported **Small Business Innovation Research** (SBIR) program provides four categories of support to qualified SBIR applicants. The partnership pays for free consulting that is provided by the Rhode Island Small Business Development Center to help applicants develop quality proposals. A Rhode Island company that submits a valid Phase I SBIR proposal to the federal government will receive a $1,000 grant to help defray the cost of preparing an application. A matching grant of 50 percent (up to a maximum of

$2,500) is available to a Phase I recipient that uses a consultant who is a faculty member from any Rhode Island university or college. A Rhode Island Phase I SBIR grant recipient who submits a Phase II proposal is eligible to receive a matching state grant of 50 percent of the Phase I award, up to a maximum of $25,000.

Governor's Advisory Council or Task Force

Contact:
Ms. Stephanie Morris, Director
Small Business Development Division
Rhode Island Department of Economic
    Development
7 Jackson Walkway
Providence, RI 02903
(401) 277–2601

The **Governor's Small Business Advisory Council** serves as a communication link between the governor and the small business community. The council studies special problems of small businesses; evaluates existing programs and legislation, making recommendations as appropriate; and monitors local, national, and international small business issues.

Legislative Committees and Subcommittees

Contacts:
Mr. Raymond W. Fogarty, Chairman
Mr. William Enos, Vice Chairman
Joint Committee on Small Business
State House
Providence, RI 02903
(401) 277–6596

The Rhode Island Legislature has a joint committee of the House and Senate to act on small business issues.

Legislation

Two bills affecting small business were passed by the Rhode Island State Legislature in fiscal year 1991. The first provided for expeditious permit processing by the Department of Economic Development for any project of critical economic concern. The other bill created the Enterprise Zone Council and amended laws relating to Enterprise Zones including tax credits and preferences.

State Small Business Conferences

Contacts:
Mr. Douglas Jobling, State Director
Rhode Island Small Business Development
    Center
Bryant College
1150 Douglas Pike
Smithfield, RI 02917–1284
(401) 232–6111

Mr. William J. Parsons, Associate Director
Rhode Island Department of Economic
    Development
7 Jackson Walkway
Providence, RI 02903
(401) 277–2601

Several conferences were held in Rhode Island during 1991, including **SBA Assistance in the Reconstruction of Kuwait, Women in the '90's, Providence Business to Business EXPO,** and the **International Trade Task Force Summit.**

South Carolina

Small Business Offices, Programs, and Activities

Enterprise Development, Inc., of South Carolina

Contact:
Mrs. Grace McKown, President
Enterprise Development, Inc., of South
   Carolina
P.O. Box 1149
Columbia, SC 29202
(803) 737–0888

Enterprise Development, Inc., of South Carolina is a Columbia-based private, not-for-profit corporation formed to focus attention on the start-up and development of high-growth business ventures. The company seeks out private and public sources of business knowledge, expertise, and financing and works to bring these resources together to nurture new businesses. Stimulating the commercialization of technology in South Carolina also is part of the company's economic development agenda. The Business Information Center of Enterprise Development, Inc., offers information to those thinking of starting or expanding a business in South Carolina.

Existing Business and Industry Services Department

Contact:
Mr. Mark Williams, Associate Manager
The Existing Business and Industry Services
   Department
South Carolina State Development Board
P.O. Box 927
Columbia, SC 29202
(803) 737–0400
(800) 922–6684 (toll-free, in-state)

The **Existing Business and Industry Services Department** of the South Carolina State Development Board is charged with promoting economic stability and development through a strategy of encouraging existing industries to expand, and to retain existing jobs. Assistance and information are provided on resources and services available to help industries grow. A quarterly newsletter, *BusinessLine*, is produced to keep businesses up to date on programs and activities available to them.

319

Small Business Development Centers

Contact:
Mr. John M. Lenti, State Director
The Frank L. Roddey Small Business
   Development Center
University of South Carolina
College of Business Administration
1710 College Street
Columbia, SC 29208
(803) 777–4907

South Carolina's **Frank L. Roddey Small Business Development Center** (SBDC) was established in 1978 and was formally chartered on June 6, 1979. In a cooperative spirit, state-supported colleges and universities joined to form the SBDC Consortium, which reflects the growing awareness of the small business manager's vital role in South Carolina's economy. Through the consortium schools, regional and area centers provide one-to-one consultation, develop management and technical assistance courses, provide information services, and offer specialized programs to assist those clients with specific needs. Also, the **Small Business Innovation Research** (SBIR) program is supported by SBDC consultants who provide assistance to interested small firms. A list of all Small Business Development Centers and subcenters in South Carolina, including their addresses and telephone numbers, is in Appendix A of this directory.

Loans and Capital Formation

Contact:
Mr. Elliott Franks, Director
South Carolina Jobs–Economic
   Development Authority
1201 Main Street
AT&T Capital Center, Suite 1750
Columbia, SC 29201
(803) 737–0079

An 11-member quasi-public **Jobs Economic Development Authority** raises capital and provides technical assistance to aid small businesses in creating jobs. The authority is authorized to sell general and industrial revenue bonds.

The governor has designated a portion of block grant funds to provide loans and technical assistance for small business development. The emphasis is on businesses that would create new jobs in a community, and preference is given to less developed areas of the state.

Carolina Investment Corporation, a mirror corporation of the Jobs Economic Development Authority, is empowered to make loans or equity investments in South Carolina small businesses. The maximum amount per investment is $75,000.

Office of Small and Minority Business Assistance

Contact:
Mr. Cleve Thomas, Director
Rural Improvement–Small and Minority
  Business Assistance
Edgar A. Brown Building
1205 Pendleton Street, Room 441
Columbia, SC 29201
(803) 734–0562

The Office of Small and Minority Business Assistance conducts research on a variety of small business issues, provides advocacy and referral services for small and minority business within state government, provides training and other educational activities for small and minority businesses, certifies minority-owned businesses for the state, and makes policy recommendations to the governor.

Small Farms Program

Contact:
Ms. Brenda Lee, Small Farm Manager
South Carolina Department of Agriculture
P.O. Box 11280
Columbia, SC 29211
(803) 734–2200

The **Small Farms Program** was designed to assist small farm owners in marketing and production techniques. In conjunction with this program, the Department of Agriculture operates the Small Farms Marketing Cooperative Education Program.

Procurement Program

Contact:
Mr. Larry Sorrell, Manager
Administrative Services
Material Management Office
South Carolina Division of General Services
1201 Main Street
AT&T Capital Center, Suite 600
Columbia, SC 29201
(803) 737–0621

The **South Carolina Consolidated Procurement Code** establishes procedures for increasing small and minority business participation in state procurement. The law contains a South Carolina preference provision that mandates that if an out-of-state firm offers the lowest bid for a state contract valued at less than $1 million, and an in-state firm offers a bid for this contract within 2 percent of the lowest bid, the state agency must award the contract to the in-state firm. For contracts more than $1 million, the in-state firm must be within 1 percent of the lowest bid.

The measure directs the Office of Small and Minority Business Assistance to maintain and disseminate a directory of minority firms to state agencies to assist them in developing a minority business utilization procurement plan. State agencies must also publish a weekly list of all procurement activities valued at more than $2,500.

Finance

Contact:
Mr. Richard Bannon, President
Palmetto Seed Capital Corporation
1330 Lady Street, Suite 607
Columbia, South Carolina 29201
(803) 779–5759

The **Palmetto Seed Capital Corporation** is a $25 million venture capital fund targeted primarily to South Carolina start-up companies.

Contact:
Mr. Meriwether Jones
Enterprise Development
P.O. Box 1149
Columbia, SC 29202
(803) 737–0888

The **Annual Southeast Capital Connection** is a 2-day conference that brings professional and informal investors together with companies seeking equity capital. Investors get training in how to make deals, and attend business plan presentations by a prescreened group of growth companies.

Contact:
Private Investor Network
Economic Enterprise Institute
University of South Carolina at Aiken
171 University Parkway
Aiken, SC 29801
(803) 648–6851

The **Private Investor Network** is an electronic "dating service" that matches professional and individual investors with companies seeking capital.

Technology

South Carolina has designated three research parks within the state: (1) the Clemson University area; (2) the University of South Carolina/Columbia area and the Charleston area near the Medical University; and (3) the College of Charleston.

Contacts:
Dr. Robert Henderson, Director
South Carolina Research Authority
P.O. Box 12025
Columbia, SC 29211
(803) 799–4070

Mr. Richard W. Fralick, Research Parks
    Manager
South Carolina Research Authority
P.O. Box 12025
Columbia, SC 29211
(803) 799–4070

Contact:
Enterprise Development, Inc.
P.O. Box 1149
Columbia, South Carolina 29202
(803) 737–0888

The **Center for Applied Technology** (CAT) concentrates on the formation and development of technology-based companies. CAT provides an incubator environment to nurture new companies spinning off of research and development efforts associated with the universities in the state.

Contact:
Mr. William C. Chard, Director
Emerging Technology Development and
   Marketing Center
115 North Palmetto Boulevard (Moorman
   House)
Clemson, SC 29634–5703
(803) 656–4237

Clemson University has developed the **Emerging Technology Development and Marketing Center** in an effort to help South Carolina entrepreneurs and small products manufacturing industries working in the advanced technology areas.

SBA 504 Certified Development Company

Contact:
Ms. Theresa Singleton, Supervisory Loan
   Specialist
Finance Division
U.S. Small Business Administration
1835 Assembly Street, Room 358
Columbia, SC 29201
(803) 253–3121

Certified Development Companies (CDCs) are local or statewide corporations or authorities—both for-profit and nonprofit, depending on the situation—that package SBA, bank, state, and private money into a financial assistance package for existing business capital improvement. Each state has at least one CDC.

All areas of South Carolina have CDCs, either through various councils of governments or local CDCs that provide service to a specific area.

Governor's Advisory Council or Task Force

Contact:
Mr. Cleve Thomas, Director
Rural Improvement–Small and Minority
   Business Assistance
Edgar A. Brown Building
1205 Pendleton Street, Room 441
Columbia, SC 29201
(803) 734–0562

The 15-member **Small and Minority Business Expansion Council** is made up of trade and business association representatives, members of the academic community, small business owners and managers, and state legislators representing each house of the State Legislature. The council brings together a cross section of experts whose primary responsibility is to advise the governor on small business policies in the next legislative session.

Legislative Committees and Subcommittees

The Joint Liaison Committee on Small Business was created in 1984 and amended in 1987. It is charged with the responsibility of conducting a continuous review of the problems confronting small business and reporting annually to the General Assembly concerning these problems.

Contacts:

Senator Verne Smith
Chairman
Senate Committee on Labor, Commerce, and Industry
Gressette Building
P.O. Box 142
Columbia, SC 29202
(803) 734–2792

Representative Thomas C. Alexander
Chairman
House, Labor, Commerce and Industry Committee
Blatt Building
P.O. Box 11867
Columbia, SC 29211
(803) 734–3015

Legislation

The following legislation was enacted in 1988:

- A measure creating a $10–16 million Seed Capital Fund to promote growth businesses in the state. The fund would be a private, for-profit business, not a new public agency.

- A measure that simplifies the process of beginning an aquaculture operation.

- Legislation calling for a constitutional amendment that would allow counties to jointly develop an industrial and business park with other counties and to share the revenues that are generated. Because this is a constitutional amendment, a public referendum is required.

- The South Carolina Business Corporation Act of 1988—establishing a $110 flat fee to incorporate—implements a less technical method to incorporate and adopts the American Bar Association's Close Cooperation Section, which allows firms to operate in a less formal corporate structure.

The following legislation was enacted in 1989:

- A reduction in the tax on workers' compensation insurance premiums from 4.5 percent to 2.5 percent by fiscal year 1991–1992. This bill's estimated annual savings to the business community are $10.5 million.

State Small Business Conferences

Contact:
Mr. Tony M. Smith, Director
Special Events
State Board for Technical and
   Comprehensive Education
111 Executive Center Drive
Columbia, SC 29210
(803) 737–9352

Several conferences are held in South Carolina: **Entrepreneur Women,** a conference focused on women in business, is held bi-annually. **Expo** is a conference that attempts to match small and minority businesses with private industry, and state and local governments. "Expo" is held each fall.

South Dakota

Small Business Offices, Programs, and Activities

Governor's Office of Economic Development

Contact:
Mr. Roland Dolly, Commissioner
Governor's Office of Economic Development
711 East Wells Avenue
Pierre, SD 57501–3369
(605) 773–5032

The **Governor's Office for Economic Development** (GOED) assists and promotes new and existing small businesses. The office is charged with integrating small business concerns into state economic development policies and plans. The office also serves as an advocate for South Dakota's small business community regarding policy determinations and questions concerning other state agencies. South Dakota does not have an agency or division devoted solely to women and minority business enterprises.

A multitude of **financial packaging** options are available to new and expanding businesses in South Dakota. These services are available through GOED and five planning districts throughout the state. Financial packagers prepare financing schemes for businesses, utilizing a combination of local, state, and federal sources offering the most appropriate terms and rates.

Contacts:
Governor's Office of Economic Development
711 East Wells Avenue
Pierre, SD 57501–3369
(605) 773–5032
(800) 872–6190 (toll-free)

South Eastern Council of Governments
P.O. Box 843
Sioux Falls, SD 57101–0843
(605) 339–6515

Northeast Council of Governments
P.O. Box 1985
Aberdeen, SD 57402–1985
(605) 622–2595

First District Association of Governments
P.O. Box 1207
Watertown, SD 57201
(605) 886–7224

Third Planning and Development District
P.O. Box 687
Yankton, SD 57078
(605) 665–4408

Black Hills Council of Local Governments
P.O. Box 1586
Rapid City, SD 57709
(605) 394–2681

Contact:
Governor's Office of Economic Development
711 East Avenue
Pierre, SD 57501–3369
(605) 773–5032

Business location services are available through GOED industrial development representatives who work closely with local development corporations to assist businesses looking to expand or relocate in South Dakota. Representatives provide pertinent information on available buildings, tax advantages, area labor forces, utility rates, zoning requirements, and transportation.

Contact:
Governor's Office of Economic Development
711 East Wells Avenue
Pierre, SD 57501–3369
(800) 773–5032

The **Revolving Economic Development and Initiative Fund** (REDI Fund) was created in 1987 by the South Dakota legislature to encourage economic development and job creation. The fund was financed by a 10-month, 1-percent sales tax. The legislation authorized the Board of Economic Development, appointed by the governor, to develop and implement the criteria for making loans from the REDI fund. Loans are made to any for-profit firm or nonprofit business cooperative that is either a start-up firm, an existing South Dakota firm, or an existing business that creates primary jobs, generates capital investment in South Dakota, helps to diversify state and local economies, and which does not compete with existing local businesses. Eligible costs for the program include land purchases, building construction and renovation and associated fees, equipment purchases and installation, trade receivables, inventory, and other working capital needs. Ineligible costs are debt refinancing, short-term financing for construction or acquisition, and preliminary design-stage costs. Interest rates are set at 3 percent. The loans are amortized over a period of time, up to 20 years, with a balloon after five years.

Contacts:
Mr. Ken Schaack, Director of Enterprise
  Initiation
Governor's Office of Economic Development
711 East Wells Avenue
Pierre, SD 57501–3369
(605) 773–5032

Dr. Randalei Ellis
Small Business Institute
Black Hills State University
Spearfish, SD 57783
(605) 642–6869

Mr. Francis McGowan, Director
Enterprise Development Center
Dakota State University
Madison, SD 57042
(605) 256–5555

Mr. Sam Gingerich
Associate Vice President for Research and
  Planning
Northern State University
South Jay Street
Aberdeen, SD 57401
(605) 622–2558

The **Future Fund** was created to incorporate the state's higher education institutions into the state's overall economic development plan by encouraging research and development activities on the state's campuses. Each eligible state-funded institution has a **Center for Innovation Technology and Enterprise** (CITE) responsible for collecting and analyzing applied research and service proposals for funding and submitting them to the director of **Enterprise Initiation**. Proposals are judged on how they relate to the overall economic development program for the state. If a proposal is accepted, a contract is drawn up to fund the work on a reimbursable basis.

Dr. S.L. Iyer
South Dakota School of Mines and
  Technology
501 East St. Joseph Street
Rapid City, SD 57701–3995
(605) 394–2445

Dr. Richard Barnes
University of South Dakota
Office of Research
108 Slagle Hall
Vermillion, SD 57069
(605) 677–5513

Dr. Ed Hogan
President's Office
South Dakota State University
Box 2201
Brookings, SD 57007
(605) 688–4173

The **Export, Trade, and Marketing Division** is designed to assist South Dakota manufacturers and value-added processors in reaching foreign markets. Programs offered include economic development outreach, trade missions, trade shows, education, consultation, promotion of South Dakota businesses, and the computerized trade leads network. Businesses may also have their company's name added into the South Dakota export directory.

Economic Development Finance Authority

In March 1986, the state legislature authorized the **Economic Development Finance Authority** to pool tax-exempt or taxable development bonds for the purpose of constructing facilities and services for the storage, distribution, or manufacture of industrial or agricultural products. The act was amended to include equipment purchases in 1987. Eligible project costs include building construction; land; financing charges; expenses incidental to determining the feasibility of development projects; and the costs of machinery, equipment, and installation. Working capital and refinancing costs do not apply. Generally, the authority will not consider loan requests for enterprises below $300,000 and will not pool projects unless the pool volume is $1 million or more. Maximum terms for loans run for 20 years or for the useful life of the assets purchased, whichever is less. Loan amounts will not exceed 80 percent of the market value of property and 75 percent the market value of equipment.

Training and Job Assistance

The **South Dakota Department of Labor** offers several training programs. On-the-job training is used with private, private non-profit, and public sector employers who agree to hire an eligible individual for permanent employment before training begins and who are responsible for all of the employee's salary and fringe benefits during the training period. Under this program, employers may be reimbursed for up to 50 percent of the wages paid to the trainee. Industrial-based training—through classroom instruction, on-the-job training, and performance-based contracts—allows new or expanding businesses to acquire trained personnel before or during a company's start-up. Rehabilitation training is also available for persons whose mental or physical disabilities are considered handicaps to employment and who can reasonably expect to be employed from the services provided by the program.

Contact:
Department of Labor, Private Industry
   Council
700 North Illinois
Kneip Building
Pierre, SD 57501
(605) 773–5017

The Department of Labor administers 19 **Job Service** offices throughout South Dakota, which can provide employers one-stop shopping in recruiting, testing, training, and hiring productive personnel. The Job Service will advertise company positions free of charge, screen qualified applicants before referring them to jobs, and administer aptitude testing of applicants. The Job Service also administers the Department of Labor's training programs and helps firms design programs for their specific needs. The **Targeted Jobs Tax Credit** (TJTC) program, implemented through the Job Service offices, is a federal income tax credit that private employers can claim when they hire employees in targeted groups.

Business and Industry Training

The **Business and Industry Training** (BIT) program is administered by the state's **Office of Adult Vocational and Technical Education** and was established to provide employee training services to business and industry in South Dakota. Individual businesses dictate the contents, location, and time of the training. Training is coordinated through the state's four vocational-technical institutes.

Contacts:

Mr. Chris Paustian, Director
Mitchell Vo-Tech Institute
821 North Capital Street
Mitchell, SD 57301
(605) 996–6671

Mr. Larry P. Zikmund, State Supervisor of
   Adult Programs
Office of Adult Vocational and Technical
   Education
Department of Education and Cultural Affairs
700 Governor's Drive
Pierre, SD 57501
(605) 773–3423

Dr. Ken Gifford, Director
Western Dakota Vo-Tech Institute
1600 Sedivy Lane
Rapid City, SD 57701
(605) 394–4034

Mr. Terry Sullivan, Director
Southeast Vo-Tech Institute
2301 Career Place
Sioux Falls, SD 57107
(605) 331–7624

Mr. Gary Williams, Director
Lake Area Vo-Tech Institute
230 11th Street N.E.
Watertown, SD 57201
(605) 886–5872

Assistance for Rural Small Businesses

Contact:
Dr. Mylo A. Hellickson, Director
Cooperative Extension Service
South Dakota State University
Agriculture Hall, Room 152E
P.O. Box 2207
Brookings, SD 57007–9988
(605) 688–4792

Contact:
Mr. Randy Englund, Administrator
South Dakota Department of Agriculture
Agriculture Enterprise Program
445 East Capitol
Pierre, SD 57501
(605) 773–3375

Contact:
Mr. Sandy Weeldryer
Economic Development Finance Authority
Governor's Office of Economic Development
711 East Wells Avenue
Pierre, SD 57501–3369
(800) 872–6190

The **Cooperative Extension Service** of the South Dakota State University in Brookings, in cooperation with the U.S. Small Business Administration, has a program through which agricultural agents advise small business persons in their respective counties on general business matters and government assistance programs available to them.

The **Agricultural Development Loan Participation Program** supplements existing credit. Loans are administered and serviced through local lenders, with the South Dakota Department of Agriculture's Agriculture Enterprise Office providing up to 80 percent of the loan for the enterprise. Applicants must be at least 21 years of age and have derived at least 60 percent of their gross income for the past year from farming. The program is designed to assist in new agricultural developments that add value to agricultural products. Money may not be used to construct, purchase, or renovate a personal dwelling.

The purpose of the **Agricultural Processing and Export** (APEX) loan program is to encourage and assist the development of companies engaged in value-added processing to raw agricultural products in communities of 2,000 or less. The program also assists in the export of these products. Under the program, loans for land, construction and associated fees, inventory, trade receivables and other working capital are eligible. Debt refinancing and loans for crop and livestock production are not allowed. Eligible applicants must locate in a community with fewer than 2,000 persons, employ to the extent feasible low income persons, families or displaced families, use the funds for a project that will use or add value to South Dakota agricultural products, and demonstrate the positive economic impact of the project upon the community and state. The APEX fund will cover up to 70 percent of the total project costs, but applicants must secure other funds before applying for the program, including a 10-percent equity contribution. The APEX fund grants maximum loans of $150,000, with interest rates varying between 5 and 7 percent and loan terms between 5 and 10 years.

SBA 504 Certified Development Companies

Contacts:

Statewide
Mr. Sandy Weeldryer, Staff Coordinator
South Dakota Development Corporation
711 East Wells Avenue
Pierre, SD 57501–3369
(605) 773–5032

South Dakota has three **certified development companies,** located in Pierre, Spearfish, and Watertown. These companies lend to small businesses at fixed rates for terms of 10 to 20 years. Companies must create one job for every $35,000 received in financing. A 504 loan is funded through the sale of a debenture guaranteed by the U.S. Small Business Administration up to $750,000, or 40 percent of the total cost of land, buildings, and equipment.

For Brookings, Clark, Codington, Deuel, Grant, Hamlin, Kinsbury, Lake, Minor, and Moody counties
Mr. Earl Monnens, Economic Development Coordinator
First District Association of Governments
P.O. Box 1207
Watertown, SD 57201
(605) 886–7224

For Butte, Lawrence, Meade, and Pennington counties
Mr. Craig Johnson, Executive Director
Northern Hills Community Development, Inc.
P.O. Box 218
Sturgis, SD 57785
(605) 347–5837
fax: (605) 347–5223

Procurement Technical Assistance Center

The **Procurement Technical Assistance Center**, located at the School of Business, University of South Dakota in Vermillion, provides assistance to firms interested in selling products to the federal government. One-on-one consulting is provided to South Dakota businesses, in addition to seminars that are conducted statewide. The center houses a microfilm library of government standards and specifications, complete with a microfilm reader/printer.

Contacts:

Mr. Kent Rufer, Area Director
226 Citizens Building
Aberdeen, SD 57401
(605) 622–2433

Mr. Melvin Ustad, SBIR/PTAC Director
Business and Education Institute
Dakota State University
Madison, SD 57042
(605) 256–5313

Mr. Carl Gustafson, Area Director
2525 West Main Street, Suite 105
P.O. Box 7715
Rapid City, SD 57709
(605) 394–5312

Ms. Kareen Dougherty, Acting Director
Procurement Technical Assistance Program
414 East Clark, Patterson 115
Vermillion, SD 57069
(605) 677–5498

Ms. Kareen Dougherty, Area Director
231 South Phillips, Room 365
Sioux Falls, SD 57101
(605) 334–8553

Business Research Bureau

Contact:
Mr. Stephen Tracy, Director
Business Research Bureau
University of South Dakota
414 East Clark
Vermillion, SD 57069–2390
(605) 677–5287

The **Business Research Bureau** serves as a depository for business and economic data, such as city sales tax data, county level income data, and employment data. On a quarterly basis, the bureau publishes the *South Dakota Business Review*.

Small Business Development Centers

Contact:
Mr. Don Greenfield, State Director
South Dakota Small Business Development
   Center
University of South Dakota
School of Business
414 East Clark
Vermillion, SD 57069
(605) 677–5272
fax: (605) 677–5427

The **Small Business Development Center** is located at the University of South Dakota in Vermillion. The center provides assistance to existing and new businesses, primarily through individual consulting and through specific training programs and seminars. The Small Business Development Center has subcenters in Aberdeen, Pierre, Rapid City, Sioux Falls, and Vermillion. A listing of all Small Business Development Centers and subcenters in South Dakota is provided in Appendix A of this directory.

FASTRACK

Contact:
Mr. Norm Lingle
Governor's Office of Economic Development
711 East Wells Avenue
Pierre, SD 57501–3369
(605) 773–5032

The **FASTRACK Loan Guarantee** program allows students with ideas for new businesses to obtain bank financing through the **FASTRACK Foundation**. The foundation provides guarantees of 80 percent, or up to a maximum of $2,000, on bank loans to high school students starting businesses. Students in grades 9 through 12 are eligible to participate in the program.

Governor's Advisory Council or Task Force

Contact:
Mr. Roland Dolly, Commissioner
Governor's Office of Economic Development
711 Wells Avenue
Pierre, SD 57501–3335
(605) 773–5032

The governor does not have a small business advisory council or task force, but has designated Roland Dolly as the state's small business advocate.

Legislative Committees and Subcommittees

The South Dakota Legislature has no committee or subcommittee focusing solely on small business issues. Most small business-related matters are referred to the House and Senate Commerce Committees.

Contacts:
Senator Harold W. Halverson
Chairman
Senate Committee on Commerce
State Capitol
Pierre, SD 57501
(605) 773–3251

Representative John D. Sears
Chairman
House Committee on Commerce
State Capitol
Pierre, SD 57501
(605) 773–3251

Legislation

Legislation affecting small business from the 1989 legislative session includes the following:

- H.B. 116 reduces the unemployment insurance contribution rates paid by South Dakota employers.

- S.B. 39 adds "religious belief" to the list of "good causes" for voluntarily leaving employment and still remaining eligible for unemployment insurance.

- S.B. 160 expands the provisions in the worker's compensation law to allow a claimant to collect workers compensation for up to 60 days while waiting to get into a vocation rehabilitation program. S.B. 160 also extends coverage for the repair or replacement of prosthetic devices if the device was damaged or destroyed in a work-related accident.

- H.B. 1049 expands the length of time a taxpayer (business owner) has to reclaim overpaid taxes from the state Department of Revenue. Individuals and businesses now have three years (formerly only one year) from the day the tax was paid or the tax was due, whichever is earlier, to file a claim to recover overpaid taxes, penalties, and interest. This law makes the refund period correspond to the time frame the Department of Revenue has to collect taxes from a business.

- H.B. 1037 provides that advertisers cannot advertise price reductions without complying with one of the following: (1) the item must be offered for sale at a higher price for any seven consecutive days during the 60-day period prior to the sale; or (2) the advertiser must specify, in writing or orally, how the product has become a better buy than it was in the past. The measure benefits both consumers and business owners, as it will prevent consumers from being lured into buying a sale item whose price may have been the same or only slightly higher.

The following laws were enacted during the 1990 legislative session:

- S.B. 255 raises the state minimum wage to match the scheduled increase in the federal minimum wage. On April 1, 1990, the state minimum wage was raised to $3.80 an hour; on April 1, 1991, the minimum wage was raised to $4.25 an hour. S.B. 255 also provides that any employee 18 or 19 years of age may be paid a training wage as outlined in Section 6 of the Fair Labor Standards Amendments of 1989.

- H.B. 1197 permits employees to create employee day cooperatives. Organized by and for employees, a cooperative is to serve only employees and their dependents. Each cooperative will be duly licensed, requiring employees to comply with guidelines as specified by the Department of Social Services. H.B. 1197 allows employers to assist their employees in creatively developing in-house day care facilities by removing civil liability.

- S.B. 44 spells out the rights of South Dakota taxpayers in the "taxpayer's bill of rights." Specifically, S.B. 44 grants taxpayers the right to appeal by written notification; asserts that taxpayers may rely on written advice or opinion about the taxability of a given product or service, unless otherwise rescinded by changes in statutory law or court decisions; directs the Secretary of the Department of Revenue to reduce or abate a penalty or interest on taxes owed if the department unduly delayed its notice to the taxpayer of an assessment; and allows taxpayers to pay by electronic transmission.

- H.B. 1231 establishes a mechanism by which interested businesses may become involved in the workers' compensation rate-making process.

- S.B. 257 creates an environmental evaluation review committee to evaluate the mining industry's impact on the Blacks Hills. The governor proposed a two-year moratorium on new gold and silver mining permits in South Dakota.

- S.B. 322 was introduced to allow employers to use deductibles to ease the rise in their workers' compensation rates. Under S.B. 322, insurance companies can offer deductibles to businesses of up to $2,500 per occurrence.

- H.B. 1344 makes it easier for businesses to garnishee wages of delinquent bill payers. Debtors may now exempt 80 percent of their wages, with the remaining 20 percent available for garnishment by creditors.

The following laws were enacted during the 1991 legislative session:

- S.B. 120 amends current law to allow employers to reduce their workers' compensation premiums by selecting an insurance plan with a deductible. S.B. 120 removes the cap of $2,500 on the deductible amount.

- S.B. 157 establishes that if an employee injury or death is due to the employee's willful misconduct, including intentional self inflicted injury, intoxication, illegal use of any schedule I or II drug, or willful failure to perform a duty required by statute, no compensation shall be allowed. Illegal drug use was added to the list.

- S. 20 directs the Department of Social Services to establish a program of child care services to assist families with child care needs and to aid in the improvement of quality and services for the care of children in day care.

- S.B. 21 sets up a child care task force, to be appointed by the governor. Of the members, there is to be one senator and representative—one from each political party—one employer, one early childhood development professional, one representative of licensed day care centers, one representative of registered family day care homes, one representative of unregulated day care providers, and one user of child care services. The purpose of the task force is to advise the office of child care coordinator in developing a five-year plan to accomplish the objectives of finding affordable, quality, available, and nontraditional day care, with a yearly plan thereafter.

- H.B. 1386 reduces unemployment insurance tax rates for all employers. The bill also raises the maximum weekly benefit from $140 to $154.

- S. 229 addresses problems between insurance companies competing for new clients. When clients come into a plan healthy, it is usually about two years before they begin to file claims. As these claims develop, the rates for the group those clients are in start to go up, making it harder for new clients to be brought into that group. Sick people stay in that plan, as it is difficult for them to find insurance elsewhere, while healthy people are free to "shop around." South Dakota has allowed insurance companies to "block business" to get healthy individuals into a block, while unhealthy people stay together in a block with premiums going up. This bill says if an insurance company is going to block insurance, the company cannot discriminate against the unhealthy block with unreasonable rates. The bill forces insurance companies to spread the risk across the different blocks of insurance.

- H.B. 1407 requires insurance companies to include mammography screening in all general group health policies.

- H.B. 1044 requires franchises that are exempt from registering with the Department of Commerce to file a notice of exemption and pay a $250 fee. This notice of exemption allows the department to track the exempt corporation.

State Small Business Conferences

Contacts:
Mr. Roland Dolly, Commissioner
Governor's Office of Economic Development
711 Wells Avenue
Pierre, SD 57501–3335
(605) 773–5032

Ms. Charlotte Conway, Program Director
Industry and Commerce Association of
    South Dakota
(605) 224–6161

The **Governor's Conference on Economic Development** was held in February 1992 in Pierre, and was attended by economic development officials and business leaders from across the state.

The Industry and Commerce Association (ICA) of South Dakota hosted **Business Day at the Legislature** in February 1992, also in Pierre.

Tennessee

Small Business Offices, Programs, and Activities

Department of Economic and Community Development

Contact:
Mr. David Weber, Small Business Consultant
Small Business Office
Department of Economic and Community
  Development
7th Floor, Rachel Jackson Building
320 6th Avenue North
Nashville, TN 37243–0405
(615) 741–2626
(800) 872–7201 (toll-free, in-state)
(800) 251–8594 (toll-free, out-of-state)

The **Small Business Office** operates within the Department of Economic and Community Development, Business Services Division. The office coordinates with other agencies—state, local, and federal—to offer complimentary programs.

The office has embarked on a long-term program with the Tennessee Board of Regents, the Tennessee Valley Authority, and others to promote the state's 14 community colleges as the primary source for instruction and information transfer. In support of this effort, the Service Corps of Retired Executives (SCORE) has begun establishing branch offices at selected campuses.

The office engages in research projects on conditions affecting the state's 93,000 small businesses, which employ approximately 800,000—or 42 percent—of the total work force. The Small Business Office also publishes *Small Business Information*, a 132-page book of rules, guidelines, and technical assistance for starting a business in Tennessee.

Contact:
Mr. John Birdsong, Director
Minority Business Enterprise
Department of Economic and Community
  Development
7th Floor, Rachel Jackson Building
320 6th Avenue North
Nashville, TN 37243–0405
(615) 741–2545

The **Office of Minority Business Enterprise** coordinates economic development activities within the overall state economic development program. It provides minority businesses with greater access to state and local economic planning data, to resources of local governments, and to assistance with loan packaging and business plan preparation. The office publishes a business newsletter for minority businesses in the state.

Contact:
Mr. Leigh Wielund, Director
Export Office
Department of Economic and Community
 Development
7th Floor, Rachel Jackson Building
320 6th Avenue North
Nashville, TN 37243–0405
(615) 741–5870
(800) 342–8470 (toll-free, in-state)

The **Export Office** of the Department of Economic and Community Development currently has a data base of more than 800 foreign corporations that have requested information regarding Tennessee products and services. Another data base contains more than 1,500 Tennessee companies that have made inquiries about exporting or sought assistance to increase their export market share. The office also publishes the *Tennessee International Trade Directory*, a master listing of all state manufacturers engaged in export trade. The office represents state manufacturers engaged in export trade at foreign trade shows and missions and is a frequent cosponsor of seminars and workshops with the U.S. Small Business Administration and the U.S. Department of Commerce.

Tennessee Child Care Loan Guarantee Corporation

Contact:
Ms. Ruth Reinhardt
Executive Director
Tennessee Child Care Loan Guarantee
 Corporation
6th Floor, Rachel Jackson Building
320 6th Avenue North
Nashville, TN 37243–0405
(615) 741–4046

This nonprofit corporation was initiated in 1989 by the Tennessee Legislature to promote the creation of additional child care facilities. Housed within the Department of Economic and Community Development, the corporation issues loan guarantees for small and medium-sized day care centers.

Department of Agriculture

Contact:
Mr. Joe Gaines, Director
Division of Marketing
Tennessee Department of Agriculture
P.O. Box 40627
Ellington Agriculture Center
Nashville, TN 37204
(615) 360–0160

The **Marketing Division** of the Department of Agriculture develops domestic and international markets for Tennessee farmers and agribusinesses.

Tennessee Technology Foundation

Contact:
Dr. David Patterson, President
Tennessee Technology Foundation
P.O. Box 23184
Knoxville, TN 37933
(615) 694–6772

The High Technology Task Force concluded in 1981 that Tennessee had an active high technology industry and that a private sector organization was needed to take advantage of this economic asset. The **Tennessee Technology Foundation**, a not-for-profit, private-sector organization, was chartered in 1982 to assist entrepreneurs and others with ideas in high technology and to do a better job in high technology industry recruitment. This foundation has been responsible for the start-up of many small businesses since 1982.

The Tennessee Technology Foundation holds **Small Business Innovation Research** (SBIR) conferences at various sites across the state. Improved effort has resulted in the targeting of the conferences to include only companies that are worthwhile candidates for winning awards. The foundation also offers face-to-face consultation in the assistance of SBIR proposals. Prior to the consultations with foundation staff, applicants are sent a pre-application package, developed by the foundation, to gain preliminary information. After the pre-application package is reviewed by foundation staff, assistance is provided in proposal submittal. The foundation also produces a monthly SBIR newsletter highlighting proposal information.

Procurement Programs

Contact:
Ms. Deborah King, Staff Coordinator
Small and Minority Businesses
Department of General Services
C2–214 Central Services Building
Nashville, TN 37219
(615) 741–1035

The purpose of the **Small Business Purchasing and Contracting Act**, enacted in 1980, is to expedite local procurement from small business and increase the percentage of state purchases from small businesses to as much as 25 percent, the goal set by the Tennessee Board of Standards. In implementing the act, the Board of Standards increased the authority of state agencies to purchase goods and services locally, and narrowed its definition of small business to more accurately reflect the business environment in Tennessee.

The **Department of General Services** has taken steps to increase the visibility of the central purchasing office among small and minority businesses. The department attends trade shows and conferences across the state seeking additional small business suppliers. All bids are advertised through statewide branches of the Office of Minority Business Enterprise. The state legislature now requires an annual report on small minority business purchases.

Small Business Development Centers

Contact:
Dr. Kenneth J. Burns, State Director
Tennessee Small Business Development
   Center
Memphis State University
Memphis, TN 38152
(901) 678–2500

Small Business Development Centers (SBDCs) provide practical management and technical assistance to present and prospective small business owners. SBDCs offer courses, seminars, and one-on-one counseling as well as access to information on marketing, managing, and financing a small business. SBDCs are partially funded by the U.S. Small Business Administration, and are usually affiliated with a state college or university. In Tennessee, SBDCs or subcenters are located in Memphis, Chattanooga, Columbia, Dyersburg, Johnson City, Murfreesboro, Knoxville, Nashville, Cookeville, Martin, and Morristown. A complete listing of all these centers, including addresses and telephone numbers, is in Appendix A of this directory.

Governor's Advisory Council or Task Force

Contact:
Mr. David Weber, Small Business Consultant
Small Business Office
Department of Economic and Community
   Development
320 6th Avenue North
7th Floor, Rachel Jackson Building
Nashville, TN 37219–5308
(615) 741–2626
(800) 872–7201 (toll-free, in-state)
(800) 251–8594 (toll-free, out-of-state)

The Small Business Office, Department of Economic and Community Development, assists the governor by monitoring legislation and development strategies for economic development.

Legislative Committees and Subcommittees

There are no committees in the Tennessee Legislature that focus solely on small business issues. Most small business legislation is handled by the Senate Committee on Commerce, Labor, and Agriculture and the House Committee on Commerce.

Contacts:

Senator Carl Koella
Chairman
Senate Committee on Commerce, Labor,
    and Agriculture
309 War Memorial Building
Nashville, TN 37219
(615) 741–3011

Representative Shelby Rhinehart
Chairman
House Committee on Commerce
34 Legislative Plaza
Nashville, TN 37219
(615) 741–3011

Legislation

The 1989 session of the Tennessee General Assembly passed the following legislation:

- Unemployment insurance will maintain $7,000 taxable wage for the next four years.

- Public Chapter 244 requires that all bills mandating employee benefits be accompanied by a fiscal impact statement.

- Legislation was adopted that would allow courts to award up to $10,000 in attorney's fees to small businesses that prevail in legal actions against local government agencies.

The 1990 session passed the following legislation:

- The "Employment-at-Will" doctrine was modified to prohibit the firing of employees who refuse to participate in or remain silent about illegal activities and those employees who smoke away from the workplace.

The 1991 session passed the following legislation:

- The Workman's Compensation Act was amended to allow insurers to allow deductibles.

State Small Business Conferences

The state actively encourages and participates in regional small business conferences conducted by such groups as chambers of commerce and Small Business Development Centers.

Contact:
Mr. David Weber, Small Business Consultant
Division of Business Services
Department of Economic and Community
   Development
7th Floor, Rachel Jackson Building
320 6th Avenue North
Nashville, TN 37219
(615) 741–2626
(800) 872–7201 (toll-free, in-state)
(800) 251–8594 (toll-free, out-of-state)

Texas

Small Business Offices, Programs, and Activities

Texas Department of Commerce

Contact:
Mr. William D. Taylor, Executive Director
Texas Department of Commerce
816 Congress Avenue
P.O. Box 12728
Austin, TX 78711
(512) 472–5059

The **Texas Department of Commerce** is working to diversify the state's economy by establishing programs to promote business development and retention, tourism, financial resources, small business, and job training. Nine separate state entities merged to form the new Texas Department of Commerce, created by the Texas Legislature in September 1987. The agency's mission is to encourage a climate that will stimulate business and other economic activities resulting in the retention and creation of jobs for Texas residents.

Program divisions include Business Development, Small Business, Finance, Tourism, and Work Force Development. Support divisions include Research and Planning, Information Services, Program Compliance, and Administration. The department is governed by a six-member board appointed by the governor with the advice and consent of the Senate.

Finance

Contact:
Mr. Reagan Houston, Director
Business Finance Division
Texas Department of Commerce
816 Congress Avenue
P.O. Box 12728
Austin, TX 78711
(512) 320–9634

The **Office of Business Finance Services** offers professional guidance to new businesses and existing companies wishing to expand their operations. Services include technical expertise, financial analysis, recommendations on appropriate private and public-sector funding programs, loan packaging, and more.

The **Texas Rural Economic Development Program** is designed to attract manufacturing and industrial jobs to rural areas of the state by providing guarantees on loans made by private lenders to Texas businesses for eligible projects.

The **Texas Exporters Loan Guarantee Program** assists small and medium-sized businesses entering or expanding into export markets in acquiring capital by guaranteeing loans from commercial lenders to Texas businesses for eligible costs. The Texas Export Credit Umbrella Insurance Program involves a policy underwritten by the Export-Import Bank of the United States (Ex-Im Bank), designed to stimulate the expansion of Texas exports by insuring a company's eligible export credit sales against loss due to political and commercial reasons. As a recipient of the Ex-Im Bank City/State Program, Commerce also offers Ex-Im Bank's services.

The **Texas Enterprise Zone Program** is designed to create jobs and induce capital investment in areas of economic distress by removing unnecessary governmental regulations, offering tax incentives, and other economic program benefits to businesses locating in these areas.

The division is required to maintain a central registry of designated reinvestment zones and executed *ad valorem* tax abatement agreements, and to provide technical assistance.

The **Development Corporation Act of 1979** allows cities, counties, and conservation and reclamation districts to form non-profit industrial development corporations or authorities on their behalf. The purpose of these corporations is to issue tax-exempt and taxable bonds for eligible projects in their jurisdictions. Under the Act, the Department of Commerce is authorized to review and approve the lease, sale, or loan agreement and the bonds issued by local industrial development corporations.

The **Business Finance Division** tracks the state's volume cap for Private Activity Bonds, and provides technical assistance in the issuance and approval of Industrial Revenue Bonds.

The **Texas Capital Fund**, a component of the Community Development Block Grant Program, helps create new jobs and retain existing ones—primarily for individuals of low and moderate income—by encouraging business development and expansions.

Business Development

Contact:
Mr. John C. Anderson, Director
Business Development Division
Texas Department of Commerce
815 Congress Avenue
P.O. Box 12728
Austin, TX 78728
(512) 320–9699

The **Office of National/International Business Development** promotes Texas nationally and internationally to encourage businesses to locate, relocate, or expand in Texas. The office assists new business and industry with site selection and with information on incentives for investing in Texas.

Companies can get assistance in promoting their products and services overseas through the **Office of International Trade**. Information on foreign markets, financing, trade shows, and supplying maquiladora industries is available.

The state of Texas foreign offices encourage—and actively pursue—business investment and trade opportunities for Texas products and tourism. Foreign offices are open in Mexico City and Monterrey, Mexico; Tokyo, Japan; Taipei, Taiwan; Frankfurt, West Germany; and Seoul, Korea. The **Office of Foreign Representation** is the administrative/reporting organization for all state of Texas offices.

The **Office of Advanced Technology** enhances the Texas science and technology infrastructure by networking public and private research needs and capabilities with federal, state, and industry resources. The office also administers the Product Commercialization and Development funds, established to aid in the financing of new or improved products or processes for which financing is not reasonably available from private sources. The office also provides information and technical assistance for Texas small technology companies interested in receiving federal funds for innovative research through the **Small Business Innovation Research Program**.

Office of the Employer Representative

Contact:
Commissioner Mary Scott Nabers, Employer
    Representative
Texas Employment Commission
101 East 15th Street, Room 614
TEC Building
Austin, TX 78778
(512) 463–2826

The **Office of the Employer Representative** on the Texas Employment Commission provides information and assistance to Texas businesses on minimizing tax liability under the unemployment insurance system.

Texas Agricultural Finance Authority

Contact:
Mr. Lindsey Dingmore,
Deputy Assistant Commissioner for
    Intergovernmental Affairs
Texas Department of Agriculture
P.O. Box 12408
Austin, TX 78711
(512) 463–7427

The **Texas Agricultural Finance Authority** program provides financial assistance through the use of the proceeds of the issuance of bonds for the expansion, development, and diversification of production, processing, marketing, and export of Texas agricultural products.

Small Business Development Centers

Small Business Development Centers (SBDCs) coordinate federal, state, university, and private resources to counsel and train owners of small businesses. SBDCs offer assistance through courses, seminars, one-on-one counseling, and by making research facilities available. They are organized by the U.S. Small Business Administration, and are usually affiliated with a state college or university. A complete list of Small Business Development Centers and subcenters in Texas appears in Appendix A of this directory.

Job Training Partnership Program

Contact:
Ms. Kathy Bonner, Interim Director
Job Training Partnership Program
Texas Department of Commerce
816 Congress Avenue, Suite 1200
Austin, TX 78701
(512) 472–5059

The **Job Training Partnership Program** operates with funding from the U.S. Department of Labor. The program provides job training and other employment-related services.

Governor's Advisory Council or Task Force

The **Small Business Advisory Committee** advises the Texas Department of Commerce Board on issues affecting small business. The committee makes recommendations on legislative and policy-oriented issues.

Contact:
Mr. Price Arredondo, Director
Small Business Division
Texas Department of Commerce
410 East Fifth Street, 4th Floor
P.O. Box 12728
Austin, TX 78711
(512) 320–0110

In 1987, the 29-member **Governor's Commission for Women** was appointed to "promote the goal of achieving equal legal, economic, political, educational, and social opportunity and advancement of women." The commission consists of four committees: Hall of Fame, Economic Development, Program, and Sponsorship. The commission has formed partnerships with academic institutions, nonprofit organizations, state agencies, and women's groups throughout the state in pursuit of its goals.

Contact:
Ms. Ann Wallace, Executive Director
Commission for Women
Office of the Governor
P.O. Box 12428
Austin, TX 78711
(512) 463–1782

Legislative Committees and Subcommittees

Small business issues are considered by the Senate Economic Development Committee and the House Business and Commerce Committee. Regular sessions convene on the second Tuesday of January in odd-numbered years. The governor may call special sessions.

Contacts:
Senator Temple Dickson
Chairman
Senate Economic Development Committee
State Capitol
P.O. Box 12068
Austin, TX 78711
(512) 463–0365

Representative Steve Wolens
Chairman
House Business and Commerce Committee
State Capitol, Room G12–A3
P.O. Box 2910
Austin, TX 78768–2910
(512) 463–0766

Contact:
Representative Harold Dutton
P.O. Box 2910
Austin, TX 78768–2910
(512) 463–0510

During the 71st legislative session, an interim study committee on women and minorities in business was formed to hear testimony from interested parties on problems they have had in doing business in Texas. A report was submitted to the 72nd legislature.

Legislation

Legislation recently passed by the Texas Legislature includes the following:

- A workers' compensation package that completely restructures the workers' compensation system.

- A constitutional amendment, passed by the voters, to finance a state incubator program, a micro enterprise program, a product development program, and an agricultural diversification program.

State Small Business Conferences

Contact:
Commissioner Mary Scott Nabers
Employer Representative
Texas Employment Commission
101 East 15th Street, Room 614
TEC Building
Austin, TX 78778
(512) 463–2826
1–800–TEC–MARY (toll-free, in-state)

The **Texas Conference on Small Business** was held April 2–3, 1990, hosted by the city of Dallas. More than 1,000 people attended, and a legislative agenda was prepared for the 72nd Texas Legislature.

The **Texas Business Council** (TBC) is a coalition of state agencies that presents seminars for business people on how to work more effectively with state government. Since its inception in the fall of 1987, more than 18,000 Texas taxpayers have attended TBC meetings across the state.

Utah

Small Business Offices, Programs, and Activities

Department of Community and Economic Development

The Department of Community and Economic Development has several programs that provide assistance to small businesses throughout the state.

Contact:
Mr. Dan Mabey, Director
International Business Development Office
324 South State Street, Suite 200
Salt Lake City, UT 84111
(801) 538–8737

The **International Business Development Office** assists businesses by developing marketing efforts, providing technical assistance in exporting, and matching foreign market opportunities with Utah sources.

Contact:
Mr. James Odle, Director
Federal Procurement Office
324 South State Street, Suite 235
Salt Lake City, UT 84111
(801) 538–8790

The **Utah Procurement Outreach Program** helps Utah small businesses bid on federal contracts. The office maintains a bid board for all major federal agencies operating within the state. In addition, this program assists companies in obtaining commercial contracts.

Contact:
Mr. L. Edward Meyer, Director
Utah Rural Development Program
324 South State Street, Suite 230
Salt Lake City, UT 84111
(801) 538–8781

The **Utah Rural Development Program** provides employment alternatives that are not dependent solely on agriculture markets or energy-related industries. The primary goal of this program is to identify and market the economic strengths of rural Utah in a way that will encourage the creation and expansion of Utah businesses.

Contacts:
Mr. Ruben J. Jiminez, Director
Office of Hispanic Affairs
324 South State Street, Suite 250
Salt Lake City, UT 84111
(801) 538–8815

Mr. Will Numkena, Director
Office of Indian Affairs
324 South State Street, Suite 250
Salt Lake City, UT 84111
(801) 538–8808

Ms. Betty Sawyer, Director
Office of Black Affairs
324 South State Street, Suite 250
Salt Lake City, UT 84111
(801) 538–8815

Mr. Louie Tong, Director
Office of Asian Affairs
324 South State Street, Suite 250
Salt Lake City, UT 84111
(801) 538–8815

The **Office of Hispanic Affairs**, the **Office of Asian Affairs**, the **Office of Black Affairs**, and the **Office of Indian Affairs** work to improve the educational, employment, and economic status of minorities in the state. The Office of Hispanic Affairs is charged with overseeing economic development and business-related issues for all minority enterprises in the state. The office works with Utah's Federal Procurement Assistance Office to match federal contracts with Utah minority-owned businesses. The office also sponsors workshops to help minorities do business with the federal government, and publishes the *Minority Business Directory*, a list of more than 400 minority businesses that is mailed to federal procurement agencies.

SBA 504 Certified Development Companies

Three Utah development companies, located in Salt Lake City and Ogden, lend to small and medium-sized businesses at fixed rates for terms of 10 to 20 years. Companies must create one job for every $35,000 received in financing. A 504 loan is funded through the sale of a debenture that is guaranteed by the U.S. Small Business Administration for up to $750,000 or 40 percent of the total cost of land, buildings, and equipment.

Contacts:
Mr. Scott Davis, President
Deseret Certified Development Company
7050 Union Park Center, Suite 570
Midvale, UT 84047
(801) 566–1163
fax: (801) 566–1632

Mr. Robert Richards, Director
Weber Capital Development Company
2404 Washington Boulevard, Suite 1100
Ogden, UT 84401–2316
(801) 627–1333
fax: (801) 392–7609

Centers of Excellence Program

Contact:
Mr. G. Michael Alder, Director
Mr. Jerold L. Foote, Deputy Director
Center of Excellence Program
324 South State Street
Salt Lake City, UT, 84111
(801) 538–8771

In 1986 Utah began the **Centers of Excellence Program**, which focuses on high-technology research that is being conducted in colleges and universities throughout the state. The primary goals are (1) to accelerate the growth of targeted technologies by assisting research activities within Utah's colleges and universities; (2) to expedite the translation of research products from university laboratories to Utah's economy; and (3) to enhance the image of Utah as a center for technological growth and economic development.

To receive state funding, a center must identify the type of research it will be doing, show that its research has industrial sponsorship, and show that the product will have an impact on Utah's economy. Another requirement is that the research must attract at least $2 of private or federal funds for each dollar of state funds used. At the present time, there are 26 centers conducting research in the following four targeted areas: (1) aerospace technology; (2) biomedical and biotechnology; (3) information technology; and (4) natural resources, including agriculture.

Utah Technology Finance Corporation

Contact:
Dr. Richard E. Turley, Executive Director
Utah Technology Finance Corporation
419 Wakara Way, Suite 215
Salt Lake City, UT 84111
(801) 583–8832
fax: (801) 583–5902

The purpose of the **Utah Technology Finance Corporation** is to encourage the growth of new and emerging high technology businesses throughout Utah and assist with product commercialization.

Committee of Consumer Services

Contact:
Dr. Joseph L. Ingles, Administrative
  Secretary
Committee of Consumer Services
408 Heber M. Wells Building
160 East 300 South
Salt Lake City, UT 84145
(801) 530–6645

The **Committee of Consumer Services** represents Utah small business and agricultural consumers of gas, electric, or telephone services in utility matters before the Utah Public Service Commission. The committee studies the impact of utility rates and regulatory actions on businesses and advocates those actions that will be most beneficial to consumers.

Small Business Development Centers

Contact:
Mr. David A. Nimkin, State Director
Utah Small Business Development Center
University of Utah
102 West 500 South, Suite 315
Salt Lake City, UT 84101
(801) 581–7905
fax: (801) 581–7814

The **Utah Small Business Development Center's** (USBDC) lead office is hosted by the University of Utah and is located in downtown Salt Lake City. The USBDC provides assistance to existing and new businesses, primarily through one-on-one consulting and through specific training programs and seminars. Currently the USBDC has subcenters located at Snow College in Ephraim, Utah State University in Logan, Weber State University in Ogden, College of Eastern Utah in Price, Brigham Young University in Provo, Southern Utah University in Cedar City, and Dixie College in St. George. A listing of all Small Business Centers and subcenters in Utah is provided in Appendix A of this directory.

Governor's Advisory Council or Task Force

Contact:
Lieutenant Governor W. Val Oveson
Office of the Lieutenant Governor
State Capitol Building, First Floor
Salt Lake City, UT 84114
(801) 538–1040

The **Small Business Advisory Council**, consisting of small business leaders from throughout the state, provides a forum that allows small business owners to bring their views to the attention of the state. The council seeks to identify small business problems, recommend solutions, and generally advise the governor on small business matters. The council is chaired by the lieutenant governor.

Legislative Committees and Subcommittees

The Utah Legislature does not have a committee or subcommittee focusing solely on small business issues. Most small-business related matters are referred to the Committee on Business and Labor.

Contacts:

Representative Donald R. LeBaron
Chairman
House Business, Labor, and Economic
    Development Committee
State Capitol Building
Salt Lake City, UT 84114
(801) 538–1029

Senator David H. Steele
Chairman
Senate Business, Labor, and Agriculture
    Committee
State Capitol Building
Salt Lake City, UT 84114
(801) 538–1035
fax: (801) 538–1414

Legislation

Legislation affecting small business that was adopted by the 1989 state legislature includes the following:

- H.B. 261 establishes a Privatization Policy Board, appointed by the governor, to review the appropriateness of privatizing existing state agencies and/or the services they provide. To the extent current state operations are privatized, small business will benefit from new contracting opportunities with the state.

- S.B. 189 creates a state-administered petroleum storage tank fund, to be used to pay part of an owner's or operator's costs for damage caused by releases of petroleum. S.B. 189 sets an annual petroleum storage tank fee.

- S.B. 24 provides that punitive damages may be awarded if it is established by clear and convincing evidence that a person's actions were willful and malicious or intentionally fraudulent, or that the conduct manifested a knowing and reckless indifference toward the rights of others. Evidence of a party's wealth is not admissible until a finding of liability for punitive damages has been made. S.B. 24 further provides that 50 percent of a punitive damage award above $20,000, after payment of attorneys' fees and cost, be remitted to the state. This law should discourage the awarding of excessive punitive damage awards, which in turn should reduce pressure on insurance companies to increase their liability insurance premiums.

- S.B. 25 benefits employers by limiting their exposure to liability suits stemming from the products they produce. The legislation repeals the unconstitutional "statute of repose" and establishes a statute of limitations of two years from the time both the harm and its cause are discovered.

- H.B. 220 establishes employee and employer rights surrounding an employee's invention.

Legislation adopted by the 1990 session of the state legislature affecting small business includes the following:

- H.B. 65 enables several changes to the labor code, including the repeal of unconstitutional statutes in the Child Labor law and increasing the state minimum wage to $3.80.

- H.B. 67 sets up the actuaries for a state-funded pool for coverage of uninsurables.

- S.B. 9 creates a reemployment program for injured workers without mandating rehabilitation benefits.

- S.B. 26 imposes a surcharge of ½ cent per gallon on all petroleum products contained in underground storage tanks, removes the current soil test requirement, and lengthens the period of time allowed for tank testing and compliance.

- S.B. 235 creates the Utah Health Data Committee and empowers it to collect and disseminate data on health care costs, quality, and accessibility.

- S.B. 175 grants counties the option to impose a tax to provide maintenance and operations revenues for tourism, recreation, and convention facilities. S.B. 175 was targeted to assist the renovation of the Salt Palace. Through this bill, a 3-percent tax may be imposed on short-term leases and rental of motor vehicles.

Legislation adopted by the 1991 session of the state legislature affecting small business includes the following:

- H.B. 51 enables financial institutions to make loans more readily to new and expanding businesses in Utah that may not otherwise obtain conventional loans. The increased risk is offset by creating a loan loss fund from fees paid by the borrower and matched with state monies.

- H.B. 438 allows counties to impose a 1-percent statewide restaurant tax on food prepared by restaurants for immediate consumption. The revenues are to be used for the purposes of financing, developing, operating, and maintaining tourism, recreation, cultural, and convention facilities and tourism promotion. It also allows certain counties to impose an additional ½ percent transient room tax on hotel rooms to be used only for tourism promotion.

- H.B. 344 authorizes a legislative appropriation for distribution to each of the state's 40 school districts, colleges, and universities for ongoing support of technology programs. Public and higher education may solicit funds from private and federal sources or establish partnerships to obtain additional resources. The legislation provides for an annual review and updating of the progress made through the technology programs. An appropriation of $11.9 million was made to public education and $1.15 million to higher education.

- H.J.R. 2 urges Congress to amend tax laws to allow taxpayers to deduct from their federal income tax, or take as a credit, paid health insurance premiums.

- S.B. 34 creates the Department of Environmental Quality and outlines its makeup, powers, and duties. The bill requires the new department to administer programs that focus on air quality, solid and hazardous waste, water pollution, drinking water, radiation control, and general sanitation. The bill requires the Department of Environmental Quality and local health departments to coordinate efforts to define a comprehensive service delivery system for statewide environmental services.

- H.B. 295 provides additional types of business and manufacturing activities that may qualify for enterprise zone incentives.

- H.B. 147 requires that whenever the State Tax Commission contacts taxpayers about the determination or collection of any tax, it notify them of their rights and obligations and of the commission's procedures for appeal, refund claims, and collections. The bill clarifies audit interview and installment payment procedures. If the commission disregards its published procedures, laws, or rules, taxpayers now have the right to sue the commission for actual damages and court costs, not to exceed $100,000. A $10,000 penalty for frivolous law suits is also imposed.

- H.B. 397 amends state and county assessment practices to allow a 5-percent reduction in value for intangibles, adjusts the homeowner's exemption, establishes in 1992 a statewide uniform tax on cars and other registered personal property, and puts a one-year restriction on certain levies. The bill also provides for a study of the state's property assessment practices.

- H.B. 394 creates the Utah Dineh Committee to direct the expenditures of federal Indian monies; creates the Utah Indian Cooperative Council and the Outreach Subcommittee to promote Indian affairs; and revises the functions and duties of the Division of Indian Affairs.

State Small Business Conferences

Contact:
Mr. Stanley Parrish, Executive Director
Department of Community and Economic
  Development
324 South State Street, Suite 300
Salt Lake City, UT 84111
(801) 538–8708

The **Governor's Conference on Economic Development and Education** was held April 29–30, 1991, in Salt Lake City. The conference provided an opportunity for business owners to discuss with government leaders the importance of economic development to all of Utah.

Vermont

Small Business Offices, Programs, and Activities

Department of Economic Development

Contact:
Mr. William E. Kenerson, Commissioner
Department of Economic Development
109 State Street
Montpelier, VT 05602
(802) 828-3221

The mission of the **Vermont Department of Economic Development** is to promote quality employment opportunities for Vermonters through programs that support existing businesses, help create and sustain new ventures, and recruit companies to the state.

The **International Business Program** conducts regional workshops and statewide seminars on the fundamentals of exporting. Areas of assistance include marketing, finance, and trade practices. The program's efforts focus largely on Canada. The Vermont/Quebec Commission promotes economic and cultural ties with Quebec. The department also operates the Vermont/Canada Free Trade Office to help Vermont and Canadian companies take advantage of opportunities resulting from the U.S.-Canada Free Trade Agreement.

Contact:
Mr. Phil Fagan, Director
Labor Training Program
Department of Economic Development
109 State Street
Montpelier, VT 05602
(802) 828-3221

Through the **Vermont Labor Training Program**, the state helps companies find and train manufacturing employees by paying up to 100 percent of the cost of pre-employment and classroom training, and up to half of the wages of employees taking part in on-the-job training.

Contact:
Mr. Curt Carter, Director
Job Zones Program
Department of Economic Development
109 State Street
Montpelier, VT 05602
(802) 828-3221

The **Job Zones Program** has targeted three areas of the state that have below-average income and above-average unemployment for financial assistance for economic development-related infrastructure projects and help in recruiting new employers.

Contact:
Mr. William E. Kenerson, Commissioner
Department of Economic Development
109 State Street
Montpelier, VT 05602
(802) 828–3221

Contact:
Ms. Patricia Moolton, Deputy Commissioner
Department of Economic Development
109 State Street
Montpelier, VT 05602
(802) 828–3221

Contact:
Mr. Greg Lawson
Agency for Development and Community
 Affairs
Department of Economic Development
109 State Street
Montpelier, VT 05602
(802) 828–3221

Contact:
Mr. Peter Varty, Director
Financial Services Recruiting
Department of Economic Development
109 State Street
Montpelier, VT 05602
(802) 828–3221

Contact:
Mr. Thomas Schroeder, Job Start
 Coordinator
Office of Economic Opportunity
103 South Main Street
Waterbury, VT 05676
(802) 241–2450

Regional Development Corporations provide financial and technical assistance to 14 regional development corporations as part of a cooperative effort that includes business call, early warning, and business adjustment programs.

Led by the Department of Economic Development, **Market Vermont** is an interagency effort to assist Vermont businesses in promoting their products and services. The Departments of Agriculture, Forests and Parks, Fish and Wildlife, and the Travel Division are also involved in the program.

The **Government Assistance Program** assists Vermont businesses, including minority- and women-owned and small businesses, to become involved in the government procurement process. Participating businesses will gain a better understanding of the federal marketplace and knowledge necessary for success in government contracting.

Financial Services Recruiting is done by 188 captive insurance companies in the state. A favorable regulatory climate, combined with Vermont's special quality of life, have made the state the national leader in the industry.

Vermont Job Start is a state-funded economic opportunity program aimed at increasing self-employment of low-income Vermonters. The program lends up to $10,000 to start, strengthen, or expand a small business. The interest rate is 9 percent adjusted quarterly, with a maximum term of four years.

To be eligible, applicants must be residents of Vermont, have sufficient access to other sources of credit, lack adequate personal financial resources for their business, and, depending on the size of their household, have an annual income of between $16,000 and $29,000. The program was established in 1978. Since that time, over $2 million in loans have been made. A recent study found that the state was spending approximately $3,500 to help create or sustain each full-time job under the program.

Vermont Industrial Development Authority

Contact:
Mr. Robert E. Fletcher, Manager
Vermont Industrial Development Authority
56 East State Street
Montpelier, VT 05602
(802) 223–7226

The **Vermont Industrial Development Authority** has several financing programs to assist small and medium-sized manufacturing firms in the state. Under Subchapter 2, the authority can provide mortgage insurance for up to 90 percent of the principal balance of the mortgage loan to finance the acquisition of land, building, machinery, and equipment or provide working capital in an amount not to exceed $10 million. Through its Subchapter 4 program, the authority can issue tax-exempt revenue bonds to fund the acquisition of land, buildings, machinery and equipment for use in a manufacturing facility. In the Subchapter 5 program, the authority provides direct loans for fixed asset financing. The maximum Subchapter 5 loan is $500,000 ($300,000 for land and buildings and $200,000 for machinery and equipment) or 40 percent of a project, whichever is less. In determining how much to lend, the authority considers, among other things, the needs of the borrower, the number and quality of jobs created, and the funds currently available to the authority.

Small Business Development Centers

Contact:
Mr. Norris Elliot, State Coordinator
Vermont Small Business Development
    Center
University of Vermont
Extension Service
Morrill Hall
Burlington, VT 05405–0106
(802) 656–4479

The Vermont **Small Business Development Center** (SBDC) system assists new and existing small businesses. With offices in St. Johnsbury, Morrisville, Rutland, West Brattleboro, and Winooski, the centers provide individual counseling and educational programs to entrepreneurs. The system is funded by the state, the University of Vermont, and the U.S. Small Business Administration.

Governor's Advisory Council or Task Force

Contact:
Ms. Anya Rader, Director
Office of Policy and Research
Pavilion Office Building
109 State Street
Montpelier, VT 05602
(802) 828–3336

The **Council of Economic Advisors** meets regularly with the governor to advise on economic conditions and actions state government might take to improve economic conditions.

Contact:
Mr. Curt Carter
Agency of Development and Community
    Affairs
109 State Street
Montpelier, VT 05602
(802)828–3221

The **Governor's Advisory Council on Technology** reviews the relationship between technology and economic development in the state. The council advises the governor on state policy to increase the use of advanced technology in Vermont's industries, in order to stimulate new, technologically oriented industry to Vermont.

Legislative Committees and Subcommittees

Contact:
Chairman
Senate Committee on Finance
State House
Montpelier, VT 05602
(802) 828–2231

The Vermont Legislature has no committee or subcommittee focusing on small business. Small business issues are considered by the House Committee on Commerce and the Senate Committee on Finance. The legislature meets annually from January through April.

Legislation

Recent legislation in Vermont includes the following:

- Small Business Ombudsman—S.345—This act authorizes the creation of the position of Small Business Ombudsman within the Vermont Department of Economic Development.

- Termination of Business Name—S.199—This act states that if the secretary of state declines to register a business name, the applicant may request the secretary to determine whether or not the person to whom the business name is registered is doing business or taking steps to do business in Vermont. If the secretary finds that the person is not doing business or intending to do business in Vermont, the secretary may terminate that registration and register the business name to the applicant. A person aggrieved by a final decision of the secretary under this section may appeal to the superior court of Washington County, which shall consider the matter *de novo*.

- Vermont Job Start Loan Fund—H.519—This act establishes a revolving loan fund for the job start program with the state Economic Opportunity Office of the Agency of Human Services. Interest earnings may be used for administration of this program. With the approval of the Joint Fiscal Committee, the agency may accept contributions and loans to the revolving loan fund created by this act.

- Small Business Partnership Pilot—H.848—This act creates a small business partnership program with the state to assist certain employers in their efforts to make health insurance benefits available to employees. The act creates the Vermont Health Insurance Plan Board, composed of 15 members including the commissioner of the Department of Social Welfare, the secretary of the Development and Community Affairs or designee, and the executive director of the Health Policy Council. The board shall file a report annually on or before January 15 describing its activities during the previous year, including updates on the number of employers and employees enrolled in the partnership. "Employees," "employers," and "partnership" are defined for the purposes of this act. In addition, the act establishes a Small Business Partnership Pilot Program.

State Small Business Conferences

Contact:
Mr. William E. Kenerson, Commissioner
Department of Economic Development
109 State Street
Montpelier, VT 05602
(802) 828–3221

Entrepreneurship forums are conducted regularly through the Department of Economic Development.

Virgin Islands

Small Business Offices, Programs, and Activities

Small Business Development Agency

Contact:
Mr. Rhudel A. George, Director
Small Business Development Agency
P.O. Box 6400
St. Thomas, VI 00601
(809) 774–8784

The **Small Business Development Agency** was created within the Department of Commerce in 1969 and is charged to assist local small-business men and women in establishing profitable operations through management counseling and financial and loan assistance. The agency is headed by an executive director appointed by the governor with the advice and consent of the legislature.

To be eligible for assistance, a person must own at least 50 percent legal or equitable interest in a small business either established or to be established in the Virgin Islands. The owner must be active in the management or operation of the small business on a full-time basis; the small business must be his or her principal means of support. In addition, the owner must be a native-born or continuous resident of the Virgin Islands for at least 10 years. If one parent is native-born, the 10-year residency requirement is reduced to five years.

Contact:
Mr. Rhudel A. George, Director
Small Business Development Agency
1131 King Street, Suite #301
Christiansted
St. Croix, VI 00820–4970
(809) 773–2161

The **Fredriksted Small Business Revolving Loan Fund** provides financial assistance to small businesses located in the Fredriksted district of St. Croix. The maximum amount for loans is $20,000.

Small Business Development Centers

Contact:
Dr. Solomon S. Kabuka, Jr., Director
Small Business Development Center
University of the Virgin Islands
P.O. Box 1087
St. Thomas, VI 00804
(809) 776–3206

Located on St. Thomas, the University of the Virgin Islands **Small Business Development Center** (SBDC) offers technical assistance in financial analysis, loan application processing, and business management. Courses are offered in financial record-keeping, marketing, and feasibility studies, with a strong emphasis on accounting. A subcenter is located in Christiansted on St. Croix. A complete listing of SBDCs and subcenters, including addresses and telephone numbers, is in Appendix A of this directory.

Minority Business Development Center

Contact:
Mr. Valencio Jackson, Executive Director
Minority Business Development Center
P.O. Box 838
St. Thomas, VI 00804
(809) 774–7215

Through the Virgin Islands **Minority Business Development Centers** (MBDC), students are assisted in acquiring contracts set aside for minority-owned firms and in obtaining development assistance. The St. Thomas MBDC offers courses in market analysis and financial planning and assists in preparing business plans.

Governor's Advisory Council or Task Force

There is no formal body that advises the governor on small business matters.

Legislative Committees and Subcommittees

Contact:
Chairman
Committee on Housing, Planning, and Health
P.O. Box 477
St. Thomas, VI 00801
(809) 774–6210

The Virgin Islands has a unicameral legislature. No small business committee or subcommittee exists; small business issues are handled by the Committee on Commerce.

Legislation

No recent legislation directly related to small business has been reported.

State Small Business Conferences

Contact:
Dr. Solomon S. Kabuka, Director
Small Business Development Center
University of the Virgin Islands
P.O. Box 1087
St. Thomas, VI 00801
(809) 776–3206

The Small Business Development Center sponsors hands-on training conferences, workshops, and managerial and technical assistance throughout the year in conjunction with the Virgin Islands Networking Committee, which is made up of the Virgin Islands Chamber of Commerce, the U.S. Small Business Administration, the Minority Business Development Center, and, on occasion, the Small Business Development Agency.

Virginia

Small Business Offices, Programs, and Activities

Office of Small Business and Financial Services

Contact:
Mr. David V. O'Donnell, Director
Office of Small Business and Financial
    Services
Virginia Department of Economic
    Development
P.O. Box 798
Richmond, VA 23206–0798
(804) 371–8100

The **Office of Small Business and Financial Services** provides assistance and information to the state's small businesses. It manages the Small Business Development Center program, through which management and technical assistance is made available to small business on a local basis; directs the Small Business Ombudsman program; provides leadership to the Interagency Small Business Alliance to improve state government's responsiveness to small companies; provides information and referral services on state laws and regulations affecting small companies; conducts the Small Business Roundtable program to determine business climate factors impacting the health and profitability of small businesses; works in partnership with the Virginia Small Business Advisory Board, which recommends programs, services, and policies to improve the small business environment; offers financial services; manages the Virginia Small Business Financing Authority, which provides financial assistance programs for small firms; provides financial consultation and referral services to economic development professionals and business clients; and, directs the Rural Virginia Development Foundation program to enhance economic growth in rural areas.

Small Business Development Centers

Contact:
Dr. Robert Smith, State Director
Virginia Small Business Development Center
Virginia Department of Economic
    Development
1021 East Cary Street, 11th Floor
Richmond, VA 23219
(804) 371–8258

Small Business Development Centers (SBDCs) provide management and technical assistance to start-up and existing businesses. SBDCs are partially funded by the U.S. Small Business Administration and are usually affiliated with a state college or university. A complete list of Small Business Development Centers, including addresses and telephone numbers, is in Appendix A of this directory.

Virginia Small Business Financing Authority

Contact:
Ms. Cynthia H. Arrington
Financial Services Representative
Virginia Small Business Financing Authority
P.O. Box 798
Richmond, VA 23206–0798
(804) 371–8254

The **Virginia Small Business Financing Authority** (VSBFA) was created in 1984 to assist small businesses in obtaining financing needed for their growth and expansion. The VSBFA currently operates the following programs:

Loan Guaranty Program. This program is designed to reduce the risk to banks in making loans and, thereby, increase the availability of short-term capital for small businesses. Under the program, the VSBFA will guarantee up to $150,000 or 50 percent of a bank loan, whichever is less. Typical borrowing includes revolving lines of credit to finance accounts receivable and inventory, and short-term loans for working capital and fixed-asset purchases, such as office equipment.

Export Financing. This program provides guaranties of short-term bank loans extended to small businesses primarily for pre-export working capital. This includes loans to finance inventory, labor, marketing, and other services needed for processing orders before actual shipment. The maximum guaranty is $150,000 or 50 percent of the loan amount, whichever is less. In addition, in partnership with the Export-Import Bank of the United States (Ex-Im Bank), the VSBFA markets Ex-Im Bank's full array of export finance programs and packages Ex-Im Bank applications. These programs include short-term working capital financing for the U.S. exporter and long-term financing for foreign buyers to facilitate the U.S. exporter's sales. The VSBFA also assists small Virginia exporters in obtaining export credit insurance from Ex-Im Bank's agent, the Foreign Credit Insurance Association (FCIA).

Industrial Development Bonds (IDBs) and Umbrella IDB Program. Tax-exempt revenue bonds are issued to small businesses to finance land, buildings, and new equipment for manufacturing facilities. In addition, the Umbrella IDB Program provides a means for these small firms to sell their IDBs in the public tax-exempt bond market, thus gaining access to the lowest interest rates available.

Virginia Business Opportunities

Contact:
Mr. Donald F. Moore, Director
Department of General Services
Division of Purchases and Supply
P.O. Box 1199
Richmond, VA 23209–1199
(804) 786–5494

No matter how large or small your company is, you are probably making a product or providing a service the Commonwealth of Virginia needs. A weekly newsletter, **Virginia Business Opportunities**, is published to help companies do business with the state by listing procurement opportunities. A subscription fee is charged for the publication.

The Virginia Department of Economic Development

Contact:
Mr. Hugh D. Keogh, Director
Virginia Department of Economic
  Development
P.O. Box 798
Richmond, VA 23206–0798
(804) 371–8106

The **Virginia Department of Economic Development's** trade service group assists Virginia firms in exploring, developing, and expanding business opportunities in the international market place. The group's efforts are enhanced by its understanding of these markets as they relate to Virginia's business and political environment.

The Virginia Department of Economic Development brings together existing resources conducting international trade functions throughout Virginia state government. By incorporating export development, research, and education into a single unified force, a shared vision is created.

Through educational support, information sharing, and one-on-one counseling, the Virginia Department of Economic Development assists firms in optimizing their potential for building foreign markets. Specific programs include participation in overseas trade shows, hosting foreign buying missions, providing market leads, and presenting seminars on current issues.

The department works closely with its affiliated agencies, the Virginia Department of Agriculture and Consumer Services, and the Virginia Port Authority. Together, these agencies provide a comprehensive range of assistance, maintaining offices in Tokyo, Hong Kong, Seoul, Brussels, and São Paulo. To further help Virginia firms export products and services, the department consults with the U.S. Department of Commerce and its foreign commercial service officers worldwide.

High Technology

Contact:
Honorable A. Lynwood Holton, President
Center for Innovative Technology
2214 Rockhill Road, Suite 600
13783 Park Center Road
Herndon, VA 22070
(703) 689–3000

The **Center for Innovative Technology** (CIT) is a nonprofit organization created by the Commonwealth of Virginia with a mission to enhance, mobilize, and transfer the state's science and technology resources to promote economic development in the Commonwealth. In order to fulfill this mission, CIT, working with businesses and universities, has developed programs in three main areas: technology development, technology transfer, and technology commercialization.

Technology Development—A business can access technology development resources by participating in CIT cosponsored cooperative research. If a business finds university research helpful in its R&D process, CIT can help match the needs of the business with the resources of Virginia's colleges and universities. With the business, CIT can cosponsor university research to answer the needs of the business. Cosponsored research is administered through CIT's four Research Institutes in the following areas: biotechnology, computer-aided engineering, information technology, and materials science and engineering. Additional resources for businesses are the four CIT-funded technology development centers for electro-fiber optics, power electronics, semicustom integrated circuits, and bioprocess/product development.

Technology Transfer—Businesses can access the technology and resources of Virginia's educational system through a new pilot program of community college-based technology transfer agents. Local businesses can draw upon these resources to link with local and statewide economic development programs; the resources of public institutions of higher education; new and under-utilized innovative technology; and business growth, management, and problem-solving resources. The CIT is also involved in setting up the Commonwealth Technology Information Service, a set of data bases comprising information on Virginia's technology resources, the first of which will describe faculty expertise and research interests at Virginia's institutions of higher education. Tapping into this data base, a firm will be able to identify faculty members who could be valuable resources to the business.

Technology Commercialization—CIT's network of entrepreneurial centers and incubators is of particular significance to small businesses. CIT has cosponsored entrepreneurial centers or incubators associated with seven colleges and universities in Virginia. The entrepreneurial centers provide outreach services in the form of management, technical, and financial advice to technology-based entrepreneurs in their localities. The incubators provide shared physical space and support services to reduce start-up costs for technology-based businesses. They also provide an environment in which resident businesses can share common problems and experiences and access on-site management assistance and sources of financial assistance and professional services. Access to schools' faculty, equipment, and libraries may also be provided. The entrepreneurial centers and incubators are in various stages from planning to implementation.

Contact:
Mr. David J. Miller, Director
Small Business Development
Center for Innovative Technology
2214 Rock Hill Road, Suite 600
Herndon, VA 22070–4005
(703) 689–3000

CIT matches industrial sponsors' contributions to research, including **Small Business Innovation Research** (SBIR) subcontracts. CIT also cosponsors individual research projects at Virginia universities, and CIT program managers can assist SBIR winners by identifying university faculty members and resources that will support the SBIR project.

Virginia Department of Agriculture

Contact:
Dr. Clinton V. Turner, Commissioner
Department of Agriculture and Consumer
  Services
1100 Bank Street, Suite 210
Richmond, VA 23219
(804) 786–3501

The Division of Markets administers the **Agricultural Products Exchange** (APEX), a program that informs subscribing buyers and sellers of Virginia agricultural products about one another. Assistance is also available for locating transportation for agricultural products. In addition to Virginia farmers, access to APEX is open to food cooperatives, wholesalers, processors, brokers, grocery chains, and others who wish to buy direct from farmers.

Department of Minority Business Enterprise

Contact:
Ms. Esther H. Vassar, Director
Department of Minority Business Enterprise
9th Street Office Building, 11th Floor
Richmond, VA 23219
(804) 786–5560

The **Department of Minority Business Enterprise** (DMBE) provides technical and educational assistance and information to minority business owners and prospective business owners. The DMBE distributes *Let Us Guide You*, a marketing guide for doing business with the Commonwealth of Virginia, and DMBE referral services offer assistance in virtually all business areas, including accounting, bookkeeping, bid preparation, bonding, and applications. Also available to encourage minority enterprise success are business courses and workshops, business information and literature, contracting and procurement assistance, marketing and advertising counseling, and loan packaging help.

In addition, the highway component of the DMBE provides management and technical assistance to prospective and existing minority firms seeking contractual opportunities available through the Virginia Department of Highways and Transportation. The highway component provides supportive services in bidding, estimating, and highway specification; financial packaging in accordance with requirements of the Virginia Department of Highways and Transportation for prequalification, bonding, lines of credit, and other operating capital needs; and identifying highway procurement opportunities.

It also offers workshops and seminars, and keeps entrepreneurs apprised of highway conferences.

Governor's Advisory Council or Task Force

Contact:
Mary Elesser, Manager
Small Business Services
Virginia Department of Economic
   Development
P.O. Box 798
Richmond, VA 23206–0798
(804) 371–8252

The **Virginia Small Business Advisory Board** advises the Department of Economic Development on small business programs, assists and develops small business, and makes recommendations concerning actions the department and state government might take to enhance small businesses growth. The board, which meets biannually, represents rapidly growing industries, private small business organizations, and state and federal agencies.

Legislative Committees and Subcommittees

The Senate Committee on Commerce and Labor handles many small business issues. The Virginia House Committee on Commerce and Labor focuses on state small business issues and concerns.

Contacts:

Senator Charles J. Colgan, Chairman
Senate Committee on Commerce and
   Labor
P.O. Box 1650
Manassas, VA 22110
(804) 786–6987

Delegate Joan Munford, Chairman
House Subcommittee on Small Business
706 General Assembly Building
State Capitol
Richmond, VA 23219
(804) 786–8425

Legislation

The following legislation affecting small businesses was recently enacted in Virginia:

- S.J.R. 181 requests that the Bureau of Insurance develop proposals to increase health insurance access for small businesses. The legislation also asks the small business advisory board to recommend ways to promote existing low cost insurance packages for small businesses.

- H.J.R. 448 establishes a joint subcommittee to study incentives and obstacles for businesses making location decisions in Virginia. The committee will examine required permitting processes and identify ways to streamline and expedite such procedures. Laws related to business operations as they affect the expansion of existing facilities also will be reviewed.

State Small Business Conferences

No recent statewide small business conferences have been reported.

Washington

Small Business Offices, Programs, and Activities

Department of Trade and Economic Development

Contact:
Business Information Coordinator
Business Assistance Center
Department of Trade and Economic
  Development
919 Lakeridge Way, S.W., Suite A
Olympia, WA 98502
(206) 586–3021

Contact:
Mr. Brian Teller, Business Ombudsman
Business Assistance Center
Department of Trade and Economic
  Development
919 Lakeridge Way, S.W., Suite A
Olympia, WA 98502
(206) 586–3022

Contact:
Mr. Jonathan Hayes, Bond Program
  Administrator
Department of Trade and Economic
  Development
2001 6th Avenue, Suite 2700
Seattle, WA 98121
(206) 464–7350

Washington's **Department of Trade and Economic Development** aids small firms through its Business Assistance Center, Business Ombudsman, and bond programs.

The **Washington Business Assistance Center** provides a central source of information on the requirements for doing business in Washington and on the public programs available to assist firms in the state. Trained business advisors answer questions on starting and operating a business, and coordinate available resources to fit particular business situations.

The **Business Ombudsman** is available to intercede with government agencies on behalf of businesses experiencing difficulties in areas such as licensing, taxation, and regulation. By bringing the involved parties together and acting as mediator, the ombudsman prevents or resolves a variety of problems for individual businesses.

Industrial Revenue Bonds (IRBs) can be issued to finance the acquisition, construction, enlargement, or improvement of industrial development facilities. Interest paid to the buyer of the bonds is not subject to federal income tax. Beginning in 1987, eligible industrial projects are limited to manufacturing facilities.

The **State Umbrella Bond Program** is available to firms whose borrowing needs are too small to warrant packaging a single-borrower bond issue or who are unable to find a purchaser for the bonds because of new federal tax code changes. Bond pooling allows the costs of issuing tax-exempt bonds to be divided among several borrowers, making bonds a more economical means of financing and enabling borrowers to benefit from lower rates.

Department of Community Development

Contact:
Mr. Bill Davison, Community Programmer
Department of Community Development
9th and Columbia Building
Olympia, WA 98504
(206) 753–4900

Washington's **Department of Community Development** offers finance and incubator programs to assist businesses.

The **Finance Program** helps business and industry to secure needed financing by combining private financial loans with federal and state "gap financing" loans. Existing businesses can secure loans that afford long-term financing, reasonable rates, and low down payments.

The **Incubator Program** has developed resource guides on both small business incubators and home-based businesses that are used by local communities, and offers one-to-one technical assistance on these and other subjects.

Export Assistance

Contact:
Mr. Kenneth L. Keach, President
Small Business Export Finance Assistance
    Center
2001 6th Avenue, Suite 1700
Seattle, WA 98121
(206) 464–7123

The **Small Business Export Finance Assistance Center** is a nonprofit corporation established by the state to encourage exports by small and medium-sized companies. The center provides assistance to prospective exporters statewide in the mechanics and financing of exports.

Minority Business Emphasis

Contact:
Mr. James A. Medina, Director
Office of Minority and Women's Business
    Enterprises
406 South Water, No. K–11
Olympia, WA 98504–4611
(206) 753–9693

The **Office of Minority and Women's Business Enterprises** was created in 1983 to increase opportunities for minorities and women wishing to obtain state contracts. The office sets annual overall goals and monitors participation on contracts awarded to businesses owned by women and minorities. To be counted toward a state agency or educational institution's annual goal, the business must be certified by the office as a bona fide minority and women's business enterprise.

375

High Technology

Contact:
Mr. Dean Ray Bowen, Interim Director
The Washington Technology Center
University of Washington Campus
Mail Stop: FJ–10
Seattle, WA 98195
(206) 685–1920

The **Washington Technology Center** is a joint industry-state-university enterprise engaged in commercially promising research and technology development. Offices and labs are located at the University of Washington, Washington State University, and Tri-Cities University Center. Industry and federal agencies can contract to train advanced students or to develop new technologies through the center. In licensing or transferring rights to intellectual property created and owned by the center to outside businesses, a priority is given to business applications within Washington.

Contact:
Mr. Jim Van Orsow, Business Development
   Assistant
Innovation Assessment Center
c/o Small Business Development Center
2001 6th Avenue, Suite 2608
Seattle, WA 98121–2518
(206) 464–5450

The **Innovation Assessment Center** offers business and technical assistance to investors and innovators of all types. For a modest fee, inventions are evaluated confidentially by experts in the specific field of the invention. The evaluations provide information to the inventor on the invention's potential commercial viability.

Small Business Development Centers

Contact:
Mr. Lyle M. Anderson, State Director
Washington Small Business Development
   Center
Washington State University
College of Business and Economics
441 Todd Hall
Pullman, WA 99164–4740
(509) 335–1576

Small Business Development Centers (SBDCs) coordinate federal, state, university, and private resources to counsel and train owners of small businesses. They offer this assistance through courses, seminars, one-on-one counseling, and by making available research facilities. They are organized by the U.S. Small Business Administration and are usually affiliated with a state college or university. The lead SBDC in Washington is located at Washington State University in Pullman. Subcenters are located in Bellevue, Moses Lake, Kennewick, Vancouver, Spokane, Everett, Lynnwood, Seattle, Tacoma, Olympia, Yakima, Wenatchee, Bellingham, Mt. Vernon, and Omak. A listing of Small Business Development Centers and subcenters in Washington is in Appendix A of this directory.

Publications

Contact:
Ms. Diana Caldwell, Office Manager
Small Business Development Center
Washington State University
College of Business and Economics
441 Todd Hall
Pullman, WA 99164–4740
(509) 335–1576

Several booklets on business activities in Washington are published jointly by the Department of Trade and Economic Development and the Small Business Development Center: *Business Assistance in Washington State*, *Financing a Business in Washington State*, *Operating a Home Based Business in Washington State*, *Selling to the Government in Washington State*, and *A Guide to Starting a Business in Washington State*.

Governor's Advisory Council or Task Force

Contact:
Ms. Robin Swenson, Staff Consultant
Small Business Improvement Council
c/o Office of Financial Management
400 Insurance Building
Olympia, WA 98504
(206) 753–1879

The **Governor's Small Business Improvement Council** was created to identify and recommend ways to improve the small business climate in the state. Council members are small business owners from across the state.

Legislative Committees and Subcommittees

The Senate Commerce and Labor Committee, the primary business committee in the Senate, has a small business subcommittee. In the House, the Trade and Economic Development Committee handles business issues.

Contacts:
Senator Frank Warnke
Chairperson
Senate Commerce and Labor Committee
John Cherberg Building, Room 102B
Olympia, WA 98504
(206) 786–7428

Representative Max Vekich
Chairperson
House Trade and Economic Development
  Committee
Room 212C, House Office Building
Olympia, WA 98504
(206) 786–7107

Legislation

Washington State 1990 legislative actions affecting small business development and growth include the following:

- A reserve fund of $430,000 was appropriated to the Washington Economic Development Finance Authority, whose programs are directed towards assistance to small businesses.

- The governor has directed the Department of Trade and Economic Development to create cooperative networks to help small businesses become more competitive. He has also directed the department to explore ways to provide bid information to small businesses through the electronic bulletin board.

- The Washington Marketplace program, a voluntary program that matches buyers with nearby suppliers through a competitive and confidential bidding process, is modified to include linkages between urban and rural areas and to assist businesses in identifying new markets. For this expansion, $150,000 is appropriated.

State Small Business Conferences

No state small business conferences were reported.

West Virginia

Small Business Offices, Programs, and Activities

Small Business Development Center Division

Contact:
Ms. Eloise Jack, State Director
Small Business Development Center
    Division
Governor's Office of Community and
    Industrial Development
1115 Virginia Street, East
Charleston, WV 25310
(304) 348–2960

The **Small Business Development Center Division** (SBDCD) of the Governor's Office of Community and Industrial Development (formerly known as the Small and Minority Business Services Office) assists small and minority businesses with their filing of state and federal forms. It also coordinates programs with other agencies serving as a one-stop center for going into business.

The SBDCD has a network of 11 subcenters located across the state on academic campuses to offer assistance and counseling on a one-to-one basis. Services include start-up counseling, loan packaging, ombudsmanship, procurement assistance, managerial and technical assistance, education, and training.

The SBDCD certifies minority- and women-owned businesses, and maintains and distributes a directory for federal and state agencies and the private sector that provides access to businesses with federal compliance goals. Assistance is available in areas such as 8(a) certification to businesses classified as disadvantaged. The SBDCD also mails a weekly notice of all issued state procurement and federal bids. A list of small business development centers, including addresses and telephone numbers, is in Appendix A of this directory.

West Virginia Economic Development Authority

Contact:
Mr. David Warner, Associate Director
West Virginia Economic Development
    Authority
Building 6, Room 525
State Capitol
Charleston, WV 25305
(304) 348–3650

The **West Virginia Economic Development Authority** (WVEDA) provides low-interest loans for land acquisition, building construction, and equipment purchases. It may participate in up to 45 percent of the project cost for new or expansion projects. The loan programs are directed to manufacturing firms, with an emphasis on new job creation.

Under the **West Virginia Capital Company Act**, there are currently 28 qualified venture capital companies in the state, with a total capitalization of $43 million. A list of qualified venture capital companies is available from the West Virginia Economic Development Authority (WVEDA).

SBA 504 Certified Development Company

Contact:
Mr. David Warner, President
West Virginia Certified Development
　Corporation
1900 Washington Street E, Building 6,
　Room 525
Charleston, WV 25305
(304) 348–3650

The **West Virginia SBA 504 Certified Development Corporation** provides long-term fixed rate loans for small and medium-sized firms. Interest rates are tied to U.S. Treasury bond rates of comparable maturity.

Governor's Advisory Council or Task Force

West Virginia has no specific advisory council to make recommendations on small business.

Legislative Committees and Subcommittees

A joint interim small business committee meets when the state legislature is in recess. The committee, which consists of seven Senate and eight House members, may prepare and present bills, as well as undertake studies on issues of concern to West Virginia's small businesses.

Contacts:
Senator Thais Blatnik, Chairman
Senate Small Business Committee
State Capitol (West Wing)
Charleston, WV 25305
(304) 357–7918

Delegate James H. Morgan, Chairman
House Small Business Committee
State Capitol, (East Wing)
Charleston, WV 25305
(304) 340–3150

Legislation

Small business interests are lobbied through the SBDCD and the West Virginia Coalition for Small Business. Problems and concerns of small business are reviewed and reports submitted to the governor and legislature with recommendations.

Contact:
Mr. John Hodges, Chairman
West Virginia Coalition for Small Business
P.O. Box 1774
Huntington, WV 25718
(304) 529–1412

State Small Business Conference

A small business conference was scheduled in West Virginia for October 1992.

Contact:
Ms. Eloise Jack, Director
Small Business Development Center
    Division
Governor's Office of Community and
    Industrial Development
State Capitol
Charleston, WV 23505
(304) 348–2960

Wisconsin

Small Business Offices, Programs, and Activities

Wisconsin Department of Development

Contact:
Mr. Philip Albert, Director
Office of Development Finance
Wisconsin Department of Development
123 West Washington Avenue
P.O. Box 7970
Madison, WI 53707
(608) 266–7099

In Wisconsin, the Department of Development is the chief agency providing assistance to businesses, including development financing, business development services, permit information, and other specialized services.

The **Office of Development Finance** administers the following economic development financing programs:

Wisconsin Development Fund/Economic Development Component. This program is funded through the federal Small Cities Community Development Block Grant Program. Its purpose is job creation and retention with a special emphasis on creating job opportunities for persons of low and moderate income. The applicant must be an eligible unit of local government making an application on behalf of a business. The assistance to the business is in the form of a loan with terms and conditions that may vary based on the business' demonstrated need.

Customized Labor Training Fund. This fund was established in 1984 to meet the critical skill needs of Wisconsin businesses when training for their labor force is not available through federal, state, or local resources. It works to stimulate expansion of existing businesses, the creation of new businesses, and the retooling of Wisconsin's industrial base through the introduction of new products and processes. The fund can provide grants for up to 50 percent of the cost of training or retraining workers in emerging occupations for expanding or retooling firms.

Technology Development Fund. This fund was created in 1984 to provide financial support for research and development of new products and processes through a consortia of businesses and institutions of higher education. The goals of the program are the promotion of business development in Wisconsin, the encouragement of business retooling and diversification, and the expansion of business access to the universities of the state. A match provision limits total awards to a maximum of 40 percent of the total project's value and requires a 20- to 90-percent contribution, cash or in-kind, from the business.

Employee-Ownership Assistance Loan Program. Under this program, financial assistance is provided to a group of employees to determine the feasibility of employee ownership of a business. To qualify, the business must have experienced substantial layoffs or a closing not more than one year before the date of application.

Major Economic Development Projects Program. The purpose of this program is to retain or increase employment in Wisconsin through the support of projects likely to have a substantial positive economic impact. Assistance can take the form of a grant or loan, depending on the circumstances. Applicants must make a commitment to locate in Wisconsin and not displace workers or relocate out of state. A match is required.

Rural Economic Development Program. This program was established in 1989 by the Wisconsin Legislature to promote business development and create jobs by assisting small businesses (those with fewer than 25 employees) located in rural or small communities. The program can provide grants or loans for certain expenses related to business start-up or expansion.

Community-Based Economic Development Program. This program was established in 1989 to provide funds to local governments and community-based organizations for the purpose of encouraging the creation of jobs in distressed areas of the state. Grants are available to promote small business development and to assist the start-up and operation of business incubators.

Minority Business Finance Program. This program was established in 1989 to provide flexible financing to minority-owned businesses. It assists with start-up, expansion, or acquisition of a business. The program provides early planning grants to assist business start-ups, and development project grants or loans once plans are completed.

Small Business Innovation Research Support Programs

Contacts:
Mr. Todd A. Boehm, Development Finance
   Specialist
Office of Development Finance
Wisconsin Department of Development
123 West Washington Avenue
P.O. Box 7970
Madison, WI 53707
(608) 266–7099

Ms. Carboline Gabber, Technology
   Development Finance Specialist
Office of Development Finance
Wisconsin Department of Development
123 West Washington Avenue
P.O. Box 7970
Madison, WI 53707
(608) 267–9383

The Department of Development's (DOD) **Small Business Innovation Research** (SBIR) Bridge Financing Program helps SBIR Phase I winners continue their research operations during the waiting period between the completion of Phase I and the start of Phase II research. Eligible firms must have completed Phase I research and submitted a Phase II proposal under the federal SBIR program, have 250 or fewer employees, and intend to perform the research primarily in Wisconsin. Also, Wisconsin must be the major place of business.

The DOD's technology-based **incubator grants and loans** assist in the feasibility study, or the initial design, development, and operation of a proposed technology-based incubator. Eligible costs include costs of the feasibility study and the purchase of equipment or the purchase and rehabilitation of a building, as well as staff costs.

Bureau of Business Development

Contact:
Mr. Hampton Rothwell, Director
Bureau of Business Development
Wisconsin Department of Development
123 West Washington Avenue
P.O. Box 7970
Madison, WI 53707
(608) 267–0313

The **Bureau of Business Development** coordinates and facilitates business creation, expansion, and retention efforts in Wisconsin. The bureau's area-development managers assist communities in developing programs that will attract and retain businesses. They provide assistance to businesses opening new facilities, expanding operations, or recovering from business setbacks. Services include identifying financial resources, suppliers, customers, and sites and buildings. Information is also provided on labor markets, training resources, utility services, transportation, taxes, and related subjects.

In addition, the bureau has a small business assistance office that encourages entrepreneurism and assists new ventures; provides specialized assistance to women-owned businesses; and assists businesses with permitting processes.

Small Business Ombudsman

Contact:
Ms. Sara Burr, Small Business Ombudsman
Bureau of Business Development
Wisconsin Department of Development
123 West Washington Avenue
P.O. Box 7970
Madison, WI 53707
(608) 266–0562

The state's **Small Business Ombudsman** assists business owners with specific complaints about state laws, administrative rules, or agency interpretations; provides information and referrals on special programs; monitors the progress of legislation and rules and acts as a small business advocate; conducts training and organizes local networks to encourage entrepreneurship; and administers Wisconsin's Regulatory Flexibility Act, which provides for special consideration of small businesses in state administrative rules.

Women's Business Services

Contact:
Ms. Mary Strickland, Director
Women's Business Services
Bureau of Business Development
Wisconsin Department of Development
123 West Washington Avenue
P.O. Box 7970
Madison, WI 53707
(608) 266–0593

The **Women's Business Services** office provides help to women business owners and prospective owners. Support includes business consultation, training, conferences, coordination of public and private resources, and loan packaging assistance. In addition, the office maintains a comprehensive data base of the 12,000 largest women-owned businesses in Wisconsin.

Permit Information Center

Contact:
Mr. Dennis Leong, Director
Permit Information Center
Bureau of Business Development
Wisconsin Department of Development
123 West Washington Avenue
P.O. Box 7970
Madison, WI 53707
(608) 266–9869
(800) HELP–BUS
(800) 435–7287 (toll-free, in-state)

The **Permit Information Center** coordinates and facilitates state regulatory participation and involvement in economic development projects. The center provides information on business permit processes; expedites the issuance of permits; resolves delays, miscommunications, and other problems; identifies needed improvements; and reports monthly and annually to the governor and the secretary of the Department of Development on state regulatory issues affecting business. The Permit Information Center serves businesses of all sizes.

Bureau of Minority Business Development

Contact:
Mr. Robert Wynn, Director
Bureau of Minority Business Development
Wisconsin Department of Development
123 West Washington Avenue
P.O. Box 7970
Madison, WI 53707
(608) 266–8380

The **Bureau of Minority Business Development** provides existing and potential minority-owned businesses assistance in market assessment, access to credit, capital formation, and coordination of public and private resources. The bureau also certifies minority vendors, maintains a data base on minority businesses in Wisconsin, and publishes an annual directory of certified minority-owned firms.

Division of Community Development

Contact:
Mr. Terry Groesenheider, Administrator
Division of Community Development
Wisconsin Department of Development
123 West Washington Avenue
P.O. Box 7970
Madison, WI 53707
(608) 267–7200

The **Division of Community Development** works with local communities and community-based organizations to promote economic development. The division is responsible for administering the Wisconsin Main Street Program, the Development Zone Program, and the Community Preparedness Program.

Bureau of International Development

Contact:
Ms. Barbara Rothwell, Manager
Bureau of International Development
Wisconsin Department of Development
123 West Washington Avenue
P.O. Box 7970
Madison, WI 53707
(608) 266–1480
fax: (608) 266–5551

The **Bureau of International Development** assists Wisconsin producers and service providers in promoting export sales, joint ventures, and foreign licensing, and invites foreign investors to establish productive ventures in Wisconsin. The Madison-based bureau also operates offices in Milwaukee, and in Frankfurt, Germany (for Europe and the Middle East); Hong Kong (for the Pacific Rim, except Japan and Korea); Tokyo (exclusively for Japan); and Seoul (exclusively for Korea). In addition, the bureau benefits from the services of the Canada Liaison of the Council of Great Lakes Governors (in Toronto) for export promotion efforts.

The bureau provides individual export counseling to Wisconsin firms; sponsors participation in foreign trade fairs and shows; organizes trade and reverse investment missions abroad—many of them led by the governor; publishes a variety of materials, including the bi-monthly *Wisconsin International Trade* magazine,

Wisconsin International Trade Handbook, and *Wisconsin Exporter's Directory*; organizes and participates in seminars; arranges programs for visiting foreign buyers; serves as liaison with chambers of commerce, world trade associations, vocational and technical colleges, and elements of the University of Wisconsin System on international economic matters; sponsors sister-state and sister-city agreements and exchanges; provides pre-export development loans; and distributes trade leads generated abroad.

Council on Small and Minority Business Opportunities

Contacts:
Mr. Robert Wynn, Director
Bureau of Minority Business Development
Wisconsin Department of Development
123 West Washington Avenue
P.O. Box 7970
Madison, WI 53707
(608) 266–8380

Ms. Hermetta Williams, Director
Minority Business Programs
Wisconsin Department of Administration
101 East Wilson Street (6th Floor)
Madison, WI 53703
(608) 267–7806

The **Council on Small and Minority Business Opportunities** is charged with the following responsibilities: (1) review the extent of small business purchasing by the state and its subdivisions; (2) advise the Department of Administration's purchasing agent about methods for increasing small business participation in state purchasing; (3) advise the Department of Administration's purchasing agent of methods to simplify compliance with the forms and procedures required to obtain contracts with the state; and (4) submit to the governor and the legislature an annual report with recommendations for improving small and minority business opportunities.

Wisconsin Innovation Service Center

Contact:
Ms. Debra Malewicki, Program Manager
Wisconsin Innovation Service Center
University of Wisconsin-Whitewater
402 McCutchan Hall
Whitewater, WI 53190
(414) 472–1365

The **Wisconsin Innovation Service Center** performs low-cost, preliminary market feasibility evaluations of inventions and new product ideas. The evaluation process utilizes a computer model, but its primary value lies in its access to a network of technical and specialized consultants with a variety of expertise and an in-house staff capable of performing quality secondary market research.

The center provides invention evaluations for other university and private programs, as well as for small businesses and independent inventors from across the United States and some foreign countries.

Statewide SBA 504 Certified Development Corporation

Contact:
Mr. John Giegel, Executive Director
Wisconsin Business Development Finance
   Corporation
3 S. Pinckney Street
Suite GL3
P.O. Box 2717
Madison, WI 53701
(608) 258–8830

The **Wisconsin Business Development Finance Corpora-tion** (WBDFC) is a private, nonprofit U.S. Small Business Administration Certified Development Corporation. Its program provides small business financing for the purchase of land, buildings, machinery, and equipment, and the construction and modernization of facilities. Businesses must obtain private financing for at least 50 percent of each project. WBDFC provides up to $750,000 or 40 percent of the fixed-asset project, whichever is less. The program offers long-term fixed-rate financing with maturities of 10 and 20 years.

Procurement Program

Contact:
Ms. Jan Abrahamsen, Director
State Bureau of Procurement
Wisconsin Department of Administration
P.O. Box 7867
Madison, WI 53707
(608) 266–2605

Wisconsin's state offices and institutions annually purchase nearly $500 million in parts, machinery, supplies, equipment, printing, and services. These purchases are made from private firms that have completed the standard bidder's list application form. A significant share of the state's purchases are made from small Wisconsin businesses.

Wisconsin's **Bureau of Procurement** offers a slide show to advise small firms on opportunities for doing business with the state. The slide show is available for presentation to business groups, economic development entities, individual businesses, or any other group with an interest in selling to the state of Wisconsin.

Community Resource Development Agents

Contact:
Mr. David Sprehn, Acting State Program
   Leader
Community, Natural Resource, and
   Economic Development
University of Wisconsin-Extension
432 North Lake Street
Madison, WI 53706
(608) 262–1748

The University of Wisconsin-Extension operates the **Cooperative Extension Service**, which, with the cooperation of counties, shares the cost of extension office staffing, including community resource development agents. These agents provide assistance in community development, natural resource management, and economic development programs. Community resource development agents provide services to new and existing businesses and serve as the link to the resources of the University of Wisconsin system.

Wisconsin Community Capital, Inc.

Contact:
Mr. Paul Eble, President
Wisconsin Community Capital, Inc.
1 South Pinckney, Suite 500
Madison, WI 53703
(608) 256–3441

Wisconsin Community Capital, Inc., (WCC) is a job creation and retention program for low-income communities of Wisconsin. WCC makes loans to, and invests in, expanding companies.

Small Business Development Centers

Contact:
Mr. William H. Pinkovitz, State Director
Wisconsin Small Business Development
 Center
University of Wisconsin-Extension
432 North Lake Street, Room 423
Madison, WI 53706
(608) 263–7794

The University of Wisconsin-Extension has a network of **Small Business Development Centers** (SBDCs) that offer noncredit management education for small business owners, managers, and entrepreneurs. Workshops and conferences are offered through the SBDC delivery network at 10 University of Wisconsin campuses. Topics are designed to strengthen the economic health of small businesses. Free one-on-one counseling is provided for those businesses in need of specific management assistance.

The Wisconsin SBDCs also conduct research, publish information, and provide special assistance in the areas of entrepreneurship, feasibility, innovation, federal and state procurement, and recreation and tourism. A minority scholarship program is available to minority entrepreneurs. SBDCs provide business assistance to members of 11 Wisconsin Indian tribes and individuals through the Wisconsin American Indian Economic Development (WAIED) Program. A complete listing of the Wisconsin SBDC delivery network is in Appendix A of this directory.

Wisconsin Housing and Economic Development Authority

Contact:
Mr. Richard Longabaugh, Director
Economic Development Group
Wisconsin Housing and Economic
 Development Authority
1 South Pinckney Street, Suite 500
Madison, WI 53703
(608) 266–7884

The **Wisconsin Housing and Economic Development Authority** has several programs within its Economic Development Group that assist Wisconsin's small businesses. The programs are available through participating lending institutions.

The **Linked Deposit Loan** (LiDL) program is designed to assist small Wisconsin businesses that are more than 50 percent owned and controlled by women or minority group members. The program, administered through Wisconsin lenders, assists in reducing the cost of borrowing on new bank loans ranging from $10,000 to $99,000 for periods of two years or less. These loans may be used only for the purchase or rehabilitation of land, buildings, and business equipment, and the project undertaken must result in the creation of jobs. Loans for working capital, inventory purchases, or acquisitions between family members are not eligible expenditures under this program.

The Contract Fund provides small businesses with an opportunity to enter into government contracts or contracts with businesses having gross annual sales of at least $10 million. Eligible businesses include those located in blighted areas or owned by women, minority group members, or the physically disabled. The fund provides loan guarantees of up to $200,000 on eligible loan proceeds obtained through a lender. Loan proceeds can be applied towards expenses necessary to perform on awarded contracts. Refinancing existing debt is not permitted.

The **Tourism Fund** assists in the expansion of tourism-related businesses. In addition, a business that derives more than 50 percent of its sales from furnishing goods or services to a tourism-related business may be eligible to participate in the fund. The fund provides loan guarantees up to $200,000 in eligible loan proceeds obtained through a lender, as well as providing a 3.5-percent interest subsidy. Loan proceeds can be applied towards upgrading, renovating, or expanding existing businesses. Eligible expenditures include the purchase or improvement of land, building, equipment, and inventory. Refinancing existing debt is not permitted.

The **Rural Development Unit** manages programs that support development of rural areas and environmentally attractive projects, including recycling and energy conservation.

The **Credit Relief Outreach Program** (CROP) is a state-funded loan guarantee and interest-rate reduction program for Wisconsin farmers. The program helps farmers obtain agricultural production loans of up to $20,000 through their lenders.

The **Agribusiness Fund** provides loan guarantees of up to $750,000 for projects that seek to develop new or more viable methods for processing or marketing a Wisconsin-grown commodity. Agribusinesses located in communities having a population of 50,000 or less can access the fund through their lenders. Loan proceeds can be applied towards working capital, the purchase of a building or equipment, or marketing expenses. Refinancing existing debt is not permitted.

The **Business Energy Fund** provides low-cost financing to commercial and industrial businesses for energy conservation improvements. Program participation is open to Wisconsin businesses having gross annual sales of less than $35 million. Using the fund, the Wisconsin Housing and Economic Development Authority assists businesses in one of two ways: (1) providing a subsidy to reduce the loan interest rate to the 3- to 5-percent range for up to five years for businesses financing pre-approved energy-related projects costing between $5,000 and $500,000; or (2) providing direct cash rebate payments equal to 25 percent of a project's cost to those businesses making pre-approved purchases for energy projects costing between $1,000 and $5,000.

The **Recycling Fund** was established in 1990 as part of a statewide recycling initiative. The program provides loan guarantees to Wisconsin businesses that emphasize alternative uses of products recovered through a recycling process. The program also encourages the expansion or start-up of businesses that supply and launder cloth diapers.

The **Secondary Market Unit** supports the purchase and resale of loans.

The **Business Development Bond Program** is an industrial revenue bond program for small and medium-size businesses. Businesses obtain fixed-rate financing through the issuance of tax-exempt bonds, which are enhanced by bank letters of credit. Bond proceeds must be used to purchase, develop, or improve buildings and land, or to purchase new machinery and equipment. Eligible borrowers must be manufacturers or first-time farmers.

Governor's Advisory Council or Task Force

There is no formal body that advises the governor on small business matters.

Legislative Committees and Subcommittees

Small business issues are considered by various committees of the Wisconsin Assembly and Senate, including the Assembly Committee on Small Business, Employment, and Training; the Senate Committee on Education, Economic Development, Financial Institutions, and Fiscal Policies; and the Senate Committee on Labor, Business, Insurance, Veterans, and Military Affairs.

Contacts:

Representative Mary Lou Van Dreel
Chair
Assembly Committee on Small Business and Education or Training for Employment
State Capitol, 32 West
Madison, WI 53702
(608) 266–5840

Senator Barbara Ulichny
Chair
Senate Committee on Education, Economic Development, Financial Institutions and Fiscal Policies
State Capitol, 33 South
Madison, WI 53702
(608) 266–5830

Legislation

Recently approved Wisconsin legislation affecting small firms includes the following:

- Establishment of a grant program for community-based organizations to promote small business and provide assistance to businesses or entrepreneurs within distressed areas. The program also provides funds for the operation and development of business incubators.

- Legislation authorizing a rural economic development program to help businesses cover the costs of professional services or management assistance related to starting or expanding a business in a rural area.

- Establishment of a Minority Business Development Fund to assist start-up minority-owned businesses and to provide grants or loans to fund expansion or acquisition of businesses that are or will be minority businesses.

- Authorization to establish a technology development center to develop a manufacturing modernization program.

- Authorization to create four additional development zones, using tax incentives to encourage businesses to locate and create jobs in distressed areas.

- Establishment of a Business Improvement Loan Guarantee Program to assist small businesses in upgrading, renovating, or expanding a business primarily engaged in providing services, goods, lodging, or amusement to tourists.

- Creation of a Business Development Initiative Program to provide technical assistance and grants to individuals and businesses for the start-up or expansion of businesses that are likely to employ persons with severe disabilities. The program also authorizes grants to the Community Development Finance Company for short-term investments in businesses that are or will be at least 51 percent owned by handicapped persons or by nonprofit organizations that provide services to handicapped persons.

- Legislation that (1) establishes a loan program to fund the production of products made from materials recovered from post-consumer waste and equipment to make such products, and to fund diaper services; (2) establishes a similar grant or loan program specifically for minority businesses that would include funding for waste-processing facilities; and (3) establishes a recycling rebate program that allows businesses to be reimbursed for costs associated with recycling.

State Small Business Conferences

Contact:
Lt. Governor Scott McCallum
State Capitol, 22 East
Madison, WI 53702
(608) 266–3516

The **Governor's Conference on Small Business** convened in October 1991, following a series of regional meetings that were held throughout Wisconsin to develop issues for a state agenda. The conference report, prepared February 5, 1992, presented priority recommendations to the legislature.

Wyoming

Small Business Offices, Programs, and Activities

Division of Economic and Community Development

Contact:
Mr. John Sedgwick, Block Grant Manager
Division of Economic and Community
    Development
Herschler Building, 2nd Floor West
Cheyenne, WY 82002
(307) 777–7284

The **Division of Economic and Community Development** serves as a liaison between Wyoming business and government on matters crucial to the growth of the small business community. The division provides a number of services.

Funds from the **Wyoming Community Development Block Grant** (CDBG) program help communities attract or expand local industry by providing low-interest loans to businesses for low- and moderate-income job creation and retention. There are also grant funds of $25,000 to $40,000 for technical assistance needs of small businesses.

Contact:
Mr. Rusty Smith, Financial Analyst
Division of Economic and Community
    Development
Herschler Building, 2nd Floor West
Cheyenne, WY 82002
(307) 777–7284

The state-funded **Economic Development Loan Program** provides direct loans and loan guarantees with flexible rates and terms to Wyoming businesses.

Contact:
Mr. John Logan, Federal Procurement
    Officer
Economic Development Division
Division of Economic and Community
    Development
Herschler Building, 2nd Floor West
Cheyenne, WY 82002
(307) 777–7284

The **Federal Procurement Assistance Office** encourages and assists Wyoming businesses to participate in federal procurement opportunities.

Contact:
Director of International Trade
Division of Economic and Community
  Development
122 West 25th Street, 2nd Floor West
Cheyenne, WY 82002
(307) 777–6412

The **Governor's International Trade Program** assists Wyoming businesses with exporting to international markets. An international data base stores information about Wyoming exporters and allows quick access to pertinent international trade information. This office also publishes the *Wyoming International Trade Directory*, which lists Wyoming exporters, export marketing consultants, freight forwarders, international banks, and foreign contacts. An **Export Incentive Program** offers limited financial support to businesses to conduct research assessing the foreign market potential for specific Wyoming products and industries.

Contact:
Mr. Paul Howard, Business Permit
  Coordinator
Division of Economic and Community
  Development
122 West 25th Street, 2nd Floor West
Cheyenne, WY 82002
(307) 777–7284

The **Business Permit Coordinator** helps both new and expanding businesses with the processes of obtaining the licenses and permits necessary to do business in the state. The office also publishes a comprehensive guide to permitting and licensing in Wyoming.

Contact:
Mr. John Logan,
Business Development and Federal
  Procurement Officer
Division of Economic and Community
  Development
122 East 25th Street, 2nd Floor West
Cheyenne, WY 82002
(307) 777–6432

The **Government Marketing Assistance Program** (GMAP) seeks to provide Wyoming companies with a greater share of government procurement spending. Through the GMAP data base, a company's products and services can be matched to the needs of several levels of government procurement.

Contact:
Ms. Barbara Stafford, Marketing Director
Wyoming First Program
Division of Economic and Community
  Development
122 East 25th Street, 2nd Floor West
Cheyenne, WY 82002
(307) 777–7286

The **Wyoming First Program** helps Wyoming companies to better market their Wyoming produced, manufactured, or substantially enhanced products and services through trade shows, campaigns, and other assistance.

Loans/Capital Formation

Contact:
Mr. Scott Weaver, Executive Director
Wyoming Industrial Development
  Corporation
P.O. Box 3599
Casper, WY 82602
(307) 234–5351

The **Wyoming Retirement System** (WRS) and the **Wyoming Industrial Development Corporation** (WIDC) have agreed to purchase from Wyoming financial institutions the guaranteed portion of U.S. Small Business Administration (SBA) and Farmer's Home Administration loans. This allows small businesses to obtain loans at more reasonable rates and terms than would otherwise be available.

Small Business Assistance Act

Under Wyoming's **Small Business Assistance Act**, the state treasurer is authorized to buy the guaranteed portion of SBA loans, then pool, package, and sell them on the secondary money market to obtain a reduced interest rate for small business borrowers.

Contacts:
Mr. Stan Smith, Wyoming State Treasurer
State Capitol Building
Cheyenne, WY 82002
(307) 777–7408

Mr. Scott Weaver, Executive Director
Wyoming Industrial Development
  Corporation
P.O. Box 3599
Casper, WY 82602
(307) 234–5351

State Linked Deposit Plan

Contact:
Mr. Glenn Shaffer, Deputy State Treasurer
Office of the State Treasurer
State Capitol Building
Cheyenne, WY 82002
(307) 777–7408

The Wyoming state treasurer can contract for deposits with Wyoming financial institutions at a rate of up to 3 percent below market rates. This program provides businesses with 5-year fixed-rate loans of up to $750,000. Loan proceeds may be used for structures, equipment, land, livestock, and working capital.

Job Training Administration

Contact:
Mr. Matt Johnson
Job Training Administration
Employment Security Commission
P.O. Box 2760
Casper, WY 82602
(307) 235–3601

The **Job Training Administration** provides funds to Wyoming businesses to support worker training and retraining. Direct subsidies can reach 50 percent of an employee's wages during the training period. Funds can be used for on- or off-site classroom training, on-the-job training, or support services.

Disadvantaged Business Assistance

Contact:
Mr. Floyd Freeman, Construction Staff
    Engineer
Wyoming Department of Transportation
P.O. Box 1708
Cheyenne, WY 82003–1708
(307) 777–4456

The **Wyoming Department of Transportation** offers assistance to minority and women contractors in competitive bidding on highway construction contracts.

Small Business Development Centers

Contact:
Mr. Jim Glover, State Director
Wyoming Small Business Development
    Center
111 West 2nd Street, Suite 416
Casper, WY 82601
(307) 235–4825

Small Business Development Centers (SBDCs) serve both new and existing business owners. They provide assistance in management skills, financial records management, business plan development, procurement, international trade, and marketing. The services are provided through one-on-one counseling, resource center video training, evening classes, and seminars. In addition to a lead SBDC in Casper, eight subcenters are operated in Casper, Cheyenne, Douglas, Lander, Laramie, Gillette, Powell, and Rock Springs. A listing of all Small Business Development Centers and subcenters in Wyoming is provided in Appendix A of this directory.

Publications

The following **publications** address a variety of issues pertaining to small business in Wyoming:

Doing Business in Wyoming

The Business Entity Pamphlet and *A Guide to Business Permitting and Licensing in Wyoming*

Contact:
Ms. Kathy Karpan, Wyoming Secretary of
 State
(307) 777–7378

Contact:
Mr. Paul Howard, Business Permit
 Coordinator
Division of Economic and Community
 Development
Department of Commerce
(307) 777–7284

Governor's Advisory Council or Task Force

The governor does not have a small business advisory council or task force, but has designated Paul Howard as the state's small business advocate.

Contact:
Mr. Paul Howard, Business Permit
 Coordinator
Division of Economic and Community
 Development
122 West 25th Street, 2nd Floor West
Cheyenne, WY 82002
(307) 777–7284

Legislative Committees and Subcommittees

Small-business related matters are referred to several standing committees.

Contacts:

Senator Charles K. Scott
Chairman
Senate Corporations, Elections and Political
    Subdivisions Committee
State Capitol
Cheyenne, WY 82002
(307) 777–7881

Representative Patti L. MacMillan
Chairwoman
House Corporations, Elections and Political
    Subdivisions Committee
State Capitol
Cheyenne, WY 82002
(307) 777–7881

Senator Jim Twiford
Chairman
Senate Minerals, Business and Economic
    Development Committee
State Capitol
Cheyenne, WY 82002
(307) 777–7881

Representative Melvin ZumBrummin
Chairman
House Minerals, Business and Economic
    Development Committee
State Capitol
Cheyenne, WY 82002
(307) 777–7881

Senator Allan D. Howard
Chairman
Senate Labor and Federal Relations
    Committee
State Capitol
Cheyenne, WY 82002
(307) 777–7881

Representative Dorothy A. Perkins
Chairwoman
House Labor, Health and Social Services
    Committee
State Capitol
Cheyenne, WY 82002
(307) 777–7881

Legislation

Legislation passed in 1989 of interest to small business includes the following:

- The 1989 Wyoming Business Corporation Act was one of the most important accomplishments of the legislative session because it successfully updated Wyoming's basic business statute—which had not been substantially revised in 30 years. S.F. 137 and S.F. 98, which allow use of facsimile signatures, photocopies, and telephone conference calls, add up to an easier way for business to operate in Wyoming. For example, the new laws permit the creation of a standard corporation by a simple-to-prepare one-page document.

- S.F. 5 increases the maximum amount for damages that could be heard in small claims court from $750 to $2,000. This change allows small business owners to resolve more of their small dollar disputes quickly and with less expense than using county courts.

- S.F. 211 authorizes the use of link deposits for loans to replace, modify, or clean up leaking underground storage tanks.

- H.B. 374 directs the University of Wyoming to operate a technology transfer program to assist small business owners in the development and commercialization of technology-based Wyoming products.

- S.F. 131 extends for five years the state treasurer's authority to invest in U.S. Small Business Administration loans. By purchasing the guarantee portion of small business loans, the state makes more capital available for loans to business enterprises.

- S.F. 144 enables a corporation to set up a subsidiary, which can own as much as 40 percent of the parent corporation's stock. This allows the firm's management, with the support of just 10 percent of the outstanding shareholders, to keep total control of a company.

Legislation adopted during the 1990 session includes the following:

- H.B. 50 obligates up to $200 million in state funds for cleanup of leaking underground storage tanks and surrounding contaminated sites. H.B. 50 imposes a one cent per gallon tax, plus a $200 per tank annual fee to fund the state's cleanup costs.

- S. 104 regulates control share acquisitions, but allows corporations to opt out of the control share acquisition regulations. S. 104 also addresses voting rights of control shares, including redemption of control shares and dissenter rights.

- Also, government reorganization continued. The legislature approved creation of the following new departments: Transportation, Health and Family Service, Administration, and Revenue.

Legislation passed in 1991 of interest to small business includes the following:

- H.B. 287 extends the tax reduction on new uranium production through December 31, 1995, to continue to encourage development of this basic industry.

- H.B. 207 establishes a "taxpayer's bill of rights" in dealing with the state of Wyoming. The bill provides rights to: (1) confidentiality; (2) assurance that no employee is rewarded based on the amount of assessments of collections; (3) accountability on written information given by the state; (4) consideration for installment payment agreements on tax assessments; and (5) descriptive tax notices, whereby the Department of Revenue is required to publish these rights and install a toll-free tax information telephone service.

- S.F. 175 imposes a penalty equal to 1 percent of the taxable value of a well, mine, or mining claim for the late or inaccurate reporting of certain information required by statute or rule.

- S.F. 214 allows persons to file a written objection to property tax assessments with the county assessor and county commissioners 30 days before the final determination of assessed value with an estimate of the tax amount at question based upon the previous year's tax levy. It allows credits on refunds for a period of up to 5 years and allows interest on refunds if the taxes are paid under protest and the taxpayer prevails in the appeal. The county treasurer is also required to place protested taxes in an earmarked account pending outcome of the appeal.

- H.B. 240 appropriates an additional $1.5 million to the Amendment IV program from the Budget Reserve Account. These funds may be used for loans and investments in Wyoming businesses.

- S.F. 280 authorizes the state to invest up to $25 million in industrial development bonds of local governments for certain purposes.

- H.J. 16 states that the management principles outlined in the "Vision Document for the Greater Yellowstone Area" document could have a crippling effect on the state's economy.

State Small Business Conferences

Contact:
Mr. Bill Schilling, Executive Director
Wyoming Heritage Society
(307) 577–8000

The **Annual Issues Conference of the Wyoming Heritage Foundation** was held November 1, 1991, in Casper.

Appendix A

Small Business Development Centers and Subcenters

This list of Small Business Development Centers and subcenters is arranged alphabetically by town or city within each state. The lead office—or "Lead SBDC"—for each state is marked by an asterisk. Specialized centers—such as those targeted at high technology firms, minority-owned firms, etc.—are marked by a double asterisk.

ALABAMA

Auburn University
Small Business Development
Center
College of Business
226 Thach Hall
Auburn, AL 36849–5243
(205) 844–4220

University of Alabama at
Birmingham*
Alabama Small Business
Development Center
1717 11th Avenue South, Suite 419
Birmingham, AL 35294
(205) 934–7260

Alabama Small Business
Procurement System**
Small Business Development
Center
1717 11th Avenue South, Suite 419
Birmingham, AL 35294
(205) 934–7260

University of Alabama at
Birmingham
Small Business Development
Center
Mathematics and Criminal Justice Building
901 South 15th Street, Room 143
Birmingham, AL 35294
(205) 934–6760

University of North Alabama
Small Business Development
Center
P.O. Box 5017
Keller Hall
Florence, AL 35632
(205) 760–4629

North East Alabama
Regional Small Business
Development Center
225 Church Street
P.O. Box 343
Huntsville, AL 35804–0343
(205) 535–2061

Jacksonville State University
Small Business Development
Center
113–B Merrill Hall
Jacksonville, AL 36265
(205) 782–5271

Livingston University
Small Business Development
Center
Station 35
Livingston, AL 35470
(205) 652–9661, ext. 439

University of South Alabama
Small Business Development
Center
College of Business and Management
  Studies
BMSB 101
Mobile, AL 36688
(205) 460–6004

Alabama State University
Small Business Development
Center
915 South Jackson Street
Montgomery, AL 36195
(205) 293–4137

*Denotes recipient organization (Lead SBDC)
**Denotes specialized Center

405

Troy State University
Small Business Development
Center
Sorrell College of Business
Troy, AL 36082–0001
(205) 670–3771

University of Alabama
Small Business Development
Center
P.O. Box 870397
400–S Martha Parham West
Tuscaloosa, AL 35487–0397
(205) 348–7011

Alabama International Trade
Center**
University of Alabama
Box 870396
400–N Martha Parham West
Tuscaloosa, AL 35487–0396
(205) 348–7621

ALASKA

University of Alaska Anchorage*
Alaska Small Business
Development Center
430 West 7th Avenue, Suite 110
Anchorage, AK 99501
(907) 274–7231

University of Alaska at Fairbanks
Small Business Development
Center
510 Second Avenue, Suite 316
Fairbanks, AK 99701
(907) 456–1701

University of Alaska Southeast
Small Business Development
Center
School of Business
1108 F Street
Juneau, AK 99801
(907) 463–3789

University of Alaska Mat-Su
Small Business Development
Center
Mat-Su Economic Development
Corporation
P.O. Box 873542
Wasilla, AK 99687
(907) 376–1063

ARIZONA

Northland Pioneer College
Small Business Development
Center
P.O. Box 610
Holbrook, AZ 86025
(602) 537–2976

Mohave Community College
Small Business Development
Center
1977 West Acoma Boulevard
Lake Havasu City, AZ 86403
(602) 453–1836

Gateway Community College*
Arizona Small Business
Development Center
108 North 40th Street, Suite 148
Phoenix, AZ 85034
(602) 392–5224

Rio Salado Community College
Small Business Development
Center
301 Roosevelt, Suite D
Phoenix, AZ 85003
(602) 238–9603

Yavapai College
Small Business Development
Center
1100 East Sheldon Street
Prescott, AZ 86301
(602) 776–2374

Central Arizona College
Small Business Development
Center
Gila Career Center
P.O. Box 339
Sacaton, AZ 85247
(602) 723–5522

Eastern Arizona College
Small Business Development
Center
1111 Thatcher Boulevard
Safford, AZ 85552
(602) 428–7603

Cochise College
Small Business Development
Center
901 North Colombo, Room 411
Sierra Vista, AZ 85635
(602) 459–9778

Pima Community College
Small Business Development
Center
655 North Alvernon, #112
Tuscon, AZ 85711
(602) 884–6306

Arizona Western College
Small Business Development
Center
Century Plaza
281 West 24th Street, #128
Yuma, AZ 85364
(602) 341–1650

*Denotes recipient organization (Lead SBDC)
**Denotes specialized Center

ARKANSAS

Henderson State University
Small Business Development
Center
P.O. Box 2231
Arkadelphia, AR 71923
(501) 246–5511, ext. 327

Arkansas State University
Beebe Branch
Small Business Development
Center
Beebe, AR 72012–1008
(501) 882–6452, ext. 25

University of Central Arkansas
Small Business Development
Center
College of Business Administration
Burdick Business Administration Bldg.
Conway, AR 72032
(501) 450–3190

University of Arkansas at
Fayetteville
Small Business Development
Center
College of Business—BA 117
Fayetteville, AR 72701
(501) 575–5148

University of Arkansas at Little
Rock*
Arkansas Small Business
Development Center
Little Rock Technology Center Building
100 South Main, Suite 401
Little Rock, AR 72201
(501) 324–9043

Harding University
Small Business Development
Center
Mabee School of Business
Blakeny and Center Streets
Searcy, AR 72143
(501) 268–6161, ext. 497

Arkansas State University
Small Business Development
Center
P.O. Drawer 2650
Jonesboro, AR 72467
(501) 972–3517

CALIFORNIA

Central Coast
Small Business Development
Center
6500 Soquel Drive
Aptos, CA 95003
(408) 479–6136

Sierra College
Small Business Development
Center
550 High Street, #3
Auburn, CA 95603
(916) 885–5488

Weill Institute
Small Business Development
Center
2101 K Street Mall
Bakersfield, CA 93301
(805) 395–4148

Butte College Tri-Counties
Small Business Development
Center
260 Cohasset Avenue
Chici, CA 95927
(916) 895–9017

Southwestern College
Small Business Development and
International Trade Center
900 Otay Lakes Road, Bldg. 1600
Chula Vista, CA 91910
(619) 421–2156

*Denotes recipient organization (Lead SBDC)
**Denotes specialized Center

North Coast
Small Business Development
Center
882 H Street
Crescent City, CA 95531
(707) 464–2168

Gavilan College
Small Business Development
Center
5055 Santa Teresa Boulevard
Gilroy, CA 95020
(408) 479–0373

Small Business Development
Center of Lake and Mendocino
Counties
341 North Main Street
Lakeport, CA 95453
(707) 263–0630

Southern California Export
Assistance**
Small Business Development
Center
124 East Olympic Boulevard, Suite 517
Los Angeles, CA 90015
(213) 749–8698

Valley Sierra
Small Business Development
Center
1012 Eleventh Street, Suite 210
Modesto, CA 95354
(209) 521–6177

Napa Valley College
Small Business Development
Center
100 Combs Street
Napa, CA 94559
(707) 253–3210

East Bay
Small Business Development
Center
2201 Broadway, Suite 814
Oakland, CA 94612
(415) 893–4114

Inland Empire
Small Business Development
  Center
800 North Haven Avenue, Suite 100
Ontario, CA 91764
(714) 941–7877

Eastern Los Angeles
Small Business Development
  Center
363 South Park Avenue, Suite 105
Pomona, CA 91766
(714) 629–2247

Department of Commerce*
California Small Business
  Development Center
Office of Small Business
1121 L Street, Suite 600
Sacramento, CA 95814
(916) 324–9234

Greater Sacramento
Small Business Development
  Center
1787 Tribute Road, Suite A
Sacramento, CA 95815
(916) 920–7949

Greater San Diego Chamber of
  Commerce
Small Business Development
  Center
4275 Executive Square, Suite 920
San Diego, CA 92037
(916) 450–1518

Silicon Valley, San Mateo County
Small Business Development
  Center
380 North First Street, Suite 202
San Jose, CA 95112
(408) 298–8455

San Joaquin Delta College
Small Business Development
  Center
5151 Pacific Avenue
Stockton, CA 95207
(209) 474–5089

Solano County
Small Business Development
  Center
320 Campus Lane
Suisun, CA 94585
(707) 864–3382

Northern Los Angeles
Small Business Development
  Center
14540 Victory Boulevard, Suite 200
Van Nuys, CA 91411
(818) 989–4377

COLORADO

Adams State College
Small Business Development
  Center
Alamosa, CO 81002
(719) 589–7372

Community College of Aurora
Small Business Development
  Center
791 Chambers Road, #302
Aurora, CO 80011
(303) 360–4745

Burlington City Hall
Small Business Development
  Center
480 15th Street
Burlington, CO 80807–1624
(719) 346–9311

Pikes Peak Community College
Colorado Springs Chamber of
  Commerce
Small Business Development
  Center
P.O. Drawer B
Colorado Springs, CO 80901–3002
(719) 635–1551

Colorado Northwestern
  Community College
Small Business Development
  Center
50 Spruce Drive
Craig, CO 81625
(303) 824–7071

Delta Montrose Vocational
  School
Small Business Development
  Center
1765 U.S. Highway 50
Delta, CO 81416
(303) 874–7671

Community College of Denver
Small Business Development
  Center
1445 Market Street
Denver, CO 80202
(303) 620–8076

Office of Business Development*
Colorado Small Business
  Development Center
1625 Broadway, #1710
Denver, CO 80202
(303) 892–3840

Fort Lewis College
Small Business Development
  Center
Miller Student Center, Room 108
Durango, CO 81301
(303) 247–7188

*Denotes recipient organization (Lead SBDC)
**Denotes specialized Center

Morgan Community College
Small Business Development
  Center
300 Main Street
Fort Morgan, CO 80701
(303) 867–3351

Grand Junction Business
  Incubator
Small Business Development
  Center
304 West Main Street
Grand Junction, CO 81505–1606
(303) 248–7314

Greeley/Weld Chamber of
  Commerce
Small Business Development
  Center
1407 Eighth Avenue
Greeley, CO 80631
(303) 352–3661

Red Rocks Community College
Small Business Development
  Center
13300 West Sixth Avenue
Lakewood, CO 80401–5398
(303) 987–0710

Lamar Community College
Small Business Development
  Center
2400 South Main
Lamar, CO 81052
(719) 336–8141

Arapahoe Community College
Small Business Development
  Center
South Metro Denver Chamber of
  Commerce
1101 West Mineral Avenue, Suite 160
Littleton, CO 80120
(303) 795–5855

Pueblo Community College
Small Business Development
  Center
900 West Orman Avenue
Pueblo, CO 81004
(719) 549–3224

Trinidad State Junior College
Small Business Development
  Center
600 Prospect Street
Davis Science Building
Trinidad, CO 81081
(719) 846–5645

Colorado Mountain College
Small Business Development
  Center
1310 Westhaven Drive
Vail, CO 81657
(303) 476–4040
(800) 621–1647

Front Range Community College
Small Business Development
  Center
3645 West 112th Avenue
Westminster, CO 80030
(303) 466–8811

CONNECTICUT

Business Regional B.C.
Small Business Development
  Center
10 Middle Street, 14th Floor
Bridgeport, CT 06604
(203) 335–3800

University of Bridgeport
Small Business Development
  Center
141 Linden Avenue
Bridgeport, CT 06601
(203) 576–4572

*Denotes recipient organization (Lead SBDC)
**Denotes specialized Center

University of Connecticut
Small Business Development
  Center
Administration Building, Room 313
1084 Shennecossett Road
Groton, CT 06340–6097
(203) 449–1188

Greater New Haven Chamber of
  Commerce
Small Business Development
  Center
195 Church Street
New Haven, CT 06506
(203) 773–0782

University of Connecticut*
Connecticut Small Business
  Development Center
School of Business Administration
Box U-41, Room 422
368 Fairfield Road
Storrs, CT 06269–2041
(203) 486–4135

Greater Waterbury Chamber of
  Commerce
Small Business Development
  Center
83 Bank Street
Waterbury, CT 06702
(203) 757–0701

University of Connecticut/MBA**
Community Accounting Aid and
  Services
Small Business Development
  Center
1800 Asylum Avenue
West Hartford, CT 06117
(203) 241–4984

DELAWARE

University of Delaware*
Delaware Small Business
   Development Center
Purnell Hall, Suite 005
Newark, DE 19716
(302) 451–2747

DISTRICT OF COLUMBIA

Gallaudet University
Small Business Development
   Center
Management Institute
800 Florida Avenue, N.E.
Washington, DC 20002–3625
(202) 651–5312

Howard University*
Metropolitan Washington
Small Business Development
   Center
2600 Sixth Street, N.W.
Washington, DC 20059
(202) 806–1550

FLORIDA

Product Innovation Center*
The Progress Center
Small Business Development
   Center
#1 Progress Blvd., Box 7
Alachua, FL 32615
(904) 462–3942

Seminole Community College
Small Business Development
   Center
P.O. Box 150784
Altamonte Springs, FL 32715–0784
(407) 834–4404

Florida Atlantic University
Small Business Development
   Center
Building T–9
P.O. Box 3091
Boca Raton, FL 33431
(407) 367–2273

Florida Atlantic University**
Energy Conservation Assistance
   Program
Small Business Development
   Center
Building T–9
P.O. Box 3091
Boca Raton, FL 33431
(407) 367–2273

Florida Atlantic University**
Office of International Trade
Small Business Development
   Center
Building T–9
P.O. Box 3091
Boca Raton, FL 33431
(407) 367–2271

Small Business Development
   Center
1519 Clearlake Road
Cocoa, FL 32922
(407) 951–1060, ext. 2045

Small Business Development
   Center
46 S.W. First Avenue
Dania, FL 33304
(305) 987–0100

Stetson University
Small Business Development
   Center
School of Business Administration
P.O. Box 8417
Deland, FL 32720
(407) 822–7326

*Denotes recipient organization (Lead SBDC)
**Denotes specialized Center

Florida Atlantic University
Commercial Campus
Small Business Development
   Center
1515 West Commercial Blvd., Room 11
Fort Lauderdale, FL 33309
(305) 771–6520

University of South Florida
Small Business Development
   Center
Sabel Hall, Rooms 219 and 220
8111 College Parkway
Fort Myers, FL 33907
(813) 489–4140

Indian River Community College
Small Business Development
   Center
3209 Virginia Avenue, #114
Fort Pierce, FL 34981–5599
(305) 468–4756

Small Business Development
   Center
414 Mary Esther Cutoff
Fort Walton Beach, FL 32548
(904) 244–1036

Central Florida Community
   College
Small Business Development
   Center
214 W. University Avenue
P.O. Box 2518
Gainesville, FL 32601
(904) 377–5621

University of North Florida
Small Business Development
   Center
College of Business
4567 St. John's Bluff Road, South
Building 11, Room 2163
Jacksonville, FL 32216
(904) 646–2476

Brevard Community College
Small Business Development
Center
3865 North Wickham Road
Melbourne, FL 32935
(407) 254–0305

Florida International University
Small Business Development
Center
Trailer M01
Tamiami Campus
Miami, FL 33199
(305) 348–2272

Florida International University
Small Business Development
Center
N.E. 151 and Biscayne Blvd.
North Miami Campus
Academic Building #1, Room 350
Miami, FL 33181
(305) 940–5790

University of Central Florida
Small Business Development
Center
P.O. Box 25000
Building CEBA II
Orlando, FL 32816
(407) 823–5554

University of West Florida*
Florida Small Business
Development Center
11000 University Parkway
Pensacola, FL 32514
(904) 474–3016

Procurement Technical
Assistance Program**
Small Business Development
Center
11000 University Parkway
Building 8
Pensacola, FL 32514
(904) 474–2919

University of South Florida
Small Business Development
Center
St. Petersburg Campus
830 First Street South, Room 113
St. Petersburg, FL 33701
(813) 893–9529

Small Business Development
Center
5700 North Tamiami Trail
Sarasota, FL 33580
(813) 359–4292

Florida A&M University
Small Business Development
Center
1715–B South Gadsdey Street
Tallahassee, FL 32301
(904) 599–3407

Florida State University
Small Business Development
Center
Business Building, Room 426
College of Business
Tallahassee, FL 32306
(904) 644–2053

Florida State University
(Downtown Office)
Small Business Development
Center
1605 Eastwood Office Plaza, Suite #1
Tallahassee, FL 32308
(904) 644–6524

University of South Florida
Small Business Development
Center
College of Business Administration
4202 East Fowler Avenue, BSN 3403
Tampa, FL 33620
(813) 974–4274

*Denotes recipient organization (Lead SBDC)
**Denotes specialized Center

Small Business Development
Center
Prospect Place, Suite 123
3111 South Dixie Highway
West Palm Beach, FL 33405
(407) 837–5311

GEORGIA

Southwest Georgia Regional
Small Business Development
Center
230 South Jackson Street, Suite 333
Albany, GA 31701
(912) 430–4303

University of Georgia*
Georgia Small Business
Development Center
Chicopee Complex
1180 East Broad Street
Athens, GA 30602
(404) 542–5760

North Georgia Regional
Small Business Development
Center
Chicopee Complex
1180 East Broad Street
Athens, GA 30602
(404) 542–7436

Georgia State University
Small Business Development
Center
Box 874
University Plaza
Atlanta, GA 30303
(404) 651–3550

Augusta College
Small Business Development
Center
1180 East Broad Street
Augusta, GA 30602
(404) 737–1790

South Georgia Regional Small Business Development Center
1107 Fountain Lake Road
Brunswick, GA 31520
(912) 264–7343

West Central Georgia District Small Business Development Center
P.O. Box 2441
Columbus, GA 31902
(404) 649–7433

Decatur Area Office Small Business Development Center
750 Commerce Drive
Decatur, GA 30030
(404) 378–8000

Gainesville Area Office Small Business Development Center
Brenau College, Butler Hall
Box 4517
Gainesville, GA 30501
(404) 536–7984

Gwinnett Area Office Small Business Development Center
1250 Atkinson Road
Lawrenceville, GA 30246
(404) 963–4902

Central Georgia Region Small Business Development Center
P.O. Box 13212
Macon, GA 31209
(912) 751–6592

Kennesaw State College Small Business Development Center
P.O. Box 444
Marietta, GA 30061
(404) 423–6450

Clayton State College Small Business Development Center
P.O. Box 285
Morrow, GA 30260
(404) 961–3440

Floyd College District Small Business Development Center
P.O. Box 1864
Rome, GA 30163
(404) 295–6326

Savannah District Small Business Development Center
6555 Abercorn Extension, Suite 224
Savannah, GA 31405
(912) 356–2755

Georgia Southern College Small Business Development Center
Landrum Center Box 8156
Statesboro, GA 30460
(912) 681–5194

HAWAII

University of Hawaii at Hilo* Hawaii Small Business Development Center
523 West Lanikaula Street
Hilo, HI 96720
(808) 933–3515

University of Hawaii at West O'ahu Small Business Development Center
1130 North Nimitz Highway, Suite A254
Honolulu, HI 96817
(808) 543–6695

*Denotes recipient organization (Lead SBDC)
**Denotes specialized Center

Maui Community College Small Business Development Center
310 Kaahumanu Avenue
Kahului, HI 96732
(808) 242–7044

Kaua'i Community College Small Business Development Center
3–1901 Kaumualii Highway
Lihue, HI 96766
(808) 245–8287

IDAHO

Boise State University* Idaho Small Business Development Center
College of Business
1910 University Drive
Boise, ID 83725
(208) 385–1640
(800) 225–3815

Idaho Small Business Development Center
7270 Potomac Drive
Boise, ID 83704
(208) 323–1154

Idaho Small Business Development Center
1110 Airport Drive
Hayden, ID 83835
(208) 772–0587

Idaho State University Small Business Development Center
2300 North Yellowstone
Idaho Falls, ID 83401
(208) 523–1087

Lewis-Clark State College
Idaho Small Business
Development Center
Eighth Avenue and Sixth Street
Lewiston, ID 83501
(208) 799–2465

Idaho State University
Small Business Development
Center
1651 Alvin Ricken Drive
Pocatello, ID 83201
(208) 232–4921

Panhandle Area Council
Small Business Development
Center
Sandpoint Unlimited
P.O. Box 724
Sandpoint, ID 83864
(208) 263–4073

College of Southern Idaho
Small Business Development
Center
P.O. Box 1844
Twin Falls, ID 83303–1844
(208) 734–9554, ext. 477

ILLINOIS

Black Hawk College
Small Business Development
Center
207 College Avenue
Aledo, IL 61231
(309) 582–5373

Waubonsee Community College
Small Business Development
Center
Aurora Campus, 5 East Galena Blvd.
Aurora, IL 60506
(708) 892–3334, ext. 141

Illinois State University
Small Business Development
Center
c/o McClean County Chamber of
   Commerce
210 South East Street
P.O. Box 1586 (mailing address)
Bloomington, IL 61702
(309) 829–6632

Southern Illinois University at
Carbondale
Small Business Development
Center
Carbondale, IL 62901
(618) 536–2424

Spoon River College
Small Business Development
Center
R.R. #1
Canton, IL 61520
(309) 647–4645, ext. 320

Kaskaskia College
Small Business Development
Center
Shattuc Road
Centralia, IL 62801
(618) 532–2049

Parkland College
Small Business Development
Center
2400 West Bradley Avenue
Champaign, IL 61821–1899
(217) 351–2556

Back of the Yards Neighborhood
Council
Small Business Development
Center
1751 West 47th Street
Chicago, IL 60609
(312) 523–4419

*Denotes recipient organization (Lead SBDC)
**Denotes specialized Center

Chicago Area Neighborhood
Development Organizations
(CANDO)
Small Business Development
Center
343 South Dearborn Street
Suite 910
Chicago, IL 60604–3808

Chicago State University
Small Business Development
Center
95th and King Drive
Chicago, IL 60628
(312) 995–3944

Cosmopolitan Chamber of
Commerce
Small Business Development
Center
1326 South Michigan Avenue
Chicago, IL 60605
(312) 786–0212

Daley College
Small Business Development
Center
7500 South Pulaski Road
Building 200
Chicago, IL 60652
(312) 838–0300

Eighteenth Street Development
Corporation
Small Business Development
Center
1839 South Carpenter
Chicago, IL 60608
(312) 733–2287

Greater North Pulaski Economic
Development Commission
Small Business Development
Center
4054 West North Avenue
Chicago, IL 60639
(312) 384–2262

Greater Southwest Development Corporation
Small Business Development Center
2358 West 63rd Street
Chicago, IL 60636
(312) 436–4448

Hyde Park-Kenwood Development Corporation
Small Business Development Center
5307 South Harper
Chicago, IL 60615
(312) 667–2610

Illinois International Trade Center**
Department of Commerce and Community Affairs
Small Business Assistance Bureau
100 West Randolph, Suite 3–400
Chicago, IL 60601
(312) 814–2092

Latin/American Chamber of Commerce
Small Business Development Center
2539 North Kedzie, Suite 11
Chicago, IL 60647
(312) 252–5211

The Neighborhood Institute
Small Business Development Center
2255 East 75th Street
Chicago, IL 60649
(708) 933–2021

North River Commission
Lawrence Avenue Development Corporation
Small Business Development Center
4745 North Kedzie
Chicago, IL 60625
(312) 478–0202

Olive-Harvey Community College
Small Business Development Center
10001 South Woodlann Avenue
Chicago, IL 60628
(312) 660–4839

Southeast Chicago Development Commission
Small Business Development Center
9204 South Commercial, #212
Chicago, IL 60617
(312) 731–8755

University Village Association
Small Business Development Center
925 South Loomis Street
Chicago, IL 60607
(312) 243–4045

Women's Business Development Center
Small Business Development Center
230 North Michigan Avenue, Suite 1800
Chicago, IL 60601
(312) 853–3477

Danville Area
Small Business Development Center
28 West North Street
Danville, IL 61832
(217) 442–7232

Richland Community College
Small Business Development Center
One College Park
Decatur, IL 62521
(217) 875–7200

Northern Illinois University
Small Business Development Center
Department of Management
305 East Locust
Dekalb, IL 60115
(815) 753–1403

Sauk Valley Community College
Small Business Development Center
173 Illinois Route #2
Dixon, IL 61021–9110
(815) 288–5605

Southern Illinois University at Edwardsville
Small Business Development Center
Campus Box 1107
Center for Advanced Manufacturing and Production
Edwardsville, IL 62026
(618) 692–2929

Southern Illinois University at Edwardsville**
International Trade Center
Small Business Development Center
Campus Box 1107
Edwardsville, IL 62026
(618) 692–2452

Elgin Community College
Small Business Development Center
1700 Spartan Drive, Office B-15
Elgin, IL 60123
(708) 697–1000, ext. 7923

Evanston Business Investment Corporation
Small Business Development Center
1840 Oak Avenue
Evanston, IL 60201
(312) 866–1841

*Denotes recipient organization (Lead SBDC)
**Denotes specialized Center

College of DuPage
Small Business Development
Center
22nd Street and Lambert Road
Glen Ellyn, IL 60137
(312) 858–2800, ext. 2771

College of DuPage**
International Trade Center
Small Business Development
Center
22nd Street Development Center
Glen Ellyn, IL 60137
(708) 858–2800, ext. 3052

College of Lake County
Small Business Development
Center
19351 West Washington
Grayslake, IL 60030
(312) 223–3614

Rend Lake Community College
Small Business Development
Center
Upper Level, Student Center
Route #1
Ina, IL 62846
(618) 437–5321, ext. 267

Joliet Junior College
Small Business Development
Center
Renaissance Center, Room 319
214 North Ottawa Street
Joliet, IL 60431
(815) 727–6544, ext. 1313

Kankakee Community College
Small Business Development
Center
Box 888 River Road
Kankakee, IL 60901
(815) 933–0374

Blackhawk Community College
(East Campus)
Small Business Development
Center
Business Resource Assistance Center
P.O. Box 489
Kewanee, IL 61443
(800) 798–5671, ext. 260

Lake Land College
Small Business Development
Center
South Route #45
Mattoon, IL 61938–9366
(217) 235–3131

Mid-Metro Economic
Development Group
Small Business Development
Center
1505 West Lake Street
Melrose Park, IL 60160
(708) 343–9205

Blackhawk Community College
Small Business Development
Center
c/o Quad-Cities Chamber of Commerce
622 19th Street
Moline, IL 61265
(309) 762–3661

Maple City Business and
Technology Center
Small Business Development
Center
620 South Main Street
Monmouth, IL 61462
(309) 734–4664

Illinois Valley Community College
Small Business Development
Center
Building 11, Route One
Oglesby, IL 61348
(815) 223–1740

Illinois Eastern Community
Colleges
Small Business Development
Center
1110 South West Street
Box 576
Olney, IL 62450
(618) 395–3011

Moraine Valley Community
College
Small Business Development
Center
Employment Training Center
10900 South 88th Avenue
Palos Hills, IL 60465
(708) 974–5468

Bradley University
Small Business Development
Center
Lovelace Hall
1501 West Bradley
Peoria, IL 61625
(309) 677–2309

Bradley University**
International Trade Center
Small Business Development
Center
Lovelace Hall
Peoria, IL 61625
(309) 677–3075

John Wood Community College
Small Business Development
Center
301 Oak
Quincy, IL 62301
(217) 228–5510

Rock Valley College
Small Business Development
Center
1220 Rock Street, Suite 180
Rockford, IL 61101–1437
(815) 968–4087

*Denotes recipient organization (Lead SBDC)
**Denotes specialized Center

Department of Commerce and Community Affairs*
Illinois Small Business Development Center
620 East Adams Street, 5th Floor
Springfield, IL 62701
(217) 524–5856

Shawnee College Small Business Development Center
Shawnee College Road
Ullin, IL 62992
(618) 634–9618

Governors State University Small Business Development Center
University Park, IL 60466
(312) 534–3713

INDIANA

Greater Bloomington Chamber of Commerce Small Business Development Center
116 West Sixth Street
Bloomington, IN 47404
(812) 339–8937

Columbus Enterprise Development Center, Inc. Small Business Development Center
4920 North Warren Drive
Columbus, IN 47203
(812) 379–4041

Evansville Chamber of Commerce Small Business Development Center
Second Street, N.W., Suite 206
Evansville, IN 47708
(812) 425–7232

Forth Wayne Enterprise Center Small Business Development Center
1830 Wayne Trace
Fort Wayne, IN 46803
(219) 426–0040

Northlake Small Business Development Center
504 Broadway, Suite 710
Gary, IN 46402
(219) 882–2000

Economic Development Council*
Indiana Small Business Development Center
One North Capitol, Suite 420
Indianapolis, IN 46204–2248
(317) 264–6871

Indiana University Small Business Development Center
1317 West Michriver
Indianapolis, IN 46202
(317) 274–8200

Hoosier Valley Economic Opportunity Corporation Small Business Development Center
1613 East Eight Street
P.O. Box 1567
Jeffersonville, IN 47130
(812) 288–6451

Kokomo-Howard County Chamber of Commerce Small Business Development Center
P.O. Box 731
106 North Washington
Kokomo, IN 46903
(317) 457–5301

Greater Lafayette Area Small Business Development Center
224 Main Street
Lafayette, IN 47901
(317) 742–0095

LaPorte Small Business Development Center
321 Lincolnway
LaPorte, IN 46350
(219) 326–7232

Madison Area Chamber of Commerce Small Business Development Center
301 East Street
Madison, IN 47250
(812) 265–3127

Northwest Indiana Forum, Inc. Small Business Development Center
8002 Utah Street
Merrillville, IN 46410
(219) 942–3496

Muncie/Delaware County Chamber of Commerce Small Business Development Center
P.O. Box 842
401 South High Street
Muncie, IN 47308
(317) 284–8144

Southern Indiana Small Business Development Center
P.O. Box 653
1702 East Spring Street
New Albany, IN 47150
(812) 945–0054

*Denotes recipient organization (Lead SBDC)
**Denotes specialized Center

416

Richmond Area Chamber of Commerce
Small Business Development Center
600 Promenade Street
Richmond, IN 47374
(317) 962–2887

Project Future
Small Business Development Center
300 North Michigan
South Bend, IN 46601
(219) 282–4350

Indiana State University
Small Business Development Center
Terre Haute, IN 47809
(812) 237–3232

IOWA

Iowa State University*
Iowa Small Business Development Center
College of Business Administration
137 Lynn Avenue
Ames, IA 50010
(515) 292–6351

Iowa State University
Small Business Development Center
111 Lynn Avenue, Suite One
Ames, IA 50010
(515) 292–6355

Audubon Branch Office
Small Business Development Center
405 Washington Street
Audubon, IA 50025
(712) 563–3165

University of Northern Iowa
Small Business Development Center
Suite 5, Business Building
Cedar Falls, IA 50614–0120
(319) 273–2696

Iowa Western Community College
Small Business Development Center
2700 College Road, Box 4C
Council Bluffs, IA 51502
(712) 325–3260

Southwestern Community College
Small Business Development Center
1501 West Townline
Creston, IA 50801
(515) 782–4161

Eastern Iowa Community College
Small Business Development Center
304 West Second Street
Davenport, IA 52801
(319) 322–4499

Drake University
Small Business Development Center
Professional and Business Development Center
Des Moines, IA 50311
(515) 271–2655

Dubuque Area Chamber of Commerce
N.E. Iowa Small Business Development Center
770 Town Clock Plaza
Dubuque, IA 52001
(319) 588–3350

University of Iowa Oakdale Campus
Small Business Development Center
106 Technology Innovation Center
Iowa City, IA 52242
(800) 253–7232

Kirkwood Community College
Small Business Development Center
2901 Tenth Avenue
Marion, IA 52302
(319) 377–8256

North Iowa Area Community College
Small Business Development Center
500 College Drive
Mason City, IA 50401
(515) 421–4342

Indian Hills Community College
Small Business Development Center
525 Grandview Avenue
Ottumwa, IA 52501
(515) 683–5127

Western Iowa Tech Community College
Small Business Development Center
5001 E. Gordon Drive, Box 265
Sioux City, IA 51102
(712) 274–6400

Iowa Lakes Community College
Small Business Development Center
Highway 71 North
Spencer, IA 51301
(712) 262–4213

*Denotes recipient organization (Lead SBDC)
**Denotes specialized Center

417

**Southeastern Community College
Small Business Development
Center**
Burlington Branch Office
Drawer F
West Burlington, IA 52655
(319) 752–2731, ext. 103

KANSAS

**Cowley County Community
College
Small Business Development
Center**
125 South Second
Arkansas City, KS 67005
(316) 442–0430, ext. 251

**Butler County Community College
Small Business Development
Center**
420 Walnut
Augusta, KS 67010
(316) 775–1124

**Colby Community College
Small Business Development
Center**
1255 South Range
Colby, KS 67701
(913) 462–3984, ext. 239

**Dodge City Community College
Small Business Development
Center**
2501 North 14th Avenue
Dodge City, KS 67801
(316) 225–1321, ext. 247

**Emporia State University
Small Business Development
Center**
207 Cremer Hall
Emporia, KS 66801
(316) 343–5308

**Barton County Community
College
Small Business Development
Center**
115 Administrative Building
Great Bend, KS 67530
(316) 792–2701, ext. 267

**Fort Hays State University
Small Business Development
Center**
1301 Pine
Hays, KS 67601
(913) 628–5340

**Hutchinson Community College
Small Business Development
Center**
Ninth and Walnut, #225
Hutchinson, KS 67501
(316) 665–4950

**Kansas City Kansas Community
College
Small Business Development
Center**
7250 State Avenue
Kansas City, KS 66112
(913) 334–1100, ext. 228

**University of Kansas
Small Business Development
Center**
734 Vermont Street
Lawrence, KS 66054
(913) 843–8844

**Seward County Community
College
Small Business Development
Center**
1801 North Kansas
Liberal, KS 67901
(316) 624–1951, ext. 148

**Kansas State University
Small Business Development
Center**
College of Business Administration
204 Calvin Hall
Manhattan, KS 66506
(913) 532–5529

**Ottawa University
Small Business Development
Center**
College Avenue, Box 70
Ottawa, KS 66067
(913) 242–5200, ext. 342

**Johnson County Community
College
Small Business Development
Center**
CEC Building, Room 3051
Overland Park, KS 66210
(913) 469–3878

**Pittsburg State University
Small Business Development
Center**
Shirk Hall
Pittsburg, KS 66762
(316) 231–8267

**Pratt Community College
Small Business Development
Center**
Highway 61
Pratt, KS 67124
(316) 672–5641

**Kansas College of Technology
Small Business Development
Center**
2409 Scanlan Avenue
Salina, KS 67402
(913) 825–0275, ext. 445

*Denotes recipient organization (Lead SBDC)
**Denotes specialized Center

Washburn University
Small Business Development
Center
School of Business
101 Henderson Learning Center
Topeka, KS 66621
(913) 295–6305

Wichita State University*
Kansas Small Business
Development Center
Campus Box 148
Wichita, KS 67208
(316) 689–3193

KENTUCKY

Ashland Small Business
Development Center
Boyd-Greenup County Chamber of
　Commerce Bldg.
P.O. Box 830
207 15th Street
Ashland, KY 41105–0830
(606) 329–8011

Western Kentucky University
Bowling Green Small Business
Development Center
245 Grise Hall
Bowling Green, KY 42101
(502) 745–2901

Southeast Community College
Small Business Development
Center
Room 113, Chrisman Hall
Cumberland, KY 40823
(606) 589–4514

Elizabethtown Small Business
Development Center
238 West Dixie Highway
Elizabethtown, KY 42701
(502) 765–6737

Northern Kentucky University
Small Business Development
Center
BEP Center, Room 463
Highland Heights, KY 41076–0506
(606) 572–6524

Hopkinsville Small Business
Development Center
300 Hammond Drive
Hopkinsville, KY 42240
(502) 886–8666

University of Kentucky*
Kentucky Small Business
Development Center
205 Business and Economics Building
Lexington, KY 40506–0341
(606) 257–7668

Bellarmine College
Small Business Development
Center
School of Business
2001 Newburg Road
Louisville, KY 40205–0671
(502) 452–8282

University of Louisville**
Small Business Development
Center
Center for Entrepreneurship and Technology
School of Business, Belknap Campus
Louisville, KY 40292
(502) 588–7854

Morehead State University
Small Business Development
Center
207 Downing Hall
Morehead, KY 40351
(606) 783–2895

Murray State University
West Kentucky Small Business
Development Center
College of Business and Public Affairs
Murray, KY 42071
(502) 762–2856

Owensboro Small Business
Development Center
3860 U.S. Highway 60 West
Owensboro, KY 42301
(502) 926–8085

Pikeville Small Business
Development Center
222 Hatcher Court
Pikeville, KY 41501
(606) 432–5848

Eastern Kentucky University
South Central Small Business
Development Center
107 W. Mt. Vernon Street
Somerset, KY 42501
(606) 678–5520

LOUISIANA

Alexandria Small Business
Development Center
5212 Rue Verdun
Alexandria, LA 71306
(318) 487–5454

Southern University
Capital Small Business
Development Center
9613 Interline Avenue
Baton Rouge, LA 70809
(504) 922–0998

*Denotes recipient organization (Lead SBDC)
**Denotes specialized Center

419

Southeastern Louisiana University
Small Business Development Center
College of Business Administration
Box 522, SLU Station
Hammond, LA 70402
(504) 549-3831

University of Southwestern Louisiana
Acadian Small Business Development Center
College of Business Administration
P.O. Box 43732
Lafayette, LA 70504
(318) 265-5344

McNeese State University
Small Business Development Center
College of Business Administration
Lake Charles, LA 70609
(318) 475-5529

Northeast Louisiana University*
Louisiana Small Business Development Center
College of Business Administration
Room 2-57
Monroe, LA 71209-6435
(318) 342-5506

Northeast Louisiana University
Small Business Development Center
College of Business Administration
Monroe, LA 71209
(318) 342-1224

Northeast Louisiana University**
Louisiana Electronic Assistance Program
College of Business Administration
Monroe, LA 71209
(318) 342-1215

Northwestern State University
Small Business Development Center
College of Business Administration
Natchitoches, LA 71209
(318) 357-5611

Loyola University
Small Business Development Center
College of Business Administration
Box 134
New Orleans, LA 70118
(504) 865-3474

University of New Orleans**
International Trade Center
Small Business Development Center
368 Business Administration
New Orleans, LA 70148
(504) 286-7197

Southern University at New Orleans
Small Business Development Center
College of Business Administration
New Orleans, LA 70126
(504) 286-5308

University of New Orleans
Small Business Development Center
College of Business Administration
Lakefront Campus
New Orleans, LA 70148
(504) 286-6978

Louisiana Tech University
Small Business Development Center
College of Business Administration
Box 10318, Tech Station
Ruston, LA 71272-0046
(318) 257-3537

Louisiana State University at Shreveport
Small Business Development Center
College of Business Administration
One University Place
Shreveport, LA 7115
(318) 797-5144

Nicholls State University
Small Business Development Center
College of Business Administration
P.O. Box 2015
Thibodaux, LA 70310
(504) 448-4242

MAINE

Androscoggin Valley Council of Governments (AVCOG)
Small Business Development Center
125 Manley Road
Auburn, ME 04210
(207) 783-9186

Eastern Maine Development Corporation
Small Business Development Center
One Cumberland Place, Suite 300
Bangor, ME 04402-2599
(207) 942-6389

Northern Maine Regional Planning Commission
Small Business Development Center
P.O. Box 779
Caribou, ME 04736
(207) 498-8736

*Denotes recipient organization (Lead SBDC)
**Denotes specialized Center

University of Maine at Machias Small Business Development Center
Math and Science Building
Machias, ME 04654
(207) 255–3313

University of Southern Maine*
Maine Small Business Development Center
15 Surrenden Street
Portland, ME 04101
(207) 780–4420

Southern Maine Regional Planning Commission Small Business Development Center
P.O. Box Q
255 Main Street
Sanford, ME 04073
(207) 324–0316

North Kennebec Regional Planning Commission Small Business Development Center
7 Benton Avenue
Winslow, ME 04901
(207) 873–0711

Coastal Enterprises Incorporated Small Business Development Center
Water Street
Box 268
Wiscasset, ME 04578
(207) 882–7552

MARYLAND

Department of Economic and Employment Development*
Maryland Small Business Development Center
217 East Redwood Street, 10th Floor
Baltimore, MD 21202
(410) 333–6996
(800) 873–7273

Central Region Small Business Development Center
1414 Key Highway
Suite 310, Box #9
Baltimore, MD 21230
(410) 234–0505

Montgomery College Small Business Development Center
7815 Woodmount Avenue
Bethesda, MD 20814
(301) 656–7482

Western Region Small Business Development Center
Three Commerce Drive
Cumberland, MD 21502
(301) 724–6716

National Business League of Southern Maryland Small Business Development Center
9200 Basil Court, Suite 210
Landover, MD 20785
(301) 772–3683

Salisbury State University Small Business Development Center
1101 Camden Avenue
Salisbury, MD 21801
(800) 999–SBDC

*Denotes recipient organization (Lead SBDC)
**Denotes specialized Center

Southern Region Small Business Development Center
235 Smallwood Village Shopping Center
Waldorf, MD 20602
(301) 932–4155
(800) 762–SBDC

MASSACHUSETTS

University of Massachusetts*
Massachusetts Small Business Development Center
Room 205, School of Management
Amherst, MA 01003
(413) 545–6301

University of Massachusetts**
International Trade Program Small Business Development Center
Room 205, School of Management
Amherst, MA 01003
(413) 545–6301

University of Massachusetts**
Minority Business Assistance Center
Small Business Development Center
250 Stuart Street, 12th Floor
Boston, MA 02116
(617) 287–7018

Boston College
Metropolitan Boston Regional Small Business Development Center
96 College Road, Rahner House
Chestnut Hill, MA 02167
(617) 552–4091

Boston College
Capital Formation Service
**Small Business Development
Center**
96 College Road, Rahner House
Chestnut Hill, MA 02167
(617) 552–4091

Southeastern Massachusetts
University
**Small Business Development
Center**
200 Pocasset Street
P.O. Box 2785
Fall River, MA 02722
(508) 673–9783

Salem State College
North Shore Regional Small
Business Development Center
292 Loring Avenue, Alumni House
Salem, MA 01970
(508) 741–6639

University of Massachusetts
Western Regional Small Business
Development Center
101 State Street, Suite 424
Springfield, MA 01103
(413) 737–6712

Clark University
Central Regional Small Business
Development Center
950 Main Street
Worcester, MA 01610
(508) 793–7615

MICHIGAN

Ottawa County Economic
Development Office, Inc.
**Small Business Development
Center**
6676 Lake Michigan Drive
P.O. Box 539
Allendale, MI 49401
(616) 892–4120

MERRA**
**Small Business Development
Center**
2200 Commonwealth, Suite 230
Ann Arbor, MI 48105
(313) 930–0034

Kellogg Community College
**Small Business Development
Center**
450 North Avenue
Battle Creek, MI 49107–3397
(616) 965–3023
(800) 955–4KCC

Lake Michigan Community
College
**Small Business Development
Center**
Corporation and Community Development
2755 East Napier
Benton Harbor, MI 49022–1899
(616) 927–3571, ext. 247

Ferris State College**
**Small Business Development
Center**
Alumni 226
Big Rapids, MI 49307
(616) 592–3553

Comercia Small Business
Development Center
8300 Van Dyke
Detroit, MI 48213
(313) 371–1680

NILAC—Marygrove College
**Small Business Development
Center**
8425 West McNichols
Detroit, MI 48221
(313) 345–2159

Manufacturers Reach Small
Business Development Center
1829 Pilgrim
Detroit, MI 48223
(313) 869–2120

Wayne State University*
Michigan Small Business
Development Center
2727 Second Avenue
Detroit, MI 48201
(313) 577–4848

Wayne State University
**Small Business Development
Center**
2727 Second Avenue
Detroit, MI 48201
(313) 577–4850

Michigan State University**
International Trade Business
Development Center
Six Kellogg Center
East Lansing, MI 48824–1022
(517) 353–4336, (800) 852–5727

First Step, Inc.
**Small Business Development
Center**
2415 14th Avenue, South
Escanaba, MI 49829
(906) 786–9234

Grand Rapids Community College
**Small Business Development
Center**
Applied Technology Center
Grand Rapids, MI 49503
(616) 771–3600

Michigan Technological
University
**Small Business Development
Center**
1400 Townsend Drive
Houghton, MI 49931
(906) 487–2470

*Denotes recipient organization (Lead SBDC)
**Denotes specialized Center

422

Michigan Technological University**
Forest Products Industry Assistance Center
Small Business Development Center
Bureau of Industrial Development
1700 College Avenue
Houghton, MI 49931
(906) 487–2470

Livingston County Small Business Development Center
404 East Grand River
Howell, MI 48843
(517) 546–4020

Kalamazoo College
Small Business Development Center
Stryker Center
1327 Academy Street
Kalamazoo, MI 49007
(616) 383–8602

Handicapper Small Business Association
Small Business Development Center
1900 South Cedar, Suite 112
Lansing, MI 48910
(517) 484–8440

Lansing Community College
Small Business Development Center
P.O. Box 40010
Lansing, MI 48901
(517) 483–1921

Thumb Area Community Growth Alliance
Small Business Development Center
3270 Wilson Street
Marlette, MI 48453
(517) 635–3561

Northern Michigan University
Small Business Development Center
1009 West Ridge Street
Marquette, MI 49855
(906) 228–5571

Macomb County Small Business Development Center
115 South Groesbeck Highway
Mt. Clemens, MI 48043

Muskegon Economic Growth Alliance
Small Business Development Center
349 W. Webster Avenue, Room 104
Muskegon, MI 49443–1087
(616) 722–3751

Saint Clair County Community College
Small Business Development Center
323 Erie Street
Port Huron, MI 48060
(313) 984–3881, ext. 457

Saginaw Area Growth Alliance
Small Business Development Center
301 East Genesse
Fourth Floor
Saginaw, MI 48607
(517) 754–8222

Downriver Small Business Development Center
15100 Northline Road
Southgate, MI 48192
(313) 281–0700

Northwestern Michigan College
Small Business Development Center
1701 East Front Street
Traverse City, MI 49685
(616) 922–1719

Walsh/O.C.C. Business Enterprise Development Center
3838 Livernois Road
Troy, MI 48007–7006
(313) 689–4094

MINNESOTA

Bemidji State University
Small Business Development Center
1500 Birchmont Drive, N.E.
Bemidji, MN 56601
(218) 755–2750

Normandale Community College
Small Business Development Center
9700 France Avenue South
Bloomington, MN 55431
(612) 830–6395

Brainerd Technical College
Small Business Development Center
300 Quince Street
Brainerd, MN 56401
(218) 828–5302

University of Minnesota at Duluth
Small Business Development Center
10 University Drive, 150 SBE
Duluth, MN 55811
(218) 726–8761

*Denotes recipient organization (Lead SBDC)
**Denotes specialized Center

**Faribault City Hall
Small Business Development
Center**
208 N.W. First Avenue
Faribault, MN 55021
(507) 334–2222

**Itasca Development Corporation
Grand Rapids Small Business
Development Center**
19 Northeast Third Street
Grand Rapids, MN 55744
(218) 285–2255

**Hibbing Community College
Small Business Development
Center**
1515 East 25th Street
Hibbing, MN 55746
(218) 262–6700

**Rainy River Community College
Small Business Development
Center**
Highway 11 and 17
International Falls, NM 56649
(218) 285–2255

**Mankato State University
Small Business Development
Center**
Box 145
Mankato, MN 56001
(507) 389–1648

**Southwest State University
Small Business Development
Center**
Science and Technical Resource Center
Marshall, MN 56258
(507) 537–7386

Minnesota Project Innovation
Small Business Development
Center**
Supercomputer Center, Suite M100
1200 Washington Avenue, South
Minneapolis, MN 55415
(612) 338–3280

**Moorhead State University
Small Business Development
Center**
P.O. Box 303
Moorhead, MN 56563
(218) 236–2289

**Pine Technical College
Small Business Development
Center**
1100 Fourth Street
Pine City, MN 55063
(612) 629–7340

**Hennepin Technical College
Small Business Development
Center**
1820 North Zenuim Lane
Plymouth, MN 55441
(612) 550–7153

**Red Wing Technical Institute
Small Business Development
Center**
Highway 58 at Pioneer Road
Red Wing, MN 55066
(612) 388–4079

**Rochester Community College
Small Business Development
Center**
Highway 14 East
851 30th Avenue, SE
Rochester, MN 55904
(507) 282–2560

**Dakota County Technical College
Small Business Development
Center**
1300 145th Street East
Rosemount, MN 55068
(612) 423–8262

**St. Cloud University
Small Business Development
Center**
Business Resource Center
1840 East Highway 23
St. Cloud, MN 56304
(615) 255–4842

**University of St. Thomas
Small Business Development
Center**
23 Empire Drive
St. Paul, MN 55103
(613) 223–8663

**Department of Trade and
Economic Development*
Minnesota Small Business
Development Center**
900 American Center Building
150 East Kellogg Boulevard
St. Paul, MN 55101
(612) 297–5770

**Thief River Falls Technical
Institute
Small Business Development
Center**
Highway One East
Thief River Falls, MN 56701
(218) 681–5424

**Mesabi Community College
Small Business Development
Center**
9th Avenue and West Chestnut Street
Virginia, MN 55792
(218) 749–7729

**Wadena Technical College
Small Business Development
Center**
222 Second Street, S.E.
Wadena, MN 56482
(218) 631–3530, ext. 371

*Denotes recipient organization (Lead SBDC)
**Denotes specialized Center

Northeast Metro Technical College
Small Business Development Center
3554 White Bear Avenue
White Bear Lake, MN 55110
(612) 779–5764

Mid Minnesota Development Commission
Small Business Development Center
P.O. Box 1097
Willmar, MN 56201
(612) 235–5114

Winona State University
Small Business Development Center
Somsen Hall, Room 101
Winona, MN 55987
(507) 457–5088

MISSISSIPPI

Northeast Mississippi Community College
Cunningham Boulevard
Stringer Hall, 2nd Floor
Booneville, MS 38829
(601) 728–7751, ext. 317

Delta State University
Small Business Development Center
P.O. Box 3235 DSU
Cleveland, MS 38733
(601) 846–4236

Mississippi Delta Community College
Small Business Development Center
1656 East Union Street
Greenville, MS 38702
(601) 378–8183

Pearl River Community College
Small Business Development Center
Route 9, Box 1325
Hattiesburg, MS 39401
(601) 544–0030

Jackson State University**
International Trade Center
Small Business Development Center
Suite A–1, Jackson Enterprise Center
Jackson, MS 39204
(601) 968–2795

Jackson State University
Small Business Development Center
Suite A–1, Jackson Enterprise Center
931 Highway 80 West
Jackson, MS 39204
(601) 968–2795

Mississippi Department of Economic and Community Development
Small Business Development Center
P.O. Box 849
Jackson, MS 39205
(601) 359–3179

University of Southern Mississippi
Small Business Development Center
USM—Gulf Park Campus
Long Beach, MS 39560
(601) 865–4544

Meridian Community College
Small Business Development Center
5500 Highway 19 North
Meridian, MS 39307
(601) 482–7445

Mississippi State University
Small Business Development Center
P.O. Drawer 5288
Mississippi State, MS 39762
(601) 325–8684

Copiah-Lincoln Community College
Small Business Development Center
Natchez Campus
Natchez, MS 39120
(601) 445–5254

Itawamba Community College
Small Business Development Center
653 Eason Boulevard
Tupelo, MS 38801
(601) 680–8515

University of Mississippi*
Mississippi Small Business Development Center
Old Chemistry Building, Suite 216
University, MS 38677
(601) 232–5001

University of Mississippi
Small Business Development Center
Old Chemistry Building, Suite 216
University, MS 38677
(601) 234–2120

Hinds Community College
Small Business Development Center
1624 Highway 27
Vicksburg, MS 39180
(601) 638–0600

*Denotes recipient organization (Lead SBDC)
**Denotes specialized Center

425

MISSOURI

**Southeast Missouri State University
Small Business Development Center**
222 North Pacific
Cape Girardeau, MO 63701
(301) 290–5965

**University of Missouri at Columbia*
Missouri Small Business Development Center**
300 University Place
Columbia, MO 65211
(314) 882–0344

**University of Missouri at Columbia
Small Business Development Center**
1800 University Place
Columbia, MO 65211
(314) 882–7096

**Mineral Area College
Small Business Development Center**
P.O. Box 1000
Flat River, MO 63601
(314) 431–4593, ext. 283

University Extension
Business and Industrial Specialists
Small Business Development Center**
2507 Industrial Drive
Jefferson City, MO 65101
(314) 634–2824

Missouri Product Finder
Small Business Development Center**
P.O. Box 118
301 West High, Room 720
Jefferson City, MO 65102
(314) 751–4892

**Missouri Southern State College
Small Business Development Center**
107 Matthews Hall
3950 Newman Road
Joplin, MO 64801–1595
(417) 625–9313, ext. 557

**Rockhurst College
Small Business Development Center**
1100 Rockhurst Road
Kansas City, MO 64110–2599
(816) 926–4572

**Northeast Missouri State University
Small Business Development Center**
207 East Patterson
Kirksville, MO 63501
(816) 785–4307

**Northwest Missouri State University
Small Business Development Center**
127 South Buchanan
Maryville, MO 64468
(816) 562–1701

**Three Rivers Community College
Small Business Development Center**
3019 Fair Street
Poplar Bluff, MO 63901
(314) 686–3499

Center for Technology Transfer
Small Business Development Center**
Room 104, Bldg. 1, Nagogami Terrace
Rolla, MO 65401
(314) 341–4559

*Denotes recipient organization (Lead SBDC)
**Denotes specialized Center

**University of Missouri at Rolla
Small Business Development Center**
Engineering Management
Building, Room 223
Rolla, MO 65401–0249
(314) 341–4561

**St. Louis University
Small Business Development Center**
3642 Lindell Boulevard
St. Louis, MO 63108
(314) 534–7232

**Southwest Missouri State University
Small Business Development Center**
901 South National
Springfield, MO 65804–0089
(417) 836–5685

**Central Missouri State University
Small Business Development Center**
Grinstead #80
Warrensburg, MO 64093–5037
(816) 543–4402

Central Missouri State University
Center for Technology
Small Business Development Center**
Grinstead #80
Warrensburg, MO 64093–5037
(816) 429–4402

MONTANA

**Billings Incubator
Small Business Development Center**
P.O. Box 7213
Billings, MT 59101
(406) 245–9989

426

Gallatin Development Corporation College Small Business Development Center
321 East Main, Suite 413
Bozeman, MT 59715
(406) 587–3113

REDI Small Business Development Center
305 West Mercury, Suite 211
Butte, MT 59701
(406) 782–7333

Dawson Community College Small Business Development Center
Box 421
Glendive, MT 59330
(406) 365–2377

High Plains Development Authority Small Business Development Center
Procurement
#2 Railroad Square Building
Great Falls, MT 59403
(406) 454–1934

Montana Department of Commerce* Montana Small Business Development Center
1424 Ninth Avenue
Helena, MT 59620
(406) 444–4780

Flathead Valley Community College Small Business Development Center
777 Grandview Drive
Kalispell, MT 59901
(406) 756–3833

Missoula Incubator Small Business Development Center
127 North Higgins, Third Floor
Missoula, MT 59802
(406) 728–9234

NEBRASKA

Chadron State College Small Business Development Center
Administration Building
Chadron, NE 69337
(308) 432–6282

Kearney State College, West Campus Small Business Development Center
Business Department Office Building
Kearney, NE 68849
(308) 234–8344

University of Nebraska at Lincoln Small Business Development Center
Suite 302, Cornhusker Bank
11th & Cornhusker Highway
Lincoln, NE 68521
(402) 472–3358,
(800) 742–8800

Mid-Plains Community College Small Business Development Center
416 North Jeffers, Room 26
North Platte, NE 69101
(308) 534–5115

Nebraska Small Business Development Center University of Nebraska at Omaha
College of Business Administration
Suite 407D
Omaha, NE 68182–0248
(402) 554–2521

University of Nebraska at Omaha* Nebraska Small Business Development Center
Peter Kiewit Center
1313 Farnam-on-the-Mall
Suite 132
Omaha, NE 68182–0248
(402) 595–2381

Peru State College Small Business Development Center
T.J. Majors Hall, Room 248
Peru, NE 68421
(402) 872–2274
(800) 742–4412

Western Nebraska Community College Small Business Development Center
Nebraska Public Power Building
1721 Broadway, Room 408
Scottsbluff, NE 69361
(308) 635–7513

Wayne State College Small Business Development Center
Connell Hall
Wayne, NE 68787
(402) 375–2004

*Denotes recipient organization (Lead SBDC)
**Denotes specialized Center

NEVADA

**Carson City Chamber of Commerce
Small Business Development Center**
1900 South Carson Street, #100
Carson City, NV 89701
(702) 882–1565

**Northern Nevada Community College
Small Business Development Center**
901 Elm Street
Elko, NV 89801
(702) 738–8493

**University of Nevada at Las Vegas
Small Business Development Center**
College of Business and Economics
4505 Maryland Parkway
Las Vegas, NV 89154
(702) 739–0852

**University of Nevada Reno*
Nevada Small Business Development Center**
College of Business Administration
Room 411
Reno, NV 89557–0100
(702) 784–1717

**University of Nevada at Reno
Cooperative Extension Service
Small Business Development Center**
College of Agriculture
Reno, NV 89557–0016
(702) 784–1679

**Tri-County Development Authority
Small Business Development Center**
50 West Fourth Street
Winnemucca, NV 89445
(702) 623–5777

NEW HAMPSHIRE

**University of New Hampshire*
New Hampshire Small Business Development Center**
108 McConnell Hall
Durham, NH 03824
(603) 862–2200

**University of New Hampshire
Small Business Development Center**
Seacoast Subcenter
Kingman Farm
Durham, NH 03824
(603) 743–3995

**Keene State College
Small Business Development Center**
Blake House
Keene, NH 03431
(603) 358–2602

**North County Subcenter
Small Business Development Center**
P.O. Box 786
Littleton, NH 03561
(603) 444–1053

**Merrimack Valley Subcenter
Small Business Development Center**
400 Commercial Street, Room 311
Manchester, NH 03101
(603) 625–5691

*Denotes recipient organization (Lead SBDC)
**Denotes specialized Center

**Plymouth State College
Small Business Development Center**
Hyde Hall
Plymouth, NH 03264
(603) 536–2523

NEW JERSEY

**Greater Atlantic City Chamber of Commerce
Small Business Development Center**
1301 Atlantic Avenue
Atlantic City, NJ 08401
(609) 345–5600
(800) 252–4322

**Rutgers University at Camden
Small Business Development Center**
Business and Science Building, Room 243
Camden, NJ 08102
(609) 757–6221

**Brookdale Community College
Business/Management Team
Small Business Development Center**
Newman Springs Road
Lincroft, NJ 07738
(201) 842–1900, ext. 551

**Rutgers University at Newark*
New Jersey Small Business Development Center**
Ackerson Hall, 3rd Floor
180 University Street
Newark, NJ 07102
(201) 648–5950

**Mercer County Community College
Small Business Development and Management Training Center**
120 Old Trenton Road
Trenton, NJ 08690
(609) 586–4800

Kean College of New Jersey
Small Business Development
  Center
East Campus, Room 242
Union, NJ 07083
(908) 527–2954

Warren County Community
  College
Skylands Small Business
  Development Center
Route 57 West, RD #1 Box 55A
Washington, NJ 07882
(201) 689–7613

NEW MEXICO

New Mexico State University at
  Alamogordo
Small Business Development
  Center
1000 Madison
Alamogordo, NM 88310
(505) 434–5272

Albuquerque Technical
  Vocational Institute
Small Business Development
  Center
525 Buena Vista, S.E.
Albuquerque, NM 87106
(505) 768–0651

New Mexico State University at
  Carlsbad
Small Business Development
  Center
301 South Canal
P.O. Box 1090
Carlsbad, NM 88220
(505) 887–6562

Clovis Community College
Small Business Development
  Center
417 Schepps Boulevard
Clovis, NM 88101
(505) 769–4136

Northern New Mexico Community
  College
Small Business Development
  Center
1002 North Onate Street
Espanola, NM 87532
(505) 753–7141

San Juan College
Small Business Development
  Center
203 West Main, Suite 201
Farmington, NM 87401
(505) 326–4321

University of New Mexico at Gallup
Small Business Development
  Center
103 W. Highway 66
P.O. Box 1395
Gallup, NM 87305
(505) 722–2220

New Mexico State University at
  Grants
Small Business Development
  Center
709 East Roosevelt Avenue
Grants, NM 87020
(505) 287–8221

New Mexico Junior College
Small Business Development
  Center
5317 Lovington Highway
Hobbs, NM 88240
(505) 392–4510

University of New Mexico at Los
  Alamos
Small Business Development
  Center
901 18th Street, #18
P.O. Box 715
Los Alamos, NM 87544
(505) 662–0001

*Denotes recipient organization (Lead SBDC)
**Denotes specialized Center

New Mexico State University at
  Dona Ana
Small Business Development
  Center
Box 30001 Department 3DA
3400 South Espina Street
Las Cruces, NM 88003–0001
(505) 527–7566

University of New Mexico at
  Valencia
Small Business Development
  Center
280 La Entrada
Los Lunas, NM 87031
(505) 865–9596, ext. 317

Luna Vocational Technical Institute
Luna Campus
Small Business Development
  Center
P.O. Drawer K
Las Vegas, NM 88701
(505) 454–2595

Eastern New Mexico University at
  Roswell
Small Business Development
  Center
#57 University Avenue
P.O. Box 6000
Roswell, NM 88201–6000
(505) 624–7133

Santa Fe Community College*
New Mexico Small Business
  Development Center
South Richards Avenue
P.O. Box 4187
Santa Fe, NM 87502–4187
(505) 438–1343

Western New Mexico University
Small Business Development
  Center
Phelps Dodge Building
P.O. Box 2672
Silver City, NM 88062
(505) 538–6320

Tucumcari Area Vocational School
Small Business Development Center
824 West Hines
P.O. Box 1143
Tucumcari, NM 88401
(505) 461–4413

NEW YORK

State University of New York (SUNY)*
Downstate and Upstate New York
Small Business Development Center
SUNY Plaza, S-523
Albany, NY 12246
(518) 443–5398
(800) 732–SBDC

State University of New York at Albany
Small Business Development Center
Draper Hall, 107
135 Western Avenue
Albany, NY 12222
(518) 442–5577

State University of New York at Binghamton
Small Business Development Center
P.O. Box 6000
Vestal Parkway East
Binghamton, NY 13902–6000
(607) 777–4024

Long Island University
Small Business Development Center
One University Plaza
Humanities Building, 7th Floor
Brooklyn, NY 11201
(718) 852–1197

State University of New York at Buffalo
Small Business Development Center
BA 117
1300 Elmwood Avenue
Buffalo, NY 14222
(716) 878–4030

Corning Community College
Small Business Development Center
24–28 Denison Parkway West
Corning, NY 14830
(607) 962–9461

State University College of Technology at Farmingdale
Small Business Development Center
Laffin Administration Building
Room 007
Farmingdale, NY 11735
(516) 420–2765

York College/City University of New York
Small Business Development Center
Jamaica, NY 11451
(718) 262–2880

Jamestown Community College
Small Business Development Center
P.O. Box 20
Jamestown, NY 14702–0020
(716) 665–5220
(800) 522–7232

Pace University
Small Business Development Center
Pace Plaza
New York, NY 10038
(212) 346–1899

*Denotes recipient organization (Lead SBDC)
**Denotes specialized Center

State University College at Plattsburgh
Small Business Development Center
Plattsburgh, NY 12901
(518) 564–7232

Manhattan College
Small Business Development Center
Farrell Hall
Riverdale, NY 10471
(212) 884–1880

Monroe Community College
Small Business Development Center
1000 East Henrietta Road
Rochester, NY 14623
(716) 424–5200, ext. 3030

Niagara County Community College
Small Business Development Center
3111 Saunders Settlement Road
Sanborn, NY 14132
(716) 693–1910

Ulster County Community College
Small Business Development Center
Stone Ridge, NY 12484
(914) 687–5272

State University at Stony Brook
Small Business Development Center
Harriman Hall, Room 109
Stony Brook, NY 11794
(516) 632–9070

Rockland Community College
Small Business Development Center
145 College Road
Suffern, NY 10901
(914) 356–0370

Greater Syracuse Incubator Center**
Small Business Development Center
1201 East Fayette Street
Syracuse, NY 13210
(315) 475–0083

State University Institute of Technology at Utica/Rome
Small Business Development Center
P.O. Box 3050
Utica, NY 13504–3020
(315) 792–7546

Jefferson Community College
Small Business Development Center
Watertown, NY 13601
(315) 782–9262

NORTH CAROLINA

Appalachian State University
Northwestern Region Small Business Development Center
Walker College of Business
Boone, NC 28608
(704) 262–2095

University of North Carolina at Charlotte
Southern Piedmont Region Small Business Development Center
c/o The Ben Craig Center
8701 Mallard Creek Road
Charlotte, NC 28213
(704) 548–1090

Western Carolina University
Western Region Small Business Development Center
c/o Center for Improving Mountain Living
Cullowhee, NC 28723
(704) 227–7494

Elizabeth City State University
Northeastern Region Small Business Development Center
P.O. Box 874
Elizabeth City, NC 27909
(919) 335–3247

Fayetteville State Continuing Education Center
Cape Fear Region Small Business Development Center
P.O. Box 1334
Fayetteville, NC 28302
(919) 486–1727

North Carolina A&T State University
Northern Piedmont Center (Eastern Office)
C.H. Moore Agricultural Research Center
Greensboro, NC 27411
(919) 334–7005

Eastern Carolina University
Eastern Region Small Business Development Center
Willis Building
First and Reade Streets
Greenville, NC 27834
(919) 757–6157

University of North Carolina*
North Carolina Small Business Development Center
Research Triangle Park SBDC
4509 Creedmoor Road, Suite 201
Raleigh, NC 27612
(919) 571–4154

University of North Carolina at Wilmington
Southeastern Region Small Business Development Center
601 South College Road
Room 131, Cameron Hall
Wilmington, NC 28403
(919) 395–3744

Winston-Salem State University
Northern Piedmont Region Small Business Development Center
P.O. Box 13025
Winston-Salem, NC 27110
(919) 750–2030

NORTH DAKOTA

Bismarck Regional
Small Business Development Center
400 East Broadway, Suite 421
Bismarck, ND 58501
(701) 223–8583

Dickinson State College
Small Business Development Center
314 3rd Avenue West
Drawer L
Dickinson, ND 58602
(701) 227–2096

University of North Dakota*
North Dakota Small Business Development Center
Gamble Hall, University Station
Grand Forks, ND 58202–7308
(701) 777–3700

Grand Forks Regional
Small Business Development Center
1407 24th Avenue South, Suite 201
Grand Forks, ND 58201
(701) 772–8502

*Denotes recipient organization (Lead SBDC)
**Denotes specialized Center

**Jamestown Area Business and
Industrial Development
Small Business Development
Center**
121 First Avenue West
P.O. Box 1530
Jamestown, ND 58402
(701) 252–9243

**Minot Chamber of Commerce
Small Business Development
Center**
1020 20th Avenue Southwest
P.O. Box 940
Minot, ND 58702
(701) 852–8861

OHIO

**Akron Regional Development
Board
Small Business Development
Center**
One Cascade Plaza, 8th Floor
Akron, OH 44308
(216) 379–3170

**Akron–WEGO
Small Business Development
Center**
58 West Center Street
P.O. Box 544
Akron, OH 44309
(216) 535–9346

**Northwest Technical College
Small Business Development
Center**
St. Route One, Box 246–A
Archbold, OH 43502
(419) 267–5511

**Ohio University Innovation
Center**
Small Business Development
Center**
1 President Street
Athens, OH 45701
(614) 593–1797

**Athens Small Business
Development Center**
900 East State Street
Athens, OH 45701
(614) 592–1188

**WSOS Community Action
Commission, Inc.
Small Business Development
Center**
P.O. Box 48
118 East Oak Street
Bowling Green, OH 43402
(419) 352–7469

**Wright State University Lake
Campus
Small Business Development
Center**
7600 State Route 703
Celina, OH 45822
(419) 586–2365

**Chillicothe-Ross Chamber of
Commerce
Small Business Development
Center**
165 South Paint Street
Chillicothe, OH 45601
(614) 772–4530

**Cincinnati Small Business
Development Center**
IAMS Research Park–MC189
1111 Edison Avenue
Cincinnati, OH 45216–2265
(513) 948–2082

**Clermont County Chamber of
Commerce
Small Business Development
Center**
4440 Glen Este-Withamsville Road
Cincinnati, OH 45245
(513) 753–7141

**Greater Cleveland Growth
Association
Small Business Development
Center**
200 Tower City Center/50 Public Square
P.O. Box 94095
Cleveland, OH 44115
(216) 621–3300

**Columbus Area Chamber of
Commerce
Small Business Development
Center**
37 North High Street
Columbus, OH 43216
(614) 221–1321

**Ohio Department of
Development*
Ohio Small Business
Development Center**
30 East Broad Street
P.O. Box 1001
Columbus, OH 43226
(614) 466–2711

**Coshocton Area Chamber of
Commerce
Small Business Development
Center**
124 Chestnut Street
Coshocton, OH 43812
(614) 622–5411

**Dayton Area Chamber of
Commerce
Small Business Development
Center**
Chamber Plaza 5th and Main
Dayton, OH 45402–2400
(513) 226–8230

*Denotes recipient organization (Lead SBDC)
**Denotes specialized Center

Terra Technical College
Small Business Development
Center
1220 Cedar Street
Fremont, OH 43420
(419) 332–1002

Lima Technical College
Small Business Development
Center
Perry Building
545 West Market Street, Suite 305
Lima, OH 45801
(419) 229–5320

Ashtabula County Economic
Development Council, Inc.
Small Business Development
Center
36 West Walnut Street
Jefferson, OH 44047
(216) 576–9126

Logan-Hocking Chamber of
Commerce
Small Business Development
Center
11½ West Main Street
Box 838
Logan, OH 43138
(614) 385–7259

Lorain County Chamber of
Commerce
Small Business Development
Center
6100 South Broadway
Lorain, OH 44053
(216) 246–2833

Mid-Ohio Small Business
Development Center
193 North Main Street
Mansfield, OH 44902
(419) 525–1614

Marietta College
Small Business Development
Center
Marietta, OH 45750
(614) 374–4649

Marion Area Chamber of Commerce
Small Business Development
Center
206 Prospect Street
Marion, OH 45750
(513) 382–2181

Lakeland Community College
Lake County Economic
Development Center
Small Business Development
Center
Mentor, OH 44080
(216) 951–1290

Tuscarawas Chamber of
Commerce
Small Business Development
Center
1323 Fourth Street, N.W.
P.O. Box 232
New Philadelphia, OH 44663
(216) 343–4474

Miami University
Department of Decision Sciences
Small Business Development
Center
336 Upham Hall
Oxford, OH 45056
(513) 529–4841

Upper Valley Joint Vocational
School
Small Business Development
Center
8811 Career Drive
North Country Road 25–A
Piqua, OH 45356
(513) 778–8419

Portsmouth Area Chamber of
Commerce
Small Business Development
Center
P.O. Box 509
Portsmouth, OH 45662
(614) 353–1116

Department of Development of
the CIC of Belmont County
Small Business Development
Center
100 E. Main Street
St. Clairsville, OH 43950
(614) 695–9678

Sandusky City Schools
Small Business Development
Center
407 Decatur Street
Sandusky, OH 44870
(800) 548–6507

Lawrence County Chamber of
Commerce
Small Business Development
Center
U.S. Route 52 and Solida Road
P.O. Box 488
Southpoint, OH 45680
(614) 894–3838

Greater Steubenville Chamber of
Commerce
Small Business Development
Center
630 Market Street
P.O. Box 278
Steubenville, OH 43952
(614) 282–6226

Toledo Area Chamber of Commerce
Small Business Development
Center
218 North Huron Street
Toledo, OH 43604
(419) 243–8191

*Denotes recipient organization (Lead SBDC)
**Denotes specialized Center

**Youngstown State University
Cushwa Center
Small Business Development
Center**
Youngstown, OH 44555
(216) 742–3495

**Zanesville Area Chamber of
Commerce
Small Business Development
Center**
217 North Fifth Street
Zanesville, OH 43701
(614) 452–4868

OKLAHOMA

**East Central University
Small Business Development
Center**
1036 East 10th
Ada, OK 74820
(405) 436–3190

**Northwestern Oklahoma State
University
Small Business Development
Center**
Alva, OK 73717
(405) 327–1700
(405) 327–5883

**Southeastern Oklahoma State
University***
**Oklahoma Small Business
Development Center**
517 University
Durant, OK 74701
(405) 924–0277
(800) 522–6154

**University of Central Oklahoma
Small Business Development
Center**
100 North Boulevard
Edmond, OK 73034
(405) 359–1968

**Phillips University
Small Business Development
Center**
100 South University Avenue
Enid, OK 73701
(405) 242–7989

Langston University**
Minority Assistance Center
Small Business Development
Center**
P.O. Box 667
Langston, OK 73050
(405) 466–3256

**American National Bank Building
Small Business Development
Center**
601 S.W. "D", Suite 209
Lawton, OK 73501
(405) 248–4946

Rose State College**
Small Business Development
Center**
6420 Southeast 15th Street
Midwest City, OK 73110
(405) 733–7348

**Albert Junior College
Small Business Development
Center**
1507 South McKenna
Poteau, OK 74953
(918) 647–4019

**Northeastern Oklahoma State
University
Small Business Development
Center**
Tahlequah, OK 74464
(918) 458–0802

*Denotes recipient organization (Lead SBDC)
**Denotes specialized Center

**Tulsa State Office Building
Small Business Development
Center**
440 South Houston, Suite 206
Tulsa, OK 74107
(918) 581–2502

**Southwestern Oklahoma State
University
Small Business Development
Center**
100 Campus Drive
Weatherford, OK 73096
(405) 774–1040

OREGON

**Linn-Benton Community College
Small Business Development
Center**
6500 S.W. Pacific Boulevard
Albany, OR 97321
(503) 967–6112

**Southern Oregon State
College/Ashland
Small Business Development
Center**
Regional Service Institute
Ashland, OR 97520
(503) 482–5838

**Central Oregon Community
College
Small Business Development
Center**
2600 N.W. College Way
Bend, OR 97701
(503) 385–5524

**Southwestern Oregon Community
College
Small Business Development
Center**
340 Central
Coos Bay, OR 97420
(503) 267–2300

Lane Community College*
Oregon Small Business
    Development Center
99 West Tenth, Suite 216
Eugene, OR 97401
(503) 726–2250

Lane Community College
Small Business Development
    Center
1059 Willamette Street
Eugene, OR 97401
(503) 726–2255

Rouge Community College
Small Business Development
    Center
290 N.E. "C" Street
Grants Pass, OR 97526
(503) 474–0762

Mount Hood Community College
Small Business Development
    Center
323 N.E. Roberts Street
Gresham, OR 97030
(503) 667–7658

Oregon Institute of Technology
Small Business Development
    Center
3201 Campus Drive, South 314
Klamath Falls, OR 97601
(503) 885–1760

Eastern Oregon State College
Small Business Development
    Center
Regional Services Institute
LaGrande, OR 97850
(800) 452–8639

Oregon Coast Community College
    Service District
Small Business Development
    Center
P.O. Box 419
4157 N.W. Highway 101
Lincoln City, OR 97367
(503) 994–4166

Southern Oregon State
    College/Medford
Small Business Development
    Center
Regional Services Institute
229 N. Bartlett
Medford, OR 97501
(503) 772–3478

Clackamas Community College
Small Business Development
    Center
7616 S.E. Harmony Road
Milwaukie, OR 97222
(503) 656–4447

Treasure Valley Community
    College
Small Business Development
    Center
88 S.W. Third Avenue
Ontario, OR 97914
(503) 889–2617

Blue Mountain Community
    College
Small Business Development
    Center
37 S.E. Dorian
Pendleton, OR 97801
(503) 276–6233

Portland Community College
Small Business Development
    Center
123 N.W. 2nd Avenue, Suite 321
Portland, OR 97209
(503) 273–2828

Portland Community College**
Small Business International
    Trade Program
121 S.W. Salmon Street, Suite 210
Portland, OR 97204
(503) 274–7482

*Denotes recipient organization (Lead SBDC)
**Denotes specialized Center

Umpqua Community College
Small Business Development
    Center
744 S.E. Rose
Roseburg, OR 97470
(503) 672–2535

Chemeketa Community College
Small Business Development
    Center
365 Ferry Street, S.E.
Salem, OR 97301
(503) 399–5181

Clatstop Community College
Small Business Development
    Center
1240 South Holladay
Seaside, OR 97138
(503) 738–3347

Columbia George Community
    College
Small Business Development
    Center
212 Washington
The Dalles, OR 97058
(503) 296–1173

Tillamook Bay Community
    College
Small Business Development
    Center
401 B Main Street
Tillamook, OR 97141
(503) 842–2551

PENNSYLVANIA

Lehigh University
Small Business Development
    Center
301 Broadway, Route 230
Bethlehem, PA 18015
(215) 758–3980

**Clarion University of Pennsylvania
Small Business Development
  Center**
Dana Still Building
Clairon, PA 16214
(814) 226–2060

**Gannon University
Small Business Development
  Center**
Carlisle Building, 3rd Floor
Erie, PA 16541
(814) 871–7714

**St. Vincent College
Small Business Development
  Center**
Alfred Hall, 4th Floor
Latrobe, PA 15650–2690
(412) 537–4572

**Bucknell University
Small Business Development
  Center**
126 Dana Engineering Building
Lewisburg, PA 17837
(717) 524–1249

**St. Francis College
Small Business Development
  Center**
Business Resource Center
Loretto, PA 15940
(814) 472–3200

**Pennsylvania State University
Small Business Development
  Center**
The Capital College
Crags Building, Route 230
Middletown, PA 17057
(717) 948–6069

**LaSalle University
Small Business Development
  Center**
19th and West Olney Avenue
Box 365
Philadelphia, PA 19141
(215) 951–1416

**Temple University
Small Business Development
  Center**
Room 6, Speakman Hall, 006–00
Philadelphia, PA 19122
(215) 787–7282

**University of Pennsylvania*
Pennsylvania Small Business
  Development Center**
The Wharton School
444 Vance Hall
3733 Spruce Street
Philadelphia, PA 19104
(215) 898–1219

**University of Pennsylvania
Small Business Development
  Center**
The Wharton School
409 Vance Hall
Philadelphia, PA 19194–6357
(215) 898–4861

**Dequesne University
Small Business Development
  Center**
Rockwell Hall, Room 10, Concourse
600 Forbes Avenue
Pittsburgh, PA 15282
(412) 434–6233

**University of Pittsburgh
Small Business Development
  Center**
Room 343 Mervis Hall
Pittsburgh, PA 15260
(412) 648–1544

**University of Scranton
Small Business Development
  Center**
St. Thomas Hall, Room 588
Scranton, PA 18510
(717) 941–7588

*Denotes recipient organization (Lead SBDC)
**Denotes specialized Center

**Wilkes College
Small Business Development
  Center**
Hollenback Hall
192 South Franklin Street
Wilkes-Barre, PA 18766
(717) 824–4651, ext. 4340

PUERTO RICO

**University of Puerto Rico
Humacao Small Business
  Development Center**
Antonio Lopez Street
Casa Roig Annex
Box 10226–CUH Station
Humacao, PR 00661
(809) 850–2500

**Interamerican University
San Juan Metro II
Small Business Development
  Center**
One Francisco Sein Street
Casa Llompart
Box 1293
Hato Rey, PR 00919
(809) 765–2335

**University of Puerto Rico*
Puerto Rico Small Business
  Development Center**
Mayaguez Campus
Box 5253—College Station
Mayaguez, PR 00680
(809) 834–3590

**University of Puerto Rico
Small Business Development
  Center**
San Juan Metro I
11 Margarida Street
Box 21417 U.P.R. Station
Rio Piedras, PR 00918–1417
(809) 763–5880
(809) 763–5933

RHODE ISLAND

University of Rhode Island Small Business Development Center
24 Woodward Hall
Kingston, RI 02881
(401) 792–2451

Community College of Rhode Island Small Business Development Center
One Hilton Street
Providence, RI 02905
(401) 455–6042

Downtown Providence Small Business Development Center
270 Weybosset Street
Providence, RI 02903
(401) 831–1330

Bryant College* Rhode Island Small Business Development Center
1150 Douglas Pike, Route 7
Smithfield, RI 02917–1284
(401) 232–6111

Opportunities Industrialization Center Small Business Development Center
1 Hilton Street
South Providence, RI 02905
(401) 272–4400

SOUTH CAROLINA

University of South Carolina at Beaufort Small Business Development Center
800 Carteret Street
Beaufort, SC 29902
(803) 524–7112, ext. 4143

Trident Technical College Small Business Development Center
66 Columbus Street
P.O. Box 20339
Charleston, SC 29413–0339
(803) 727–2020

Clemson University Small Business Development Center
College of Commerce and Industry
425 Sirrine Hall
Clemson, SC 29634–1301
(803) 656–3227

University of South Carolina* South Carolina Small Business Development Center
College of Business Administration
1710 College Street
Columbia, SC 29208
(803) 777–5118

Coastal Carolina College Small Business Development Center
School of Business Administration
Conway, SC 29526
(803) 347–2169

Florence Darlington Technical College Small Business Development Center
P.O. Box 100548
Florence, SC 29501
(803) 661–8324

Greenville Technical College Small Business Development Center
Station B GHEC
Box 5616
Greenville, SC 29606
(803) 271–4259

*Denotes recipient organization (Lead SBDC)
**Denotes specialized Center

Upper Savannah Council of Government Small Business Development Center
Exchange Building
222 Phoenix Street, Suite 200
Greenwood, SC 29648
(803) 227–6110

Aiken/North Augusta Small Business Development Center
Triangle Plaza, Highway 25
North Augusta, SC 29841
(803) 442–3670

South Carolina State College Small Business Development Center
School of Business Administration
P.O. Box 1676
Orangeburg, SC 29117
(803) 536–8445

Winthrop College Small Business Development Center
School of Business Administration
119 Thurman Building
Rock Hill, SC 29733
(803) 323–2283

Spartanburg Chamber of Commerce Small Business Development Center
P.O. Box 1636
Spartanburg, SC 29304
(803) 594–5080

SOUTH DAKOTA

Aberdeen Small Business Development Center
226 Citizens Building
Aberdeen, SD 57401
(605) 622–2252

**Pierre Small Business
Development Center**
105 South Euclid, Suite C
Pierre, SD 57501
(605) 773–5941

**Rapid City Small Business
Development Center**
2525 West Main, Suite 105
P.O. Box 7715
Rapid City, SD 57709
(605) 394–5311

**Sioux Falls Small Business
Development Center**
231 South Phillips, Room 365
Sioux Fall, SD 57101
(605) 339–3366

**University of South Dakota*
South Dakota Small Business
Development Center**
School of Business
414 East Clark, Patterson 115
Vermillion, SD 57069
(605) 677–5272

TENNESSEE

**Tennessee Technological
University
Small Business Development
Center**
College of Business Administration
P.O. Box 5023
Cookeville, TN 38505–0001
(615) 372–3648

**Dyersburg State Community
College
Small Business Development
Center**
Office of Extension Services
P.O. Box 648
Dyersburg, TN 38024
(901) 286–3201

**East Tennessee State University
Small Business Development
Center**
College of Business
P.O. Box 23, 440A
Johnson City, TN 37614–0002
(615) 929–5630

**Pellissippi State Technical
Community College
Small Business Development
Center**
Business/Industrial Services
P.O. Box 22990
Knoxville, TN 37933–0990
(615) 694–6660

**University of Tennessee at Martin
Small Business Development
Center**
School of Business Administration
402 Elm Street
Martin, TN 38237–3415
(901) 587–7236

**Memphis State University*
Tennessee Small Business
Development Center**
Memphis, TN 38152
(901) 678–2500

Memphis State University
International Trade Center
Tennessee Small Business
Development Center**
320 South Dudley Street
Memphis, TN 38152
(901) 678–4174

**Walters State Community College
Small Business Development
Center**
Business/Industrial Services
500 S. Davy Crockett Parkway
Morristown, TN 37813–6889
(615) 587–9722, ext. 447

*Denotes recipient organization (Lead SBDC)
**Denotes specialized Center

**Middle Tennessee State
University
Small Business Development
Center**
School of Business
P.O. Box 487
Murfreesboro, TN 37132
(615) 898–2745

**Tennessee State University
Small Business Development
Center**
School of Business
10th and Charlotte Avenue
Nashville, TN 37203
(615) 251–1178

TEXAS

**Abilene Christian University
Small Business Development
Center**
College of Business Administration
ACU Station, Box 8307
Abilene, TX 79699
(915) 674–2776

**Alvin Community College
Small Business Development
Center**
3110 Mustang Road
Alvin, TX 77511–4898
(713) 388–4686

**West Texas State University
Small Business Development
Center**
T. Boone Pickens School of Business
1800 South Washington, Suite 110
Amarillo, TX 79102
(806) 372–5151

**Trinity Valley Community College
Small Business Development
Center**
500 South Prairieville
Athens, TX 75751
(214) 675–6230

Texas Association of Mexican-American
Small Business Development Center
Chamber of Commerce
2211 South IH35, Suite #103
Austin, TX 78741
(512) 326–2256

Lee College
Small Business Development Center
511 South Whiting Street
Rundell Hall
Baytown, TX 77520–4796
(713) 425–6309

Lamar University
Small Business Development Center
855 Florida Avenue
Beaumont, TX 77705
(409) 880–2367
(800) 722–3443

Blinn College
Small Business Development Center
902 College Avenue
Brenham, TX 77833–1059
(409) 830–4137

Bryan/College Station Chamber of Commerce
Small Business Development Center
401 South Washington
Bryan, TX 77803
(409) 823–3034

Texas Engineering Experiment Station
Small Business Development Center
310 Engineering Research Center
College Station, TX 77843–3369
(409) 845–0538

Navarro Small Business Development Center
120 North 12th Street
Corsicana, TX 75110
(903) 874–0658

Corpus Christi Chamber of Commerce
Small Business Development Center
1201 North Shoreline
Corpus Christi, TX 78403
(512) 882–6161

Dallas County Community College*
Northeastern Texas Small Business Development Center
1402 Corinth Street
Dallas, TX 75215
(214) 747–0555

International Trade Center**
Small Business Development Center
World Trade Center, Suite #150
2050 Stemmons Freeway
P.O. Box 58299
Dallas, TX 75258
(214) 653–1777

Grayson County College
Small Business Development Center
6101 Grayson Drive
Denison, TX 75020–8299
(214) 465–6030
(903) 463–8654

University of Texas–Pan American
Small Business Development Center
1201 West University Drive
Edinburg, TX 78539–2999
(512) 381–3361

*Denotes recipient organization (Lead SBDC)
**Denotes specialized Center

El Paso Community College
Small Business Development Center
103 Montana Avenue, Room 202
El Paso, TX 79902–3929
(915) 534–3410

Tarrant County Junior College
Small Business Development Center
Mary Owen Center
1500 Houston Street, Room 163
Fort Worth, TX 76102
(817) 877–9254

Cooke County Community College
Small Business Development Center
1525 West California
Gainesville, TX 76240
(817) 665–4785

Galveston College
Small Business Development Center
4015 Avenue Q
Galveston, TX 77550
(409) 740–7380

University of Houston*
Texas Small Business Development Center
Park 601 Jefferson, Suite 2330
Houston, TX 77002
(713) 752–8444

University of Houston**
Texas Information Procurement Service
401 Louisiana Street, 7th Floor
Houston, TX 77002
(713) 752–8477
(800) 252–7232

University of Houston**
International Trade Center
601 Jefferson, Suite 2330
Houston, TX 77002
(713) 752–8404

University of Houston
Texas Product Development
   Center
401 Louisiana, 7th Floor
Houston, TX 77002
(713) 752–8400

Central Texas Small Business
   Development Center
P.O. Box 1800
Killeen, TX 76540–9990
(817) 609–8848

Kingsville Chamber of Commerce
Small Business Development
   Center
635 East King
Kingsville, TX 78363
(512) 592–6438

North Harris Montgomery
   Community College District
Small Business Development
   Center
Administration Building
20000 Kingwood Drive, Room 104
Kingwood, TX 77339
(713) 359–1677
(800) 443–SBDC

Brazoport College
Small Business Development
   Center
500 College Drive
Lake Jackson, TX 77566
(409) 265–6131, ext. 380

Laredo Development Foundation
Small Business Development
   Center
Division of Business Administration
616 Leal Street
Laredo, TX 78041
(512) 722–0563

Kilgore College
Small Business Development
   Center
300 South High
Longview, TX 75601
(903) 753–2642

Texas Tech University*
Northwestern Texas Small
   Business Development Center
Center for Innovation
2579 South Loop 289, Suite 210
Lubbock, TX 79423
(806) 745–1637

Angelina Chamber of Commerce
Small Business Development
   Center
1615 South Chestnut
P.O. Box 1606
Lufkin, TX 75901
(409) 634–1887

Northeast/Texarkana
Small Business Development
   Center
P.O. Box 1307
Mt. Pleasant, TX 75455
(214) 572–1911

University of Texas/Permian
   Basin
Small Business Development
   Center
College of Management
4901 East University, Room 298
Odessa, TX 79762–8301
(915) 563–0400

Paris Junior College
Small Business Development
   Center
Alford Learning Center
2400 Clarksville Street
Paris, TX 75460
(903) 784–1802

Angelo State University
Small Business Development
   Center
2610 West Avenue N
Campus Box 10910
San Angelo, TX 70909
(915) 942–2098

University of Texas at San
   Antonio*
South Texas Border Small
   Business Development Center
College of Business
San Antonio, TX 78249–0660
(512) 224–0791

Houston Community College
Small Business Development
   Center
13600 Murphy Road
Stafford, TX 77477
(713) 499–4870

Tarleton State University
Small Business Development
   Center
School of Business
Box T-158
Stephenville, TX 76402
(817) 968–9330

College of the Mainland
Small Business Development
   Center
8419 Emmett F. Lowry Expressway
Texas City, TX 77591
(409) 938–7578

Tyler Junior College
Small Business Development
   Center
1530 South S.W.
Loop 323, Suite 100
Tyler, TX 75701
(903) 510–2975

*Denotes recipient organization (Lead SBDC)
**Denotes specialized Center

University of Houston
Small Business Development
Center
700 Main Center, Suite 102
Victoria, TX 77901
(512) 575–8944

McLennan Community College
Small Business Development
Center
4601 North 19th Street, Suite A–15
Waco, TX 76708
(817) 750–3600

Wharton County Junior College
Small Business Development
Center
Administration Building, Room 102
911 Boling Highway
Wharton, TX 77488–0080
(409) 532–2201

Midwestern State University
Small Business Development
Center
Division of Business Administration
3400 Taft Boulevard
Wichita Falls, TX 76308
(817) 696–6738

UTAH

Southern Utah University
Small Business Development
Center
351 West Center
Cedar City, UT 84720
(801) 586–5401

Snow College
Small Business Development
Center
345 West First North
Ephraim, UT 84627
(801) 283–4021

Utah State University
Small Business Development
Center
East Campus Building
College of Business
Logan, UT 84322–8330
(801) 750–2277

Weber State College
Small Business Development
Center
School of Business and Economics
3750 South Harrison
Ogden, UT 84408–3806
(801) 626–7232

College of Eastern Utah
Small Business Development
Center
Applied Sciences
451 East 400 North
Price, UT 84501
(801) 637–1995

Brigham Young University
Small Business Development
Center
Graduate School of Management
790 Tanner Building
Provo, UT 84602
(801) 378–4022

University of Utah*
Utah Small Business
Development Center
102 West 500 South, Suite 315
Salt Lake City, UT 84101
(801) 581–7905

Dixie College
Small Business Development
Center
225 South 700 East
St. George, UT 84770
(801) 673–4811, ext. 455

VERMONT

University of Vermont Extension
Service*
Vermont Small Business
Development Center
Morrill Hall
Burlington, VT 05405
(802) 656–4479

University of Vermont Extension
Office
Central Small Business
Development Center
RFD One, Box 2280
Morrisville, VT 05661
(802) 888–4972

University of Vermont Extension
Office
Southwestern Small Business
Development Center
Box 489
Rutland, VT 05701
(802) 773–3349

University of Vermont Extension
Office
Northeastern Small Business
Development Center
HCR 31, Box 436
St. Johnsbury, VT 05819
(802) 748–5512

University of Vermont Extension
Office
Southeastern Small Business
Development Center
411 Western Avenue, Box 2430
West Brattleboro, VT 05301
(802) 257–7967

*Denotes recipient organization (Lead SBDC)
**Denotes specialized Center

441

University of Vermont Extension Office
Northwestern Small Business Development Center
4A Laurette Drive
Winooski, VT 05404
(802) 655-9540

VIRGIN ISLANDS

University of the Virgin Islands Small Business Development Center
United Plaza Shopping Center
Suite #5-6, Sion Farm
St. Croix, VI 00820
(809) 778-8270

University of the Virgin Islands*
Virgin Islands Small Business Development Center
Grand Hotel
Box 1087
St. Thomas, VI 00804
(809) 776-3206

VIRGINIA

Mountain Empire Community College
Small Business Development Center
Drawer 700, Route 23
Big Stone Gap, VA 24219
(703) 523-2400

Central Virginia Small Business Development Center
700 Harris Street, Suite 207
Charlottesville, VA 22901-4553
(804) 295-8198

Northern Virginia Small Business Development Center
4260 Chainbridge Road, Suite B-1
Fairfax, VA 22030
(703) 993-2131

Longwood College
Small Business Development Center
Farmville, VA 23901
(804) 395-2086

James Madison University
Small Business Development Center
College of Business Building, Room 523
Harrisonburg, VA 22807
(703) 568-6334

Lynchburg Small Business Development Center
147 Mill Ridge Road
Lynchburg, VA 25402-4341
(804) 582-6100

Flory Small Business Development Center
10311 Sudley Manor Drive
Manassas, VA 22110
(703) 335-2500

Small Business Development Center of Hampton Roads, Inc.
420 Bank Street
P.O. Box 327
Norfolk, VA 23501
(804) 622-6414
(804) 825-2957

Southwest Virginia Community College
Small Business Development Center
P.O. Box SVCC
Richlands, VA 24641
(703) 964-7345

*Denotes recipient organization (Lead SBDC)
**Denotes specialized Center

Capital Area Small Business Development Center
801 East Main Street, Suite 501
Richmond, VA 23219
(804) 648-7838

Blue Ridge Small Business Development Center
310 First Street, S.W. Mezzanine
Roanoke, VA 24011
(703) 983-0719

Commonwealth of Virginia Department of Economic Development*
Virginia Small Business Development Center
1021 East Cary Street, 11th Floor
Richmond, VA 23219
(804) 371-8258

Longwood College
Small Business Development Center
South Boston Branch
3403 Halifax Road
P.O. Box 739
South Boston, VA 24592
(804) 575-0044

WASHINGTON

Bellevue Small Business Development Center
13555 Bel-Red Road #208
Bellevue, WA 98005
(206) 643-2888

Western Washington University Small Business Development Center
College of Business and Economics
415 Parks Hall
Bellingham, WA 98225
(206) 676-3899

Edmonds Community College
Small Business Development
Center
917 134th Street, S.W.
Everett, WA 98204
(206) 745–0430

Columbia Basin College Tri-Cities
Small Business Development
Center
901 N. Colorado
Kennewick, WA 99336
(509) 735–6222

Big Bend Community College
Small Business Development
Center
7662 Chanute Street, Building 1500
Moses Lake, WA 98837–3299
(509) 762–6289

Skagit Valley College
Small Business Development
Center
2405 College Way
Mt. Vernon, WA 98273
(206) 428–1282

Department of Trade and
Economic Department
Small Business Development
Center
919 Lakeridge Way, Suite A
Olympia, WA 98502
(206) 586–4854

Wenatchee Valley College
Small Business Development
Center
P.O. Box 1042
Omak, WA 98841
(509) 826–5107

Washington State University*
Washington Small Business
Development Center
College of Business and Economics
441 Todd Hall
Pullman, WA 99164–4740
(509) 335–1576

Small Business Development
Center
2001 Sixth Avenue, Suite 2608
Seattle, WA 98121–2518
(206) 464–5450

North Seattle Community
College**
International Trade Institute
Small Business Development
Center
9600 College Way North
Seattle, WA 98103
(206) 527–3733

Small Business Development
Center
Duwamish Industrial Educational Center
6770 East Marginal Way South
Seattle, WA 98108–1499
(206) 764–5375

Washington State University
Spokane Small Business
Development Center
West 601 First
Spokane, WA 99204–0399
(509) 456–2781

Small Business Development
Center
Financial Center
950 Pacific Avenue, #300
Tacoma, WA 98402
(206) 272–7232

Columbia River Economic
Development Council
Small Business Development
Center
100 East Columbia Way
Vancouver, WA 98660–3156
(206) 694–2190

*Denotes recipient organization (Lead SBDC)
**Denotes specialized Center

Wenatchee Valley Community
College
Small Business Development
Center
Grand Central Building
25 North Wenatchee Avenue
Wenatchee, WA 98801
(509) 662–8016

Yakima Valley Community
College
Small Business Development
Center
P.O. Box 1647
Yakima, WA 98907
(507) 575–2284

WEST VIRGINIA

Concord College
Small Business Development
Center
Center for Economic Action
Box D-125
Athens, WV 24712
(304) 384–5103

Bluefield State College
Small Business Development
Center
219 Rock Street
Bluefield, WV 24701
(304) 327–4107

Governor's Office of Community
and Industrial Development*
West Virginia Small Business
Development Center
1115 Virginia Street, East
Charleston, WV 25310
(304) 348–2960

Fairmount State College
Small Business Development
Center
Fairmount, WV 26554
(304) 367–4125

443

Marshall University
Small Business Development
Center
1050 Fourth Avenue
Huntington, WV 25755–2126
(304) 696–6789

Potomac State College
Small Business Development
Center
75 Arnold Street
Keyser, WV 26726
(304) 788–3011

West Virginia Institute of
Technology
Small Business Development
Center
Engineering Building, Room 102
Montgomery, WV 25136
(304) 442–5501

West Virginia University
Small Business Development
Center
P.O. Box 6025
Morgantown, WV 26506
(304) 293–5839

West Virginia University at
Parkersburg
Small Business Development
Center
Route 5, Box 167–A
Parkersburg, WV 26101
(304) 424–8277

Shepherd College
Small Business Development
Center
120 North Princess Street
Shepherdstown, WV 25443
(800) 344–5231, ext. 261

West Virginia Northern
Community College
Small Business Development
Center
College Square
Wheeling, WV 26003
(304) 233–5900, ext. 206

WISCONSIN

University of Wisconsin at Eau
Claire
Small Business Development
Center
Schneider Hall, #113
Eau Claire, WI 54701
(715) 836–5811

University of Wisconsin at Green
Bay
Small Business Development
Center
2420 Nicolet Drive
460 Wood Hall
Green Bay, WI 54311–7001
(414) 465–2089

University of Wisconsin at
Parkside
Small Business Development
Center
234 Tallent Hall
Kenosha, WI 53141
(414) 553–2189

University of Wisconsin at La
Crosse
Small Business Development
Center
School of Business Administration
La Crosse, WI 54601
(608) 785–8782

*Denotes recipient organization (Lead SBDC)
**Denotes specialized Center

University of Wisconsin*
Wisconsin Small Business
Development Center
432 Northlake Street, Room 423
Madison, WI 53706
(608) 263–7794

University of Wisconsin**
International Trade Program
423 North Lake Street
Madison, WI 53706
(608) 263–7810

University of Wisconsin
Small Business Development
Center
905 University Avenue
Madison, WI 53715
(608) 263–0221

University of Wisconsin at
Milwaukee
Small Business Development
Center
929 North Sixth Street
Milwaukee, WI 53203
(414) 224–3240

University of Wisconsin at
Oshkosh
Small Business Development
Center
Clow Faculty Building, Room 157
Oshkosh, WI 54901
(414) 424–1541

WIS–BID (Procurement Match
Program)**
W9859 Highway 16 and 60
Reeseville, WI 53579
(414) 927–5484

University of Wisconsin at
Stevens Point
Small Business Development
Center
012 Old Main Building
Stevens Point, WI 54481
(715) 346–2004

University of Wisconsin at Stevens Point**
Wisconsin American Indian Economic Development
Main Building
Stevens Point, WI 54481
(715) 346-2004

University of Wisconsin at Superior
Small Business Development Center
29 Sundquist Hall
Superior, WI 54880
(715) 394-8351

University of Wisconsin at Whitewater
Small Business Development Center
2000 Carlson Building
Whitewater, WI 53190
(414) 472-3217

University of Wisconsin at Whitewater**
Wisconsin Innovation Service Center
402 McCutchan Hall
Whitewater, WI 53190
(414) 472-1365

WYOMING

Casper Community College*
Wyoming Small Business Development Center
111 West Second Street, Suite 416
Casper, WY 82601
(301) 235-4825

Casper College
Small Business Development Center
350 West "A" Street, Suite 200
Casper, WY 82601
(307) 235-4827

Laramie County Community College
Small Business Development Center
1400 East College Drive
Cheyenne, WY 82007
(307) 778-1222

Eastern Wyoming Community College
Small Business Development Center
Douglas Branch
203 North Sixth Street
Douglas, WY 82633
(307) 358-4090

Northern Wyoming Community College District
Gillette Campus
Small Business Development Center
720 West Eighth
Gillette, WY 82716
(307) 686-0297

Central Wyoming College
Small Business Development Center
360 Main Street
Lander, WY 82502
(307) 332-3394
(800) 735-8394

University of Wyoming
Small Business Development Center
University Station Box 3275
Laramie, WY 82071
(307) 766-2363

Northwest Community College
Small Business Development Center
146 South Bent, #103
Powell, WY 82435
(307) 754-3746

Western Wyoming Community College
Small Business Development Center
P.O. Box 428
Rock Springs, WY 82902
(307) 382-1830

*Denotes recipient organization (Lead SBDC)
**Denotes specialized Center

Appendix B

State Regulatory Flexibility Acts

Federal and state regulation continues to be a major problem for small businesses. To counter the imposition of overly burdensome paperwork, record-keeping, and other regulatory requirements, 25 states as well as the federal government had adopted regulatory flexibility acts as of 1992. These laws, while differing in their specific provisions, have one central theme in common—they direct government agencies to consider the effects their regulation will have on small businesses and to look at other, less onerous, ways to regulate.

The following table, prepared by the Small Business Administration's Office of Advocacy, compares in summary fashion the state regulatory flexibility statutes, specifically the following provisions:

- **Size Definition:** whether the law specifically defines what constitutes a small business for purposes of regulation.

- **Exemptions:** whether certain types of proposed rules (for example, emergency rules, rules required by federal law, public health rules, etc.) are exempted from coverage of the state's act.

- **Judicial Review:** whether judicial review of agency rulemaking is specifically provided for, disallowed, or "not precluded."

- **Periodic Review:** whether a periodic review of the rules promulgated by the state's regulatory agencies is mandated by the legislation.

- **Alternatives:** whether regulatory agencies are required to consider alternatives to the proposed rule which accomplish the stated objectives of applicable laws and which minimize any significant economic impact of the proposed rule on small entities.

- **Agenda:** whether the state requires periodic publication or notification of proposed rulemaking by an agency prior to implementation of the regulation. This may or may not include a public comment period.

More detailed information on current state regulatory flexibility acts—including citations to state codes and brief descriptions of the applicable statutes or executive orders—can be found in the appendix to the *Annual Report of the Chief Counsel for Advocacy on Implementation of the Regulatory Flexibility Act*. The latest edition of this report is available upon request from the Small Business Administration's Office of Advocacy.

State Regulatory Flexibility Statutes

State	Contact	Size Definition	Exemptions	Judicial Review	Periodic Review	Alternatives	Agenda
Arizona	Margaret Fernandez (602) 542-5381	Yes	Yes	No	Yes	Yes	No
California	Craig Tarpenning (916) 323-6225	Yes	Yes	Not Precluded	No	Yes	Yes
Colorado	Geoff Hier (303) 894-7839	Yes	Yes	Not Precluded	Yes	No	No
Connecticut	Joseph McGee (203) 258-4202	Yes	Yes	Not Precluded	No	No	No
Delaware	John J. Casey, Jr. (302) 736-4271	Yes	Yes	Not Precluded	Yes	No	No
Florida	Laurice Thompson (904) 487-4698	Yes	Yes	Yes	No	Yes	No
Illinois	Linda Brand (217) 524-1516	Yes	Yes	Not Precluded	Yes	Yes	Yes
Indiana	John Humes (317) 232-5296	No	No	Not Precluded	No	Yes	No
Iowa	Joseph Royce (515) 281-3084	Yes	Yes	Not Precluded	Yes	Yes	No
Kansas	Norman Furse (913) 296-2321	Yes	Yes	Not Precluded	No	Yes	No
Kentucky	Randy Bacon (502) 564-8100	Yes	Yes	Yes	No	Yes	No
Michigan	Debra Tomburrini (517) 373-6476	Yes	Yes	Not Precluded	Yes	No	No
Minnesota	Charles Schaffer (612) 296-3871	Yes	Yes	Not Precluded	Yes	No	No
Nevada	Legislative Counsel (702) 687-6800	No	Yes	Yes	No	No	No
New Hampshire	Helen Goodman (603) 271-3658	Yes	Yes	Yes	No	Yes	No

State Regulatory Flexibility Statutes

State	Contact	Size Definition	Exemptions	Judicial Review	Periodic Review	Alternatives	Agenda
New Jersey	Charles Jones III (609) 292-3860	Yes	Yes	Yes	No	No	No
New York	William Redmond (518) 473-0620	Yes	Yes	Yes	No	No	No
Ohio	Evelyn Golding (614) 466-2535	Yes	Yes	Yes	Yes	No	No
Oregon	Mike Shabolt (503) 373-1241	Yes	Yes	Yes	Yes	No	No
Pennsylvania	Richard Spiegelman (717) 783-6563	No	Yes	No	Yes	Yes	Yes
Rhode Island	William Parson (401) 277-2600	Yes	Yes	Not Precluded	No	Yes	Yes
Texas	Robert Velasquez (512) 472-5059	Yes	Yes	Yes	No	No	No
Vermont	Herb Olson (802) 828-2231	Yes	Yes	Not Precluded	Yes	Yes	No
Washington	Richard Paulson (206) 586-4853	No	Yes	Yes	Yes	No	Yes
Wisconsin	Dennis Fay (608) 266-1018	Yes	No	Not Precluded	Yes	Yes	No

Appendix C

SBA Regional Advocates

Supplementing its Washington staff, the SBA's Office of Advocacy has a representative in each of the 10 SBA regional offices. The regional advocates handle casework, deal with federal and state agencies in their districts, and inform local organizations and associations about the Office of Advocacy, the SBA, and government policies that may benefit small business owners. Regional advocates can be reached at the following offices of the U.S. Small Business Administration:

Region I:
Connecticut, Maine, Massachusetts, New Hampshire, Rhode Island, Vermont

Mr. Harry Bellardini (Acting)
U.S. Small Business Administration
60 Batterymarch Street, 10th Floor
Boston, MA 02110
(617) 565-5590

Region II:
New Jersey, New York, Puerto Rico, Virgin Islands

Mr. Harry Bellardini
Regional Advocate
U.S. Small Business Administration
100 South Clinton, Room 1071
Federal Building
Syracuse, NY 13260
(315) 423-5350

Region III:
Delaware, District of Columbia, Maryland, Pennsylvania, Virginia, West Virginia

Mr. Rich Johnson
Regional Advocate
U.S. Small Business Administration
Allendale Square, Suite 201
475 Allendale Road
King of Prussia, PA 19406
(215) 962-3751

Region IV:
Alabama, Florida, Georgia, Kentucky, Mississippi, North Carolina, South Carolina, Tennessee

Mr. Sam Lindsey
Regional Advocate
U.S. Small Business Administration
1375 Peachtree Street, N.W.
Atlanta, GA 30367
(404) 347-7757

Region V:
Illinois, Indiana, Michigan, Minnesota, Ohio, Wisconsin

Ms. Katy Oliver
Regional Advocate
U.S. Small Business Administration
300 South Riverside Plaza, Room 1975
Chicago, IL 60606-6611
(312) 353-5000

Ms. Sharon Erb
Assistant Regional Advocate
U.S. Small Business Administration
212 East Washington Avenue, Room 213
Madison, WI 53703
(608) 264-5559

Region VI:
Arkansas, Louisiana, New Mexico, Oklahoma, Texas

Ms. Mary Fae Kamm
Regional Advocate
U.S. Small Business Administration
8625 King George Drive, Building C
Dallas, TX 75235-3391
(214) 767-7635

Region VII:
Iowa, Kansas, Missouri,
Nebraska

Ms. Judy Krueger
Regional Advocate
U.S. Small Business Administration
911 Walnut Street, 13th Floor
Kansas City, MO 64106
(816) 426-2803

Region VIII:
Colorado, Montana,
North Dakota, South Dakota,
Utah, Wyoming

Mr. Jim Henderson
Regional Advocate
U.S. Small Business Administration
999 18th Street, Suite 701
Denver, CO 80202
(303) 294-7003

Region IX:
Arizona, California, Guam,
Hawaii, Nevada

Mr. Frank Toti
Regional Advocate
U.S. Small Business Administration
71 Stevenson Street, 20th Floor
San Francisco, CA 94105-2939
(415) 744-6405

Region X:
Alaska, Idaho, Oregon,
Washington

Mr. Dan Cummings
Regional Advocate
U.S. Small Business Administration
2615 Fourth Avenue, Room 440
Seattle, WA 98121
(206) 442-5231

452

Appendix D

SBA District Offices

The Small Business Administration's district offices serve as the contact point for the agency's many assistance programs for small businesses. They also make available upon request small business start-up kits.

The following list of SBA district offices is arranged alphabetically by town or city within each state. For further information about SBA programs, you can also call the Small Business Answer Desk at (800) 827-5722. (For the hearing impaired, the TDD number is (202) 205–7333.)

Alabama

U.S. Small Business Administration
2121-8th Avenue North, Suite 200
Birmingham, AL 35203-2398
(205) 731-1338

Alaska

U.S. Small Business Administration
Federal Building Annex
222 West 8th Avenue, #67
Anchorage, AK 99513-7559
(407) 271-40221

Arizona

U.S. Small Business Administration
2828 North Central Avenue, Suite 800
Phoenix, AZ 85004-1025
(602) 640-2316

Arkansas

U.S. Small Business Administration
2120 Riverfront Drive, Suite 100
Little Rock, AR 72202
(501) 740-5871

California

U.S. Small Business Administration
2719 North Fresno Drive, #101
Fresno, CA 93727
(209) 487-5189

U.S. Small Business Administration
330 North Brand Boulevard, Suite 1200
Glendale, CA 91203-2304
(213) 894-2956

U.S. Small Business Administration
Federal Building, Suite 4-S-290
880 Front Street
San Diego, CA 92188
(619) 895-7269

U.S. Small Business Administration
211 Main Street, 4th Floor
San Francisco, CA 94102-1988
(415) 484-6804

U.S. Small Business Administration
901 West Civic Center Drive, Suite 160
Santa Ana, CA 92703
(714) 836-2492

Colorado

U.S. Small Business Administration
721 19th Street, Room 426
Denver, CO 80202
(303) 844-3984

Connecticut

U.S. Small Business Administration
330 Main Street, 2nd Floor
Hartford, CT 06106
(203) 240-4700

District of Columbia

U.S. Small Business Administration
1111 18th Street N.W., 6th Floor
Washington, DC 20036
(202) 634-1500

Florida

U.S. Small Business Administration
1320 South Dixie Highway, Suite 501
Coral Gables, FL 33146-2911
(305) 536-5521

U.S. Small Business Administration
7825 Baymeadows Way, Suite 100-B
Jacksonville, FL 32256-7504
(904) 443-1900

Georgia

U.S. Small Business Administration
1720 Peachtree Road N.W., Suite 600
Atlanta, GA 30309
(404) 347-4749

Hawaii

U.S. Small Business Administration
300 Ala Moana, Room 2213
Honolulu, HI 96850
(808) 541-2990

Idaho

U.S. Small Business Administration
1020 Main Street, Suite 290
Boise, ID 83702
(208) 334-9635

Illinois

U.S. Small Business Administration
500 West Madison, Room 1250
Chicago, IL 60661
(312) 353-4528

Indianapolis

U.S. Small Business Administration
Federal Building, Suite 100
429 North Pennsylvania Street
Indianapolis, IN 46204-1584
(317) 226-7272

Iowa

U.S. Small Business Administration
210 Walnut Street, Room 749
Des Moines, IA 50309
(515) 284-4422

U.S. Small Business Administration
373 Collins Road N.E., Room 100
Cedar Rapids, IA 52402-3118
(319) 393-8630

Kansas

U.S. Small Business Administration
110 East Waterman Street
Wichita, KS 67202
(316) 269-6273

Kentucky

U.S. Small Business Administration
600 Dr. Martin Luther King, Room 188
Louisville, KY 40202
(502) 582-5971

Louisiana

U.S. Small Business Administration
Ford-Fisk Building
1661 Canal Street, Suite 2000
New Orleans, LA 70112
(504) 589-2354

Maine

U.S. Small Business Administration
Federal Building, Room 512
40 Western Avenue
Augusta, ME 04330
(207) 622-8378

Maryland

U.S. Small Business Administration
Equitable Building, 3rd Floor
10 North Calvert Street
Baltimore, MD 21202
(301) 962-2235

Massachusetts

U.S. Small Business Administration
10 Causeway Street, Room 265
Boston, MA 02222-1093
(617) 565-5590

Michigan

U.S. Small Business Administration
477 Michigan Avenue
515 Patrick V. McNamara Building
Detroit, MI 48226
(313) 226-6075

Minnesota

U.S. Small Business Administration
610-C Butler Square
100 North 6th Street
Minneapolis, MN 55403
(612) 370-2324

Mississippi

U.S. Small Business Administration
101 West Capitol Street, Suite 400
Jackson, MS 39269
(601) 965-4378

Missouri

U.S. Small Business Administration
323 West 8th Street, Suite 501
Kansas City, MO 64105-1500
(816) 374-6762

U.S. Small Business Administration
815 Olive Street, Room 242
St. Louis, MO 63101
(314) 539-6600

Montana

U.S. Small Business Administration
301 South Park, Room 528
Federal Office Building, Drawer 10054
Helena, MT 59626
(406) 449-5381

Nebraska

U.S. Small Business Administration
11145 Mill Valley Road
Omaha, NE 68154
(402) 449-5381

Nevada

U.S. Small Business Administration
P.O. Box 7527, Downtown Station
301 East Stewart
Las Vegas, NV 89125
(702) 388-6611

New Hampshire

U.S. Small Business Administration
143 North Main Street, Suite 202
Concord, NH 03301
(603) 225-1400

New Jersey

U.S. Small Business Administration
Military Park Building
60 Park Place, 4th Floor
Newark, NJ 07102
(201) 645-2434

New Mexico

U.S. Small Business Administration
625 Silver Avenue S.W., Suite 320
Albuquerque, NM 87102
(505) 766-1870

New York

U.S. Small Business Administration
111 West Huron Street, Room 1311
Buffalo, NY 14202
(716) 846-4301

U.S. Small Business Administration
26 Federal Plaza, Room 3100
New York, NY 10278
(212) 264-2454

U.S. Small Business Administration
Federal Building, Room 1071
100 South Clinton Street
Syracuse, NY 13260
(315) 423-5377

North Carolina

U.S. Small Business Administration
222 South Church Street, Room 300
Charlotte, NC 28202
(704) 344-6563

North Dakota

U.S. Small Business Administration
Federal Office Building, Room 218
657 Second Avenue North
Fargo, ND 58108-3086
(701) 239-5131

Ohio

U.S. Small Business Administration
AJC Federal Building, Room 317
1240 East Ninth Street
Cleveland, OH 44199
(216) 522-4180

U.S. Small Business Administration
Federal Building-U.S. Courthouse
85 Marconi Boulevard, Room 512
Columbus, OH 43215
(614) 469-5548

Oklahoma

U.S. Small Business Administration
200 N.W. 5th Street, Suite 670
Oklahoma City, OK 73102
(405) 231-4301

Oregon

U.S. Small Business Administration
222 S.W. Columbia Street
Portland, OR 97201-6605
(503) 326-5213

Pennsylvania

U.S. Small Business Administration
Allendale Square, Suite 201
475 Allendale Road
King of Prussia, PA 19406
(215) 962-3846

U.S. Small Business Administration
960 Penn Avenue, 5th Floor
Pittsburgh, PA 15222
(412) 644-2780

Puerto Rico

U.S. Small Business Administration
Federico Degatau Federal Building,
    Room 691
Carlos Chardon Avenue
Hato Rey, PR 00918
(809) 766-5002

Rhode Island

U.S. Small Business Administration
380 Westminster Mall, 5th Floor
Providence, RI 02903
(401) 528-4561

South Carolina

U.S. Small Business Administration
1835 Assembly Street, Room 358
Columbia, SC 29202
(803) 765-5376

South Dakota

U.S. Small Business Administration
Security Building, Suite 101
101 South Main Street
Sioux Falls, SD 57102-0577
(605) 330-4231

Tennessee

U.S. Small Business Administration
50 Vantage Way, Suite 201
Nashville, TN 37228-1504
(615) 736-7176

Texas

U.S. Small Business Administration
1100 Commerce Street, Room 3C36
Dallas, TX 75242
(214) 767-0608

U.S. Small Business Administration
10737 Gateway West, Suite 320
El Paso, TX 79935
(915) 541-5560

U.S. Small Business Administration
222 East Van Buren, Suite 500
Harlingen, TX 78550
(512) 427-8533

U.S. Small Business Administration
2525 Murworth, Suite 112
Houston, TX 77054
(713) 660-4421

U.S. Small Business Administration
Regency Plaza
1611-10th Street, Suite 200
Lubbock, TX 79401
(806) 743-7462

U.S. Small Business Administration
7400 Blanco Road, Suite 200
San Antonio, TX 28216
(512) 229-4535

Utah

U.S. Small Business Administration
Wallace F. Bennett Federal Building
125 South State Street, Room 2237
Salt Lake City, UT 84138-1195
(801) 524-5800

Vermont

U.S. Small Business Administration
87 State Street, Room 205
Montpelier, VT 05602
(802) 828-4422

Virginia

U.S. Small Business Administration
Federal Building, Room 3015
400 North 8th Street
Richmond, VA 23240
(804) 771-2400

Washington

U.S. Small Business Administration
915 Second Avenue
Federal Building, Room 1792
Seattle, WA 98174-1088
(206) 442-1420

U.S. Small Business Administration
Farm Credit Building, 10th Floor East
West 601 First Avenue
Spokane, WA 99204
(509) 353-2810

West Virginia

U.S. Small Business Administration
168 West Main Street, 5th Floor
Clarksburg, WV 26301
(304) 623-5631

Wisconsin

U.S. Small Business Administration
212 East Washington Avenue, Room 213
Madison, WI 53703
(608) 264-5205

Wyoming

U.S. Small Business Administration
Federal Building, Room 4001
100 East B Street
Casper, WY 82602-2839
(307) 261-5761

Glossary

Business development corporation (BDC): a business financing agency, usually comprising financial institutions in an area or state that are organized to help finance industrial enterprises unable to obtain such assistance through normal channels. The risk is spread among various BDC members; interest rates may vary from those charged by the member institutions.

Business and industrial development company (BIDCO): a private, for-profit financing corporation chartered by the state to provide both equity and long-term debt capital to small business owners.

Capital: (1) assets less liabilities, representing the ownership interest in a business; (2) a stock of accumulated goods, especially at a specified time and in contrast to income received during a specified time period; (3) accumulated goods devoted to the production of goods; (4) accumulated possessions calculated to bring in income.

Certified Development Company (CDC): a local area or statewide corporation or authority—for profit or nonprofit, depending on the situation—that packages SBA, bank, state, and private money into a financial assistance package for existing business capital improvement. The SBA holds the second lien on its maximum share of 40 percent involvement. Each state has at least one CDC. *See also* SBA 504 loans.

Certified lenders: banks that participate in the SBA's guaranteed loan program and agree to certain conditions set forth by the SBA. In return, the SBA agrees to process any guaranteed loan application within three business days.

Collateral: securities, evidence of deposit, or other property pledged by a borrower to secure repayment of a loan.

Community development corporation: a corporation established to develop economic programs for a community and, in most cases, to provide financial support for such development.

Consortium: a coalition of organizations—such as banks and corporations—set up to fund ventures requiring large capital resources.

Corporation: a group of persons granted a charter legally recognizing them as a separate entity having its own rights, privileges, and liabilities distinct from those of its members. The process of incorporating should be completed with the state's secretary of state or state corporate counsel and usually requires the services of an attorney.

Debenture: (1) a certificate given as acknowledgement of a debt secured by the general credit of the issuing corporation; (2) a bond, usually without security, issued by a corporation and sometimes convertible to common stock.

Equity: an ownership interest in a business. Equity securities such as stocks, for example, afford ownership in a company without any guaranteed return, but with the opportunity to share in the company's profits.

Equity partnership: a limited partnership arrangement for providing start-up and seed capital to businesses.

Incubator: a facility designed to encourage entrepreneurship and minimize obstacles to new business formation and growth, particularly for high technology firms, by housing a number of fledgling enterprises that share an array of services. These shared services may include meeting areas, secretarial services, accounting services, research libraries, on-site financial and management counseling, and word processing facilities.

Industrial development authority: the financial arm of a state or other political subdivision established for the purpose of financing economic development in an area, usually through loans to nonprofit organizations, which in turn provide facilities for manufacturing and other industrial operations.

Industrial revenue bond (IRB): a tax-exempt bond issued by a state or local government agency to finance industrial or commercial projects that serve a public good. The bond usually is not backed by the full faith and credit of the government that issues it, but is repaid solely from the revenues of the project and requires a private sector commitment for repayment.

Innovation: introduction of a new idea into the marketplace in the form of a new product or service, or an improvement in organization or process.

IRB: *see* Industrial revenue bond.

Job Training Partnership Act (JTPA): a federal law, passed in 1983, providing for publicly financed training from private-sector experts for economically disadvantaged adults and youths.

Minority-owned businesses: generally, businesses owned by blacks or persons of Hispanic, American Indian, or Asian descent. The definition will vary from state to state.

Patent: a patent secures to an inventor the exclusive right to make, use, and sell an invention for 17 years. Inventors should contact the U.S. Department of Commerce, Patent Office.

Procurement assistance: programs or services offered by government to aid small businesses in bidding on government procurement contracts. Such assistance can take the form of counseling, procurement service centers, set-asides, and sheltered-market bidding.

Product liability: type of tort, or civil liability, that applies to product manufacturers and sellers.

Prompt Payment Act: federal law that requires federal procuring agencies to pay interest to contractors on bills not paid within 30 days of invoicing or completion of work.

Regulatory Flexibility Act: federal law that requires federal agencies to evaluate the impact of their regulations on small businesses before the regulations are issued and to consider less burdensome alternatives.

SBA 504 loans: an economic development loan program offered by the SBA and administered by Certified Development Companies certified by the SBA. *See also* Certified Development Company.

SBIC: *see* Small Business Investment Company.

SBIR: *see* Small Business Innovation Research Program.

SCORE: the Service Corps of Retired Executives is a volunteer business development program of the SBA. SCORE volunteers (and ACE volunteers still active in careers) provide business counseling, workshops, and seminars.

Section 8(a) program: a program designed to assist socially and economically disadvantaged small firms to become more competitive. The SBA provides for business development by entering into contracts with federal agencies to supply goods and services, and then subcontracts the actual performance of this work to 8(a) certified firms. To be eligible for 8(a) certification, a company must be managed, controlled, and at least 51 percent owned by American citizens who are socially and economically disadvantaged individuals.

Small Business Development Center (SBDC): university-based program, organized and cofinanced by the SBA and run in conjunction with individual states and state universities, that provides faculty and student counseling to small business owners.

Small Business Innovation Research (SBIR) program: program mandated by the federal Small Business Innovation Development Act of 1982, requiring federal agencies with R&D budgets of $20 million or more to set aside a fixed percentage of these funds for small businesses. Contract awards are made in three phases: Phase I awards feasibility studies; Phase II awards product development of Phase I projects; Phase III involves private funds for commercial marketing of Phase II projects.

Small Business Institute (SBI): small business counseling program, offered nationally at 530 colleges and universities, that provides in-depth management counseling to small businesses by student teams under faculty guidance.

Small Business Investment Company (SBIC): a privately owned institution licensed by the SBA. The SBIC operates under SBA regulations, but its transactions with small companies are private arrangements and have no direct connection with the SBA. An SBIC may be formed by three or more parties, and must be chartered by the state in which it is formed. No individual bank may own more than 49 percent of an SBIC. Minimum initial private capitalization is $1 million.

SBICs may lend or invest a maximum of 20 percent of their initial private capital to any one company. After 75 percent of the initial private capital has been loaned out, the SBIC may then borrow additional capital from the SBA at an average rate of $3 for each $1 loaned out.

Surety bonding assistance: an SBA program that helps qualified small businesses to obtain bid, payment, or performance bonds on government and commercial contracts otherwise unobtainable from commercial sources.

Targeted Jobs Tax Credit: federal legislation enacted in 1978 that provides a tax credit to an employer who hires structurally unemployed individuals.

Venture capital: money used to support new or unusual commercial undertakings; equity, risk, or speculative investment capital. This funding is provided to new or existing firms that exhibit above-average growth rates, a significant potential for market expansion, and the need for additional financing for business maintenance or expansion.

Workers' compensation: a state-mandated form of insurance covering workers injured in job-related accidents. In some states the state is the insurer; in other states insurance must be acquired from commercial insurance firms. Insurance rates are based on a number of factors including salaries, firm history, and risk of occupation.

☆ U.S. GOVERNMENT PRINTING OFFICE: 1993 332-986/80105